Disability and Social Policy in Britain since 1750

Disability and Social Policy in Britain since 1750

A History of Exclusion

Anne Borsay

palgrave
macmillan

First published 2005 by
PALGRAVE MACMILLAN
Houndmills, Basingstoke, Hampshire RG21 6XS and
175 Fifth Avenue, New York, N.Y. 10010
Companies and representatives throughout the world

PALGRAVE MACMILLAN is the global academic imprint of the Palgrave
Macmillan division of St. Martin's Press, LLC and of Palgrave Macmillan Ltd.
Macmillan® is a registered trademark in the United States, United Kingdom
and other countries. Palgrave is a registered trademark in the European
Union and other countries.

ISBN 0–333–91254–3 hardback
ISBN 0–333–91255–1 paperback

This book is printed on paper suitable for recycling and made from fully
managed and sustained forest sources.

A catalogue record for this book is available from the British Library.

A catalog record for this book is available from the Library of Congress.

10   9   8   7   6   5   4   3   2   1
14   13   12   11   10   09   08   07   06   05
Printed in China

Contents

Illustrations

Foreword

Centre for Disability Studies, University of Leeds

Over the latter half of the twentieth century interest in the social and political dynamics of the experience of disability has intensified considerably, both at the general level and in universities and academic institutions. Since the end of the 1939–45 War the systematic inclusion of people with accredited impairments, whether physical, sensory, and/or cognitive and labelled 'disabled', into the mainstream of every day life has become a major consideration for politicians and policy makers across the globe. In the closing decades of the last century there was a flurry of political and policy initiatives at both the national and international levels, designed specifically to address the multiple deprivations encountered by disabled people. Several nation-states, including both wealthy nations such as Britain and the USA and poorer countries like South Africa and China, now have some form of legislative and policy framework with which to combat discrimination on the grounds of impairment.

This has been paralleled by a corresponding growth of interest in the complex process of disablement amongst academics and researchers in universities and colleges the world over. This has generated an increasingly expansive literature from a variety of perspectives within the social sciences, humanities and related disciplines, and a burgeoning interdisciplinary field of enquiry rooted in political science and sociology generally referred to as 'Disability Studies'.

Much of the inspiration for these developments came from outside the academy. In the 1970s and 1980s the politicization of disability by disabled activists, both nationally and internationally, had a significant impact on many politicians, policy makers and scholars in Britain, Canada and the United States. The United Nations designated 1981 as the 'The International Year of Disabled People', and the years 1982 to 1993 'The Decade of

Disabled Persons'. This heightened emphasis on the social and political situation of the growing numbers of disabled people was given a further boost by the development of a radical new socio-political analysis of disablement, commonly referred to as the 'social model of disability', by disabled activists and writers in the UK.

Unlike previous approaches, the social model of disability focuses exclusively on the various environmental barriers: economic, political and cultural, as the major cause of disabled people's individual and collective disadvantage. Hitherto, orthodox thinking, which is often summarized by the phrase 'the individualistic medical model of disability', has explained this unfortunate and unacceptable situation in terms of biology. Here impairment or 'chronic illness', whether real or culturally determined, was presented as the root cause of the problem rather than socially determined exclusionary policies and practices.

An explanatory tool rather than a full-blown sociological theory, a social model analysis explains society's responses to impairment with reference to a complex and pernicious form of institutional discrimination that is rooted in history and culture. Although a social model approach is not without its detractors, there is now an expanding literature on the various barriers to inclusion, and the ensuing experience of disablement from an explicitly or otherwise social model perspective.

However, many of these works are couched within a rather generalized and superficial account of history. Studies that provide a comprehensive and accessible synthesis of social model inspired theorizing along with detailed historical evidence are conspicuous by their absence. Anne Borsay's study of *Disability and Social Policy in Britain since 1750: A History of Exclusion* provides a much welcomed and scholarly example of how to fill this gap.

Drawing on expansive data from a variety of sources, this book chronicles the formulation of contemporary social policy in Britain from the late eighteenth century through to the present day. This is especially relevant to the acquisition of a thorough knowledge of contemporary disability policy. This is because, whilst debates about the origins and nature of capitalism persist within academic circles, there can be little doubt that the period covered by this study has had an enormous influence on modern day perceptions of, and assumptions about, disabled people. Notwithstanding that the philosophical roots of discrimination were well established in western culture before the eighteenth century, the economic and social upheavals that accompanied capitalist development precipitated its institutionalization throughout British society.

Through a well argued, clearly structured and, most importantly, readable account of history, Anne Borsay shows how the bourgeoning ideologies of economic rationality, liberal utilitarianism and scientific medicine, have impacted on, and continue to shape, disability policy in the UK. This is important, not simply because it helps us to understand how and why people with impairments continue to be excluded from the mainstream of economic and social activity, but also because it provides a meaningful insight into the various and complex social forces that have and continue to influence the creation of conventional individual and collective disabled, or dependent, identities.

It is important to point out too that the lessons of history clearly indicate that the more technically and socially sophisticated a society becomes the more impairment and disability it creates. Due to various factors including changing work patterns, relative affluence, medical advances, and violence and war, the number of people with 'long-term illness or disability' has increased substantially over the last 50 years. Moreover, because the incidence of acquired impairment increases significantly with age, it is likely to increase still further over the coming decades if only because of Britain's rapidly ageing population; a phenomenon common to most western societies.

All of which make the contents of this book an essential read for everyone with an interest in disability, disabled people and social policy generally. It is unequivocal that an understanding of history is fundamental if we are to avoid the exclusionary policies and practices of the past. This book provides a well-argued and well-researched foundation upon which that understanding can be based.

Acknowledgements

My involvement in disability studies dates back to the 1970s when I undertook a postgraduate thesis on contemporary community care. A decade later I turned to the social history of medicine and wrote a monographic study of the General Infirmary at Bath during the long eighteenth century. *Disability and Social Policy in Britain since 1750* combines my interests in history and the social sciences, and I thank all those whose work has influenced my thinking in these areas. The majority of the book was prepared during 2000/2001 when I was a beneficiary of the AHRB Research Leave Scheme, and I am grateful both to the Board and to the Department of History at the University of Wales, Lampeter, where I was then employed. The Wellcome Trust also provided valuable research expenses. I am likewise indebted to the School of Health Science at the University of Wales Swansea, for granting me a period of leave to finish the manuscript so soon after my appointment. In the past six months, my research assistant, Dr Alison Golby, has helped enormously in tracking down references. Since the book is based on primary as well as secondary materials, I have gained much from staff at the following libraries and record offices: the British Library; the Wellcome Library for the History and Understanding of Medicine; the Local Studies Library, Derby; the Local Studies Library, Nottingham; the Birmingham City Record Office; the Devon County Record Office, Exeter; the Glamorgan Record Office, Cardiff; the Shropshire Records and Research Service, Shrewsbury; and the West Glamorgan Record Office, Swansea. In addition, I am obliged to the following organizations for their permission to reproduce illustrations: National Museums Liverpool – The Walker (Figure 1); Birmingham Library Services – LP46.323 (Figure 2); Birmingham City Archives – MS 1060/54 (Figure 4); and West Glamorgan Archive Service – D/D PRO/ch/82/20/1 (Figure 5). Terka Acton and the team at Palgrave, and Penny Simmons of Password Publishing Services, have been extremely efficient and supportive, an anonymous reader has offered helpful feedback, and I am grateful to Colin Barnes for his foreword. However, my greatest debt is to my family. I dedicate this book to my father, Horace Howard, and to the memory of my mother, Peggy Howard, who died as it was nearing completion after living for more than three years with the consequences of a severe stroke. Their support over the years has been invaluable. My daughters, Clare and Sarah, have been wonderfully tolerant of my hours at the computer and suitably sceptical of the output. Above all, my husband, Peter, has been a constant source of intellectual and emotional support, and willingly assumed the extra domestic responsibilities that my move to Swansea has entailed.

Anne Borsay

For my Father, and in memory of my Mother

1 Introduction

In 1995 it became illegal in Britain to discriminate against disabled people 'in connection with employment, the provision of goods, facilities and services or the disposal or management of premises'. Though hailed as a major breakthrough by the Equal Opportunities Commission,[1] the Disability Discrimination Act that parented these changes was fundamentally flawed. Disabled people with 'invisible, indecipherable, and unstable' impairments were unable to demonstrate 'a substantial and long-term adverse effect on... normal day-to-day activities'. Those who met this condition were identified in a demeaning way through their deviance from an able-bodied norm that was medically defined.[2] And only direct discrimination was prohibited, leaving untouched the more subtle forms of indirect oppression brought about by 'in-built or institutional *patterns* of inequality'.[3] Therefore, the legislation was too 'weak and toothless' to reverse the economic and political, social and cultural exclusion that prevented disabled people from claiming the full rights of citizenship.[4]

This book offers a historical interpretation of how since the Industrial Revolution social policies have created and sustained the discrimination that continues to make disabled people excluded citizens. We begin by developing a conceptual framework, which distils the key characteristics of modern Britain between 1750 and the election of a Conservative government under Margaret Thatcher in 1979. The shifting mixed economy of social policy and the evolution of citizenship are assessed, along with the size of the disabled population, current historiographies of impairment, and the influence of economic rationality, power and resistance. Subsequent chapters engage with these issues via an exploration of institutional and community living. The rise of the institution is examined with reference to the growing array of workhouses

(Chapter 2), hospitals (Chapter 3), asylums (Chapter 4) and schools (Chapter 5) into which disabled people were decanted. Life in the community, the location of the majority even at the height of incarceration, is discussed with reference to work (Chapter 6), financial relief (Chapter 7) and community care (Chapter 8). The book concludes by relating past experiences of exclusion to contemporary social policies and suggesting a role for disability histories in strategies for political change.

The challenge to modernity

By the time the Disability Discrimination Act reached the statute book, the principles of modernity that had underpinned British society for over 300 years were being severely challenged.[5] Dating from the seventeenth-century Enlightenment, modernity had four essential characteristics. First and foremost, there was a commitment to rational, objective or truthful knowledge that jettisoned the *a priori* reasoning of pre-modern societies and promoted secular sciences of humanity which were dedicated to the achievement of social improvement or progress. Second, an already developing capitalist economy became increasingly industrialized and structured around a rigid division of labour. Third, the social relations built upon this economic base solidified into sharply demarcated class and gender groupings. And, finally, a code of rights for citizens evolved that culminated in the post-war welfare state. Modernity survived the shock waves of world recession and world war. From the 1970s, however, the economy went from crisis to crisis, class relations engendered industrial conflict, and the rights of citizenship were not delivering political institutions and social services that won public confidence. It was this disintegration that enabled postmodernism to question the Enlightenment project, attacking the rationality upon which the whole edifice rested.

Though sociologists dispute whether a new age of postmodernity has in fact dawned, the debate points up a series of economic and political, social and cultural changes that are too profound to ignore. National autonomy, for example, is being eroded by economic globalization, and by the information and communication technologies that are also permitting flexibility at the work place. Power is becoming more fluid as political loyalties are constructed around lifestyles, regions or particular issues rather than determined by fixed party allegiances. And personal identities are becoming more fragmented as ascription by class and gender weakens, and the consumption of goods and services takes on greater significance. Social policy has not escaped unscathed. In particular, the loss of confidence in rational thinking has revivified individualism at the expense of collectivism, bringing about a fragmentation of service provision and a reconfiguration of citizenship. Historiography – what historians write about the past – has similarly responded by overturning the progressive narrative that dominated scholarship from the early twentieth century. Therefore, policy development is no longer understood as a morality tale in which 'heroic medical experts and reformist politicians' embarked upon a journey of improvement that led unequivocally from charity and poor relief to the post-war welfare state.[6]

The mixed economy of welfare

This abandonment of a linear trajectory means that disabled people's experiences of exclusion have to be assessed with reference to a 'moving frontier' in a mixed economy of welfare.[7] Service provision in modern Britain was never the monopoly of a unitary state. On the contrary, the separate national identities recently acknowledged through devolution were grounded in the administrative structures that Scotland retained after the Act of Union in 1707, whilst Wales – part of the British polity since its earlier union in 1536 – nevertheless possessed distinctive institutions that mediated policy. The eighteenth-century state governing these kingdoms was characterized as 'under-funded', 'amateurish' and 'weak',[8] but levels of taxation were high and an effective system of public administration was in operation, which included sophisticated mechanisms for transferring and servicing troops around the world.[9] Increasingly perceived as corrupt, this apparatus was dismantled in the early nineteenth-century era of *laissez-faire*,[10] leaving in place the decentralized network that had previously delivered domestic policy. Consequently, legislation was largely permissive and its enforcement relied heavily upon an unpaid army of unpaid JPs, local councillors and servants of the poor law.[11]

Complementing these loose statutory arrangements, however, was a commercial sector, a voluntary sector of charitable and mutual aid organizations, and an informal sector consisting of relatives, friends and neighbours. This mixed economy was not overturned by the Victorian expansion of collectivist legislation. On the contrary, Martin Daunton has argued that 'both the expenditure and personnel of voluntarism [alone] were greater than the central and local state.'[12] The social reforms carried out by Liberal governments in the decade before 1914 did not diminish the significance of the non-statutory sectors. And in the years between the First and Second World Wars, voluntary organizations benefited from the growing flow of finance to local authorities, which rewrote their partnership and enabled innovative co-operation.[13] The arrival of the welfare state caused a temporary eclipse. Though Clement Attlee, Labour Prime Minister in the late 1940s, shared Beveridge's belief in the continuing value of voluntarism, the Labour Party as a whole was more sceptical, fearing the reassertion of '[p]ast moralizing and class condescension'. Therefore, with the endorsement of universal services, charity was 'restricted merely to supplementing and complementing state welfare'.[14]

By the 1960s, confidence in the public sector was stalling. The state had only limited resources to invest in welfare; the costs were rising relentlessly; and users complained that services were insensitive to their requirements. Social policy gained an extra-national dimension in 1973 when Britain joined the European Economic Community, now the European Union. However, this did not halt the resurgence of interest in the voluntary sector, which engulfed the political spectrum from left to right. The consequences were increasingly selective public services, more decentralized funding, greater reliance on the voluntary and commercial sectors, and a revised concept of citizenship.

From civil to social rights

The New Right inspired the reconfiguration of the citizen. Convinced that the post-war welfare state had undermined both the economic prosperity and the moral fibre of the nation, Conservative governments emphasized the obligations of citizenship. The duty to work, and hence avoid the curse of state dependency, was articulated through a stricter regulation of the social security system. Personal responsibility for health, education, welfare and the environment was promoted by disinvesting in the public services. And from this platform of self-help was launched a call to the needs of others, to be answered not by tolerating high rates of taxation but by offering time and money in a voluntary capacity. Decoupled from the state, citizenship became defined in terms of consumer choice and government policies measured against their achievement of this criterion. Furthermore, the contract was imported from the private sector to police the interface between the state and its citizens, extracting obligations from the recipients of support and giving rights of compensation to those whose treatment did not attain the minimum standard.[15]

This late twentieth-century 'citizenship of contribution' stood in sharp contrast to the 'citizenship of entitlement' prevalent after the Second World War.[16] In 1948, the United Nations published its Universal Declaration of Human Rights:

> Everyone has the right to a standard of living adequate for the health and well-being of himself and his family, including food, clothing, housing and medical care and the necessary social services and the right to security in the event of unemployment, sickness, disability, widowhood, old age or other lack of livelihood in circumstances beyond his control.[17]

The incorporation of disability and old age demonstrated an appreciation of impairment that was subsequently elaborated in specific Declarations on the Rights of Mentally Retarded Persons (1971) and Disabled Persons (1975).[18] Of course, without the political will of a nation state, all goals of the United Nations remain aspirations in search of enforcement.[19] In Britain, however, the human right to 'a standard of living adequate for...health and well-being' found concrete expression in the objectives of the welfare state.

It was citizenship that conferred this right. For T. H. Marshall, principal among the early theorists of state welfare, citizenship was 'a status bestowed on those who...[were] full members of a community'; and '[a]ll who possess[ed] the status...[were] equal with respect to the rights and duties with which the status...[was] endowed.' Three categories of rights were identified: civil, political and social. The 'civil element', associated with the eighteenth century, comprised 'the rights necessary for individual freedom – liberty of the person, freedom of speech, thought and faith, the right to own property and to conclude valid contracts, and the right to justice'. The 'political element', associated with the nineteenth century, involved 'the right to participate in the exercise of political power, as a member of a body invested with political authority or as an elector of the members of such a body'. And the 'social element', associated with the twentieth century, ranged ambitiously 'from the right to a modicum of economic welfare and security to the right to share to the full in the social heritage and to live the life of a civilized being according to the standards prevailing in the society'.[20]

Marshall's ideas have enjoyed an enduring influence but, as post-war optimism faded and the limitations of the welfare state came into view, his inclusive notion of social citizenship began to look 'less and less like the symptomatic expression of a progressive trend, and more and more like the product of... a short-lived ideological mood'.[21] First, Marshall saw no fundamental conflict between 'a modified form of capitalist enterprise' and 'civilized forms of collectivist social policy'.[22] Therefore, the '[d]ifferential status, associated with class, function and family, was replaced by the single, uniform status of citizenship, which provided the foundation of equality on which the structure of inequality could be built.'[23] Throughout the post-war period, however, the middle class made more effective use of even the universal services like education, health and social security; and their command of the relevant information was also an asset when claiming the selective services to which they were entitled.[24] The social rights of citizenship thus remained subservient to economic inequalities.

A second problem was Marshall's oversimplified chronology. Lynn Hollen Lees contends that before 1834 the old poor law created 'a condition of social citizenship' in England and Wales that for those with full settlement rights amounted to 'a locally organized welfare state'.[25] The threadbare patchwork of services to which these 'rights' granted access weakens her analogy. Furthermore, as Sidney and Beatrice Webb noted in their monumental history:

> The English Poor Law at no time gave the destitute a personal 'right' to relief... What was enacted was not a right at all, but an obligation

...the obligation to relieve the impotent poor and to provide the able-bodied with the means of earning their livelihood by work.[26]

Nevertheless, this paternalist rhetoric enabled the poor to perform an active role in the welfare process, assured that they had entitlements that were communally acknowledged. Marshall recognized these customary social rights, but insisted that civil rights were victorious during the eighteenth century because they were essential to the market economy. In so doing, he underestimated both the contested nature of early nineteenth-century social reform and the continuing influence of paternalism.[27]

Finally, Marshall disregarded ethnicity, gender and disability. Despite having the appearance of neutrality, his conception of citizenship was rooted in an 'idealized image' of the human being as white, male and able-bodied.[28] Whilst 'agency, capability, autonomy or responsibility' was not explicit in this 'formulation',[29] 'lesser' citizens who failed to meet these conditions[30] fell prey to a residual paternalism that undermined their social rights. Alf Morris, introducing the Chronically Sick and Disabled Persons Bill to Parliament in 1969, aspired to a world where there was both 'genuine compassion' towards disabled people and 'a fundamental right to participate in industry and society according to ability'.[31] In practice, however, this combination is incompatible. As Michael Ignatieff has argued:

> The language of citizenship is not properly about compassion at all, since compassion is a private virtue which cannot be legislated or enforced. The practice of citizenship is about ensuring everybody the entitlements necessary to the exercise of their liberty. As a political question, welfare is about rights, not caring, and the history of citizenship has been the struggle to make freedom real, not to tie us all in the leading strings of therapeutic good intentions.[32]

In the history of disability, therapeutic intentions have not always been good. But even where they were, social policies predicated on compassion have created passive recipients who bowed to professional advice, rather than active citizens who compiled support packages within 'a framework of entitlements'.[33] The outcome has been a 'needs-based' approach to welfare in which social rights are 'variable and negotiable', and groups access services according to their 'special needs'.[34]

Measuring disability

Before probing the historical antecedents of these policies, it is important to consider how we define and measure disability. The concept itself has often been confined to the physical impairments that in the past were collectively associated with 'the crippled'. More recently, the boundaries expanded to include the sensory impairments of blindness and deafness, and the intellectual impairments (or learning difficulties) that were previously described as 'idiocy', 'mental deficiency', 'mental sub-normality' and 'mental handicap'.[35] The long-term nature of some mental illnesses, and the discrimination which survivors have faced in resuming their everyday lives,[36] also justify the absorption of psychological impairments: a term preferable to 'psychiatric'[37] impairment because it does not accept uncritically the professional labelling of 'lunacy', 'madness' and 'insanity'. Furthermore, though elderly people are typically not drawn into the debate, they too warrant attention as a majority within the disabled population.[38] In adopting a wide-ranging definition, the intention is not to gloss over the differences between physical, sensory, intellectual and psychological impairments. However, it does reflect the conviction that all these disabled people share a common exclusion from the full rights of citizenship that a historical study of social policies can productively address.

Of all the parameters of impairment, old age is most easily measured because of its visibility in the mainstream demographic statistics. However, since not every elderly person was disabled, those who were have to be incorporated into a broader trawl across the life cycle that embraces physical and mental impairments caused by acute and chronic diseases, work, poverty, and environmental pollution, road traffic accidents and sporting injuries, and medical errors like thalidomide. Though from 1851 there was an attempt to pick out *sensory* impairments in the decennial census, these questions were discontinued in 1921 because they were difficult to construct for a general survey.[39] Some of the gaps were plugged by *ad hoc* investigations and official statistics compiled under poor law, factory, mental health and education legislation. Moreover, with the advent of the welfare state, local authorities – which had been required to maintain lists of blind people since 1920 – were additionally empowered under the 1948 National Assistance Act to register deafness and physical impairment. But given the partial nature of these rolls, and the limited community services that were available, such sources are of little value in gauging the size of the disabled population.

It was to provide a more reliable indicator that in the late 1960s the government commissioned a national survey from the Office of Population Censuses and Surveys (OPCS). Impairment was defined as 'lacking part or all of a limb, or having a defective limb, organ or mechanism of the body'; disablement was defined as 'the loss or reduction of functional ability'; and handicap was defined as 'the disadvantage or restriction of activity caused by disability'. From this foundation, it was estimated that in Great Britain there were 3.1 million people aged 16 or over living in private households who had some *physical* impairment.[40] The International Classification of Impairment, Disability and Handicap (ICIDH), published in 1980, extended the OPCS terminology to include sensory and intellectual impairments. Consequently, when deployed in a second government survey later in the decade, it threw up an impaired population of 6.2 million for Britain, exclusive of Northern Ireland.[41] In his monumental study of poverty, published in 1979, Peter Townsend berated the narrowness of both definitions. Delineating disability as the 'inability to perform the activities, share in the relationships and play the roles which are customary for people of broadly the same age and sex', he judged that in the late 1960s there were 9.9 million impaired adults and children within the United Kingdom.[42] For radical critics, however, all three studies were misconceived because they conformed to an 'individual' and not a 'social' model of impairment.

The individual model explained disability as a 'personal trouble'. Sharp distinctions were drawn between different types of impairment, and their causes were sought exclusively within the 'defective' individual. It was assumed that any 'deviation' from 'normal' behaviour was necessarily a tragic loss or misfortune, and parallels were commonly drawn with death and mourning. Most significantly, individuals were expected to cope with impairment by adapting themselves to society, relying on the expertise of medicine and the allied professions for treatment and cure. In contrast, the social model explained disability as a 'public issue'. Therefore, the common ground between various types of impairment was emphasized, and their joint causes sought in economic, social and political organization. Dogmatic notions of 'normality' were outlawed, allowing the celebration of 'abnormal' life experiences. And disabled people were not burdened with trimming themselves to fit the dimensions of mainstream society.[43] There were implications for terminology. In 1976, the Union of the Physically Impaired Against Segregation (UPIAS) defined impairment as 'lacking all or part of a limb, or having a defective limb, organ or mechanism of the body'. However, disability was reconfigured to become 'the disadvantage or restriction caused by a contemporary social organization which takes no or little account of people who have physical impairments and thus excludes them from the mainstream of social activities'.[44] Redrafted in this mould, the questions from the OPCS survey looked very different. 'Does your health/problem/disability prevent you from going out as often or as far as you would like?' was the transmuted into 'What are the environmental constraints which make it difficult for you to get about in your immediate neighbourhood?'[45] With this perspective in place, head counting is discredited. As Oliver and Barnes insist, 'there is no fixed number of disabled people ... [because] disability is dependent on the environments in which impaired people are placed.'[46]

Historiographies of disability

The understanding of disability as a social oppression rather than an individual pathology has informed its historiography as well as its measurement. There are three main approaches to the history of impairment: the biographical, the empirical and the material. Biographical histories tell the stories of 'great male reformers' and laud the institutions with which they were often connected. Empirical histories evaluate the 'relative effectiveness' of different 'care' strategies, assessing their performance against a yardstick of the professional service assumed to be the answer to disabled people's 'problems'.[47] Both these approaches conform to the individual model. Only materialist histories engage with the social model and locate past experiences of disability within the economic and political, social and cultural organization of society. In 1981, Peter Townsend put forward a seminal argument for the 'structured dependency' of elderly people. Attacking '[t]he bias ... towards individualistic instead of societal forms of explanation', he blamed industrial societies for creating 'the framework of institutions and rules within which the general problems of the elderly emerge and, indeed, are manufactured'.[48] However, the materialist account of disability was articulated most forcefully in histories of physical impairment.

Indebted to the Marxist legacy, materialist histories of impairment favoured a developmental approach, focusing especially on the transition from feudalism to modern industrial capitalism. Vic Finkelstein began the discourse in 1980 with his provocative but imprecise distillation of three 'phases'. In Phase 1, impaired people were congregated at the bottom of the economic pile in the company of poorly paid workers, the unemployed and the mentally ill. Attempts were made to differentiate the poverty of unfortunate 'cripples' from the poverty of sturdy beggars, but impairment was normally regarded as a consequence of sin or wanton behaviour that required no special social provision. Phase 2 saw the arrival of segregated disability institutions in response to 'a new productive technology'. '[L]arge scale industry with production-lines geared to able-bodied norms' excluded impaired people who had previously been integrated and socially active members of their class and community. Furthermore, the growth of hospital-based medicine encouraged the expansion of professionals whose expert knowledge was disabling. Yet, paradoxically, public services also helped disabled people to acquire social independence and challenge the professional control of their lives. It was this critique that triggered the birth of the social model and the onset of Phase 3.[49]

Finkelstein's schema was valuable for the way in which industrialization was highlighted. On his own admission, however, it sought 'to say something about the context in which attitudes are formed' and was not 'a historical analysis of disability'.[50] Therefore, the dynamics of the industrial process and its social and political outcomes were not made plain. In *The Disabled State*, Deborah Stone was more specific in designating 'the distributive dilemma' as central to disability. 'All societies', she declared, 'have at least two distributive systems, one based on work and one on need'; the universal predicament was 'how to reconcile...[them] without undermining the productive side of the economy'. Stone concentrated on the role of the state in defining and redefining the boundaries of dependency by establishing categories which expressed 'a culturally legitimate rationale for nonparticipation in the labor system'. Those categories that were chronologically based on childhood or old age were easily validated exemptions, but disability was not. Diverse, unstable and prone to abuse by impostors who feigned illness or impairment in order to obtain assistance, it was ripe for the picking by eighteenth- and nineteenth-century medical professionals as their status climbed. Therefore, clinical judgement overtook the old ways of detecting skulduggery.[51]

Although Stone incorporated an economic mechanism for the social construction of impairment, her polarization of work and welfare assumed too uncritically that 'the distributive dilemma' was universal and her fixation with official categories led to a narrow convergence on the state. Michael Oliver tackled both shortcomings in *The Politics of Disablement*. First, he complicated the influence of the 'economic base' by arguing that whereas fully-fledged capitalism was exclusive, 'agriculture or small-scale industry . . . did not preclude the great majority of disabled people from participating in the production process.' To the impact of the economy was added the 'mode of thought' and the problem of order. The evolution of intellectual concepts 'from a religious interpretation of reality' to a metaphysical and then a scientific one interacted with the disruption thrown up by the rise of capitalism to alter 'historical perceptions of disability' and to propagate new medical and institutional methods for subduing deviancy. This tripartite model of economy, ideology and politics presented a far more sophisticated analysis of economic development than Finkelstein or Stone, and the dissection of social policies was situated within a political matrix that reached beyond the administrative state to include beliefs and values, and the policing of disorder.[52] Nevertheless, Oliver shared the assumption that impairment in pre-industrial Britain was for the most part unproblematic: a premise that Brendan Gleeson also upheld in *Geographies of Disability*.

Gleeson envisaged disability 'as part of a broader process of social embodiment' in which 'roles and representations' were ascribed 'to body types that varie[d] in time and space'. Applying this geographical perspective to a comparison of feudal England and the industrial city, he argued that 'bodily impairment' was so accepted and commonplace among medieval peasants that it occupied a social space 'distinct from, *yet embedded within*, the general terrain of everyday life'. With the gradual shift to industrial capitalism and urban living, this inclusion was lost. 'One disabling feature of the...city was the new separation of home and work', but '[t]he rise of mechanized forms of production introduced productivity standards that assumed a "normal" (that is to say, usually male and non-impaired) worker's body and disabled all others.' The upshot of this 'labour market exclusion' was 'socio-spatial marginalisation' – whether through incarceration, home working or street trading. But though disabled people were often visible on the thoroughfares of the Victorian city, they were not engaged in the customary pedestrian activities of shopping, socializing or circulating. Rather, the street was 'a place of subsistence' which also served as a stage that 'constantly retold the story of their social difference'.[53]

Economic rationality, power and resistance

Though Gleeson was anxious not 'to dismiss or downplay' socio-cultural influences, his analysis was a structural one that used 'a political-economic historical framework'.[54] Therefore, like earlier historiographies of disability, it offers a materialist interpretation derived from the social model. Critics have alleged that this orientation omits structural factors besides impairment – social class, gender, age and ethnicity – the interplay of which also shapes experiences of exclusion. The neglect of personal pain, fatigue, depression and the internalized oppression that arises from the psychology of exclusion is also condemned.[55] Above all, the social model is accused of being too deterministic, of selling short the ability of disabled people to challenge institutional constraints, and of denying them the agency to give their lives meaning.[56] The original architects of the social model dispute that its materialism rides roughshod over the multiplicity of individual experiences. Mike Oliver and Colin Barnes are thus scathing of the view that 'the world is somehow constructed through discourse alone', and insist that social change can only be delivered by addressing the concrete reality of discrimination.[57]

Oliver and Barnes rightly stress the material underpinnings of impairment, but the social model does exaggerate the impact of industrialization. As Barnes himself has shown, negative attitudes to disability were evident both in the religions and cultures of ancient Greece and Rome, and in the art and literature of Renaissance Europe.[58] Furthermore, the work ethic was a preoccupation in pre-modern Britain, the Tudor poor law struggling to distinguish 'deserving' from the 'undeserving' applicants. And although the factory system with its heavy machinery did ultimately entrench a geographical separation of home and work that became a defining feature of industrial societies, this change was slow in coming; as late as 1851 only 6 per cent of the total labour force was working in textile factories – the sole employment sector where this mode of production had made major inroads.[59] Far more significant was the economic rationality characteristic of capitalism that was growing in importance during the pre-modern period long before the Industrial Revolution. For capitalism to thrive, 'the labour force had to be organized to achieve maximum efficiency, productivity and profitability'.[60] Rewards and sanctions were consequently applied in the pursuit of economic rationality, which was broadly 'maintained not only, or even mainly by legal systems, police forces and prisons, but... expressed through a wide range of social institutions, from religion to family life, and including, for example, leisure and recreation, education, charity and philanthropy, social work and poor relief'.[61]

Traditionally, these strategies were understood as a 'top down' process of social control[62] that assumed a consensual society where the values of the dominant class were universally accepted.[63] For Michel Foucault, power was subtler. Emerging with modernity in the seventeenth century, disciplinary power displaced sovereign power, substituting its visible, episodic and brutal mode of punishment with one that was invisible, ongoing and routinized.[64] Therefore, power was exercised and undergone simultaneously 'through a net-like organization' in which individuals moved 'between its threads'. There were two implications. First, power was not 'one individual's consolidated and homogenous domination over others, or that of one group or class over others'. Second, it was inseparable from resistance. In short, power was 'local and unstable', 'never in anybody's hands, never appropriated as a commodity or piece of wealth'.[65] But though Foucault rejected the monolithic concentration of disciplinary forces, he did concede to 'dividing practices' – 'made acceptable by claims of science and the institutional backing given to the operation of scientific discourses' – that 'separate[d] and objectif[ied] people from social groups for exhibiting difference'.[66]

David Armstrong has elaborated on these exclusionary procedures in his concept of 'surveillance medicine'.[67] Monitoring the social body as a whole, surveillance medicine spread 'its gaze over the normal person to establish early detection, to advise on appropriate behaviour and relationships and to enable the potentially abnormal to be adequately known'. '[T]echnologies' based on scientific and statistical methodologies were developed to measure the physical, psychological and social states of the population. And as additional categories were discovered varying from the normal, so new 'disciplines' arose to treat them. Armstrong argues that it was the social problems of the Second World War that brought into being a 'comprehensive surveillance network', dismantled the 'normal/abnormal divide', and 'classified bodies on a continuum'. Preventive medicine thus moved beyond sanitation and the environment to embrace 'the minutiae of social life', advising individuals on the behaviour patterns most likely to deliver good health and implying personal responsibility for illness. Professionals – bolstered by 'the way in which their...knowledge [wa]s grounded in precise, accurate and scientific information'[68] – were invested with the authority to impose their expert definitions of needs.[69] And impairment was constructed as a pathological abnormality, whose 'victims' were exposed to the 'pastoral surveillance' of health and social services.[70]

Whilst Foucault was correct to challenge the structural determinism of social control, the activities of surveillance medicine suggest that he misjudged how far 'dividing practices' concentrated power. That power was crucial in building the personal and political identities of disabled people. Consequently, social policies functioned as a type of 'power which work[ed] upon the individual's sense of self',[71] 'categories of identity' being 'articulated in welfare discourses and...inscribed in the material practices and institutional forms of welfare'.[72] Social policies were only one ingredient. For most of the modern period, personal identities were relatively fixed and unified around class and gender, ethnicity and geography, age and disability. As late twentieth-century society became more fluid and fragmented, however, so identities became constructed more reflexively by using 'technologies of the self'[73] to sustain 'coherent, yet continuously revised, biographical narratives'. But these 'technologies' did not, as Foucault argued, enable effective resistance to disciplinary power.[74] Economic, social, and political structures continued to contain opposition, preventing disabled people from orchestrating substantial change through 'a multiplicity of points of resistance'.[75]

Conclusion

In this chapter, we have examined how the modern society that emerged in Britain from the Enlightenment changed in response to the conditions of the late twentieth century. In the chapters that follow, these ideas are applied in a historical study of social policies between the Industrial Revolution and the fall of the Labour government in 1979. Rather than reducing disability to a personal pathology, the study adopts a materialist approach that recognizes the influence of societal factors. Therefore, policy developments are located within the shifting mixed economy of commercial, charitable, state and family provision. These developments are assessed with reference to the civil, political and social rights associated with citizenship. The influence of economic rationality in voluntary and statutory as well as commercial services is considered. And the imposition of disciplinary power is explored by looking at disabled people's reaction and resistance to the institutional and community care that they received.

Part I

Institutional Living

2

Workhouses

Institutional living was a phenomenon that Michel Foucault linked to the Enlightenment. Between 1660 and 1800, he argued, European society underwent a 'great confinement' during which – as 'poverty,...incapacity for work,...[and] inability to integrate with the group' were 'perceived on the social horizon'[1] – 'the sick, the mad, the handicapped, the unemployed' were increasingly incarcerated.[2] In Britain, the central state was slow to extend its powers and the institutions which grew up as a result of charitable, commercial or local government initiatives were too few in number and too small in size to justify the degree of sequestration that Foucault advocated.[3] But if he exaggerated the extent of impoundment, his emphasis on institutions flagged up what for disabled people was the ultimate 'dividing practice', a form of exclusion which denied them access to 'the normal exchanges, practices and rights'[4] of their society. Exclusion has 'a long history' in the analysis of social policy.[5] The version advanced by New Labour since 1997 diminishes the negative effects of structural inequality to specific 'problems' and accentuates the importance of individual responsibility at the expense of collective obligation.[6] In the past, however, exclusion has been a means 'of describing the ways in which not only markets, but also state welfare provisions, generate and sustain ... inequalities and discrimination'.[7] It is in this sense that we use it to examine institutional living, focusing especially on the composition of mixed economies of provision, the implications for disabled people's civil, social and political rights, the influence of economic rationality, and the effects of resistance to confinement regimes. Chapter 3 looks at hospitals, Chapter 4 at asylums, and Chapter 5 at schools, but we begin with the workhouse where the principal themes are the old and the new poor laws, the institutional environments

19

and conditions to which they gave rise, the late nineteenth-century crusade against outdoor relief, the emergence of residential care, and the perspectives of disabled inmates.

The old poor law

By the mid-eighteenth century, the workhouse was the institution with the longest history of housing disabled people. The system of statutory relief of which it formed a part was not a unitary one. In Scotland, under legislation passed in 1597, voluntary contributions made via the kirk were used to support the 'aged' and 'impotent', but the able-bodied poor had no unequivocal right to assistance.[8] In England and Wales, on the other hand, the Poor Law Act of 1601 was mandatory. Every one of the 15,000 parishes (and later some individual townships) was required to elect overseers of the poor. Their duties were threefold: to levy a compulsory property-based rate; to put the 'undeserving' able-bodied poor to work, whilst punishing those who refused to obey; and to supply outdoor relief to the 'deserving' or 'impotent' poor who were elderly, sick or 'infirm'. Laws of settlement were introduced from the mid-seventeenth century, locating responsibility for the poor with their parish of birth or with the parish where they had lived for the past three years. The existence of so many units of administration ensured that the delivery of relief was highly decentralized, despite supervision by the county magistracy and nominal monitoring by Parliament. Furthermore, this fragmentation was increased by the lack of any legal definition of 'deserving', by the failure to specify the form, level and regularity of outdoor relief, and by the piecemeal development of workhouse provision.[9]

Between 1696 and 1712, the 'Corporations of the Poor', set up by local Acts of Parliament, built workhouses in 14 towns. Knatchbull's Act of 1723 enabled, but did not require, overseers to restrict relief for able-bodied applicants to the workhouse and extract labour in return. By 1750 there were 600 workhouses in England, and in the period to 1783 a further 100 local statutes were passed whose measures to 'improve' the poor law included constructing 'houses of industry'. Although a few early projects were commercially managed, these workhouses were essentially institutions of the local state. They sought to increase the nation's manufacturing output, to reduce the poor rate by deterring requests for assistance, and to turn jobless paupers into morally virtuous labourers through regulated employment. By the later eighteenth century, however, the economic rationality of this Enlightenment plan was being undermined by the failure of workhouses to achieve self-sufficiency. Gilbert's Act of 1782 acknowledged an alternative custodial role: 'no person shall be sent to such poor house or houses, except such as are become indigent by old age, sickness or infirmities, and are unable to acquire a maintenance by their labour.' Thereafter, parishes and townships were allowed to combine and share the cost of building a common workhouse not to repel the work-shy but to accommodate the 'impotent' or disabled poor. Outdoor relief was also sanctioned where institutional care was not offered.[10]

Workhouses under the old poor law threatened the civil rights of disabled people who were compulsorily detained on grounds of mental impairment. At Tilbury near London, for example, a local magistrate sanctioned locking, and if necessary chaining, a parishioner in the workhouse after the overseers reported that he 'is so far disordered in his senses that it is dangerous for him to be permitted to go abroad'.[11] Benevolent paternalism may have informed his decision, but the 1714 vagrancy legislation under which he acted required two JPs to authorize indefinite confinement and recognized no necessity for legal redress.[12] Since the workhouse was designed to deter requests for assistance, other disabled inmates were at liberty to leave. For as long as they remained in residence, however, they were not only excluded from mainstream society but also enjoyed little freedom of movement. Determined to achieve change, nineteenth-century reformers painted an ugly picture of the workhouse environment in which disabled people were held. The 'aged and infirm and the infants', claimed Dr James Kay, one of the new poor law assistant commissioners, 'were promiscuously mingled with sturdy able-bodied paupers, idiots and the sick, in groups which presented to the eye only a picture of common misery or depravity.'[13] But, in practice, conditions in the 4800 institutions that had developed by 1834 were diverse.

Workhouses were deliberately multi-purpose. Like the House of the Rollesby Incorporation in Norfolk, established in 1775, they sought 'the Instruction of Youth, the Encouragement of

Industry, the Relief of Want, the Support of Old Age, and the Comfort of Infirmity and Pain'.[14] As relatively few able-bodied men were admitted, elderly or disabled people comprised the majority of inmates along with women and children.[15] At Ormskirk in Lancashire, the workhouse was in 1821 accommodating 'none but houseless and impotent...and...they have looked to it rather as a comfortable asylum for those really distressed and without comfort of a home than for the Idle and Disorderly'.[16] However, elderly and disabled inmates were not automatically exempt from work. Some workhouses obliged those over 60 to labour. Others excused only those incapable of employment, putting the rest to work, often at the tedious task of picking oakum: a tarry rope that lacerated the fingers.[17] Living arrangements were equally varied. In some localities, efforts were made to soften the regime for elderly inmates by providing them with a more generous diet and making allocations of tobacco and snuff; and in some larger towns – notably Liverpool – dedicated furnished apartments emerged within the workhouse. As Sir Frederick Eden observed in 1795, these apartments, 'being thus detached from the rest of the poor', enabled their occupants to feel 'comfortably lodged as in a secluded cottage...[with] the comforts of a private fireside'. Smaller workhouses, vulnerable to overcrowding, were not always as salubrious; nor did all officials endorse special privileges for elderly inmates, fearing that they would weaken family responsibility.[18]

The new poor law

The Poor Law Amendment Act of 1834 built on such anxieties, setting out to exclude its clientele from citizenship in a bid to banish inappropriate dependency. Characterized as a revolutionary measure, the Act sought to sweep away the alleged excesses of the former relief system and replace it with an efficient administrative machine. A central Poor Law Commission with three members was established, which in 1847 became the Poor Law Board, to implement national policy in the localities. The 15,000 parishes in England and Wales were amalgamated into approximately 600 poor law unions, which were serviced by relieving officers and managed by Boards of Guardians elected on the basis of property ownership. Finally, two new principles were enshrined: first, the situation of paupers was to be 'less eligible' than that of 'the independent labourer of the lowest class'; and, second, relief for able-bodied applicants and their families was to be available only in the workhouses that every union was directed to erect.[19] In the interests of economic rationality, the work ethic was to be enforced.

This grand scheme for national uniformity broke down. When the Scottish poor law was eventually reformed in 1845, poorhouses were not compulsory and parishes remained the unit of administration under a central Board of Supervision.[20] Even within England and Wales, however, there was fragmentation. Though the 1834 Act was framed with particular reference to rural pauperism, outdoor relief quickly re-emerged in country districts where farmers served as guardians and learnt to obtain the economic advantages of wage subsidies by disguising them as sickness payments. In urban areas, reactions differed. Where similar changes had already been introduced on local initiative, the reforms were welcomed. But the cyclical nature of the industrial economy led other guardians to resist constructing workhouses, which would stand empty during a boom but be inadequate to cope with a slump.[21] Lacking an independent financial base, the Poor Law Commission and its small inspectorate were unable to override such opposition and enforce compliance. Therefore, disabled people were on the receiving end of policies that evolved through processes of negotiation in which national interests were mediated by vibrant local welfare cultures.[22]

The new poor law was greeted with widespread protest, violence erupting in South Wales and the North.[23] Whereas the 1832 Reform Act expanded the parliamentary electorate, the Poor Law Amendment Act removed the vote from paupers who were enfranchised, defining them as unfit for democracy or political citizenship until the restriction was removed in 1918.[24] Disabled people who became paupers not only lost any political rights that they possessed. The workhouse test also attacked the customary social right to outdoor poor relief that paternalism underwrote. Elderly people featured prominently in the dissent expressed in popular newspapers, working-class autobiographies and ballads sold on the streets and from door-to-door. In one ballad called 'The State of Great Britain, or, a Touch of the Times for 1841', the narrator deplored the destruction of national harmony wreaked by the new poor law and called for Parliament to rectify the damage by giving 'old men and women beer and tea' and 'a half-a-crown a day.'[25] Drawing in the 'aged and infirm' may have captured public sympathy for the cause as a whole, but the reforms were driven by the imagined abuses of the able-bodied poor: always a small minority of claimants. Incarcerating the 'deserving poor', and hence shifting the balance from outdoor to indoor relief, was not envisaged. Indeed, separate workhouses were recommended to protect them from the rigorous routines designed for their unworthy counterparts. In the words of the Royal Commission that preceded the Act: 'Each class might thus receive an appropriate treatment; the old might enjoy their indulgences without torment from the boisterous; the children be educated, and the able-bodied be subjected to such courses of labour and discipline as will repel the indolent and vicious.'[26]

The marginality of the 'deserving' groups was evident in the statistical activities of the central commissioners. For the first five years of their operation, only information on expenditure was collected. From 1840, 'the basic units of analysis...[became] the forms of relief' – in other words, 'indoor versus outdoor aid'. This information was then classified according to age and gender, distinguishing adult males from adult females and children under the age of 16. Of greatest relevance to impairment, however, was the distinction between the able-bodied; the 'aged', 'infirm' or disabled; and the 'insane', 'lunatic' or 'idiot'. Whereas the economic dependency of the able-bodied poor attracted a profusion of subcategories, the other groups were simply counted and rapidly dismissed as unproductive 'defectives'.[27] Michael Rose has suggested that '[m]ost Unions regarded all paupers between the ages of sixteen and seventy as being "able-bodied" if they were not permanently incapacitated.'[28] But since no legal definitions of the categories were supplied, we cannot assume that local officials were consistent in how they allocated between them. Nevertheless, the national statistical series that were compiled from their returns mean that we have a more comprehensive picture of impaired paupers after 1834 than under the old poor law where no routine data was gathered.

During the course of the nineteenth century, resort to poor relief declined. In 1840, the mean number of recipients in all classes was 1,200,000, or 77.0 per 1000 estimated population. By the turn of the century, the mean had dropped to 797,000 and the rate to 25.0. Impaired people were a growing constituency within this contracting 'pauper host'. Between 1851 and 1901, 'aged and infirm adults' increased from 349,300 to 387,900, or from 42.1 per cent to 48.4 per cent of all recipients. With psychological impairment for the same period, the expansion was almost sevenfold, pushing the 'insane' category from 14,300 to 967,000 and its relative share from 1.7 per cent to 12.1 per cent. Like the vast majority of other paupers, these impaired people were much more likely to receive outdoor than indoor relief. Nevertheless, institutionalization became more common. Thus, whereas only 11 per cent of the 'adult non-able-bodied' were workhouse residents in 1849, 50 years later the proportion was 28 per cent.[29]

Workhouse environments

The experiences of the disabled minority confined in the workhouse were a product of the physical environment and the social processes that occurred within it. The poor law commissioners originally intended to use the existing workhouse infrastructure, and so unions like Tunbridge Wells in Kent began by adapting their old premises to corral the able-bodied from children and from elderly, 'infirm' and female inmates.[30] Very quickly, however, the commissioners were converted to the general mixed workhouse. Two model plans were published in their first *Annual Report*, one Y-shaped and the other a cruciform; and by 1841 320 unions had agreed to erect single institutions. It was within this environment that the classification of disabled inmates took place. From the outset, this was difficult because the number of categories exceeded the number of wings in which separate regimes could be easily imposed. Walls, partitions, iron grilles and gates were erected to increase the amount of discrete accommodation, but 'the need to provide each class with separate day, night and outdoor space gave rise to immense planning problems' and the barriers to inmate mobility interfered with the smooth running of the institution.[31]

The corridor plan, evident in approximately 150 workhouses built between 1840 and 1875, eased access throughout the building but continued to rely on gates to keep inmates apart. Simultaneously, however, a more dispersed plan was evolving in which different categories of pauper were placed in separate blocks on the same site. With this pavilion-style, which received official sanction in 1868, classification finally came into its own. By 1914 at least 46 such workhouses had been built, whilst many others had been modified along pavilion lines. From the turn of the century, it was the specialist institution on its own site that was gaining momentum.[32] However, neither these institutions nor the general workhouse made any concessions to the design needs of disabled people, leaving them to survive as best they could within an environment constructed for the able-bodied.

Though the pavilion-style may have lightened the image, the workhouses built in the aftermath of 1834 resembled prisons, their radiating wings and perimeter walls eloquently expressing the penalties of pauperism.[33] The deterrent effect of this architecture was compounded by the workhouse procedures, laid down like the model plans in the commissioners' first *Annual Report*. Upon admission, the paupers were to be placed in the 'probationary ward' where they were 'examined by the medical officer', 'thoroughly cleansed' and 'clothed in the workhouse dress'. Families were separated. Inmates were to start work at 7am in summer and 8am in winter, finish at 6pm and retire to bed two hours later. Fixed intervals were allowed for each meal, and menus were 'in no case to exceed...the ordinary diet of the able-bodied labourers living within the same district'. Flouting these rules led to chastisement, as did a long list of other misdemeanours: making 'any noise when silence is ordered'; using 'obscene or profane language'; reviling another pauper; being dirty, drunk or indecent; refusing to work; feigning sickness; and disobeying the workhouse officers. Inmates considered 'disorderly' or 'refractory' suffered a reduction in their diet, exclusion in a correction cell, corporal punishment or – in serious cases – referral to the magistrates.[34]

Disabled people were in theory excused the more repressive aspects of this workhouse regime. In 1836, the Poor Law Commission, echoing concerns voiced during the passage of the controversial Amendment Act, reminded their officers that it was their 'duty to treat the sick, the aged, and the infirm with marked tenderness and care'.[35] Even the harshest unions were sympathetically inclined towards these categories of pauper. In 1861, for example, the Visiting Committee of the Aylsham Workhouse in Norfolk 'having reported that the aged men in the house complained of the cold in consequence of their waistcoats not being of sufficient length,...ordered that the Master do cause the same to be altered accordingly.' General procedures and practices were also modified. The timetable was relaxed, allowing disabled inmates to rise at a later hour. Employment was not imposed. Full-day excursions on Sundays, and shorter walks throughout the week, were permitted. Dietary allowances were more generous, including tea, milk and sugar, and perhaps even extra food if considered appropriate. The medical officer, whose consent was required before disabled paupers were punished, was able to order them beer, porter, tobacco and snuff. And from 1847 unions were encouraged to provide married accommodation for elderly couples.[36]

Such 'indulgences' were sometimes, but not always forth-coming. At the Gressenhall Workhouse in Norfolk, for example, married accommodation was opened in 1853, but ten years later only 14 of the other 21 institutions in the county had such a facility. Nationwide, the proportion was slightly lower, 311 unions in England and 15 in Wales providing elderly couples with shared workhouse rooms by 1862.[37] Similarly variable was exemption from workhouse employment: a relentless, soul-destroying business. Men chopped wood, ground corn or, until 1846, crushed bones or broke stone. Women, if not engaged in domestic tasks, made sacks or picked oakum.[38] Though only the able-bodied were supposed to undertake such labour, some institutions recruited elderly inmates. On occasions they were stretched beyond rea-sonable limits, as the medical officer of Blean in Kent complained to his guardians in 1842: 'it is my opinion that women who are on the verge of 70 years should not be called upon...for such... work as the washing of an establishment of this kind.'[39] If old age absolved workhouse inmates of employment, impairment did not. The Poor Law Commission instructed local officials 'to keep the partially disabled paupers occupied to the extent of their abil-ity; and to leave none who are capable of employment idle at any time'. Therefore, at Hampshire's infamous Andover Workhouse, William Newport – a man with one leg – was among the starving paupers discovered gnawing the bones that they were required to pulverize in the labour yard.[40]

Mentally impaired inmates were also singled out. The 1834 Act defined the workhouse as a staging post for 'dangerous luna-tics' *en route* for specialized asylums, but required their removal after no more than two weeks. Those with 'harmless' mental impairments, on the other hand, were allowed to reside on a long-term basis. A shortage of asylum places, allied to the reluctance of guardians to meet their higher marginal costs, meant that not all inmates with serious mental illnesses or disruptive behaviour patterns were transferred. How to treat them was initially left to local discretion, but as quickly as 1835 Birmingham had set up separate wards for the 'insane'. Leicester followed in the early 1840s and by the early 1860s 18 per cent of all unions in England and Wales, many of them in London and the industrial North, were segregating in this way. Welcomed by the poor law authorities, these wards were deplored by the lunacy commissioners who regarded them as a cheap substitute for the proper asylum. Empowered to inspect from 1845, the commissioners prioritized wards for the 'insane', visiting those for 'idiots' less frequently. Ruth Hodgkinson has argued that this inspection, together with the appointment of medical officers, gradually fostered an increasingly humane regime tracking the reduction of physical coercion in the asylum sector. From 1853 the Poor Law Commission did prohibit the use of chains, manacles and other mechanical restraints.[41] Furthermore, at least some lunatic wards aimed to cure patients rather than allowing them to 'fester out of the public eye'.[42] However, the gentlemanly mode of inspection – inspired more by paternalist obligation than the civil liberty of inmates or any social right to adequate facilities – was too under-resourced robustly to monitor workhouse conditions.

Workhouse conditions

The poor law commissioners sought to convey a positive impression of conditions for disabled inmates, insisting in their third *Annual Report* that 'The warmth and cleanliness, the wholesomeness of the workhouse, as well as the regularity of the diet, could scarcely fail to be manifested in the general health of the infirm and the aged inmates.'[43] This view met with independent corroboration. When the French philosopher and critic, Hippolyte Taine, visited the Manchester workhouse in the early 1860s, he was full of praise for the 'beautiful, correct, and useful' institution that he saw.

> [T]he most aged and feeble women have white caps and new clothes.... One room is set apart for the lunatics, another for the female idiots; the latter do needle work for some hours daily; during the period of recreation they dance together to the sounds of a fiddle.[44]

In reality, the quality of workhouse environments was inconsistent. In 1836 the guardians of the Bradfield Union in Yorkshire congratulated themselves on not receiving a single complaint about breaching 'the just privilege or comforts of the aged, or blind'. On the contrary, 'the cleanliness of the linen and habits, the regularity of wholesome and sufficient meals, and the medical attendance' meant that their circumstances were 'ameliorated and enhanced'. A year later the Union had opened a dedicated poorhouse for the 'aged' and 'infirm', where children would not annoy them.[45] Across the Pennines at Bolton in Lancashire, on the other hand, conditions were sordid, an investigation of 1843 finding inmates with infectious diseases mingling with the healthy and 'the aged and the young covered with vermin'.[46]

The state of the workhouse provoked a rumbling discontent that was bolstered by literary and empirical representations. Charles Dickens, renowned for his portrait of workhouse cruelty in *Oliver Twist* (1837–8), also depicted the socio-psychological effects of confinement with telling insight. Describing the Sunday congregation at a workhouse chapel in a journalistic article of 1850, he observed that:

> Generally, the faces ... were depressed and subdued, and wanted colour. Aged people were there, in every variety. Mumbling, blear-eyed, spectacled, stupid, deaf, lame; vacantly winking in the gleams of sun that now and then crept in through the open doors, from the paved yard; shading their listening ears, or blinking eyes, with their withered hands; poring over their books, leering at nothing, going to sleep, crouching and drooping in corners. Upon the whole, it was the dragon, Pauperism, in a very weak and impotent position; toothless, fangless, drawing his breath heavily enough, and hardly worth chaining up.[47]

The public impact of such literary images was reinforced in the mid-1860s by the devastating results of an empirical survey of the sick poor in metropolitan workhouses, which was sponsored by the *Lancet*, a leading medical journal.

In investigating the causes of high mortality, the enquiry uncovered strengths as well as weaknesses. Take, for example, the management of mental impairment. It was 'quite an oasis in the desert, when, as at Marylebone, Newington and some other houses, we find a garden with swings, birdcages, and rabbit hutches for the amusement of these poor creatures, and a number of pretty pictures pasted upon the walls of their day-room'. In Chelsea, on the other hand, both violent 'lunatics' and the 'chronic insane' roamed 'in a melancholy objectless manner about the house and yards',[48] whilst in Shoreditch 'idiots' were found

> [m]oping about in herds, without any occupation whatever; neither classified, nor amused, nor employed; congregated in a miserable day-room, where they sit and stare at each other or at the bare walls, and where the monotony is only broken by the occasional excitement due to an epileptic [fit] or the gibbering and fitful laughter of some more excitable lunatic...[49]

The *Lancet* blamed these lapses on the principles of 1834:

> For the first time it could not be denied that the character of workhouse inmates had completely changed, and that a harsh and repulsive regime intended for the repression of idleness and imposture had been and was still applied to persons suffering from acute diseases, permanent disability, or old age brought on prematurely by sickness, starvation, intemperance and neglect.... The national sense of humanity was deeply shocked, and arousing from its usual apathy on pauper misery, society united in a determined effort to redress the evil...[50]

The response was to fall back on the separatist solution of the Royal Commission, stillborn over 30 years before. In 1867, the Metropolitan Poor Act established a Metropolitan Asylums Board charged with using its common fund to build separate isolation hospitals, infirmaries and asylums catering for serious intellectual impairments. In 1868, a second Poor Law Amendment Act encouraged separate infirmaries in the provinces, though without the facility for jointly financed projects.

In their history of the English poor law, Sidney and Beatrice Webb interpreted this specialization in therapeutic terms; 'the mere relief of destitution' was being 'progressively replaced by a policy of preventive and curative treatment'. Consequently, the strategy attempted:

> to take out of the general mixed workhouse and to transfer to special-ised institutions or other forms of treatment, one class of paupers after another; the children, the vagrants, the persons of unsound mind, those suffering from infectious disease, other sick persons, the blind,

the deaf and dumb, the crippled, the sane epileptics, the chronically infirm or even feeble-minded, the aged and even the able-bodied unemployed.[51]

When approving building plans after 1870, the Local Government Board did intensify its support for specialization as the endorsement of 'separate buildings on one site' gave way to 'separate buildings on separate sites'. Special circumstances were also met by moving paupers to more appropriate institutions. Since 1851 guardians had been permitted to send children to schools not more than 20 miles distant. From the late 1860s, they could also send adults with sensory impairments to suitable hospitals or institutions, and mentally impaired people of all ages to workhouses or establishments in other parishes.[52] However, this therapeutic model sat uneasily with the contemporary crusade against outdoor relief that inflated the workhouse population in the later nineteenth century.

The crusade against outdoor relief

The crusade against outdoor relief was triggered by its spiralling expenditure. In the 1860s, the cost of payments outside the workhouse had bucked the downward trend and jumped from £2,863,000 to £3,633,000. The number assisted similarly swelled from 695,000 to 838,000.[53] There were economic reasons, in particular trade depressions and harsh winters in London, and the Lancashire Cotton Famine caused by the American Civil War.[54] However, the reaction was an ideological restatement of the principles of 1834, embodied in the infamous Goschen Minute of 1869 written by the president of the Poor Law Board, George Goschen. The Local Government Board endorsed this Minute when it assumed responsibility for poor relief in 1871. Outdoor payments were 'in many cases granted by the Guardians too readily and without sufficient inquiry', complained one early circular; 'and . . . they give it also in numerous instances in which it would be more judicious to apply the workhouse test'.[55] A Select Committee on the Poor Law in Scotland reached similar conclusions a year later. Only the institution was capable of providing adequate relief that was not excessive. Therefore, the workhouse test was to be extended from the able-bodied to all classes of pauper and the applicant was expected to demonstrate 'why he should be excepted from the rule on indoor relief.'[56]

This crackdown was not an onslaught against the reluctant worker, to be disciplined by obnoxious employment under regimes like that at the notorious Poplar Workhouse in London. Able-bodied men, including those temporarily sick, formed less than 5 per cent of the pauper population. As a consequence, the main victims were widows and children, and the impaired adult poor.[57] These 'deserving' groups supplied new recruits for the workhouse. Between 1871 and 1901, the number of 'non-able-bodied' paupers in receipt of indoor relief climbed from 68,500 to 109,700. This increase continued an established trend, but it also exceeded growth in the older population, representing a rise from 3 per cent to 5 per cent of those over 65. Pat Thane maintains that the elderly majority of workhouse inmates suffered less than single or widowed mothers.[58] In austere unions like Brixworth in Northamptonshire, however, the 'not able-bodied' were targeted, where 'as much as anywhere...imposition and abuses prevail'. Indeed, the 'partially disabled' were singled out as particularly prone to idleness and banned from outdoor relief unless they had a 'deprivation of limbs, or eyesight', or were extremely old.[59] Upholding the work ethic was particularly important at the boundaries.

By the later nineteenth century, the specialization that had first emerged in the 1860s was amassing support from several quarters. As Anne Crowther has argued in *The Workhouse System, 1834–1929* (p. 90):

> Specialized institutions appealed to humanitarians who felt that the helpless would be 'better off' inside them; to eugenists who hoped incarceration would prevent the unfit from breeding; to the medical elite who were themselves becoming more specialized; and to a vague public sense of propriety which disliked mixing the deserving with the disreputable poor.

On the ground, the move towards separate institutions was slow. Though a number of large provincial unions set up infirmaries for the sick, only one – West Derby in Liverpool – actually built a separate workhouse for the chronic 'infirm' and when finally opened in 1914 it was as the Alder Hey Children's Hospital. In London, the Metropolitan Asylums Board stimulated more activity and two institutions for the 'harmless insane' started business at Caterham and Leavesden in 1870, each accommodating 1500 inmates. In addition, unions amalgamated under the second Amendment Act rationalized their workhouses to achieve dedicated facilities for different categories of pauper, including the 'aged and infirm', for whom large dormitories and purpose-built blocks were erected. In the late 1860s, the City Road Workhouse commissioned new premises in which the wards had no fewer than 56 beds and a hydraulic lift was installed to transport bedridden inmates, and food and other materials, to the upper levels. At the same time, the St Marylebone guardians, 'anxious that their aged poor should be made as comfortable as the rules of a workhouse will permit', constructed a three-story building with two wards per floor, each containing 40 beds. In 1898/9 they were active again, adding two ornate blocks that housed 555 old and 'infirm' men, plus 21 'imbeciles' and six 'lunatics' of both sexes.[60]

For workhouse inmates, life was monotonous. In the 1870s, a Bavarian emigrant artist called Hubert von Herkomer (1849–1914) painted *Eventide: A Scene in the Westminster Union* (Figure 1) that he exhibited at the Royal Academy. A superficial reading focuses on the cluster of well-dressed women in the foreground who were drinking tea, reading and sewing in a day-room where the walls were decked with pictures. This, however, is not a picture of a 'happy and comfortable old age'. 'The dark flat forms of two figures that seem to be shuffling forward...cast a long symbolically-laden shadow,' which is compounded by the 'plunging perspective' that heightens the impression of 'deprivation and loneliness'.[61] A leading artist of the Victorian realist school, von Herkomer took '[p]oor people...as subject-matter for a new kind of art, in which social conscience was combined with a documentary interest in accurate recording'.[62] In adopting this stance, the social realists were accused of arousing pity that confirmed the compassion of the ruling class and sanctioned charity as an adequate solution to social problems. However, originally produced as a wood engraving for a popular weekly news magazine, *Eventide* exposed the 'dreary jail-like interior' of the workhouse to a wide audience.[63] Therefore, like the literature and journalism of Dickens earlier in the century, von Herkomer's art increased public awareness and public debate, contributing to a political context that questioned the propriety of the workhouse for elderly and disabled people.[64]

Figure 1   Hubert von Herkomer, *Eventide – A Study at the Westminster Union*

Source: National Museums, Liverpool.

Quality assurance within the late Victorian workhouse remained too weak to detect when a monotonous regime became abusive. In the mid-1890s, one of the original *Lancet* commissioners oversaw an investigation of provincial workhouses. He was horrified to discover that conditions were often no better than they had been in 1866. In one case, the sick were

> lying on plank beds with chaff mattresses about three inches thick between their weary bodies and the hard uneven planks. One paralysed woman had a spring bed with a chaff mattress over the springs . . . Some idiots and imbeciles share the wards with these patients.[65]

Procedures as well as amenities were found to be unsatisfactory. In March 1892, the medical officer for the Blean Union in Kent reported that when three weeks ago 'one of the old men fell and injured his hip, . . . his skin was so dirty as to render an examination difficult and extremely disagreeable.' A decade before he had asked that 'each adult inmate be provided with a bath or some other means of thoroughly washing the whole surface of the body at least once a month, and the feet and legs at least once a fortnight'.[66]

The extension of the franchise to more working-class men in 1867 and 1884–5 created a new context for social policy. In Lynn Hollen Lees's words, '[a]s workers asserted their rights to political citizenship, they adopted a broad conception of social citizenship that made welfare in the form of "poor" laws unacceptable.'[67] Therefore, calls for a more relaxed workhouse regime accompanied the ongoing discourse about old age pensions.[68] By 1900 the *Annual Report* of the Local Government Board was recommending that guardians 'should form a special class of inmates of 65 years of age and upwards' who were worthy of this status because of 'their moral character or behaviour or previous habits'. This group was to be allowed individual sleeping cubicles, personal lockers and extra day-rooms, set apart from 'disreputable inmates', in which the sexes were permitted to mix. The daily routine also became more flexible, diet was enhanced and additional rations of tobacco, tea and sugar were granted. Finally, the pauper uniform was dropped.[69] The degree to which these 'perks' were extended to younger disabled people is unclear, given eugenic attitudes to physical and mental impairments at the beginning of the twentieth century.[70]

Despite policy changes at central level, local reform was patchy. Consequently, the Minority Report of the Royal Commission on the Poor Laws was still in 1909 expressing dismay at the 'terrible sights' witnessed in the mixed workhouse:

> We have seen feeble-minded boys growing up in the workhouse year after year, untaught, untrained, alternately neglected and tormented by other inmates . . . we have seen idiots who are physically offensive or mischievous, or so noisy as to create a disturbance by day and by night with their howls, living in the ordinary wards, to the perpetual annoyance and disgust of the other inmates . . . We have seen half-witted women nursing the sick, feeble-minded women in charge of the babies, and imbecile old men put to look after the boys out of school hours.[71]

Yet such encounters did not detract from the Commission's overall conclusion that rural workhouses were humanely managed.[72] What bothered them more were the vast, barrack-like structures in urban areas that regimented large numbers of elderly inmates. Thus the Majority Report recalled a large institution where more than 900 old people

> were congregated in large rooms, without any attempt to employ their time or cheer their lives. There was a marked absence of any human interest . . . It could not be better described than as a 'human warehouse'. The dormitories, which in some cases accommodated as many as sixty inmates, were so full of beds as to make it impossible to provide chairs, or to walk, except sideways, between them.[73]

It was difficult to transcend the principle of 'less eligibility' for groups of any age who were not economically productive.

From public assistance institutions to 'sunshine hotels'?

The First World War, and the economic problems of peace that came to a head in the Great Depression of the early 1930s, reduced resources for all social expenditure. For the poor law, cash was not the only problem. The failure of the Royal Commission to produce a single report created a hiatus that condemned indoor and outdoor relief to cosmetic alteration. Both the Majority and the Minority Reports proposed abolishing the Boards of Guardians, but whereas the former recommended replacing them with Public Assistance Committees in every borough and county, the latter recommended allocating their functions to existing local authority committees as appropriate. Opponents of reform exploited the division to stall change.[74] In 1913 the workhouse was renamed the poor law institution, and in 1918 the new Ministry of Health absorbed poor law administration. Mathew Thomson has suggested that the move to the Ministry of Health may have bettered conditions for 'mentally defective' people. However, even the eventual removal of functions from the guardians to the public assistance committees in 1929 did little to modify the stigmatizing tenor of relief.[75]

Throughout the inter-war period, 'aged and infirm' inmates continued to dominate the poor law cum public assistance institution. There was pressure to improve their quality of life by upgrading food, clothing and surroundings, and by encouraging outside visitors. Local authorities were also permitted to pay pocketmoney after 1938: a decision that epitomized the patronizing attitude towards residents. A few local authorities did begin to built separate accommodation, particularly in the years leading up to the Second World War, but only for hand-picked categories of elderly people who in Birmingham were deemed 'women of the more gentler type' or men of 'the merit class'.[76] Concerned about the isolation of deaf inmates, the National Institute called on public assistance institutions to improve opportunities for communication by bringing them together.[77] Deaf and blind institutions had since the nineteenth century offered accommodation in conjunction with their education and employment programmes,[78] and temporary hostels for ex-servicemen retained severely impaired occupants on a permanent basis after the First World War.[79] For the most part, however, charities began to develop residential homes for disabled adults from the 1920s,[80] mirroring the provision of separate accommodation for elderly people by local authorities.

The Second World War threw up a crisis of massive proportions, bomb damage and family disruption creating extra demand for residential care at the same time as hospitals were decanting their chronically sick and disabled patients into public assistance institutions. However, the middle-class members of these groups judged irrelevant to the war effort were shocked by their close encounter with the spartan environment of the old workhouse and its petty restrictions. Such experiences lent weight to the reform campaign. In 1947 the Ministry of Health issued a circular calling on local authorities to improve existing arrangements as a matter of urgency. A year later the National Assistance Act, one of the pillars of the post-war welfare state, required them to provide accommodation for all 'who by reason of age, infirmity or any other circumstances are in need of care or attention which is not otherwise available'. There were also responsibilities to register and inspect voluntary residential homes for elderly and disabled people.[81] Though the Act received a euphoric welcome, restrictions on capital expenditure condemned post-war residential care to pre-war poor law premises, frustrating construction of what the *Daily Mail* called 'sunshine hotels'.[82] Therefore, when Peter Townsend investigated residential homes in 1960, he found that 35,000 elderly people were still living in former public assistance institutions – just 5000 less than in 1949.[83]

Conditions in these homes owed much to the poor law mentality. Bureaucracy led to rigid regimes. There were few single rooms or personal possessions. Social interaction between residents was discouraged. And staff were aggressive;[84] indeed, one ex-workhouse master complained how after 1948 it was no longer possible to punish residents by stopping privileges like sweets and tobacco.[85] By 1960 207 newly built homes had been opened.[86] However, few were dedicated to younger disabled people, many of whom lived in old age institutions. Others occupied accommodation that local authorities 'bought' from established or newly emerging charities like the Cheshire Foundation.[87] These homes played an important role in the evolution of the disability movement. In the late 1960s, residents at Le Court in Hampshire invited two researchers from the Tavistock Institute to assist them in challenging the needs-based approach to service and putting the case for greater personal autonomy and greater political influence in management decisions.[88] The resulting study, which defined the first task of institutions for 'the physically handicapped and the young chronic sick' as processing 'the transition from social to physical death',[89] simply advocated 'a reworking of traditional professional practice' on the grounds that the residents' agenda was unrealistic. Le Court was subsequently the seedbed for the Hampshire Centre for Independent Living, later the Hampshire Coalition of Disabled People, one of the first organizations to promote independent living through personalized support packages.[90]

Disabled inmates

The disabled inmates who inhabited the workhouse were not necessarily permanent residents. Official statistics do not allow us to investigate length of stay, but David Thomson has calculated for elderly people that 'perhaps 1 in 6 men and 1 in 13 women', aged 65 or over at the beginning of January 1841 and living within the area of the Bedford Poor Law Union, 'were to seek at least one night's shelter in the workhouse during the next 30 years'. Furthermore, only an estimated 7 per cent of the male cohort and 4 per cent of the female cohort, both aged 55–64 in 1841, would die in the workhouse and even among those who became institutionalized the proportion was less than a half.[91] But if indoor relief was a temporary phase for some, a one-off parliamentary return for 1861 showed that disabled people predominated among the long-term population resident for at least five years. Of the 21 per cent of adult inmates who fell into this category, 42 per cent were elderly or 'infirm', 35 per cent were mentally ill, and 11 per cent were 'handicapped'.[92]

Among the older inmates, men were more numerous than women, perhaps because they were less domestically competent or less useful within the family division of labour where child care was a marketable commodity.[93] In any event, during the 12 months to 25 March 1892, there were 685,000 men over 65 inhabiting workhouses but only 457,000 women. The gap was relative as well as absolute, men in receipt of indoor relief constituting 11.3 per cent of the age group and workhouse women 6 per cent.[94] There were regional variations, London workhouses being 'much more heavily populated by the elderly than workhouses elsewhere'. Despite narrowing, however, the gender differential clearly survived the increased institutionalization of the older poor from the 1870s – a trend that was more pronounced among women than men – and in London women were still less likely to be on indoor relief than men in the 1930s.[95]

Though 'less eligibility' was difficult to enforce until working-class living standards showed significant improvement towards the end of the nineteenth-century,[96] the psychological trauma of confinement was intense. Some elderly people construed the workhouse as a medical service in an effort to reduce the pain of admission. This Martha Loane discovered during her travels as a district nurse in the late nineteenth and early twentieth centuries:

> The workhouse in all refined circles is called the Infirmary, and it seems to be a point of honour with most of the elderly inmates to speak of it as a well-managed place to which they have voluntarily retired. 'I have a day nurse and a night nurse', said an old man solemnly, although he knew that I knew that he was not in the Infirmary at all, 'and every comfort as the doctor orders. Whatever he says I'm to have is purvided without stint. Yes, it's a blessing there *is* such places, ma'am.'[97]

Other potential inmates evaded the workhouse at all costs. As Charles Booth observed in 1894, the 'aversion to the "House" is absolutely universal, and almost any amount of suffering and privation will be endured by the people rather than go into it.'[98] So terrifying was the prospect of the workhouse for one disabled man that, according to the *Dereham and Fakenham Times*, he committed suicide in 1897 rather than face admission.[99]

The 'bastilles' that evoked such fear did not always crush their inmates, despite the punitive regulatory code. Therefore, riots periodically erupted; staff and inmates were exposed to verbal abuse and physical violence; and those with the 'privilege' of temporarily leaving the institution returned in a drunken state.[100] Disabled people may have participated in these acts of protest, but they also complained through the official channels. In 1876, the Minute Book of the Mitford and Launditch Union in Norfolk noted that the elderly and 'infirm' inmates were unhappy about the pea soup and tea with which they had been supplied. When interrogated by the guardians, the master admitted that the soup 'was improperly cooked', and that the tea was defective in both quality and quantity.[101] On this occasion, the grievance was locally resolved, but inmates also wrote to and elicited responses from the central authority. In 1879 the guardians of the Cricklade and Wootton Bassett Union in Wiltshire received a communication from the Local Government Board in which their attention was drawn to a letter from Jane Richens. A married woman of 80 who was described as an 'invalid', she had discharged herself from the workhouse because she had been placed in a ward for able-bodied women with straw beds and given the basic diet that she was unable to eat. The guardians observed that she had been treated in the same way as other 'old and infirm women' because the medical officer considered that she was not a suitable case for the infirmary. She herself had not requested a separate bedroom.[102]

Conditions in the early twentieth-century workhouse are accessible through oral history. Joyce Brayne, born with cerebral palsy at a Warwickshire workhouse in 1916, was one of 50 people interviewed in depth for *Out of Sight*, a study of disability in Britain between 1900 and 1950:

> Nobody wanted me because I couldn't walk and I couldn't talk proper. Mother left me in the workhouse and I had to stay there until I was six. We didn't get much food and I had to crawl around on the floor and I slept in a big high bed and I were always scared to fall out. And I had to look after eight babies there when I could feed meself. I tested the bottles of milk on my arm. That was my job and I fed them every four hours. Never learned to write or speak properly because nobody took no notice so long as I did my work. But I were only really little then and I had to do everything I was told or I got smacked.[103]

Critics of oral history dismiss such testimony as anecdote, unreliable in comparison with the written document or statistical return. There are issues to bear in mind. Leading questions may produce distorted answers. Reminiscence may yield stereotypical responses. The meanings that individuals attach to their pasts are reconstituted over time. And their stories may lack chronological specificity.[104] But no historical source is an objective account of past reality; all were constructed with a purpose in mind that renders them subjective. Therefore, Joyce Brayne's story of exploitation and neglect is not invalid for being told orally in the first person.

Workhouse practices towards disabled people are a formidable indictment of its mentality. The infraction of rules and the registration of complaints demonstrate that they were not inevitably bullied into submission. However, acts of insubordination were easily controlled and whilst guardians may have tackled those grievances that arose from the behaviour of paid officials, they were able to deflect criticism of their own procedures with ease. Consequently, whilst resistance may have been personally empowering, structural change proved illusive.

Conclusion

The workhouse was a major instrument of institutional confinement in modern Britain. There was no mixed economy, agencies of local government becoming the sole suppliers after a handful of early commercial ventures faltered. Though the central state offered tutelage, provision was highly variable even following the efforts of the 1834 Poor Law Amendment Act to impose uniformity. In the late eighteenth century, Gilbert's Act briefly conceived of the workhouse as a refuge protecting the 'impotent' poor. For the most part, however, its purpose was to implement the principle of economic rationality by extracting labour from the able-bodied unemployed and teaching them the virtues of the work ethic. Yet the 'feckless' were always a small minority of inmates. Many more were disabled people, some of whom were compulsorily detained because of mental impairment. Inspection systems were too rudimentary to guarantee the civil rights of these inmates, who were also disenfranchised by the removal of any previous right to vote. Towards the end of the nineteenth century, increased political citizenship led to demands for social citizenship that were incompatible with the ethos of poor relief. Disabled people added their own complaints, using both the official channels and unofficial protest. Nevertheless, the regime of 'less eligibility' was resilient in the face of inmates who broke the norms of economic productivity, and the replacement of the workhouse with the public assistance institution, and later the residential home, left demeaning conditions and procedures ensconced.

3

Hospitals

Though medieval foundations had offered treatment as well as hospitality within an ecclesiastical context, the modern hospitals that sprung up in Britain after 1700 were secular institutions for which medicine was the *raison d'être*. The early modern period retained an allegiance to the humoral ideas of the classical world. Good health, physical and mental, consisted of a stable balance of blood, phlegm, yellow bile and black bile appropriate to the age and personality of the individual; illness occurred when the equilibrium was disturbed. From the 1750s, this system was displaced by a localized pathology that focused on diseased organs rather than the general constitution, and classified clinical conditions by 'correlating external symptoms with [these] internal lesions'. From the later nineteenth century, organs gave way to cells as the body's basic building block, and an emphasis on general cellular activity fused the distinction between normal and abnormal functioning.[1] The cumulative effect of these developments was to lock modern medicine into a curative mode that privileged the full repair of defective organs or cells, and stigmatized patients who were unable to return to economically rational social roles. For disabled people, hospitals were central to these 'dividing practices'. Often confined for long periods of time, they experienced institutional medicine not as a social right but as a product of medical knowledge and power that was difficult to resist. This chapter teases out these themes in relation to physical conditions, paying particular attention to the eighteenth-century voluntary infirmary, the rise of orthopaedics, and the emergence of geriatric and rehabilitation medicine. But first we look at the evolving mixed economy of hospital provision.

From charitable to state medicine

The modern hospital in Britain was a derivative of voluntary infirmaries provided by charitable effort and indoor medical relief provided by the poor law. In the voluntary infirmaries that emerged during the early eighteenth century, benefactors and subscribers were normally allowed to serve as governors, and sponsor poor but deserving patients, in return for their financial contributions. Physicians and surgeons who earned a living from paying customers offered medical services free of charge; and, in compensation, they gained access to a laboratory of patients whose compliance with clinical directions was closely supervised.[2] By 1800 there were 33 voluntary hospitals in England and Wales[3] and they expanded rapidly during the nineteenth and early twentieth centuries so that by 1938 there were 696 separate infirmaries.[4] Funding diversified to include corporate subscriptions from employers, friendly societies and poor law authorities, patient charges, collections among workmen and contributory schemes that offered a package of health care benefits for a weekly sum. But these mechanisms failed to keep pace with the costs of modern medicine and the hospitals were too jealous of their charitable independence to accept significant government intervention. Therefore, they slipped into financial crisis. Absorbed into the Emergency Medical Service during the Second World War, voluntary infirmaries became reluctant members of the NHS in 1948.[5] Like the Robert Jones and Agnes Hunt Orthopaedic Hospital at Oswestry in Shropshire, they feared being 'dragooned with a dull, even if fairly high level of mediocrity'.[6]

Complementing charitable infirmaries was indoor poor relief. Before 1834 there were separate wards or hospitals for the sick at only a few urban workhouses. The Poor Law Amendment Act made no explicit reference to health and guardians were unwilling to incur the high capital and revenue costs of infirmaries. Consequently, institutional facilities developed slowly, hospital wards and buildings were dilapidated and overcrowded, nursing standards low and amenities primitive. These conditions, brought to public prominence by the *Lancet* investigation of workhouses in 1866, triggered legislation for separate infirmaries. In London the new Metropolitan Asylums Board, with its common fund, encouraged hospital development, but provision in the provinces, without either inducement, was variable. Guardians in some towns ran pristine infirmaries; others tolerated dirty and out-dated premises; and only a few rural unions had separate facilities. The 1929 Local Government Act sought to remove hospital medicine from the shadow of the poor law by enabling the transfer of hospitals from the new Public Assistance Committees to the already established Public Health Committees of local authorities. By 1936, 46 major authorities, but only nine outside London, had 'appropriated 92 institutions.' But whilst this takeover improved the quality of acute medicine, it perpetuated both the neglect of chronic conditions and the imbalance between urban and rural areas.[7]

Like voluntary hospitals, the former poor law infirmaries were incorporated into the Emergency Medical Service during the Second World War and the National Health Service inherited both types of institution. Universally available to the population as a whole and collectivist in offering health care free of charge at the point of receipt, the brief of the NHS was 'to promote the establishment ... of a comprehensive health service designed to secure improvement in the physical and mental health of the people ... and the prevention, diagnosis and treatment of illness'.[8] However, there was no automatic social right to treatment. Rather citizens were granted a right of access, the outcome of which was dependent upon resource availability and professional judgement.[9] Escalating costs in an era of post-war austerity frustrated NHS ambitions. For hospitals, the consequence was a diversion of monies from capital to revenue expenditure, starving them of funds to replace or upgrade their decaying buildings. The 1962 Hospital Plan introduced a national network of district general hospitals with 600 to 800 beds and proposed the construction of 90 such sites within the next decade.[10] By the late 1970s, however, capital expenditure was still heavily skewed towards London and the South East, despite the implementation of a resource allocation formula aimed at achieving greater equity.[11]

The rapid advance of high-technology medicine intensified the financial pressures on the NHS, relegating to low priority the long-term requirements of disabled people who were perceived as neither medically challenging nor economically productive. But this was not a problem unique to the late twentieth century. On the contrary, hospitals – in collaboration with doctors – had privileged acute over chronic patients since the eighteenth century. Far from being an objective science, medical knowledge was unavoidably connected to professional power. 'We should admit... that power produces knowledge', wrote Foucault, 'that power and knowledge directly imply one another; that there is no power relation without the correlative constitution of a field of knowledge, nor any knowledge that does not presuppose and constitute at the same time power relations.'[12] Therefore, health care practitioners used their knowledge not simply to further the best interests of patients but also to pursue their own professional interests by engaging with dominant social values. Resistance, denied comparable knowledge and power, was limited in its impact.

The eighteenth-century voluntary hospital

Though the eighteenth-century voluntary infirmary fulfilled a series of social, cultural and political functions,[13] it shared with the workhouse a commitment to economic rationality. Instead of putting the poor to work, hospitals sought to render them healthy for useful employment, thereby increasing national prosperity and reducing the cost of relief. In this pre-anaesthetic era, most treatment involved the administration of drugs or the application of minor surgical procedures to the body surface: bleeding, blistering, the dressing of wounds or ulcers, and the manipulation of fractures.[14] But to gear the Enlightenment faith in scientific progress to the achievement of economic advance, doctors and hospitals had to demonstrate their efficacy.[15] Consequently, acute conditions were prioritized over chronic conditions where there was little prospect of major improvement, and hospital rules banned patients 'disordered in their Senses, ... [and] apprehended to be in a dying condition or incurable'.[16] The effect was inequality of access to health care, resources being skewed towards younger adults and men among whom short-term ailments were most prevalent and economic utility most pressing.[17]

The General Infirmary at Bath, specifically founded in 1739 to grant poor 'cripples and other indigent strangers' access to the spa,[18] did not escape this calculus.[19] Judging that there were few parishes without disabled people who 'by the loss of their limbs, are become a burden to themselves and their neighbours', the

Infirmary set out to restore them 'from impotence to strength, from beggary and want, to a capacity of getting an honest livelihood, and comfortable subsistence'.[20] In the mid-eighteenth century, approximately 70 per cent of patients had rheumatism, paralysis or another neurological or muscular-skeletal condition, whilst during the 60 years between 1760 and 1830 rheumatism and paralysis together accounted for 60 per cent of all patients, lameness for 15 per cent, and colica pictonum for 10 per cent. Whereas most contemporary infirmaries discharged their patients after two or three months unless there were exceptional circumstances, the Bath Infirmary operated a six-month rule and during the 1740s and 1750s mean residence was in excess of 130 days. Even when eventually discharged, however, only just over a quarter of all patients were deemed 'cured' – far less than the proportion at other voluntary hospitals.[21]

The humoral model that underpinned assessment of these treatment outcomes defined 'cure' in terms of reverting to a proper equilibrium rather than mending a defective organ or bodily function.[22] For disabled people, the apparent virtue of this approach was the assimilation of impairment into an understanding of illness free of the curative aspirations of modern medicine. However, letters recommending patients for admission to the Infirmary were written with a negative vocabulary. Thomas Thatcher of Whatley in Somerset had 'for about six years past, been afflicted with a general weakness and relaxation of the nerves, or a sort of universal palsy'. '[A]ll parts ... [were] alike afflicted, and seem[ed] to partake of the common imbecility.' Therefore, he spoke 'just intelligibly, but very lame and hesitating and walks about, but staggers like a child just learning to go'.[23] We cannot assume from this language of loss that the community as a whole embraced a calamitous view of impairment because the authors – predominantly doctors, clergymen and other major local figures – were soliciting the services of an institution whose publicity embraced such a discourse. Nevertheless, the depiction of prospective patients as the victims of 'crippling' conditions shows that, even where humoralism blurred the boundaries between sickness and health, impairments were construed as pathological.

The eighteenth-century Bath Hospital demonstrates that a forceful partnership between economic rationality and medicine was in existence before the Industrial Revolution or the modern state.

The implications for the patient were profound. Though the system of sponsorship implied a degree of co-operation over admission, rebutting the patronage of an employer or local dignitary, or even exercising the right to leave at will, ran the risk of alienating those upon whom future security might depend. An ignominious discharge for misbehaving or disobeying medical orders was still more damaging.[24] Accounts of what went on inside the eighteenth-century infirmary are few and far between, but in 1809 a minor actor called Joseph Wilde was admitted to the Devon and Exeter Hospital with an injured knee. In the long poem describing his experiences, Wilde told of the camaraderie among patients, the ambulant of whom helped to clean the wards and look after their bedridden fellows. In contrast, relations with the medical and nursing staff were cold and formal. Wilde was confused by the questions that he faced prior to admission and distressed by the ridicule that he detected among those examining him. The regular ward visits by physicians and surgeons were similarly daunting as at 'the fix'd hour, each cripple' – the 'lame recumbent, and the sick erect' – awaited inspection 'in solemn silence hush'd', his 'wounds' exposed 'all bare' to public scrutiny. The everyday insensitivities of the nursing staff compounded the trepidation of the periodic medical examination. Allocated to an upper floor despite his physical impairment, Wilde saw '[s]igns of impatience ... but none of pity' in the 'stormy eye' of the nurse who accompanied him as he climbed 'with painful steps and slow' – 'presage', he thought, of 'trouble to ensue'.[25]

Of course, this autobiographical poem is based on one personal encounter, but the ethos that it described is consistent with Mary Fissell's thesis of estrangement between doctor and patient after 1750. Taking Bristol as her example, Fissell argues that voluntary infirmaries so increased medical power over the lower orders that patients' narratives vanished from hospital consultations. More and more, she says, the doctor came to rely on 'signs and symptoms' that were conducive to 'a disease-orientated diagnosis' and to 'the demands of hospital practice'. Therefore, 'foreign' labels were attached to patients who themselves remained in the realm of humoral medicine, and the treatment of their conditions was no longer negotiable.[26] The autobiography of a textile worker called Joseph Townend challenges the total absence of negotiation.[27] In 1827, Townend sought treatment at the Manchester Infirmary for an old burn and a recently injured wrist. The burn, which was the result of a childhood accident, had healed but attached the right arm to his side as far as the elbow. Townend reports that whenever the medical staff debated the options, his doctor asked him what was to be done. He always replied that he wanted the operation and believed that this continued insistence tipped the balance in favour of performing what was a controversial procedure.

Yet if there was consultation where experimental surgery was concerned, the enforcement of medical authority was fierce when rules were broken. As in Exeter, there was great comradeship among the patients and on one occasion Townend drank

rather freely of port wine, which a friend had poured into my tin. When the wound was dressed next morning, it was very much inflamed. Mr Waterhouse said, 'What hast thou been doing? Thou hast been out of bed?' He was very much grieved; and he suddenly jerked up my shoulder, which made me sweat with pain, and it cracked like the firing of a pistol.

Patient autonomy was exercised within strict parameters.

Orthopaedic medicine

At the same time as patient narratives were disappearing from the hospital consultation, the emergence of localized pathology was fragmenting medical knowledge and furnishing an intellectual rationale for specialization. Whereas attempts at specialist work-houses failed in the 1830s, specialist hospitals grew rapidly from the turn of the century as ambitious doctors sought institutional power bases outside the general hospitals that were dominated by the professional elite. Diseases of the eye were initially a popular cause, prompting the foundation of some 20 small infirmaries and dispensaries during the first four decades of the nineteenth century.[28] Orthopaedic hospitals were slower to develop. Derived from the Greek, 'orthopaedic' literally meant 'appertaining to the straight child', but the term was extended to adults as well as children and imbued with moral as well as physical connotations.[29] In Henri-Jacques Stiker's words: 'Straightening out physically and straightening up behaviorally . . . [were] put in the same semantic field, a normative one. Educate and rehabilitate, mind and body: draw upward toward correctness.'[30]

The first hospital dedicated to orthopaedics was established in Birmingham in 1817 'for the relief of Persons labouring under Bodily Deformity'. Though 'spinal diseases', and 'contractions and distortions of the limbs' were treated, club foot was singled out for particular attention. '[T]here are 50 children born annually in the town, with club feet,' the annual general meeting was told in 1862:

> [E]ach one costs in instruments alone, £2 and requires almost constant attention for at least a year. But this year we will send forth 50 human beings who instead of being cripples will, in the majority of cases have no evidences of their deformity remaining.[31]

The reason for emphasizing club foot was the availability of a surgical operation that promised to vanquish impairment. William Little, who founded an Infirmary for the Cure of Club Foot in London in 1838, learnt the procedure after undergoing it himself in Hanover. Two further metropolitan infirmaries, opening in 1851 and 1864, joined Little's foundation, and the three institutions merged in 1905 to form the Royal National Orthopaedic Hospital.[32] By the later nineteenth century, however, these infirmaries were becoming peripheral as a result of their concentration on a narrow range of methods applied to the foot. Indeed, by 1875 Little himself was questioning the value of the surgery that he had championed.[33]

With the orthopaedic hospitals marginalized, conservative approaches to surgery captured the initiative. There were two hubs to this development. Both exploited the eighteenth-century teachings of John Hunter, who not only advocated cautious use of the scalpel but also recognized 'the curative value of fresh air, rest, the immobilization of injured limbs, and ... minimal doses of physic'. First, general surgeons in general hospitals began to practice 'subcutaneous osteotomy – the technique for cutting and dividing bones by making insertions under the skin.' Designed to prevent 'post-operative blood poisoning' by avoiding the exposure of tissues, this 'technique made possible a whole range of treatments for diseased and deformed bones' from the 1860s and was not replaced by open 'antiseptic osteotomy' until 1878. The management of fractures formed a second hub for conservative methods. Instead of amputating broken limbs, some orthopaedic surgeons began to recommend splinting. '[A] man who understands my principles will do better with a bandage and a broomstick than another can do with an instrument-maker's arsenal,' declared the Liverpool practitioner, Hugh Owen Thomas. Thomas – who came from a dynasty of bonesetters – distanced himself from the manipulative techniques derived from this tradition. However, the new emphasis on mechanical practices was accompanied by the refinement of physiotherapeutic practices like massage, medical gymnastics, electrotherapy and hydrotherapy, and by the absorption of a holistic philosophy of diet, rest and fresh air.[34]

Despite the growth of conservative orthopaedics, a fatalistic attitude often prevailed and many doctors admitted 'to a large class of "stationary cripples" who, as a result of congenital malformations, accidents of childbirth, infantile paralysis or long-standing rickets, were beyond the surgical pale and . . . capable of help only through special education and training facilities'. Attitudes gradually changed as part of a broader reconfiguration of childhood that was manifest in the extension of state education and the introduction of compulsory attendance.[35] The effect was to throw into sharp relief the existence of children with physical, sensory and intellectual impairments who were uneducated and hence considered unemployable.[36] Though schools and training colleges were promoted in response to this disclosure, their ethos was pedagogic rather than medical. Since the 1880s, however, doctors had become increasingly engaged in managing children with sub-acute chronic conditions, mainly but not entirely non-pulmonary (as opposed to respiratory) tuberculosis. Their situation was highlighted by the growth of surgery at paediatric hospitals because, as chronically impaired patients blocked beds intended for acute, short-term cases, attention turned to an alternative model of long-term treatment.[37] It was exemplified by Agnes Hunt's charitable convalescent home at Baschurch near Oswestry in Shropshire that, during the Edwardian period, pioneered an orthopaedic facility of international renown with a programme of surgery, open-air therapy and satellite after-care clinics to supply post-operative care.[38]

Between 1914 and 1918 the First World War created additional clinical opportunities. Two-thirds of all casualties suffered locomotive injuries. Drawing on techniques learnt from the treatment of 'crippled' children, orthopaedic surgeons tackled fractures, gunshot wounds and nerve lesions, all of which fell within their province. During the early stages of the war, there was insufficient hospital space to absorb the huge influx of maimed soldiers and men not fit for duty were discharged from active service when their wounds, but not their physical impairments, were healed. Worry that this policy was both damaging the national economy and wasting military manpower led to the establishment of the first orthopaedic centre in Liverpool. By 1918 there were 20 such centres in the British Isles, containing a total of 20,000 beds. Under the control of Robert Jones – a nephew of Hugh Owen Thomas and wartime Director of Orthopaedics for the Army from 1916 – each centre consisted of a team of surgeons and a series of auxiliary departments offering massage, electrical and hydrological therapies, gymnastics and therapeutic employment.[39]

The cessation of hostilities endangered this orthopaedic power. Some military hospitals shut, albeit not immediately. In London, for example, the Shepherd's Bush Military Hospital – the premier orthopaedic centre during the conflict – was transferred to the Ministry of Pensions in 1922 and closed three years later.[40] Other wartime establishments adapted to peacetime circumstances by turning their attention to 'crippled' children or to industrial injuries. The Prince of Wales Orthopaedic Hospital in Cardiff followed the first course of action and by 1924 had 'ten open-air cots in the garden'; an appeal was also under way for funds to build separate premises 'on a healthy site, where educational facilities are easily available'.[41] The Prince of Wales Hospital was plugging into a National Scheme for the cure of 'crippled' children: an ambitious project set up by Robert Jones and fellow orthopaedic surgeons upon their return to civilian life in an effort 'to recreate the power and glory of their military empire' by applying the lessons of war to peacetime 'crippledom'. They were hopeful of attracting state sponsorship because the proposal accorded with the Ministry of Health's commitment to 'preventive and curative techniques' that also revealed 'the interdependence of the health of individuals and communities'. However, the continuing influence of local authorities in medical planning made it impossible for the Ministry to oversee the Scheme and, therefore, the orthopaedists turned to the charitable sector in the form of the Central Council for the Care of Cripples.[42]

The Central Council, which eventually became the Royal Association for Disability and Rehabilitation, was set up in 1919. Whereas pre-war charities had been divided between medicine, charity and welfare, the Council brought together representation from all these constituencies. The National Scheme of which it became the co-ordinator was based on the arrangements at Baschurch and therefore advocated a network of central orthopaedic hospitals, allied to a series of affiliated local after-care clinics. The central orthopaedic hospital provided the 'crippled' child with skilled surgery and nursing, a good diet, education, and 'the benefits of the sun and open air ... for as long as his (*sic*) physical disability demands'. The local after-care clinics supplied a 'short-cut' to accurate diagnosis and hospital admission; enabled 'the surgeon to supervise his own handiwork ... and to realize the end results'; and offered him a 'wonderful school' in which to learn 'more and more all his life how best to help the crippled child'.[43] The Central Council embarked upon a vigorous promotional campaign. The schemes that emerged followed no single model, some being organized by local authorities and others by charitable effort. By 1936, however, there were 40 orthopaedic hospitals in the British Isles and 400 orthopaedic clinics.[44]

The National Scheme was an important precursor of 'surveillance medicine'.[45] Resources were too limited to sustain a comprehensive and wholly penetrating gaze, but many disabled people were exposed to intrusive socio-psychological scrutiny and painful medical intervention in the bid to police any deviation from the physical norm. First, the Scheme encouraged community monitoring. In Nottingham, for example, where an orthopaedic hospital opened in 1929, the local Cripples' Guild not only ran several after-care clinics for surgeons to follow up their work but also split the city into 15 districts, each with a group of visitors who were briefed to identify and supervise local 'cripples'.[46] Second, widespread, heroic surgery was promoted. As early as 1923, a minute to the Board of Education, supporting a proposal for an orthopaedic hospital in Yorkshire, was asserting that every disabled child required operative treatment. Superhuman qualities were even implied. 'You can help to perform this miracle', proclaimed a publicity leaflet produced by the Royal Cripples Hospital, Birmingham in 1939. On the cover was a boy pictured twice, first in leg-irons and then playing cricket. In the middle was the surgical team transforming his fate (Figure 2).[47]

Throughout the inter-war period, this mission was justified through recourse to economic rationality. As J. Herbert Lewis,

Figure 2   Birmingham Royal Cripples Hospital, *You Can Help To Perform This Miracle*

Source: Birmingham Library Services.

representing the Board of Education, told a conference organized by the Central Council and the Invalid Children's Aid Association in 1920:

> I do not appeal to the tender hearts, to be found by the thousand in this great business community, I appeal to the hard heads, which are also to be found . . . When they realize that with proper treatment, combined with education, 75 per cent of the child cripples of this country can be turned into satisfactory workers, they will also realize that the expend-iture of money on their treatment is not merely an act of merit but a sound investment. It means that thousands of children who would otherwise grow up to be a burden on their relatives and the community will become useful, self-supporting citizens.

Proponents of this strategy pictured the orthopaedic hospital as a happy, supportive, even idyllic environment for its disabled patients. 'As one approaches such a hospital', wrote G. R. Girdlestone, a pioneer of the National Scheme:

> one becomes aware of its presence by eye and by ear – an attractive sight and a most cheerful sound. One sees wards open to sun and wind, one hears happy shouts and laughter. Gaiety and fun seem to be distilled unendingly out of the children.[48]

Similarly, house visitors during their tours of inspection at the Princess Elizabeth Orthopaedic Hospital in Exeter regularly reported that the patients were 'very busy and happy'.[49]

Parents actively sought out orthopaedic and other voluntary hospital services for their children.[50] Once involved, however, they had little room for manoeuvre because withholding consent to surgical treatment not only led to boots and appliances being refused[51] but also triggered referral to the local authority for 'such legal action . . . as . . . [it] may think fit to take'.[52] Where parents agreed to hospitalization, few accounts of this hospitalization survive from patients' standpoints. However, we know from the 'memories' recorded in Maurice White's popular history of the Royal Orthopaedic Hospital in Birmingham that children were subjected to repeated surgical interventions over many years. Mr N. H. Field, for instance, recalled how he was admitted at the age of three with spinal TB in 1921 and immobilized on a spinal frame for six years. Similarly, Bobby James was admitted in 1928 with 'very serious deformities to both his legs'; only a few months old, he was to spend ten years 'on and off' in the Hospital, where he underwent 16 operations.[53] Whilst neither Mr Field nor Bobby

James complained about the treatment that they received, the study was a celebration of a revered local institution that was unlikely to elicit critical comment. Conversely, *Out of Sight* uncovered harrowing personal testimonies of excruciating surgery.

Take Bill Elvy, born in 1918 with 'severely deformed hands and feet which prevented him from walking'. Admitted to an institution for 'crippled' children, he was periodically dispatched to hospital for surgery:

> They operated on me when I was still very young. It was so frightening. In and out of hospital all the time I was. You couldn't have any visitors and anyway my parents couldn't afford to come 'cos the hospital was in London. . . . the hospital would ring up and say, 'Right, let's have him in for another op.' And off I'd be sent for some more torture at the hospital.[54]

This story, and others in the collection, cannot be specifically tied to orthopaedic hospitals under the National Scheme, but they do discredit the uniformly benign image of medical intervention. Childhood impairments declined during the inter-war period as the incidence of 'gross' rickets and tuberculosis fell.[55] However, for the children who contracted polio in the immediate post-war period before vaccination was available, hospitalization was no less of a nightmare under the National Health Service. Traumatized by separation from their families, they were exposed to painful treatments and callous nursing care. 'I had difficulty swallowing and breathing', recalled Simon Parritt, 'but when I didn't want my food they used to hold my nose and stuff greens down my throat.'[56] Standards were not quick to rise. When in the late 1960s Maureen Oswin investigated the 'Ridge Hospital', which provided long-term residential care for children with 'severe chronic handicaps', she found inadequate toilet facilities, upstairs wards with no access to the grounds, a depersonalized system of care in which possessions were numbered and tasks fragmented, and staff who neither communicated effectively with the children nor participated in any play.[57]

Rehabilitation medicine

With the inter-war decline of childhood impairment, orthopaedic surgeons shifted their focus to the rehabilitation of fractures and industrial injuries. Before 1918 industrial injuries were handled in a variety of ways. At general voluntary infirmaries, medical staffs were allowed to suspend the usual sponsorship procedure and admit accident cases as emergencies.[58] Special casualty hospitals developed as at Bath, where many patients were building workers hurt during the boom that hit the town at the end of the eighteenth century.[59] Commercial companies ran accident services like that organized by Robert Jones during the construction of the Manchester Ship Canal between 1888 and 1893.[60] And the Manor House Hospital, a temporary facility in France that moved to London to treat injured soldiers and sailors, grew into the Industrial Orthopaedic Society where annual subscribers across the country were granted access to assistance.[61] Until the First World War, however, the specialist treatment of accidents was not a field in which the medical profession showed much interest.[62]

Just as expertise gained from military casualties fed through to the treatment of 'crippled' children, so it raised the profile of accident cases because many of the locomotive injuries suffered by soldiers were fractures caused by bullets and shrapnel. Broken bones were also an important source of civilian impairment. In 1935, for example, a study by the British Medical Association found that 37 per cent of fracture patients were disabled for the rest of their lives, whilst more than half of those treated each year were maladministered and three-quarters were handled at home.[63] One story from South East Wales told of a parent splinting a fracture:

> My father set... [the] leg between two pieces of wood... there was no money for the doctor you see, and even if there was this was not one of the things the doctor was consulted about. Charlie was soon hopping about on crutches made from the branches of a tree, but he always limped after that. I expect the leg wasn't set properly.[64]

It was not only laymen who mismanaged fractures. General practitioners were also criticized for their incompetent performance, and voluntary and local authority infirmaries accused of leaving fractures to junior or under-trained staff.[65]

The proper treatment of fractures became a pre-eminent health issue during the inter-war period, the trade union movement endorsing the campaign. However, the depressed economy, with a surplus rather than a deficit of labour, offered little inducement to develop industrial rehabilitation services. The financial arrangements for supporting disabled people compounded this disincentive. For both the workmen's compensation schemes faced with the bill for industrial injuries, and the private insurance companies faced with the escalating costs of road traffic accidents, were predisposed to favour cheap lump-sum settlements rather than regular payments during an indefinite rehabilitation programme.[66] In 1939 the BMA's research did elicit government confirmation that specialist care for fracture cases was 'gravely defective', together with a warning that war injuries would aggravate these limitations;[67] and by the summer the Emergency Medical Service had requisitioned more than half of all hospital accommodation in the voluntary and statutory sectors.[68] But although there were 24 orthopaedic centres in existence by the beginning of 1940, civilian and military hospitals were failing to refer patients whom they were not staffed or equipped to cope with. The realization that enemy bombing caused fewer major orthopaedic casualties than estimated allayed some of this concern, but the extension of the Emergency Medical Service to civil defence and industrial workers intensified the pressure and in March 1941 fractures were still regarded as 'badly treated'.[69]

The response to this deficiency was soon to be revolutionized by the manpower shortage. First, the orthopaedic centres were rapidly joined by 'several hundred' fracture departments and clinics with less specialist briefs. Second, an Interim Scheme for engaging disabled people in the war industries was introduced. And this initiative was consolidated from late 1942 in a third phase after the government accepted the Report of the Inter-Departmental Committee on the Rehabilitation and Resettlement of Disabled Persons. The Committee 'recommended an extension of rehabilitation methods to all areas of the country, and to other patients besides those with fractures – medical and surgical patients, the blind, and people suffering from tuberculosis, neurosis and other illnesses.' The Ministry of Health reacted by undertaking a rehabilitation survey of the hospital services and inviting selected institutions to appoint rehabilitation officers. Equipment, clothing and supplies for physiotherapy and occupational therapy had been distributed to over 400 hundred hospitals by the end of 1943, and others had been provided with prefabricated gymnasia or with grants and licences to adapt their premises. Training courses were also set up to address the shortage of qualified staff. The scheme was dramatic in its effects, almost doubling the number of hospitals using rehabilitation methods in 12 months. Moreover, during the first half of 1945, a daily average of over 30,000 patients was being rehabilitated in emergency scheme hospitals, two-thirds of them as out-patients.[70]

For many disabled people, however, the rehabilitation ethos was fraught with difficulty. The problems stemmed from the relentless pursuit of normality. Though the Inter-Departmental Committee maintained that rehabilitation was 'not solely a medical problem',[71] its interpretation as a 'problem' of any kind invited the application of a curative model in which recovery was presumed to follow treatment. This orientation was evident in the wartime information films commissioned by government to sell industrial rehabilitation. Made in the realist tradition of the documentary movement, the films shaped 'actuality' to 'social purpose' in the same way that poverty and deprivation had been critiqued from a left-wing perspective in the 1930s.[72] Key workers were targeted through film magazines like *Worker and War-Front* that in 1944 contained a short sequence on how industrial injuries were dealt with on the South Wales coalfield. Medical personnel were an audience for longer expositions like *Life Begins Again* that in 1942 articulated the virtues of expert rehabilitation via a staged discussion between three doctors. On both occasions, however, men were shown pushed to the outer limits of endurance in a bid to return their impaired bodies to normal functioning. Conversely, fracture patients discharged from hospital without rehabilitation were pictured as helpless victims, idle and demoralized without the spur of professional advice and direction. Only the person who returned to work again became 'a useful and normal citizen'.[73]

Though orthopaedics played a leading role in the promotion of fracture clinics before 1939, the wartime rehabilitation service owed much to the manpower concerns of the Ministry of Labour and to the Inter-Departmental Committee on the Rehabilitation and Resettlement of Disabled Persons. Widely acclaimed as one of the great achievements of the Emergency Medical Service, the service did not survive the birth of the NHS because the new structure preserved 'the old division between industrial health and the rest of medicine'. Diverting its energies after 1945 to the growth of dedicated accident services,[74] orthopaedics became associated from the 1960s with advances in 'medical engineering and materials science that permitted the development of hip replacement'.[75] In the meantime, the configuration of clinical expertise was changing. Military hardware – far more destructive than during the First World War – produced multiple injuries that were more appropriately managed by groups of specialists than by the orthopaedic surgeons who had headed single-speciality teams between 1914 and 1918. Above all, the professional profile of neurology was enhanced by the development of dedicated units to treat patients with spinal injuries whose chances of survival were poor before the Second World War due to kidney and bladder disease, pneumonia and infection from bed sores.[76]

The first, and most famous, spinal unit opened in 1944 at Stoke Mandeville, the Ministry of Pensions Hospital in Aylesbury. Transferred to the National Health Service seven years later, and subsequently designated as a National Centre with a UK catchment area, Stoke Mandeville had treated over 4000 paraplegic and tetraplegic patients by 1967. Spelling out the philosophy of Stoke Mandeville, Ludwig Guttmann explained that:

> the idea [was] to provide for the spinal paraplegic and tetraplegic patients a comprehensive service . . . to rescue . . . [them] from the human scrap-heap and to return them, in spite of their profound disability, to the community as useful and respected citizens.[77]

The suggestion that without rehabilitation severely disabled people were neither 'useful' nor 'respected citizens' was indicative of an aggressive pursuit of normality. This was Vic Finkelstein's experience in the 1960s:

> The aim of returning the individual to normality is the central foundation stone upon which the whole rehabilitation machine is constructed. If, as happened to me following my spinal injury, the disability cannot be cured, normative assumptions are not abandoned. On the contrary, they are reformulated so that they not only dominate the treatment phase searching for a cure but also totally colour the helper's perception of the rest of that person's life. The rehabilitation aim becomes to assist the individual to be as 'normal as possible'.

'The result, for me', he concludes, 'was endless soul-destroying hours at Stoke Mandeville Hospital trying to approximate to able-bodied standards by "walking" with callipers and crutches.'[78]

Charles Webster has regretted the uneven development of rehabilitation services, blaming their predicament on 'falling between the stools of the established specialities'.[79] Disabled people were indeed forced to struggle for rehabilitation placements[80] or abandoned as long-stay hospital patients.[81] However, their social right to rehabilitation under the NHS was impeded less by medical boundaries than by the construction of impairment as a pathology remediable through the performance of a specified set of 'technical activities'. With this mind-set in place, the majority of disabled people with static or deteriorating conditions were excluded from rehabilitation services that differently conceived could have supported the achievement of personal autonomy within particular social contexts.[82]

Geriatric medicine

Geriatric medicine was similarly marginalized. Its heritage was the poor law infirmary. Since the 1860s the central Board had encouraged guardians to liberate health care from the spirit of 'less eligibility' and this process was taken a step further in 1885 when the receipt of medical relief ceased to be a cause for electoral disqualification.[83] Surgery was also performed at these institutions. In October 1863, for instance, Thomas Barker was admitted to Merthyr Tydfil, 18 months after having his thigh amputated, because the stump had become diseased and a second operation was necessary if he was to continue working.[84] The number of disabled people who received such treatment is unclear from the official statistics. However, there is evidence from London that they were infrequently admitted to dedicated infirmaries. Therefore, when the Local Government Board conducted a census of sick paupers in 1896, a mere 94 classified as 'aged and infirm' occupied hospital beds. Conversely, most of the 6000 paupers in workhouse sick wards fell into this category.[85]

Disregard for 'aged and infirm' patients had been recognized since the 1870s when Louisa Twining – founder of the Association for Promoting Trained Nursing in Workhouse Infirmaries – complained that poor physical amenities were being replaced by more benign neglect as a result of staff shortages:

> The old and infirm were put to bed and kept there, for there was no one to dress them, and the passive cruelty was general; the bed sores were frequent, though called 'eczema', and yet what could one nurse, much less an untrained girl, do with 80 or 90 cases under her care?[86]

McEwan and Laverty have argued, on the basis of Bradford, that access to clinical beds for elderly people deteriorated after 1929 because 'many of the new and aspiring municipal hospitals got rid of their undesirable chronic sick..., sending them to Public Assistance Institutions to upgrade their own medical services'.[87] Even for those who entered poor law infirmaries, however, conditions were grim as Marjorie Warren found at the West Middlesex County Hospital in 1935. Writing in the *Lancet* on the eve of the NHS, she recalled how:

> [h]aving lost all hope of recovery..., the patient rapidly loses morale and self-respect and develops a pathetic or peevish, irritable, sullen, morose and aggressive temperament...Lack of interest in the surroundings, confinement to bed, and a tendency to incontinence soon produce pressure sores...and an inevitable loss of muscle tone make for a completely bedridden state. Soon the well-known disuse atrophy of the lower limbs, with postural deformities, stiffness of joints, and contractures completes the unhappy picture of human forms who are not only heavy nursing cases in the ward and a drag on society but also are no pleasure for themselves and a source of acute distress to their friends.

Appalled by this institutional deprivation, Dr Warren introduced a vigorous reform campaign. Wards were redecorated, personal lockers and day rooms provided, and activities organized. Patients underwent proper diagnosis. And various types of rehabilitation were practiced to mobilize patients who were often bedridden due to strokes where the paralysis was assumed to be permanent.[88] In aiming to relieve 'a drag on society', however, Warren imposed a compassionate but professionally driven assessment of needs that reflected a patronizing attitude to elderly people

Elsewhere, 'aged and infirm' patients continued their confinement in run-down poor law infirmaries, of lessening medical interest to a profession ever more wedded to the scientific treatment of acute illness or injury.[89] Indeed, so dismal were services for chronically sick people that a report from Political and Economic Planning concluded in 1937 that 'poor standards of treatment in many institutions resulted in permanent disability which could have been avoided by better medical or surgical attention.'[90] Their denigrated status was ratified by the mass evacuation that followed the declaration of war in 1939. No fewer than 140,000 patients were ejected from hospitals in two days. Those who 'fared worst of all were the chronically sick, the bedridden, the paralysed, the aged, people suffering from advanced cancer or from tuberculosis who were discharged in their hundreds from public institutions to their own homes, where they could get little, if any, care'.[91] It was an exodus that exposed long-stay patients to what Charles Webster has called 'humiliating conditions arguably little better than the concentration camp'.[92]

In the post-war NHS, doctors who drew on the work in inter-war municipal infirmaries reduced dramatically the time that elderly people spent as in-patients. At the Cowley Road Hospital in Oxford, for example, L. Z. Cosin cut the average length of stay from 290 days to 42 days between 1950 and 1956 by preparing patients for a return to the community as soon as the treatment of their acute conditions was complete.[93] In other health author-ities, however, decrepit wards were still in use with a shortage of doctors, nurses, social workers, and physio-, occupational and speech therapists.[94] The effect on morale was devastating. There-fore, when the well-known geriatrician, Bernard Isaacs, first confronted the chronic ward at one of Glasgow's former poor law hospitals in 1958, he was shocked by the 'terrifying appearance' of the 30 or 40 old men. Dressed only in 'what answered for blue jackets and blue trousers' – 'shrunken, crumpled, shapeless, devoid of all buttons, thickly stained with dried soup, saliva, caked tobacco' – '[t]heir countenances expressed a kind of dying rage, a wrath that had been replaced by despair, now become lifeless, unmoving, as though carved out of cold, grey stone.' Bedridden patients were still more deprived, being 'appallingly malnourished and emaciated'. 'Many lay in urine and faeces, waiting to be cleaned up. Pressure sores were numerous, many of them deep and gangrenous.'[95]

The 1962 Hospital Plan inaugurated slow improvement by abolishing the distinction between acute and chronic hospitals. Each district general hospital was to include an 'active geriatric unit' taking referrals from the acute wards and from the com-munity of 'elderly people likely to require prolonged treatment'. But though the hospital was to contain 'some beds for long stay', its 'size . . . or its distance from smaller towns' was frequently seen to 'justify long-stay annexes on separate sites or geriatric provision at small hospitals'.[96] Only in the 1970s did hospital-based geriatric units arrive in all health authorities in England and Wales, albeit 'often still in outdated buildings and understaffed'. Negative cultural attitudes to old age partly explain why geriatric medicine was a Cinderella service, but doctors also had difficulty in framing an economic rationale for their specialty and in his 1953 text, *Our Advancing Years* – new editions of which were still being published in the 1970s – Trevor Howell went so far as to describe most elderly people as 'parasites' who 'consume more of our national wealth than they produce'.[97] Under these circumstances, unblocking hospital beds for those who were economically productive came to assume major importance in the development of geriatrics.

As early as 1947, the British Medical Association was arguing that unless geriatric departments were set up to carry out accurate diagnosis, classification and rehabilitation, 'the hospital services ..., already severely handicapped by shortage of beds due to insufficient nurses, will be still further crippled.'[98] This disablist terminology emboldened the subtext of the therapeutic strategies advocated by geriatricians since Warren. Elderly people in hospital were prepared for community living not because home care was most appropriate to their situation, but to release beds for acute patients.[99] Furthermore, the circumstances of elderly people at home were increasing surveyed not 'to extend the system of surveillance into the community, but to define certain sections of the elderly population as outside the realm of hospital provision and in need of social, rather than medical assistance'.[100] Therefore, elderly people's social right to appropriate NHS treatment was compromised by the priority given to younger patients.

Conclusion

In this chapter, we have explored how the development of the modern hospital has affected disabled people. Hospitals derived their influence from the medical profession, acting as a site where knowledge and power were negotiated. From their charitable origins in the early eighteenth-century – well before the emergence of the factory system or the modern state – they danced to the tune of economic rationality, promoting a curative model of treatment that aspired to full recovery and hence the resumption of productive work roles. In orthopaedics, where after 1918 doctors preserved their wartime gains by collaborating with the voluntary sector, attempts were made to bend the disabled body into the 'normal' shape, but prior to 1948 the majority of disabled people with chronic conditions were concentrated in poor law – or later local authority – infirmaries where medical intervention was minimal and neglect rampant. Though the National Health Service bestowed a right of access to treatment, funding continued to favour curative medicine. Therefore, geriatrics was fashioned less to serve the interests of elderly people than to unblock beds for acute patients, whilst rehabilitation services persisted in their quest for normality. Faced with the power of the health care professions, disabled people had little success in either resisting medical practices or achieving an equitable distribution of resources consistent with inclusive citizenship.

4 Asylums

Whereas the workhouse accommodated a variety of inmates and patients, and the hospital dealt with physical conditions, the brief of the asylum was the management of mental impairments. Though there had been 'a legal dichotomy between idiocy and lunacy' since the medieval period,[1] patients of these types were not clearly identified. Under the 1845 Lunacy Acts, the 'idiot' – classified as a person who from birth was incapable of thought or judgement – was distinguished from the 'lunatic' and the individual of 'unsound mind'. However, all three were placed within the overall category of 'insanity'.[2] The boundaries between mental and physical impairments were similarly porous because difficulties with co-ordination or communication were often defined as 'mental deficiencies' when the cause was cerebral palsy or problems with sight or vision. Therefore, physically as well as mentally disabled people were confined to asylums.[3] In this chapter, we examine the rise of these mental institutions and their rapid expansion during the nineteenth and early twentieth centuries. Particular attention is paid to the evolving mixed economy of private, voluntary, and later statutory sites, and the role of medical knowledge and medical practice in developing them as 'dividing practices'. The social rights of patients are then considered in relation to the regulation of asylum conditions, and their civil rights assessed during both the move towards legal protection and the era of psychiatric experimentation. Finally, patient perspectives and the capacity to resist asylum regimes are appraised.

The rise of the asylum

In the early modern period, popular and medical discourses on mental impairments were underpinned by the same humoral theory that was used to explain physical disease. Too much black bile produced melancholy or depression; too much yellow bile produced 'irritation and inflammation, or in extreme cases mania and frenzy'; strategies of depletion restored good health by returning the body to equilibrium.[4] Therefore, George III was bled, purged and blistered in the periods when, during his long reign from 1760–1820, porphyria[5] rendered him 'insane'. Foucault has overstated the extent to which the Age of Reason endorsed the cruel 'repudiation' of irrational behaviour.[6] Nevertheless, for much of the eighteenth century, the management of mental illness relied on the socializing potential of fear and terror, and the King – like his subjects – was restrained, beaten, starved and verbally abused to provoke the return of reason.[7] In the terminology of the early Enlightenment philosopher, John Locke, 'lunatics' were suffering from 'a form of disordered reasoning, in which random associations of ideas led to false judgements and thus to erroneous actions'.[8] The solution was to shock them out of their 'madness'.

From 1750, however, specialists treating mental impairments became more prominent, applying their personality and presence to the management of 'insanity'. So as well as being physically 'treated', the King was exposed to the penetrative psychological gaze of the Revd Dr Francis Willis, who was famous for fixing 'lunatics' in his eye to bring about their submission and control. The late Roy Porter argued that these alienists helped to open up 'a psychiatric space' that had two key characteristics. First, it was 'secular' rather than 'demoniacal',[9] rejecting religious theories of mental disorders that were popular with the labouring classes but increasingly spurned by ruling elites.[10] Second, it was 'sympathetic' to the notion that 'people might...be not just organically, but morally mad.'[11] By the 1790s, these ideas were taking shape as moral treatment that, instead of depending upon force of personality, relied on a kindly but disciplined domestic environment that encouraged patients to learn self-restraint.

The Quaker Samuel Tuke articulated this philosophy most comprehensively in *A Description of the Retreat, an Institution Near York*, published in 1813. Even 'lunatics', he explained:

> quickly perceive, or if not, they are informed on the first occasion, that their treatment depends in great measure, upon their conduct. Coercion thus flowing as a sort of necessary consequence, and being executed in a manner which marks the reluctance of the attendant, it seldom

exasperates the violence of the patient, or produces that feverish and sometimes furious irritability, in which the maniacal character is completely developed: and under which all power of self-control is utterly lost.[12]

This was no 'epistemological rupture'. Mid-eighteenth-century physicians had anticipated the basic principles of moral treatment, whilst the practices that Tuke advocated drew on the same Lockean theories of socialization that informed mainstream medicine. Moreover, though ritual bleedings and corporal punishment were less frequently applied from the 1750s,[13] doctors were designing complex apparatus to professionalize the traumatization of patients into sanity. Joseph Mason Cox's swinging chair, for example, promoted in his popular *Practical Observations on Insanity* of 1804 exploited 'the sympathy or reciprocity of action that subsists between mind and body'. Each became

in its turn the agent, and the subject acted upon, as when fear, terror, anger, and other passions, excited by the action of the swing, produce various alterations in the body, and where the revolving motion, occasioning fatigue, exhaustion, . . . vertigo, etc, effect new associations and trains of thought.

Even the most stubborn 'lunatics' were said eventually to succumb.[14]

Asylums were increasingly the sites for administering such technologies. But though medical knowledge and practice were factors in the growth of institutional psychiatry, they were by no means the only explanation. The first dedicated institution for mental as opposed to physical impairments was the Bethlem Hospital in London, a monastic foundation dating back to the thirteenth century. From the mid-seventeenth century, 'Bedlam' was joined by a number of private madhouses, which flourished as part of a market economy fuelled by the new prosperity of the middling orders and encompassing service industries in addition to manufactured goods. Initially catering for the better off, private madhouses later admitted pauper patients who were paid for by their parishes. By 1844, however, a majority of the 100 licensed commercial premises, which accommodated approximately a half of all 'lunatics' in England and Wales, were taking no paupers and after 1890 the number of patients in private houses did not increase.

The commercial sector ossified because of developments in the charitable and public sectors. With medical philanthropy thriving in eighteenth-century Britain, asylum provision for paupers and the working poor was designated a suitable cause for charity. In 1712 the Bethel Hospital was founded in Norwich at the behest of a single benefactor.[15] But it was the transmission of the subscription system from voluntary hospitals that moved the charitable asylum forward. St Luke's Hospital for Lunatics in London was established on the subscription principle in 1751 and similar institutions followed at regional centres like Newcastle, Manchester, York, Liverpool, Leicester and Exeter. In contrast to hospitals, voluntary asylums charged for their services, competing for custom with the private madhouses. In bidding for patients, they pointed out the economic advantage to the poor law authorities of paying more in the short term for specialist treatment and avoiding the cost of long-term dependency.[16] However, this economic rationality – a major narrative in the development of the workhouse as well as the infirmary – played a minor role in the promotion of voluntary asylums. 'What they offered...were practical examples, and also salutary lessons, as to what could be achieved by more direct public intervention.'[17]

Though the aspiration was humane, curative treatment in a secure and controlled environment, conditions were not always ideal and it was the suspicious death of a Quaker patient at the voluntary York Asylum that prompted the Society of Friends to open their Retreat just outside the city in 1796.[18] The York Retreat put into practice the moral treatment of Samuel Tuke, whose grandfather was highly instrumental in its foundation. Surrounded by spacious grounds with woodland, gardens, orchards and walks, the Retreat was designed to replicate the family home. Therefore, it was initially small in scale and the secure galleries, which gave access to patients' rooms and enabled them to exercise indoors, were furnished in the style of a drawing room. The social relations conducted within this physical environment rejected fear and force in favour of techniques that appealed to the patient's unimpaired mental faculties.[19] This humanitarian prototype lay at the heart of the reform campaign, which in pressing for public institutions brought together Benthamite Radicals with their utilitarian goal of social order and Evangelical Tories with their paternalist interest in the welfare of the lower orders.[20] The conditions against which reformers railed were variable. Though the York Retreat has been hallowed as a great landmark, it was by no means the only institution to implement forms of moral treatment; for by the early 1800s, many licensed madhouses and voluntary asylums were adopting methods 'probably as advanced as those of the...Retreat'.[21] On the other hand, Bethlem's damning reputation was 'justly earned'. Clothing was rough, diet insufficient for good health, and restraint widely practiced. Patients were also exposed to physical and sexual abuse, and saturated with medicines that had painful side-effects.[22] Mechanical restraint was similarly extensive at St Luke's, whilst in 1807 the *Report of the Select Committee on the State of Criminal and Pauper Lunatics* described workhouse conditions as 'revolting to humanity'.[23]

In Scotland, the reform campaign extracted no statutory obligation to construct public asylums until 1857.[24] In England and Wales, conversely, counties were permitted – but not required – under an Act of 1808 to build asylums for the pauper and criminal insane that were funded from the rates.[25] Despite allowing collaboration with 'the subscribers of existing or projected voluntary asylums',[26] Peter Bartlett has stressed the allegiance of the legislation to the poor law rather than to the charitable sector; at local if not national level, he says, the two systems shared an administrative infrastructure of JPs and paid officials who decided whether to build an asylum and who was to occupy it.[27] Yet only nine facilities were completed under the 1808 Act, prompting reformers to continue their pursuit of public provision. By the middle decades of the century, a drift away from *laissez-faire* towards greater collectivism was preparing fertile soil for the 1845 Lunacy Acts, which finally made it compulsory for counties and boroughs, singly or in combination, to erect asylums. By 1900 there were 77 such institutions housing over 74,000 patients.[28] Most but not all were paupers because the public asylums were allowed to admit private patients.[29] Therefore, a mixed economy continued.

Although nineteenth-century understandings of psychological and intellectual impairment were confused, three gigantic custodial institutions each of 2000 beds were opened by the Metropolitan Asylums Board at Caterham in Surrey, Leavesden in Hertfordshire, and Darenth in Kent. One or two county asylums also expressed interest in intellectually impaired patients, whilst the Idiots Act of

1886 enabled but did not compel local authorities to build separate institutions. Outside London, however, specialist provision remained the exception rather than the rule. As a result, the vast majority of 'idiots' who were incarcerated found themselves in the local workhouse, only those considered difficult and dangerous being dispatched to the asylum. The Devon County Asylum was thus typical in having only 7 per cent of its admissions between 1845 and 1914 'registered as "idiot" or "imbecile" by the medical superintendent'.[30]

The Mental Deficiency Act of 1913 set out to tackle this issue as part of its mission to ascertain, certify and – where necessary – compulsorily detain 'mental defectives' in specialist local authority institutions under a central Board of Control. Born of eugenic panic about racial degeneration,[31] the Act introduced an elaborate four-way classification that ranged from 'idiots' who were 'so deeply defective in mind as to be unable to guard against common physical dangers' to 'moral defectives' who exhibited 'some permanent mental defect coupled with strong vicious or criminal propensities on which punishment had little or no effect'.[32] Statistics from the Board of Control, which also assumed responsibility for mental illness, show that far fewer people were admitted to mental deficiency institutions – later 'mental handicap' hospitals – than to asylums – later psychiatric hospitals. Between 1926 and 1939, the number falling within the orbit of mental deficiency legislation climbed from 36,185 to 89,904 in England and Wales, over half being accommodated in institutions.[33] In 1934, however, there were 1,503,000 patients in asylums in England and Wales.[34]

Regulating asylum conditions

Incarceration had profound implications for the political, social and civil rights of disabled people. Though paupers regained the vote after 1918, patients in mental hospitals were still disenfranchised in 1979.[35] Mathew Thomson has argued that in imposing limits on an electorate no longer constrained by economic status, Britain was 'adjusting to democracy' rather than engaging in 'a crudely deliberate attempt to establish a new biological definition of citizenship'.[36] However, the effect was to exclude asylum residents from the political process. The regulation of asylum conditions was likewise incompatible with citizen status, being driven not by any recognition of the social rights of patients but by a paternalistic obligation to protect the vulnerable.

The Madhouses Act of 1774 was the first attempt to inspect the conditions in which disabled people were held. Charitable asylums were omitted, but the Act did establish a degree of central government control over many private premises, which had to be licensed and visited annually by a commission of five members of the Royal College of Physicians in London and by two JPs and one local physician elsewhere. Since there was no mechanism for revoking licences, however, the legislation was ineffective and abuses continued.[37] A Select Committee in 1816 thus uncovered appalling conditions. In the East London madhouses of the Warburton and Miles families, for instance, three inmates were routinely crowded into each bed; brutal forced feeding led to broken teeth; and incontinent patients were kept on straw beds that were wet, soiled and infested with vermin. One woman even had to have a foot partially amputated due to cold and neglect.[38] The revelations of a second Select Committee in 1827 suggest that few improvements followed the first investigation. 'We found a considerable number of very disgusting objects,' reported a guardian from the Marylebone parish. Several were chained to the wall, and the air was so 'oppressive and offensive' from the smell of excrement that he was 'obliged to hold my breath while I stayed to take a very short survey of the room'.[39]

This time reforms did ensue. From 1828 county asylums and charitable hospitals as well as private madhouses were required to submit annual statements of admissions, discharges and deaths to the Home Department, which, in conjunction with the Royal College of Physicians, appointed 15 rather than five metropolitan commissioners. These commissioners, and the unaltered teams of JPs and physicians in the provinces, were to visit each institution on four occasions every year. Inspection in London has been judged 'highly effective'.[40] Beyond the capital, however, scandals persisted. At Hereford, for example, a Select Committee investigated the asylum – opened in 1799 on a charitable basis but leased almost immediately to a private proprietor – in the late 1830s. Patients were overcrowded, restraint was widely practiced, and cold baths were used as a therapy but also as a punishment. The visitors reported to local justices that the asylum 'was not in that state, either as relates to ventilation, to classification, to employment, to moral treatment, to recreation and religious consolation to convalescents, which they would wish to prevail'. Yet though these county magistrates refused a licence, the city's JPs issued one and the institution remained open until 1853.[41]

The Lunacy Acts of 1845 did not resolve this particular type of confrontation because local justices remained answerable for provincial licensing. However, the new lunacy commissioners – five lay, three medical and three legal – did receive a copy of each licence that was granted and their mandate was extended to include all asylums and madhouses nationwide. 'A legal and a medical Commissioner were to visit each hospital once a year, each licensed house in the metropolis four times a year, and each licensed house in the provinces – where the justices would also continue to visit – twice a year.' Whilst the lay commissioners were unpaid, the medical and legal commissioners were salaried and so formed a permanent full-time inspectorate.[42] In the past, the efficiency of this inspectorate has been criticized for its numerical weakness, its erratic and superficial visits, and its inability to impose recommendations on local magistrates.[43] Conversely, a more recent study of the Devon Pauper Lunatic Asylum has concluded that 'the county institutions were subjected to a remarkable degree of central regulation.' From this perspective, 'The Lunacy Commission interacted effectively and subtly with local interest groups to secure its desired policy outcomes', demonstrating authority and achieving success.[44] Nevertheless, the Commission faced an uphill battle to control the conditions in which mentally impaired patients were confined during the second half of the nineteenth century.

Up to 1845, it was amongst privately lodged pauper patients that the greatest abuses occurred, hence the victorious campaign for the compulsory construction of public asylums. The private madhouses duly declined as their customers were transferred to purpose-built facilities,[45] but standards in some of the charitable institutions were slow to improve. During 1855, for instance, the lunacy commissioners scrutinizing St Luke's in London 'were struck with the cheerless and dreary aspect presented both within the building and in the airing courts.' Furthermore, there was disappointment that '[f]ew or no steps appear to have been taken to forward the recommendations made in previous reports as to out-door exercise, occupations and the purchase of land in the vicinity of London' for the erection of more suitable premises. Yet despite these setbacks, the commissioners were confident that 'if the labours of the medical gentlemen were carried on under more favourable circumstances, their efforts would be more successful.'[46]

Optimism also infused the new generation of public asylums as they aspired to replicate the regime of the York Retreat.[47] Even at the Retreat itself, however, the distinctive domestic ethos proved difficult to reconcile with the increasing size of the institution. By the 1870s moral treatment had been reduced to mere amusement, and chemical concoctions were being administered within 'an increasingly authoritarian regime'. The average real cost of drugs per patient thus more than doubled between 1806 and the decade 1890 to 1899, and gags and nasal tubes were applied to override the right to refuse medication that patients had previously enjoyed. From mid-century, moreover, the discontinuation of mechanical restraint had led to 'more pervasive but concealed techniques of social management ... in which rewards and punishments were used systematically to influence patient behaviour'.[48] Foucault berated this shift from external to internal coercion, arguing that it 'substituted for the free terror of madness the stifling anguish of responsibility'; 'fear no longer reigned on the other side of the prison gates, it now raged under the seals of conscience.'[49] Anne Digby has argued that whilst 'individuality was not crushed into helpless anonymity' by this social discipline, personal 'idiosyncrasies became too inconvenient to be tolerated' as patient numbers expanded.[50]

If moral treatment was difficult to sustain at York, it was even more difficult to export to the public asylum system where the average institution housed five times as many inmates.[51] At the Buckingham County Pauper Lunatic Asylum, which opened in 1853 with 200 beds, the commissioners in lunacy praised patient conditions after their annual inspection in 1861:

> The various dormitories and single sleeping rooms are provided generally with bedside carpets, with chairs, with muslin blinds and with curtains of

white dimity; the beds are all of horsehair and the bedding excellent...
Entertainments, comprising music and dancing, at which the patients
of both sexes associate, are now given weekly and about 100 generally
take part...We saw the patients at Dinner. It was neatly and well-
served and consisted of meat and vegetables, both very good and
supplied in abundance...[The patients] appear to be treated with
great kindness by the nurses and attendants.

But these commodious facilities were soon to be overcrowded
as a swelling body of local paupers was joined by private patients
and by those under contract from other counties. Not only were
washing and toileting facilities seriously inadequate, but single
rooms were turned into double rooms and dining rooms into
dormitories.[52]

The experiences of Buckinghamshire were repeated across the
country and reflected in the expanding capacity of asylums. In
1860, a population of 15,845 was accommodated in 41 institutions
that averaged 386 patients; 30 years later, 65 institutions were
accommodating 52,937, making the average size 802 patients.[53]
The public asylum reached its apotheosis at Colney Hatch, which
opened in 1851 with 1250 beds (Figure 3). Ten years later it was
enlarged to admit 2000 and by 1937 virtually 2700 patients were
resident.[54] Independent observers lambasted the gargantuan institution. '[T]he Middlesex County asylum at Colney Hatch is a
colossal mistake,' wrote Mortimer Granville investigating the
London asylums for the *Lancet* in the mid-1870s. '[T]he wards
are long, narrow, gloomy, and comfortless, the staircases cramped
and cold, the corridors oppressive, the atmosphere of the place
dingy, the halls huge and cheerless. The airing courts...are unin-
viting and prison-like.' The commissioners in lunacy, likewise critical
of the building's dreary utilitarianism,[55] were more condemnatory
of the mechanical restraint that was reintroduced after being
initially outlawed. Violent patients were packed into wet sheets
or held by belts, wrist scraps and locked gloves; whilst the dirty
and destructive were confined in side-rooms 'in a nude state' with
neither beds nor pillows and only 'strong quilted rugs' for comfort.
Finally, too many of the 'dirty', 'degraded' and 'destructive' were
kept in 'exceptionally strong dresses' or 'frocks' with 'locked
leather belts'. Not until 1934 did the 'better conducted patients'
finally gain access to lockers for their personal possessions, a facility
that only became universally available in the 1960s.[56]

COLNEY HATCH LUNATIC ASYLUM

Figure 3 Colney Hatch Asylum, Middlesex

Source: From the author's collection.

A 'dumping ground...for physical and mental wrecks'?[57]

In 1979 Andrew Scull published a bold explanation for the development of the nineteenth-century asylum in England. Rejecting the orthodox view that social reformers were paramount, he declared that the explosion of provision up to 1900 was primarily due to the professional ambitions of doctors, who were keen to capture a new specialist market for their services, and the political ambitions of the state, which was anxious to police a growing band of unproductive workers whose idleness threatened the order of a industrial society.[58]

This conspiratorial account is too narrow. In the first place, public asylums arose from the 'successful coalition' of central government agents and local elites, not all of whom were doctors or sympathetic to the economic logic of capitalism; and once they were in operation, medical superintendents had to interact with lay governors and county magistrates as well as the lunacy commissioners.[59] Second, institutional care expanded in response to external demand. Far from corralling patients to boost the size of their institutions and hence inflate their own 'professional prestige', superintendents 'responded to incessant public demand for secure accommodation for the insane', most of which emanated from relatives struggling to come to terms with 'the stresses of industrialization'.[60] In the case of private madhouses, families agonizing over whether to confine a disturbed member discussed the options with asylum proprietors who also offered an after-care service.[61] But the family was also instrumental in the admission of patients to public asylums.[62] In the 1860s, for example, relatives were responsible for referring 80 per cent of inmates at the Leicestershire County Asylum, 20 per cent being routed via the workhouse.[63] This institution in turn acted as a 'transit point', with different guardians, relieving officers and medical officers applying different criteria to the dispersal of patients.[64] Therefore, superintendents had 'little say' in whom was recruited to their asylums.[65]

The third strand to Scull's argument – that asylums policed the feckless poor – is bound up with the increasing size of asylums. This inflation, epitomized by Colney Hatch, rendered the therapeutic aspirations of reformers ever more unrealistic. Though medical attendance had been compulsory since 1828, it was after 1845 that the profession began its assault on 'insanity', with the help of the commissioners who showed 'a steadily growing hostility to non-medically run asylums'.[66] Far from jettisoning moral treatment, these doctors absorbed it into their disease-based therapies. However, their position became increasingly untenable. First, scientific evidence to validate the equation of 'madness' and physical disease failed to materialize prior to the First World War when a link between syphilis and mental illness was established. Second, the promised cures proved illusive. Even at the York Retreat, only 45 per cent of first admissions were said to have made a full recovery between 1796 and 1841, and by the end of the century the proportion had slumped to 26 per cent.[67] Superintendents in the public asylums estimated for the commissioners that during the years 1873 to 1898 fewer than four in ten were discharged as recovered. By this stage, it was no longer plausible to argue that a shortage of beds was preventing early treatment and hence causing acute conditions to become chronic. Therefore, it was difficult to avoid the conclusion that 'mad medicine' was not working.[68]

From mid-century, the preponderance of long-term cases in public asylums was a subject for contemporary comment. 'Of the admissions during the year', wrote the superintendent of the Buckinghamshire Asylum in 1876, 'a proportion amounting to nearly 40 per cent were from the first seen to be hopelessly incurable, and of the remaining cases in many instances there is but little chance of their recovery.'[69] The vast majority of expansion occurred within the pauper category where the ratio of lunatics per 10,000 population jumped from 15.95 in 1859 to 26.86 in 1890; in comparison, the ratio for private lunatics rose from only 2.38 to 2.81 during the same period.[70] After 1874 the poor law authorities were granted financial compensation for the 'insane' paupers whom they dispatched to specialist institutions – though asylums remained empowered under legislation of 1862 to return chronic and harmless 'lunatics' to workhouses.[71] For Scull, however, these administrative niceties were of less significance than the function of incarcerating the poor. 'Asylums', he avers,

> became a dumping ground for a heterogeneous mass of physical and mental wrecks – epileptics, tertiary syphilitics, consumptives in the

throes of terminal delirium, cases of organic brain damage, diabetics, victims of lead poisoning, the malnourished, the simple-minded, and those who had simply given up the struggle for existence.[72]

Why were these 'social deviants' confined, given that they did not – like former inmates – exhibit florid and disruptive behaviour? Because, says Scull, they failed to conform to the economic regime of an increasingly industrialized society by participating in the labour market.

If the range of patients was diverse, were they permanently deposited in the asylum, silting up beds for acute mental conditions? During the third quarter of the nineteenth century, returns to the commissioners in lunacy show that 51.6 per cent of all asylum admissions were subsequently decanted. This level of release calls into question Scull's contention that medical superintendents deliberately extended the stay of patients in order to increase the size of their institutions and hence their professional power.[73] Yet if one half of the inmate population was discharged, the other half remained in custody. It was this group that 'clogged' the asylums, their numbers accumulating over time to produce a high proportion of patients – as opposed to admissions – that were long-stay cases.[74] Therefore, we can conclude with Mark Finnane that the 'custodial functions' of the asylum were 'undeniable and alarming'.[75]

'The triumph of legalism'?[76]

The significance of confinement for civil rights had been recognized to some degree since 1744 when at least two magistrates, rather than the one needed for vagrants, were required to authorize the detention of a 'mad person'. Public concern about mistaken incarceration was reflected in the medical certification required for private patients under the 1774 Madhouses Act; and by the early nineteenth century, charitable as well as private asylums were covered and pauper as well as private patients. The effect was minimal because the release of any wrongfully detained inmates, revealed by the cursory inspection process, was unenforceable. Therefore, a more detailed certification procedure was put in place from 1828 and combined with an empowerment of the commissioners to set free any patient whom they believed to be improperly confined. The Lunacy Acts of 1845 achieved what reformers regarded as a perfect balance in which specialist medical provision was subject to a system of statutory control that included additional legal safeguards against wrongful detention: two medical certificates were now demanded, along with a petition signed by a representative of the private patient, and by a JP or clergyman and by a poor law official for the pauper patient.[77] However, the public whom these precautions were designed to reassure remained sceptical.

Though sensationalism was blamed for inflaming this anxiety, the stories of erroneous confinement told by Charles Reade in *Hard Cash* (1863) or Wilkie Collins in *The Woman in White* (1869) only aroused public opinion because there was little confidence in the protection offered by the lunacy commissioners. The extraordinary case of the eccentric Mrs Georgina Weldon – who embarked upon a tortuous legal battle after her estranged husband tried to engineer her admission to a private madhouse in 1884[78] – was likewise unsettling. The first pressure group formed to defend the liberty of the subject dated from 1845. Despite recognizing benefits from the central inspectorate, the Luke James Hansard's Alleged Lunatic's Friend Society criticized the commissioners for their inefficient liberation of the wrongly confined and complained that legitimate calls for legal changes were ignored. The Louisa Lowe's Lunacy Law Reform Association was more vitriolic. Campaigning in the 1880s, the Association declared the commissioners to be in cahoots with 'mad-doctors' and even persuaded the *New York Sunday Times* to claim that 'the sane, and especially sane women, are constantly incarcerated. The fact seems to be, that the commissioners in lunacy drive a profitable trade with the superintendents and madness mongers, by detaining patients after recovery.' Lax rather than corrupt, the commissioners had indulged in superficial investigation and inadequate reporting.[79] In this context, their failure to respond to pressure group accusations prepared fertile soil for the Lunacy Act of 1890.

The 1890 Act was 'primarily concerned to establish an elaborate system of judicial orders and medical certificates to safeguard against the inadvertent admission of a sane patient'.[80] The Local Government Act two years previously had transferred responsibility for the local management of asylums from magistrates to county councils, where it was to remain until 1948. Therefore, it was the visiting committees appointed by local authorities that oversaw the admissions procedure. Three main methods were put in place for public asylums and licensed madhouses: the urgency order, the reception order, and the summary reception order. The urgency order, which lasted for seven days, allowed the emergency admission of a private case on the basis of just a relative's petition and one medical certificate. The reception order, which only applied to non-pauper cases and could replace an urgency order, 'involved a near relative or other person stating his connection with the patient in making a statement before a justice of the peace supported by two medical certificates'. The summary reception order was used to admit the biggest constituency of the asylum population: paupers, for whom one medical certificate was enough; the poor law relieving officer normally notified a JP and obtained the necessary order. Both reception orders and summary reception orders were made for 12 months in the first instance. Thereafter, they were 'renewable after periods of two years, three years, five years, and successive periods of five years, on the report of the medical officer of the asylum to the Lunacy Commissioners'.[81]

Admissions under the Mental Deficiency Act of 1913 were rooted in similar principles. Institutionalization was permissible either at the request of a parent or guardian, or as a consequence of relatives, friends or local government officers petitioning a 'judicial authority' on the grounds that a person 'in addition to being a defective... was found neglected, abandoned, or without visible means of support, or cruelly treated or... in need of care or training which could not be provided in his home'. Other qualifying conditions included committing a criminal offence, 'undergoing imprisonment' or attending an approved school, suffering from 'habitual' drunkenness, being 'incapable of receiving education at school', or requiring 'supervision after leaving school'. Irrespective of the route, two medical certificates were required, one of which was to be supplied by a practitioner who was officially approved for the purpose. When the order expired after a year, the medical officer of the institution and its visiting committee supplied reports to the Board of Control;[82] and a decision was taken as to whether confinement should be continued for a further year, and subsequently for five-year periods.[83]

Families exercising their legal role in the admissions process were also influential in transacting discharge, release depending much less upon clinical judgement than the attitude and situation of the receiving household;[84] only when the permanency of the 'mental deficiency' institution was misunderstood were relatives thwarted.[85] But how well they represented the civil rights of disabled people is questionable. Akihito Suzuki has demonstrated for nineteenth-century Bethlem that 'the patient was not only the object of their friends' report, but also a subject who could and did refute the narrative about him or her, by telling his or her own stories.' From this perspective, 'psychiatric power' had not 'silenced the voice of the mad', but was instead enabling it to be heard. We cannot assume that all asylum superintendents either strove to reconstitute the 'triangular relationship between doctor, patient and friends', or were committed to giving their charges the opportunity for authentic expression.[86] On the contrary, the inmate inaudible during the admissions process was also the mute recipient of psychiatric intervention, consent to treatment being an alien concept to the lunacy commissioners. In 1879 they did circulate guidelines to local asylum committees recommending that 'no patient shall be placed in restraint or seclusion except by the order of the superintendent, unless found necessary in cases of extreme violence, when the fact shall be immediately communicated to him.' Bathing, 'except for the purposes of cleanliness', required the same approval. However, this was an ethical code driven not by the patient but by the medical profession. Furthermore, physical restraint was, as we have seen, being overtaken by chemical restraint, with even bastions of moral management like the York Retreat making extensive use of potent sedatives that were, if necessary, forcibly administered.[87]

The York Retreat, like other asylums, was hostile to the ideas of Freudian psychoanalysis. From the late nineteenth century, however, 'medical attention started to focus, not on unreason, but on the vagaries of apparently normal mental functioning'[88] and their elision with abnormality. This 'invention of the neuroses' was reinforced by the effects of shellshock during the First World War when 80,000 servicemen were admitted to military mental hospitals with symptoms 'ranging from deep depression, compulsive shaking and nightmares to mutism and paralysis'. Not only was Freud's emphasis on 'the sexual origins of mental illness' expanded to include broader notions of 'the unconscious mind and repressed emotion', but psychiatrists outside the asylum also began to question their inheritance of organic and eugenic explanations that jarred with a previously fit patient group, many of whom were regarded as 'belonging to the flower of the imperial race'.[89] This new thinking about mental illness sat uneasily with the stigma of compulsory, certified detention. The Maudsley Hospital in London was permitted to admit voluntary patients under a special Act of Parliament passed in 1915. And the 1890 Lunacy Act had built on an earlier, but little used provision by allowing 'any person who is desirous of voluntarily submitting to treatment' to be admitted to an approved licensed madhouse. But for the vast majority of asylum patients, certification was a pre-condition for treatment.[90]

The excessive legalism of the 1890 Act has been berated, amidst claims that it hampered 'the progress of the mental health movement for nearly seventy years'.[91] In 1926, however, the Royal Commission on Lunacy and Mental Disorder recommended that: 'The treatment of mental disorder should approximate to the treatments of physical ailments as nearly as is consistent with the special safeguards which are indispensable when the liberty of the subject is infringed.' Four years later the Mental Treatment Act tried to realize this goal by encouraging the establishment of psychiatric out-patient clinics and observation wards, and by introducing the concept of the voluntary psychiatric patient. Out-patient facilities had been offered by voluntary hospitals since the eighteenth century, but the development of non-residential services specifically aimed at mentally ill patients started in the 1880s when a number of infirmaries and asylums followed the example of St Thomas's in London and opened clinics. It was the accumulated effect of poor recovery rates – only one in three for the 1920s – that led the 1930 Act to endorse these clinics for general as well as psychiatric hospitals.[92] Seemingly, they met with some success in preventing institutionalization. At the Buckinghamshire Asylum, for example, 189 of the 276 seen as out-patients in 1943 were referred by general practitioners, 146 of these 'were subsequently treated at home by the GP with clinic advice', and a mere 38 'went on to mental hospital'.[93]

Voluntary status was one of three categories of psychiatric patient. Certified patients were admitted in accordance with the procedure laid down in 1890. Temporary patients were 'likely to benefit by temporary treatment', but were incapable of indicating their willingness. Voluntary patients, on the other hand, had to be competent to express their attitude to treatment, make a written application to their chosen asylum, and give three days' written notice if they intended to leave. Responsible medical officers were expected to satisfy themselves periodically that these patients were 'fit' to be voluntary.[94] The 1930 Act was heralded as a watershed that set the care of the mentally ill apart from the incarceration of the 'mentally deficient'. In practice, however, changes were slow to take effect. By the late 1930s, 47 per cent of all admissions to Herrison Hospital in Dorset were voluntary, but this was atypical. Even in 1948 most of the asylum population nationwide was still compulsorily detained, voluntary patients numbering 21,788 compared with 527 temporary and 145,799 certified patients.[95] Nevertheless, the existence of voluntary patients did sever 'the necessary connection between asylum inmate status and subjection to compulsory powers, raising the question of whether they could be secluded or restrained physically or chemically without their consent'.[96]

The era of experimentation

Since the late nineteenth century, the performance of surgical operations had been regarded as a matter for consent by mentally impaired people themselves or by their 'natural protectors'. Psychiatric interventions, on the other hand, were not seen in the same light and by 1913 it was 'officially accepted' that asylum doctors were able to exercise a high degree of discretion in applying their 'armamentarium'. Manipulation of the Mental Treatment Act meant that voluntary status was no defence. Therefore, when during the late 1930s Dr Douglas Macrae, president of the Medico-Psychological Association, welcomed each patient to Glengall Hospital in Ayr, he got 'him clearly to understand that in agreeing to come under my medical care he was faithfully to abide by medical orders and so help me in securing his recovery'. This utterance from the heartland of asylum medicine gives credence to Phil Fennell's assertion that the 1930 Act 'created a favourable . . . climate for a period of experimentation with a wave of new psychiatric treatments'.[97]

Experimentation was not a new phenomenon. In the 1920s, psychiatry had presided over the widespread extraction of teeth and tonsils in the belief that they acted as foci of infection, playing host to physical sepsis that was capable of generating mental impairment. The induction of malaria in patients with general paralysis of the insane (or advanced syphilis) was similarly advocated. After 1930, however, the pace quickened. One strategy involved the administration of heavy drug dosages. Barbiturates, replacing bromides as the principal sedative in psychiatric medicine, were additionally used to bring about prolonged narcosis that – it was claimed – broke faulty thought patterns, put the patients' minds at rest, and enabled a psychological exploration of their symptoms. Insulin coma therapy sought similar enlightenment from the deep state of unconsciousness that arose from the depletion of sugar levels in the blood stream. Other drug-based treatments also resurrected previous theories of shocking the 'mad' into sanity, cardiazol being injected to stimulate a type of epileptic fit that was preceded by a 'violent heartbeat and pulsating of the larger blood vessels'. In 1938, the Board of Control reported that 92 institutions had adopted insulin and/or cardiazol therapy and that 3531 patients had undergone treatment. Contemporary mental health practitioners insisted that these aggressive interventions worked.[98] 'Many treatments [of cardiazol therapy]... were given', remembered one nurse from Severalls psychiatric hospital in Essex, 'and we found a very marked improvement. The patient would start to take an interest in herself and her surroundings.'[99] More systematic evaluation was rarely conducted. Some 20 years after insulin therapy commenced, however, the first controlled study demonstrated that it 'was not the effective agent in causing therapeutic change'.[100]

On the eve of the Second World War, electro convulsive therapy and psychosurgery were poised to displace the drug-based treatments of the 1920s and 1930s. They were to reach their apotheosis, however, in the National Health Service, which from 1948 managed those institutions for mentally ill and mentally 'defective' patients that had formerly been the responsibility of local authorities.[101] Doctors believed that passing electrical currents through the brain was a cheap and easy way of inducing a shock that improved their clinical control and delivered good results. Psychosurgery was likewise regarded as a wonder cure. Its most common procedure – leucotomy – involved severing nerve fibres within the brain to reduce acute emotional dysfunction in patients whose behaviour was deeply disturbed. The Ministry of Health reported that in the 12 years from 1942 10,365 leucotomies were carried out, two-thirds of them on people with schizophrenia. But the side-effects – memorably portrayed by Ken Kesey in *One Flew Over the Cuckoos Nest* (1962) – meant that the popularity of the operation was relatively short-lived. For with the introduction from the early 1950s of tranquilizing drugs like chlorpromazine or largactil, which calmed disruptive behaviour whilst leaving the patient conscious and hence open to other therapies, psychosurgery was 'relegated largely to the sidelines'.[102]

This 'pharmacological revolution'[103] was to influence both the legal framework of mental health care and the asylum environment. Though a report from the Royal Medico-Psychological Association in 1945 argued that 'psychiatry in all essential respects' should be treated like 'other branches of medicine', the mental institutions absorbed into the NHS three years later remained isolated backwaters.[104] By 1954, when a Royal Commission on the Law Relating to Mental Illness and Mental Deficiency was finally appointed, no 'major revision and consolidation' of the legal position had taken place for 64 years and parliament had not debated the issues for almost a quarter of a century. The 1959 Mental Health Act adopted most of the Royal Commission's recommendations.[105] The maximum-security 'special' hospitals for patients considered particularly dangerous were placed under the direct control of the Minister of Health. In addition, the community services that local authorities had been empowered to offer since 1948 were spelt out more fully and the procedures for hospitalization were overhauled. Not only did the Act remove 'all remaining restraints on the admission and treatment of voluntary patients', but it also established two categories of compulsory detention apart from the exceptional emergency and court orders. Both the observation order, lasting for one month, and the treatment order, lasting for 12 months, required the written recommendations of two medical practitioners and the support of either the patient's nearest relative or a mental welfare officer. There were limited rights of appeal to a Mental Health Review Tribunal when patients felt that they had been wrongfully detained.[106]

By the mid-1950s, the new tranquilizing drugs were widely enough prescribed to create 'a totally different atmosphere' in psychiatric hospitals. The transformation has been called dramatic, there being 'no longer any justification for "refractory" wards, for wired-in airing courts, for strong-arm tactics on the part of staff'.[107] The pharmacological impact should not be exaggerated. Group psychotherapy for traumatized military personnel was extensively practiced during the Second World War. Psychiatrists increasingly saw the hospital as a therapeutic community where social relationships – along with art, music and occupational therapies – could be geared to the curative process. And studies of intellectual as opposed to psychological impairment were suggesting a greater capacity for community living among the occupants of mental deficiency institutions. In one 1954 investigation of 12 institutions, for example, the average IQ of 'feeble-minded' patients was more than 70 and half needed no nursing or supervisory care.[108] It was these trends, acting in concert with the pharmacological revolution, which altered the hospital regime and underpinned the shift from institutional to community care.

In the immediate post-war period, however, the asylum retained its appeal. Cecil French, a mental welfare officer in Bedfordshire from 1946, thus praised the local mental deficiency hospital:

> Patients used to work on the farm. They grew cereals, they had their own herds, they had their own pigs, it was completely self-contained. The idea was out of sight, out of mind by and large, and life was as comfortable as you could possibly make it.[109]

Local authorities shared this enthusiasm and there were frequent complaints about the shortage of mental deficiency beds.[110] In the aftermath of the 1959 Act, which explicitly sought a reorientation from institution to community, the constituency resident in mental 'subnormality' hospitals fell from a peak of 64,622 in 1963 to 59,918 by 1970. The psychiatric asylums contracted more rapidly, their occupants dropping from a high of 1,354,000 in 1961 to 1,033,000 in 1970.[111] This decline was already discernible when in March 1961 Enoch Powell as Minister of

Health made his famous 'water-tower' speech to the National Association of Mental Health. Announcing a programme of closure, Powell waxed lyrical about putting 'the torch to the funeral pyre'; he expected 'the acute population of mental hospitals to drop by half in the next fifteen years and the long-stay population ultimately to dwindle to zero'.[112]

The ten-year Hospital Plan, published in 1962, assimilated these predictions, the addition of extra psychiatric beds in the new district general hospitals only minimally offsetting the reduction of institutional places.[113] Baruch and Treacher have argued that whilst this integration was presented as a means of reducing the stigma of mental illness, its 'latent function' was to reassert the 'hegemony' of psychiatry by 'medicalizing' mental health problems and thus confining other professionals to 'ancillary roles'.[114] The power of the doctor in relation to the patient undergoing psychiatric treatment was incontrovertible. Though the legal reforms of 1959 may have reflected contemporary good practice, their civil rights credentials were coming under scrutiny by the early 1970s. Informal or voluntary patients in psychiatric wards and psychiatric hospitals had the same status in respect of consent as those admitted with physical illnesses.[115] Therefore, it was the potential for abusing involuntary detention that provoked particular worries.

First, the legal definition of mental conditions sufficient to invoke compulsory powers was based on contentious medical diagnoses, rather than specific acts of behaviour on the part of the patient. Second, more than half of all compulsory admissions did not use the standard observation and treatment orders but resorted to an emergency procedure that permitted hospitalization for 72 hours with only one medical recommendation. General practitioners ignorant of mental health legislation, social workers heavily influenced by psychiatrists, and a willingness on the part of all three groups to break the rules explained this abuse of 'urgent necessity'. For patients thus admitted, however, there was no right of appeal for the first month. Moreover, the Mental Health Review Tribunals to which they could subsequently turn were intimidating to those without an advocate, less than independent of the hospital psychiatrists whose cases were under consideration, and so veiled in secrecy that medical officers were entitled to withhold information that they believed the patient should not see. Therefore, by the time a new Mental Health Act was introduced in 1983, the assumption that professional discretion best protected the civil rights of mental patients had been severely dented.[116]

Patients' perspectives

The mental hospitals that accommodated disabled people in the 1970s carried the architectural burden of their past. Historical accounts of asylum design have been dominated by the influence of Bentham's panoptic wheel of cells that exposed inmates to constant surveillance.[117] However, only one early asylum was of radial design[118] and in 1847 the commissioners in lunacy condemned this 'windmill principle' on the grounds that it denied patients 'an uninterrupted view of the country and the free access of the air and sun' as well as preventing 'medical staff and others' from moving through the galleries 'without retracing their steps'.[119] Consequently, panoptic experiments coexisted with the traditional, mansion-like structure of the York Retreat that had an enduring appeal. Both forms were joined in the 1860s by the pavilion style of separate blocks that also influenced hospitals for the physically ill. And by the turn of the century the colony system had emerged with its detached villas 'scattered over the site . . . to diminish an institutional appearance'.[120] These asylums were not mere bricks and mortar; they embodied the social values and social relations that attached to mental impairment,[121] their geographical isolation aggravating the fearsome meanings of 'madness' that for those residing within the walls had to be mediated on a daily basis.[122]

The sense of abandonment conveyed by the asylum was compounded by a forceful linguistic suppression of the 'mad', which discredited their discourse and reduced them to silence. Though inmates' narratives did feed into the early nineteenth-century reform campaign, their authors voiced not their own abuse and maltreatment but that of other patients. As Allan Ingram says of Urbane Metcalf, who published *The Interior of Bethlehem Hospital* in 1818, his 'capacity . . . to control his own experience from within had been so severely curtailed that . . . we find only the lobotomized English of a man who no longer believes himself to be heir to the throne of Denmark'.[123] Therefore, the personal stories of asylum life looked very similar to the social reports that censured design and conditions. In her recent study of mental illness since 1948, Kerry Davies has likewise confirmed that whilst patients' 'voices' were not 'entirely silenced', they were 'kept within...[the] permissible boundaries' of the patient magazine, group therapy and the user-led training programme. Only in the last 20 years has this 'language of resistance and negotiation' been joined by another 'acceptable narrative' based on 'informed consent and patients' rights'.[124]

The negotiation and resistance conducted by patients was framed by the social processes of the asylum regime. Though some male psychiatric wards were run along military lines, the patriarchal Victorian family was the dominant organizational structure.[125] The York Retreat adopted this model, Samuel Tuke in his *Description* seeing 'much analogy between the judicious treatment of children, and that of insane persons'. How far the family ideal was realized is difficult to assess. Some inmates did develop close relationships with asylum staff, or intimate friendships with fellow patients. But it was the authoritarianism of the patriarchal family that most forcefully infused the regime. Despite enjoying single rooms, their own 'personal possessions and... some freedom of choice over diet, employment and amusements', patients at the Retreat were restricted by 'the moral order of [the] daily routine' and 'the obsessively high standards of cleanliness, neatness and decorum'. The more alert were not unaware of this repression, one former inmate from the Retreat recounting in 1878 how she had told the superintendent that what 'he meant by "better" was a nearer approach to that subdued and helpless condition below the power of complaint, which I saw in many of those around me'.[126]

For some patients, the controlled environment of the asylum was experienced 'as a place of safety and security' in which they felt at home and free.[127] Others, however, strived for greater independence. Even at the big state institutions, inmates achieved a modicum of individuality. 'There is no more touching sight', observed Andrew Wynter visiting the gargantuan Colney Hatch Asylum in 1857, 'than to notice the manner in which the female lunatics have endeavoured to diversify the monotonous appearance of their cell-like sleeping-rooms with rag dolls, bits of shell, porcelain, or bright cloth.'[128] Ranged against gestures like these was the 'darker side of institutional life',[129] evidenced for the second half of the twentieth century by the oral testimonies of ex-patients. 'The worst thing was, I couldn't wear my own clothes, you had to wear other people's,' complained Mabel Cooper of her period at St Lawrence's mental deficiency institution between 1952 and 1968: 'Because you never, you never got your own because the beds were too close together, so you didn't have a locker or anything, you just went to this big cupboard and helped yourself.'[130]

Personal possessions were confiscated during humiliating entry rituals. 'I got locked in', explained Isabel talking of her reception at Bromham House for intellectually impaired patients:

> I had lovely hair right down my back. And they cut it.... Tied me in a chair cos I didn't want my hair cut. They cut it all short by scissors.... Then after that got punished. They put me in a dark room on a mattress. Quarter/half hour, then they took me out and injected me. Yeah. Long while ago.[131]

Institutional routines after admission were similarly regimented and demeaning. 'One ward I was on which was – I would call it semi-locked – and it was mainly old incontinent women,' recalled a female patient, resident in Severalls psychiatric hospital:

> So there was one bath night a week and there were three baths. And everyone sort of queued up and had a bath and got a towel sort of dabbed at them, and off they went.... And on that ward as well the toilets only had half doors, so they could see people's feet and heads.[132]

Overt resistance to such indignities was expressed in bids to escape[133] or running the gauntlet of the asylum's authority. Margaret, for example, protested to the sister at Bromham House who alleged that her 'work wasn't done properly' and informed the doctor why she was scrubbing the stairs again. But not all patients were proactive,[134] choosing instead to collude over the avoidance of medication or the smoking of illicit cigarettes.[135]

In the closed world of the asylum with its vulnerable population, there was scope for staff behaviour to become abusive. 'You know if we did something wrong we had to be in us nighties all day and be punished,' said one narrator in Fido and Potts's study of a mental deficiency institution:

> Couldn't go out anywhere, couldn't have your visitors to see you. If you were bursting to go somewhere and wet yourself, you know like with me, you got punished. Say you were in a wheelchair and you couldn't talk to tell them, you still got punished![136]

Such 'punishment' on occasions degenerated into violence. 'Oh we were treated terribly, you know,' testified a male patient at Severalls. 'Night staff – some of those were bullies. I did the wrong thing really, I tried to hide away from them in the toilets – and they'd beat me up in the toilets. I thought I was gonna die.'[137]

These patients' testimonies are corroborated by staff accounts of asylum practices,[138] by a string of official enquiries,[139] and by social research that documented inhumane procedures and impoverished interpersonal relationships.[140] Of particular concern was the position of elderly people held in growing numbers in long-stay mental hospitals.[141] Individual psychiatrists like Russell Barton at Severalls may have tried to implement 'a friendly, permissive ward atmosphere' that acknowledged the need for 'individual territory', and his patients may have felt the benefit of more enlightened nursing.[142] Nevertheless, the weight of evidence discredits any assumption that the National Health Service and the reforms of the 1960s comprehensively rid mental hospitals of their abuses. Consequently, it is difficult to concur with Kathleen Jones that the 'sustained campaign of "hospital-bashing"' – provoked by the 'ideological attack' on asylums mounted by Goffman, Foucault and Szasz – was 'largely based on the description of conditions before 1900'.[143]

Conclusion

In this chapter, we have examined the development of asylums that accommodated a miscellany of disabled people with predominantly mental, but also physical impairments. Within the mixed economy that delivered these institutions, humanitarian concern and the medical profession were common elements. For private madhouses, however, commercialization supplied the catalyst, whereas for subscriber charities the economic benefits of restoring patients to sanity were articulated within a spectrum of social, cultural and political returns. The intervention of the state from 1808 was neither a simple conspiracy with psychiatry nor a crude stab at social control, but the rapid expansion of asylums after 1845 – and the emergence of mental deficiency institutions after 1913 – had the effect of incarcerating many long-term patients on the grounds that their behaviour contravened social norms. These patients, denied political citizenship for the duration of their confinement, were inadequately protected against squalid or abusive conditions by paternalistic inspection systems that showed no awareness of social rights. Civil rights were similarly endangered by illegal detention and treatment without consent that the introduction of voluntary admission did little to alleviate. Some patients found comfort in the institutional regime; others resisted its impositions, but to little effect given the societal forces that shored up asylum living.

5 Schools

Before the late eighteenth century, disabled children in Britain were generally regarded as incapable of education just as 'lunatics' were dismissed as irretrievably 'mad'; without an unimpaired mind and body, rationality and hence full personhood were impossible. In parallel with changing attitudes to mental illness, a new optimism arose in the aftermath of the Enlightenment. Blind and deaf people, denied access to the word of God, appealed to Christian sympathies, particularly since new methods of teaching them to communicate offered a justification for schools; and social experiments in the management of 'idiocy' likewise encouraged educational initiatives. However, it was the introduction of compulsory schooling after 1880 that flushed out the exclusion of many disabled children and led to legislation covering physical as well as sensory and intellectual impairments. Though not all schools were residential institutions, they did function as 'dividing practices' that exerted a formative influence on life experiences. Chapter 5 looks at how this influence came about by charting the development of commercial, charitable, and state schools for blind and deaf, and mentally and physically disabled children. More specifically, the role of economic rationality in this mixed economy is set against religious and professional interests, and the traumatic experiences of schooling that pupils were unable to resist are used to dismiss the assertion that education policies were conducted within a framework of social rights.

Blind and deaf institutions

Britain's first 'special' school opened for deaf children in 1764 under the proprietorship of Thomas Braidwood. A commercial enterprise imitating the methods of private teachers, this Academy was originally located in Edinburgh but moved to Hackney in London in 1783 because there was too little space for its 20 pupils.[1] The charitable schools that sprung up from the late eighteenth century – the first for blind pupils in Liverpool in 1791 and for deaf pupils in the London suburb of Bermondsey a year later[2] – retained a paying clientele. However, their principal aim was to extend education to the children of the respectable poor. In a variation of the patient sponsorship that operated in voluntary hospitals, benefactors and subscribers voted for pupils typically aged between six and 12 on the basis of biographical notes that were circulated in advance of electoral meetings.[3] After 1834 the poor law authorities were also empowered to subsidize pupils without their parents being pauperized,[4] and after 1879 they were 'allowed...to support institutions and societies caring for blind, deaf and dumb children'.[5] By the late nineteenth century, this mixed economy had launched 50 blind institutions in Britain outside the metropolis that were educating – and employing and relieving – 1113 people. Twenty-six institutions for deaf children were educating 2340 pupils.[6] In 1897 these institutions were re-titled Royal Schools.

In marketing themselves to their public, blind and deaf institutions hunted funds by stressing the horrors of sensory deprivation. Blind institutions maintained that blindness was 'one of the heaviest privations', making blind people 'a class which without the Divine blessing of...[charitable] assistance would be almost shut out from all knowledge and means of good'.[7] Deaf institutions insisted that deafness was 'an infinitely greater calamity, particularly if the affliction had existed from birth'.[8] Both types of impairment were put forward as occasions for philanthropic largess that would 'establish a lasting monument'[9] to 'the liberality of English benevolence'.[10] But they were also presented as an opportunity to improve disabled children. Medical treatment was specifically ruled out[11] in favour of the 'modern miracles' that were wrought by instruction.[12] Without education, blindness and deafness denied full access to the word of God and necessitated idleness. With education, 'helpless and possibly dangerous members of society' were rescued 'from their almost uncivilized state',[13] offered religious salvation, and taught 'the means of maintaining themselves by their own industry'.[14]

Communication skills were at the centre of the curriculum designed to deliver this mix of spiritual enlightenment and economic utility. Several different systems were being used to teach blind children when in 1868 the National Institute for the Blind – then known as the British and Foreign Blind Association – decided to 'end the confusion' and mass-produce all its books in Braille. This script was broadly endorsed by the Royal Commission on the Blind, the Deaf and the Dumb, which recognized in 1889 that its pattern of raised dots for each letter was preferable to the printed characters of Moon for those who had not already learnt to read. Nevertheless, the 'battle of types' was unresolved and organizations with 'considerable stocks in other systems defended their vested interests'.[15] Language acquisition for deaf children was still more controversial. Thomas Braidwood promoted the oral method, using a small silver rod, flat at one end with a marble at the other, to position the tongue for the correct articulation of vowels and consonants.[16] After the Bermondsey Asylum opened in 1792, a combined method evolved in which speaking was augmented by 'writing, reading, and drawing and natural signs'. But this labour-intensive approach was soon confined to the paying clientele, being too expensive to apply to the growing number of charity pupils. Therefore, the majority of children were taught in sign language.[17] From the 1860s, oralism fought back as pure oral schools were founded and existing schools took note of calls to revise their manual methods.[18] However, when in 1880 the First World Congress to Improve the Welfare of the Deaf and the Blind met in Milan and decided that 'only oral instruction could fully restore deaf people to society',[19] 74 per cent of British schools supported sign language above the oral or the combined method.[20]

In the wake of the Milan Congress, oralism was ruthlessly imposed. Won over by arguments that sign language was too crude for subtle, abstract expression and inimical to proper classroom control, old schools were reformed whilst new ones were set up often as day rather than residential institutions in a bid to maximize integration into the hearing community.[21] An 'explanatory booklet' issued by Birmingham's Royal School for the Deaf in the mid-1930s outlined the curriculum:

The main work throughout the school... is the teaching of the English language – its understanding and use – and speech and lip-reading so far as possible. Along with this goes the teaching of number and simple arithmetic; and in the higher classes some geography, history, health knowledge, nature study, etc.

Non-sectarian religious and moral instruction was also 'an important part of the training', and handicraft was taught 'both for its educational value and for its practical worth in preparation for after-life'. Overall, the 'general aim...was "trained adaptability," so that on leaving school a child is able to take advantage of any suitable opening that offers.'[22]

This programme was not dissimilar to the curricula of nineteenth-century institutions where children typically spent their mornings on communication, their afternoons on mathematics, and the 'forenoon' on scripture plus a little history and geography.[23] The gendered training evident in the Victorian period was also replicated. From the age of 12 boys took 'a thorough course in woodwork' whereas girls did 'domestic science, laundry, cookery, housecraft and advanced needlework, including dressmaking'. The 'separation...[was] not complete' because 'senior girls' had 'a weekly lesson in simple woodwork, and the boys similar regular instruction in housecraft and simple cookery'. But whilst these classes were justified as having 'considerable practical value', they were also said to foster 'a more sympathetic and understanding attitude' to gender roles,[24] thus reproducing the division of labour between men and women that characterized society as a whole.[25] The emphasis on handicrafts as facilitators of employment ensured that class as well as gender fissures were sustained. Blind and deaf institutions depressed the expectations of all their pupils,[26] irrespective of social background. Long criticized for offering poor job prospects, however, they perpetuated the poverty of their working-class pupils by preparing them for only lowly paid manual work.

Whereas blind and deaf institutions initially distanced themselves from medicine, they were espousing the metaphor of 'educational treatment' by the 1930s and designating the school medical officer as the professional with responsibility for deciding the appropriate course of action in cases of residual hearing.[27] Mike Oliver has argued for the post-war period that the 'medical hegemony' in special education, which legitimated the withdrawal of children from classes to receive 'medical and paramedical interventions',

HIGHLAND DANCING.

Figure 4   Highland dancing at the Birmingham Royal School for Deaf Children
Source: Birmingham City Archives.

encouraged them to acquiesce in a passive sick role.[28] However, medicine was increasingly influential in constructing the ethos of educational institutions from the late nineteenth century, embracing like orthopaedics the virtues of fresh air and physical exercise.[29] Therefore, open-air schools and classrooms multiplied rapidly as an economical means of expanding provision,[30] and gymnasia and playing fields – 'a splendid "Lung"' for children – became the location for a vigorous pursuit of games, dancing, swimming and drill (Figure 4). 'For twenty minutes every School morning', advised the Royal Institution at Birmingham in 1924, 'both boys and girls are given training in Physical Exercises, such as Free Movements, Marching, Indian Club Drill, etc.'[31] Sensory impairment was to be controlled by disciplining the material body.

'Idiot' asylums

The 'idiot' asylum and the 'mental deficiency' colony had much in common with the blind and deaf institutions. Changing attitudes to intellectual impairment emerged from post-Enlightenment France where educationalists began to concentrate on improving 'the mind through sensory experience and object association'. Transmitted to Britain during the 1840s, these ideas were applied most systematically at the National Asylum for Idiots that opened in temporary premises in North London in 1848. After migrating to Essex Hall in Colchester, the National Asylum finally took possession of completed purpose-built facilities at Earlswood in Surrey in 1863, a decade after the foundation stone had been laid and eight years after the first patients were admitted. Like the blind and deaf institutions, Earlswood operated a mixed economy in which paying patients joined with charitable patients who were elected by subscribers for up to five years on the basis of their ability to benefit from the training on offer. This programme bore a strong resemblance to the schemes of moral management under way at contemporary lunatic asylums. At its core was a belief that, in the words of the *Annual Report* for 1849, the mind was perfect but had 'imperfect and defective expression or imperfect or deranged organisation'. Therefore, the Board had implemented a 'principally physical' system in which '[t]hey have educated the eye, the mouth, the muscle, the limb; and have endeavoured to reach the better portion of our nature, that it might also be trained to moral and spiritual exercise.'[32]

Though sporting and leisure activities contributed to this organicist agenda, physical drill was central to its application, providing the means by which 'idiot' children were to learn control of the involuntary and erratic body movements – often thought to characterize 'idiocy' – through subjecting them to their will. In addition, different classes were run to cater for different abilities. According to the official schedule, children in the 'top' class were expected to read passages from the Bible 'with tolerable correctness', write sentences in copybooks, and handle simple arithmetic. At the lower levels, on the other hand, the emphasis fell on basic life skills like feeding, dressing and speech. Teaching methods were sometimes ingenious. Numbers were put to music. Letters were demonstrated with wooden aids. And clothing was even proposed to 'form a series of graduated exercises in buttoning and unbuttoning, tying and untying, lacing and unlacing, buckling and unbuckling, fastening and unfastening with hooks and eyes'. As at blind and deaf institutions, vocational training complemented the formal curriculum, underscoring fault lines of class and gender. Female pupils of charitable status undertook the institutional housework, discovering how to wash, clean and sew; male pupils were engaged in the workshops, discovering how to make mats, baskets, clothing and boots.[33]

The National Asylum became a role model for four regional asylums in England. The Essex Hall site became the Eastern Counties Asylum in 1859, recruiting patients and subscribers from its geographical hinterland. Five years later, two more institutions opened – the Northern Counties Asylum (later the Royal Albert Institution) at Lancaster and the Western Counties Asylum at Starcross near Exeter. In 1868 a Midlands County Asylum was set up at Knowle in Staffordshire[34] and a year later Scotland acquired a National Institute for Imbecile Children at Larbert near Falkirk.[35] This network of 'idiot' asylums was united in its commitment to train patients to become useful, productive members of society and adopted similar methods to achieve that goal. As the Western Counties Asylum 'came increasingly to specialise in the education and training of pauper idiots', it sought to harness this economic potential in its policy of self-sufficiency and commercial manufacture. Less hamstrung by the electoral rights of voluntary subscribers, Starcross ruthlessly selected patients deemed 'improvable' and quickly ejected those who could not meet the demands of the work regime.[36]

Asylum medical reports contained exemplary cases of how 'idiot' children had improved. 'O.P.', for instance, was described as 'very backward in all branches of learning' when he was admitted to the Western Counties Asylum at the age of 12. After 'careful and continuous training', however, he was 'able to write fairly in a copy book and to do sums of long division'. 'L.F.' was likewise unable to read or write when she was admitted, but she had been taught to 'read easy tales and write so well that her friends are delighted with the letters she sends home to them. She has moreover become quite a good housemaid.'[37] Correspondence from parents corroborated stories of betterment, praising the asylum for improving their children's 'memory and intellect' and teaching them to keep their 'clothes straight and in good order'.[38] Yet with these flagship cases, the amount of change was incremental rather than revolutionary and fell far short of early promises to turn 'idiots' into independent community members. This did not mean that the asylums became custodial institutions.

At Earlswood, for example, where between 1853 and 1886 '50 per cent of all inmates were elected for a five-year term', only 18 per cent of the 2053 admitted 'stayed in excess of ten years'.[39] However, when the principal of the Northern Counties Asylum conducted a survey of discharged patients in 1909, he found that only 33 of the 367 for whom information was received were 'earning wages or the equivalent'. Conversely, 149 were in work-houses, lunatic asylums or other institutions, and 123 were 'living at home with parents or relatives'.[40]

Even during their early optimistic phase, the 'idiot' asylums promulgated a negative image of intellectual impairment, seeking – in the words of an Earlswood founding father – to elevate the patient 'from existence to life – from animal being to manhood – from vacancy and unconsciousness to reason and reflection'. This disparaging discourse, and its underlying organicism, was easy prey for an altogether more sinister physical explanation that under the influence of Social Darwinism construed 'idiocy' as a hereditary problem. Doctors had called on phrenology before 1845 in justifying the medical control of 'lunatic' asylums, but it was in the 'idiot' asylums that the correlation of mental impairments with cranial size, structure and topography was most tenacious. John Langdon Down – the medical superintendent of Earlswood who gave his name to Down's syndrome – was a standard bearer. Writing after the publication of Charles Darwin's *Origins of the Species* in 1859, Langdon Down put forward an evolutionary model in which mental disease was capable of dissolving 'racial barriers'. Therefore, what he called the 'great Mongolian family' was a product of the spontaneous reversion by Caucasian children to an earlier, 'less developed' race. The ethnic interpretation was comprehensively discredited by statistical research in the 1930s. However, the promotion of a racial model meant that the 'idiot' asylums fed into 'an emerging discourse on degenerationism' that from the 1870s converged with 'fears over urban squalour . . . and the slow encroachment of the state' to evolve into the eugenics movement.[41]

The 'mental deficiency' colony

The term 'eugenics' – invented by Francis Galton in 1883 – named the application of biological principles to upgrade the physical and mental strength of the nation. The parent of this mind-set was Charles Darwin. Writing in his 1871 treatise on *The Descent of Man*, Darwin complained that

> We civilized men . . . do our utmost to check the process of elimination; we build asylums for the imbecile, the maimed, and the sick; we institute poor-laws and our medical men exert their utmost skill to save the life of everyone to the last moment. . . . Thus the weak members of society propagate their kind.[42]

From its foundation in 1907, the Eugenics Education Society advocated four strategies to prevent such degeneration: sterilization, marital regulation, birth control and segregation of the unfit.[43] Feeding on the long-term 'cultural and social pessimism' that afflicted late Victorian and Edwardian Britain, the eugenic ideas that informed these policies appealed across the political spectrum. For the Right, they supplied a 'scientific rationalization' with which to resist social reforms that flouted 'the laws of natural selection'; for the Left, they offered a progressive agenda with which to plan and guide social reforms in a rational way.[44] Greta Jones has challenged this unanimity, arguing that the presence of 'progressives' at meetings of the Eugenics Education Society indicated that it was 'a unique forum for discussion of human biology and genetics' rather than a movement with a 'radical, even socialist element in . . . [its] philosophy'.[45] Nevertheless, eugenic thinking enjoyed widespread endorsement that extended it beyond 'a minority of racists and extremists' and made it 'an implicit part of popular Western cultural assumptions'.[46]

The eugenics debate about intellectual impairment was fuelled by the 'feeble-minded' who were provoking anxiety well before the Eugenics Education Society was established. Though variations of this term had been used colloquially since the seventeenth century, it took on a more specific meaning in 1866 with the publication of *A Manual for the Classification, Training and Education of the Feeble-Minded, Imbecile and Idiotic*, by P. Martin Duncan and William Millard. As the title suggests, Duncan and Millard added 'feeble-mindedness' to the existing typology of 'idiocy' and 'imbecility', defining the 'feeble-minded' as a sub-group of 'idiots' with 'more or less defective voices and powers of locomotion [and] a great want of foresight, common sense, and power of self-management'. They were to be distinguished from 'backward children' who were 'really perfect in body and mind' and able to gain from 'a rational system of education'.[47] This categorization of 'feeble-minded' people according to their training and hence employment potential brought about a convergence of eugenics with the individualism that was pivotal to economic rationality.[48] Moreover, it provided a seedbed for the National Association for Promoting the Welfare of the Feeble-Minded that emerged in 1896.

A leading figure in this National Association was Mary Dendy who, through the Lancashire and Cheshire Branch, campaigned for the Sandlebridge Boarding Schools and Colony that opened at Great Warford in 1902. Deeply influenced by her experiences on the Manchester School Board, Dendy argued in her 1901 publication, *The Importance of Permanence*, that 'feeble-mindedness' was not one of many social problems but their cause; it was 'an evil which brings all other evils in its train', thus propagating crime, poverty, drunkenness, promiscuity and disease. The 'feeble-minded', she declared, formed a pathological group within society because their condition was inherited and they were incapable of acquiring social competence through education. Dendy's case was strengthened by other writers who contended that 'feeble-minded' children and adults were not simply quantitatively removed from the norm, as earlier writers had suggested, but that they were 'qualitatively different from the rest of the population'. In other words, 'the continuum that had previously stretched from the lowest to the highest intelligence was categorically broken into two distinct and incommensurable groups, the normal and the pathological.' The designation of 'feeble-mindedness' as a pathological condition allowed the medical profession to claim control of diagnosis. Therefore, Alfred Tredgold, whose *Textbook of Mental Deficiency* from 1908 was still being reissued after the Second World War, was adamant that 'feeble-mindedness' was 'not the lowest grade of the normal, but... a definite abnormality – that it... [was], in fact, a disease'.[49]

For the eugenicists of the early twentieth century, 'feeble-mindedness' was not only an inherited pathology but also a permanent state. 'No one can promise to cure the sufferers who are such a curse to themselves and to society,' declared Mary Dendy, again in *The Importance of Permanence*:

> No one can make the faulty brain into a perfect one, change the diseased rickety body for one glowing with health and beauty, strengthen the feeble will so that it has all the power of the highest and strongest of God's creatures. These things are beyond the skill of man.

But all was not lost. If 'feeble-mindedness' could not be cured, it could be managed under a regime of 'scientific morality' in a permanent institution. 'We can develop the faulty brain in those directions in which it has power', wrote Dendy; 'we can minimise the bodily weakness and suffering; we can give the feeble will right guidance and support.' Above all, incarceration would prevent the contamination of others and the propagation of 'feeble-mindedness' in subsequent generations.[50]

Although Sandlebridge was designed for permanent occupation, the children – and later adults – were engaged in education and training. In the mornings, the pupils did what the *Annual Report* for 1913 called 'head-work', which included speech therapy, spelling and reading, arithmetic and nature study. In the afternoons, they did 'hand-work', which included housework, gardening, drawing and rug making. On completing their schooling, young adults were transferred to a programme of manual instruction that not only generated vital income but also stressed the value of practical work for improving physical and mental functioning. Needless to say, labour was gendered, young men being employed on the farm, in the grounds or in the workshops and young women undertaking domestic tasks. Therefore, despite Dendy's claims to the contrary, the differences between Sandlebridge and the voluntary 'idiot' asylums were more apparent than real. Both combined training with custody. Moreover, Sandlebridge failed its own test of permanency. Some pupils were discharged as unsuitable cases; some families or poor law sponsors removed others; and so only 265 of the 380 children admitted up to 1914 were still resident in that year.[51]

Yet Sandlebridge continued to entice charitable benefactors, and donations from school boards and county councils that sought to reserve places for their pupils. Central government grants and maintenance payments from local education and poor law authorities were also forthcoming. These financial partnerships, characteristic of early twentieth-century relations between the voluntary sector and the state, allowed expansion from just 30 pupils in 1902 to 442 adults and children when the institution was transferred to Cheshire County Council in 1941.[52]

Special schools

The late Victorian commentator, D. O. Haswell, berated the 'exile principle' that underpinned institutions for instruction and training. These asylums, he argued, added to 'the imprisonment that nature has already put upon' blind people and subjected them to a 'system' that not only failed to 'develop the[ir] powers' but also weakened their physical and mental health.[53] His case is equally relevant to deafness and intellectual impairment. Not every pupil was resident, some local children living at home.[54] However, all those taught in special types of school were excluded from the 'right to partake in all the educational endowments of the country, in common with' their able-bodied peers.[55] For most of the nineteenth century these endowments were minimal. Though the provision of schooling had been obligatory in Scotland since 1696, education in England and Wales was delivered through a mishmash of charitable, commercial and statutory initiatives that ranged from public, grammar and dame schools to ragged, workhouse and factory schools. Literacy levels fell after 1780 as this motley collection failed to keep pace with the demographic growth that accompanied the Industrial Revolution.[56] At the same time, the rapid shift of population to deprived urban centres stimulated fears of social disorder. Therefore, the state began to invest in education in an effort to quell unrest.

During the early phases of industrialization, literacy was thought to stir up rather than put down insurrection by enabling the labouring classes to read subversive literature. From the 1830s, however, its pacifying potential was increasingly recognized. In parallel to education for disabled children, Christianity played a central role, being advocated not only to advance moral probity and spiritual salvation but also to impart 'humility' and 'social deference'; 'the inequity of this world... [was] counterbalanced by the equality of the next.' In 1833 the state began to offer modest grants to the two religious societies – one Anglican and the other Nonconformist – that had been developing schools since the early nineteenth century.[57] Though after 1850 the proportion of children in education rose steadily, the quality of schooling received was variable and regional disparities were marked.[58] The context was also changing. In 1867, the franchise was extended to the urban working class, triggering calls of education for democracy. Furthermore, as Britain's economic and imperial primacy was increasingly challenged, better schooling was seen as a route to enhanced national efficiency.[59] 'Upon the speedy provision of elementary education depends our industrial prosperity', W. E. Forster told the House of Commons when he introduced the 1870 Education Act; 'if we leave our work folk any longer unskilled,...they will become overmatched in the competition of the world.'[60]

The Act addressed these political and economic issues by requiring elected School Boards to set up elementary schools for all children aged between 5 and 12 in areas where the voluntary sector was delivering insufficient places. In Scotland, where legislation at the beginning of the century had anticipated reform by strengthening lay influence in parochial schools, obligatory attendance was introduced in 1872. In England and Wales, however, education did not become compulsory for pupils aged between 5 and 10 until 1880.[61] The religious societies had showed little interest in disabled children[62] and the 1870 Act did not specifically mention them, but the arrival of mandatory state schooling transformed their education. Previously, 'children had all been mixed together in school or remained at home'; 'compulsory attendance brought them all under public supervision and assessment for the first time.' Initially, disabled pupils were 'often ignored or allowed absence by "reasonable excuse"'.[63] Over time, however, their visibility grew as they became the focus of a series of increasingly divisive investigations.

Of greatest influence was the 1889 Royal Commission. The Commission recommended schooling for the 'blind, deaf and dumb, and the educable class of imbeciles' to prevent them from becoming not only 'a burden to themselves but a weighty burden to the state'. It was, went on the Report, 'in the interests of the state to educate them, so as to dry up, as far as possible, the minor streams which must ultimately swell to a great torrent of pauperism'.[64] Legislation followed in the shape of the 1893

Elementary Education (Blind and Deaf Children) Act. Under this Act, responsibility for the education of blind and deaf children was transferred from the poor law authorities to local education authorities (LEAs), which had a duty to develop their own special schools or grant-aid schools in the voluntary sector. Parents were obliged to submit their children to this service. However, the Commission's recommendation that LEAs be empowered but not mandated to provide schools for intellectually impaired children who were not in existing facilities was deferred until the Elementary Education (Defective and Epileptic Children) Act of 1899.[65]

The new legislation in no way marginalized the voluntary sector. On the contrary, the blind and deaf institutions continued under their new name and other charitable bodies continued to found new establishments into the era of the welfare state. The National Institute for the Blind thus opened its first Sunshine Home for Blind Babies in 1918, the Chorleywood College for Girls in 1921, and Condover Hall for children with multiple impairments in 1948.[66] Nevertheless, the Acts did consolidate local initiatives, which reflected a reaction against residential institutions that dated back to the 1880s. The first special school for 'feeble-minded' pupils opened in Leicester in 1892 and five years later there were 31 educating 1300 pupils.[67] Furthermore, although the 1899 Act did not make such schools compulsory, there were 116 in existence by 1904 accommodating 4307 children. The 1913 Mental Deficiency Act, which established the 'mental deficiency' institution,[68] also required local authorities to identify all 'mentally defective' children in their areas who were between 7 and 16 years old. And a year later they were compelled under the Elementary Education (Defective and Epileptic Children) Act to provide special schools or classes to which parents were obliged to send their 'feeble-minded' children. By 1916 the number of dedicated schools had risen to 179 and there were places for over 14,000 children.[69] The 1918 Education Act made schooling for mentally *and* physically 'defective' children mandatory on the same terms that had applied to blind and deaf children since 1893, but the clause did not come into force until the mid-1920s.[70]

The 1899 Act insisted that 'physical defect alone' – as opposed to sensory or intellectual impairment – was 'not sufficient cause for the admission of a child to a special class'. Therefore, physically impaired pupils were to be placed in mainstream schools or in classes for 'feeble-minded' children if their education was disrupted by ill health.[71] As a result, special schools for these children were exclusively charitable for longer. An early Cripples' Home and Industrial School for Girls opened in London in 1851, and a national Industrial Home for Crippled Boys in 1865.[72] Later foundations replicated the occupational orientation. In 1903, for example, Grace Kimmins set up what she called the 'public school of crippledom' – the Heritage Craft Schools and Hospital at Chailey in Sussex, which aimed to 'remake' the disabled child through a rigorous programme of education, vocational training, recreation and medical care.[73] The first local authority residential school for 'crippled' children opened in Manchester two years later.[74] And by 1918 there were 60 day schools and 35 residential schools for physically 'defective' pupils.[75] Overall, Britain had in excess of 500 institutions for children with sensory or physical impairments during the 1920s, among them 77 for blind, 50 for deaf and 78 for 'crippled' pupils.[76]

United in their quest for economic utility, these special schools have been represented as a progressive 'advancement' for disabled children.[77] In reality, however, they marched forward in response to an amalgam of ulterior motives. With compulsory education geared to tooling the industrial workforce, the removal of disabled pupils brought about 'the smoother running of the normal . . . system'. The medical profession used their experience in 'idiot' asylums to claim control of the service.[78] In the words of Dr G. E. Shuttleworth, superintendent of the Royal Albert Asylum in Lancaster: 'the conditions of feeble-mindedness are so mixed up with physical conditions that it is important that a person who has been trained to discriminate between various abnormal physical conditions should have the decision as to the state of the child.'[79] But by the turn of the century, educationalists were beginning to contest the role of doctors in assessment. The Board of Education saw the expansion of the special school system as one of the cornerstones of the new school medical service.[80] In addition, the 1914 Elementary Education (Defective and Epileptic Children) Act made local education authorities responsible for ascertaining 'defective' children and identifying those incapable of being taught in special schools; whilst special school teachers – who had formed a professional association to pursue their interests in 1903 – were gratified by a legal requirement compelling parents to send their children to special schools.[81]

The execution of special schooling was thwarted in several ways. First, magistrates were reluctant to impose compulsory residential education on the grounds that it was an infringement of parental rights as well as an emotional trauma for many families.[82] Second, economic motives were paramount. In 1909, George Newman, the Chief Medical Officer, challenged the curriculum for intellectually impaired children, recommending that special schools better their employment record by adopting manual training and dropping the 'diluted traditional classroom syllabus' with its pointless aim of teaching pupils to read and write.[83] As the economy flagged and public expenditure was cut,[84] the cost of special education became prohibitive. In 1922, therefore, Newman urged the Board of Education to trim spending on special schooling, restricting reductions 'as far as possible to the attempted education of the defective children whom no education will make breadwinners'.[85] Gillian Sutherland has argued that the financial climate rather than mental testing underpinned this retrenchment. The mental test, she says – 'poised for take-off in 1914 under the new profession of psychology' – 'constituted a continuum of ability', which stretched from the normal to the abnormal and so discredited segregated education.[86] The 1929 Wood Report on Mental Deficiency exemplified this position. However, its desire that special schools be seen as a 'helpful variant' of normal schooling proved wishful thinking because, tarred with the brush of eugenics, their stigmatizing reputation was unyielding.[87]

Though eugenic fears were at their strongest with intellectual impairment, other disabled children were mistakenly sent to 'feeble-minded' schools[88] and as late as 1936 the Board of Education was warning that '[t]o apply the ordinary tests of intelligence to a child who is defective in sight or hearing is to do him [*sic*] serious injustice.'[89] But education for children with sensory and physical impairments also came under the influence of eugenics. In 1904 the Report of the Inter-Departmental Committee on Physical Deterioration decided that there was 'very little real evidence on the pre-natal side to account for the widespread physical degeneracy among the poorer population'.[90] As Seth

Koven has pointed out, however, the 1899 Act had made 'crippled' children 'a protected category of persons not as victims of industrial accident but within the context of broader concerns about disease'. After the Representation of the People Act, which in 1918 increased the male British electorate threefold,[91] traces of citizenship crept into the publicity for special schools seeking to 'fit their charges to...take their places in the world as well-behaved, self-respecting citizens, able and willing to prove their worth amongst their more fortunate fellows'.[92] But this 'civic' consciousness did not signal greater inclusion. Burdensome in expecting disabled people to demonstrate their value, it was also combined with a 'racial' awareness[93] that, in the words of the Wood Report, attributed 'mental deficiency, much physical inefficiency, chronic pauperism, recidivism' to 'poor mental endowment'.[94] Therefore, the duty of local authorities to provide special schools for disabled children was 'inscribed within the rhetorical and ideological framework of eugenics' rather than of citizenship and social rights.[95]

The 1944 Education Act

The 1944 Education Act was one of the measures that forged the post-war welfare state. Committing local authorities to provide all children with schooling suited to their 'age, aptitude and ability', the Act 'extended the principle of free secondary education...to all pupils and established the modern distinction between primary and secondary schools.'[96] It was conceded that where possible these mainstream schools were the most appropriate locations in which to teach disabled pupils. Therefore, all those 'able to benefit' from education were brought into the local authority domain, leaving only 'ineducable' children under the jurisdiction of the NHS.[97] Additional facilities were made available under the Handicapped Pupils and Medical Services Regulations of 1945. As well as special attention from the teacher, disabled children in ordinary schools were to be allowed 'a favourable position in the classroom', special furniture, aids and equipment, and tuition in lip-reading if they were partially deaf.[98] Furthermore, in an effort to overcome past stigma, the derogatory term, 'mental deficiency,' was superseded by 'educational subnormality' and 'maladjustment', which were claimed to be less insulting.[99]

The impact of these reforms is easily exaggerated. Far from ushering in an equality of educational opportunity consistent with inclusive social citizenship, the 1944 Act preserved a hierarchical structure of secondary schooling in which the IQ test that demarcated intellectually impaired children was used to select 'able' children for privileged grammar schools and condemn 'less able' children to low status, under-funded secondary modern schools.[100] Methodologically flawed and indifferent to social background, the testing procedure skewed access to grammar schools in favour of pupils from middle-class families.[101] Disabled children caught up in selection were exposed to this discrimination. For many, however, the promise of mainstream schooling failed to materialize because the legislation facilitated an expansion of special education. As in the pre-war period, the teaching profession and the state saw segregation as a convenient means of regulating disruptive behaviour, whilst psychologists and special school teachers hijacked education for disabled children to wrest power from doctors. Therefore, in the decade after 1945 the number of children attending special schools in England climbed from 38,499 to 58,034, and by 1972 the figure was no fewer that 106,367.[102]

The case for segregated education was articulated within a needs-based discourse. Special schools were promoted for two main reasons. First, they had the teaching expertise and material resources to deliver curricula geared to the particular circumstances of impairment. Second, they offered a sympathetic environment where disabled pupils could acquire the interpersonal skills necessary for adult life in the able-bodied world.[103] It follows that waiting lists were deplored for leaving children to 'languish at home or sometimes block hospital beds because there is no suitable... school place available'.[104] This argument gained credibility from the endorsement of disabled children and their parents, who had experienced educational and social isolation in mainstream schooling. Deaf people in particular stressed the importance of attending a special school in order to learn the sign language that offset the dominance of hearing culture. However, the performance of disabled children in special education was undermined by narrow curricula and low teacher expectations, which meant that they left school with fewer qualifications and hence more limited opportunities for subsequent education and employment. Their self-esteem was likewise ill served by a segregated institution that exuded dependency and impeded association with non-disabled children.[105]

Separate special schools looked increasingly anomalous from the 1960s as the all-ability comprehensive gradually displaced selective secondary education and enabled children from a variety of social backgrounds to mix more easily.[106] In 1970 the junior training centres, which the NHS had set up for 'ineducable' children after 1948, were finally transferred to local education authorities.[107] Four years later the Warnock Committee was appointed to investigate the education of disabled children and young adults. Its recommendations informed the 1981 Education Act. Mainstream schools were to offer a range of special provision for which LEAs were required to assess pupils with an accredited impairment. Parents gained a small increment to their right to information. However, since there was no extra funding to meet the 'special educational needs' identified by the 'statement', the Act 'added nothing to ... the entitlements of citizenship for disabled children.'[108] Even without the financial constraints, there were limits to what more inclusive schooling could achieve, at least in the short term. Then as now 'disabled children encounter[ed] discriminatory notions of "normality" and "difference" in both "special" and "mainstream" schools.' Furthermore, 'these experiences relate[d] not simply to the structural forces that impinge on schools and teachers, but also to the everyday individual and cultural practices of adults and children.'[109] None the less, beginning to dismantle special schools tackled the social oppression of disabled people by challenging their passive self-image and confronting negative community attitudes.

Pupils' perspectives

Although the testimonies of disabled people confirm the oppression of the special school, they also disclose a positive contribution to self-esteem that eluded pupils who were reliant on mainstream education. In the 1920s, many disabled children were not attending a school of any description. For those who were, photographic images portrayed a happy, carefree existence with education interspersed with outings to the seaside. In reality, experiences were mixed. When disabled children were welcomed into ordinary classrooms, and teachers recognized their intellectual and physical requirements in a sensitive way, inclusion was successful. However, it was common for children to be punished and ridiculed for the consequences of their impairment. David Swift, whose hand movements deteriorated whilst he was at school, was caned because the teacher regarded his handwriting as a disgrace. Ernest Williams gained a reputation as the 'dunce' at his village school in Herefordshire because his partial sightedness prevented him from seeing the blackboard and participating appropriately in lessons:

> So I gave the answers when it wasn't my turn and eventually I'd get punished for that, because to the teacher it was disobedience.... I remember standing in the corner or having to sit under the teacher's table out of the way. And I used to get sent down to the infants. I felt badly about that.

Ernest was removed to a special school at the age of ten when an inspector discovered the extent of his impairment.[110]

The institutional regime to which children were admitted sought to discipline its charges. A paternalistic authority structure was adopted to steer education, training and employment in this direction. Schools for blind and deaf children were closely identified with the personalities of their charismatic headmasters,[111] whilst Dr F. D. Turner, superintendent of the Royal Eastern Counties Asylum for Idiots and Imbeciles, urged pupils as well as staff to regard him as a father: 'Every one of them...must be able to come to you with their troubles', he wrote in the *Annual Report* for 1935. '"Daddy" is the name I like best to hear.'[112] The all-powerful head of the asylum or special school presided over a 'regularised life of healthy activity with proper hours of sleep and...close attention...to each child's physical condition and diet'.[113] Teachers supervised the children's day-to-day activities, getting them up and bringing them 'downstairs in an orderly manner', ensuring that they 'behave themselves in a decent and orderly manner at the table', and checking 'any wrong-doing, cruelty, mischief, or tyranny...that may come to their notice'.[114] The photographic images that the Sandlebridge Boarding Schools chose to publish in their *Annual Reports* embodied this aspiration for order. Neat dormitories were uncluttered by their deviant occupants who were gainfully at work in the reclamation and domestication of waste land: a metaphor for their own rehabilitation.[115]

For deaf children caught in the ruthless reassertion of oralism from the 1880s, there was a savage campaign to stamp out sign language. As Joyce Nicholson recalled of her period as a pupil at the Royal School for the Deaf and Dumb in Birmingham: 'we would get smacked on the hands and our arms would be tied by our sides for the morning or afternoon just to stop us signing.' Children who were caught were called 'little monkeys'.[116] However, residential schooling in general was all encompassing. When not being taught, pupils were engaged in domestic tasks or physical exercises, and even more enjoyable excursions organized on an occasional basis were compulsory. Consequently, there was little free time for independent activities that nurtured individuality.[117] If residential provision denied children personal space, segregated education was at times an escape from poverty and mistreatment, which helped boost their self-esteem.[118] Yet some special schools were brutal with harsh discipline and living conditions reminiscent of the workhouse; indeed, children were so hungry that they ate toothpaste and sweet grasses.[119] In addition to this physical abuse, special schools failed to react appropriately to their pupils' emotional responses, shaming them into the repression of feelings about impairment and family separation. Furthermore, they practised psychological abuses that damaged essential processes of mental development.[120]

Like 'lunatic' asylums and 'mental deficiency' institutions, special schools subjected their entrants to demeaning admission rituals, scrubbing them with carbolic soap and chopping off their hair.[121] Once inside, personal identity was systematically attacked. Children were described as animals; their first names were rarely used; they were dismissed as only fit for menial employment; and girls were forced to wear tatty clothes that suppressed their femininity. Therefore, they came to believe that they were 'nothing' or 'nobody'. The significance of disability was also denied. Schools made strenuous efforts at 'normalization' by experimenting with new aids and appliances. Their staff mocked the academic abilities of pupils and their capacity for personal care. And insensitive procedures – indifferent to bodily functioning – exposed disabled children to punishment for bed-wetting.[122] This was Harriet's fate at a school for visually impaired girls in the 1950s:

> I was very unsettled... one night I wet the bed. The prefect on duty realized what had happened and she tried to cover up for me, she got me out of bed and put me in the bath, but one of the matrons came along. She picked me out of the bath, just as I was soaking wet, and gave me the hiding of my life... I yelled and screamed, it terrified me.[123]

Andrea was made to stand 'in the corner with her wet sheets tied around her neck' for committing the same offence.[124]

These hardships were made more bearable by the firm friendships that were forged with peers who shared the experiences of impairment.[125] Special schools exploited these relationships for disciplinary purposes, splitting up friends in what was 'the most devastating of punishments'. This strategy of divide and rule was also applied to pupils who were socially isolated. Sally French remembers the cruelty with which Glenda was treated. In addition to her visual impairment, Glenda had 'a heart condition, one lung and a spinal deformity'. During 'the long crocodile walks' that the pupils endured on Saturday and Sunday afternoons, she 'was pushed and shoved by the care staff... and we were encouraged, indeed sometimes forced, to join in. On many occasions she sat, exhausted, in the road and was dragged to her feet.' Colluding with staff was one way of coping.[126] Resistance was another. Disabled children were argumentative and disobedient; they organized strikes against bad food or excessive punishment; they mounted raids on the kitchen to supplement meagre diets; they made bids to escape. But if acts of defiance were possible, the structures within which they occurred were ultimately constraining. Therefore, school practices were not overturned but reasserted through the correction of 'offenders'.[127]

Conclusion

Chapter 5 has traced the development of educational institutions for disabled children. Originating in the commercial sector, schools for pupils with sensory and intellectual impairments tapped into the optimism of the post-Enlightenment era to offer a combination of spiritual salvation and employment skills. By the end of the nineteenth century, eugenic influences were casting impairment in a more negative light, but the charitable sector, and later state schooling for all categories of disabled children, perpetuated the economic rationale in a mixed economy of education where the curriculum was imbued with class and gender. Neither the decline of medical power in assessing pupils nor the rise of psychological testing managed to translate the special school into normal education. Furthermore, though the 1944 Education Act was integrative in intention, claims to professional expertise underwrote the expansion of segregated facilities from which pupils emerged with below-average qualifications. Their experiences of these paternalistic, closely supervised school regimes were often painful, with harsh discipline, poor conditions and emotional abuse against which resistance was impotent. Consequently, special education in the years to 1979 was in no way delivered as a social right. Legislation stemming from the Warnock Report began the process of breaking down segregation, but with inadequate resources the social inclusion of disabled children was a distant goal.

Part II

Community Living

6 Work

Institutions have dominated the history of disability, their position secured by a strong physical presence, the deposition of written records in public archives, the segregated lifestyle of their inmates, and the resource implications of large-scale hospital closures in the late twentieth century.[1] Yet only a small minority of disabled people was ever domiciled in workhouses, hospitals, asylums or schools. There has been a tendency to assume that their isolation was paralleled by an inclusive experience of life in the community thanks to progress towards social citizenship.[2] Recent debates about social exclusion have revealed the futility of this assumption. As Ruth Levitas argues, '[e]xclusion and marginalization are mainly construed as exclusion from and marginality to paid employment.' The 'opposite of social exclusion...is not inclusion, but integration.' And since '[i]ntegration into society is elided with integration into work', disabled people who are unable to participate in the labour market are regarded as less than full citizens.[3] The next three chapters have as a central theme the divisive effects for community living of equating citizenship with paid work. In this chapter, the performance of a mixed economy of services is assessed with reference to the persistence of segregated training and workshop facilities, the impact of economic recession for marginal employees, and the operation of the workplace legislation that in the 1940s was heralded as a social right to employment. Chapter 7 and Chapter 8 then address the diverse origins of social security and community care, and the barriers that they erect to citizenship. But first we trace the financial exclusion to which disabled people were exposed by poverty.

The incidence of poverty

Until the end of the nineteenth century, poverty was regarded as the natural predicament of the great mass of the population. It was, wrote the political economist, Patrick Colquhoun, in 1806, 'a most necessary and indispensable ingredient in society... since without poverty there would be no labour, and without labour there could be no riches, no refinement, no comfort, and no benefit to those who may be possessed of wealth'.[4] By the 1840s, however, the context was changing. First, the economy became less volatile as the initial phases of industrialization drew to a close. Second, the political situation became more stable as the Chartist campaign for universal male suffrage waned. And, third, attitudes to the economic and social plight of the working classes became more sympathetic as 'responsible opinion' participated in a lively debate about the 'Condition of England Question'.[5]

Literature, especially the 'social-problem' novels by authors like Charles Dickens and Elizabeth Gaskell, played an important part in stirring up this new social consciousness.[6] So too did the rise of empiricism. Though often attributed to the practical needs of an industrializing society, empiricism was also linked to the intellectual aspirations of the professional middle class that was an important audience for the new literary fare. Increasing in number and influence with the expansion of the democratic state, these doctors, lawyers and civil servants sought to replace the polemical discussion of social issues with a predictive science of society based on the collection of statistical data. In the later nineteenth century, this mentality found expression in the embryonic social survey,[7] but it was prefigured by the work of Henry Mayhew. Recruited by the *Morning Chronicle* in 1849 to serve as the metropolitan correspondent for a national investigation of labour and the poor, Mayhew went on to produce a multitude of detailed individual portraits, combining 'the interrogative approach of the royal commission with the reporting skills of the journalist'. Despite claiming to record the facts without bias, his accounts were infused with moral judgement. Therefore, the 'undeserving' poor were distinguished from the 'deserving' poor who could not 'live by their labour, whether from under payment, want of employment, or physical or mental incapacity'.[8]

Disabled people, if appearing only rarely in Mayhew's extensive narratives, were excused responsibility for their poverty. Take the 'maimed' Irish crossing-sweeper. A former bricklayer's labourer who had lost a leg after falling from a scaffold, he had 'no especial mode' of attracting customers, except 'hobbling a step or two towards them and sweeping away an imaginary accumulation of mud'. He explained that his income was meagre and uncertain:

> I dunno how much I earn a-day – p'rhaps I may git a shilling, and p'rhaps sixpence. I didn't git much yesterday (Sunday) – only sixpence. I was not out on Saturday; I was ill in bed, and I was at home on Friday. Indeed, I did not get much on Thursday, only tuppence ha'penny. The largest day? I dunno. Why, about a shilling. Well, sure, I might git as much as two shillings, if I got a shillin' from a lady. Some gintlemen are good – such a gintleman as you, now, might give me a shilling.[9]

Mayhew's use of the language of the poor gave his characters a compelling immediacy that not only boosted sales but also won supporters to his cause; London poverty was a public disgrace for which the more fortunate were culpable. But though the stories were transcribed as told, the careful priming of the narrators compromised spontaneity; and since his plan to survey the entire labouring population was aborted, the investigation was heavily skewed towards the most marginal occupational groups. Therefore, whilst Mayhew's study was empirical, it did not yield a systematic picture of the poor.[10]

Subsequent surveys put the measurement of poverty on firmer statistical foundations. During the 1880s, Charles Booth invented the poverty line for his classification of London life and labour. A decade later, Seebohm Rowntree refined this monolithic, static approach by distinguishing between 'primary' and 'secondary' poverty, and identifying a 'cycle' through which the working classes passed from childhood to old age.[11] Neither Booth nor Rowntree recognized disability as a social category. However, Rowntree's cyclical model did lead him to include elderly people in his three surveys of York. In 1899, old age and sickness together accounted for 5.11 per cent of those in poverty. In 1936, 14.7 per cent of the poor were elderly, whilst 4.1 per cent were sick. And in 1950 old age was responsible for no less than 68.1 per cent of poverty and sickness for another 21.3 per cent. Furthermore, this growing concentration amongst sick and elderly people occurred as the general incidence of poverty declined from almost a third of the York population in 1899 to less than 3 per cent by 1950.[12] Under the welfare state, the poor had all but vanished.

The absence of disabled people from a methodology as influential as that of Rowntree conspired to exclude them from later research. Therefore, they were still concealed in the early 1960s when Brian Abel-Smith and Peter Townsend 'rediscovered' poverty. On the basis of the scales applied to the allocation of means-tested benefits, Abel-Smith and Townsend concluded that old age was no longer the main reason for poverty because only 33 per cent of the poor were elderly. Overall, however, they estimated that more than seven million people, or 14 per cent of the total population, were living in poverty.[13] The news that the poor had increased since 1950 shocked contemporaries. Britain, though declining as a world power, had become more affluent, and this cocktail of demise and prosperity fed a challenge to traditional authority that was expressed through popular culture, sexual permissiveness and a radical critique of materialism in which the new consumer society was accused of neglecting the public services. This anxiety was reflected in the election of a Labour government after 13 years of Conservative rule. It was during the subsequent reappraisal of the welfare state that disability finally emerged as a political issue, aided by the activities of the Disablement Income Group that was founded in 1965 to press for better financial support.[14]

In response to this heightened awareness, the first national survey of disabled people was commissioned from the Office of Population Censuses and Surveys in the late 1960s. It revealed that at least a half of the impaired population was living in poverty or on the margins of poverty.[15] Peter Townsend's independent study, undertaken at much the same time, set the financial circumstances of disabled and non-disabled people side by side: '58 per cent of those with appreciable or severe incapacity, compared with 24 per cent of the non-incapacitated, were in households with incomes below or close to the government's supplementary benefit standard.' For elderly people, the figure was 64 per cent.[16] Though there are problems with the terminology of both studies,[17] they do document persuasively the financial disadvantage of disabled people. During the 1970s, a series of studies catalogued how physical and sensory impairments generated extra expenses not just for aids and adaptations but also for heating, food, laundry, travel and recreation.[18] Income deprivation was thus aggravated by the additional costs associated with impairment.

Segregated training and employment

Disabled people's increased risk of poverty made them vulnerable to financial exclusion, denying them access to the consumer goods and services purchasable by a majority of citizens. Ineffective social security strategies were one explanation for this disadvantage,[19] but resort to mutual aid, charity and state relief was itself due in part to exclusionary employment. The employment destinies of disabled people were configured through the interaction of impairment with age, gender and social class. The introduction of state pensions from 1908 gradually removed elderly workers from the job market, leaving them to serve as a reserve army in the event of a labour shortage.[20] Women were likewise marginal to paid work because 'most policy makers assumed that all females, regardless of their physical status, ought to be dependent on fathers, brothers, or husbands.'[21] Social class affected employment via access to education. Some disabled people – like the deaf lawyer, John William Lowe, who was called to the Bar in 1829 at the age of 25 – received an education that paved the way to successful professional careers.[22] However, the voluntary societies that educated many disabled children had low expectations,[23] seeking only to absorb them into skilled manual occupations at the bottom end of the labour market. Deaf workers found employment more easily than blind workers[24] and so deaf charities organized apprenticeships or paid the fees where parents or guardians were unable to afford them.[25] But the voluntary sector also pioneered segregated employment in the form of home-working schemes and sheltered workshops that identified disabled people with low status jobs.

Home-working dated from the mid-nineteenth century. The schemes were intended for the 'many capable Blind who, for various reasons, prefer to work in their own homes, or, to carry on business for themselves', and they involved a stereotyped spectrum of economic activities: basket-making, mat-making, knitting, piano tuning and music teaching.[26] Exported from the voluntary to the public sector, and from sensory to other categories of impairment, home-working like this persisted into the post-war period. Margaret Wymer recalled 'making lavender bags for a local firm' in Norwich during the late 1960s. Seeing the finished products was 'satisfying'. However, their manufacture was 'often hard and exacting'; she 'lived in a continuous muddle of organza material, buckets of lavender and ribbon bows'; and at 'one new penny a bag' the hours were long for £1 a week.[27] The economics of home-working schemes were also increasingly strained. Overheads were high because of administrative, storage and transport costs; mechanization reduced the potential for domestic production and the market for its goods; and the ensuing low profit margins meant poor rates of pay and the risk of overwork that damaged health. Therefore, by 1973 the Department of Employment was doubting whether home-working was compatible with modern industrial development.[28]

At this stage, home-working engaged approximately 1000 disabled people, or less than 10 per cent of the segregated workforce.[29] The more heavily populated sheltered workshops were of longer lineage, having been set up by charitable bodies from the late eighteenth century. Gordon Phillips maintains that whereas English institutions for the blind adopted the school model with 'a proportionately much higher recruitment of the young', Scottish institutions prioritized 'long-term employment', making the 'earning power of the blind and the profitability of their work ... the acid tests of philanthropic endeavour'. Therefore, in 1871 a guide to blind charities observed that the five Scottish institutions sold goods worth £21,930 whilst for the 40 English institutions the trading income was only £33,598. Phillips speculates that English philanthropists were less convinced by the capacity of blind people for rational self-improvement, citing in his defence 'Christian voluntarism' and 'the optimistic view of labour presented by Adam Smith', Scotland's famous *laissez-faire* economist. Only when the 1889 Royal Commission 'examined the conditions of blind labour on a national scale ... were the English schools finally compelled to confront the impoverished results of their attempts at industrial training'.[30]

It is difficult to evaluate this hypothesis without a detailed study of blind institutions south of the border. However, the workshop programme of the Swansea and South Wales Institution for the

Blind – established in the mid-1860s as the Swansea Auxiliary of the Society for Teaching the Blind to Read – suggests that economic activity was important. In its very first year, the Society had a boy 'under tuition in basket-making, at which trade, as well as mat-making, three of our Blind earn a respectable living in this town'.[31] Expansion quickly followed, with the acquisition of workshops and commercial premises from which to sell the articles made. Branches elsewhere in South Wales were also opened. By 1922/3, the Society was employing 110 blind workers and during the course of that year they manufactured over 15,000 baskets and mats, reseated almost 1000 chairs, and knitted nearly 1400 articles. 146,419 parcels of firewood were also bundled together (Figure 5).[32]

The discovery of physical and mental 'deficiency' from the late nineteenth century spread the sheltered workshop to other impaired groups.[33] At the same time, attitudes to unemployment were mutating. Before the 1880s, it was widely assumed that the market economy would deliver jobs to all who genuinely wanted

MAT MAKING.

Figure 5   Mat-making at the Swansea and South Wales Institution for the Blind

Source: West Glamorgan Archive Service.

to work, adjusting the supply of and demand for labour via wage rates. But this confidence was gradually undermined. Economic crises like the disruption of cotton imports during the American Civil War (1861–5) had already shown that external events could cause involuntary unemployment. The British economy was also undergoing relative – though not absolute – decline, after an extended period of international pre-eminence. And developments within the discipline of economics were encouraging a new theoretical focus on trade cycles and labour markets, which qualified the past obsession with the feckless poor.[34] Policy initiatives ensued. The Local Government Board praised the 'spirit of independence' widespread among the working class and pressed local poor law authorities to provide non-stigmatizing jobs for those who had previously avoided assistance. The Workmen's Unemployment Act of 1905 implemented this recommendation. In addition, local distress committees, with representatives from borough councils, boards of guardians and charitable organizations, were established in every major urban area and empowered to organize labour exchanges, maintain unemployment registers, and facilitate migration or emigration.[35]

Though too weak for the task in hand, the Workmen's Unemployment Act was a 'seminal measure' for acknowledging that joblessness was 'more than a purely personal problem'.[36] During the years preceding the Act, a threefold categorization had evolved: 'seasonal unemployment', caused by 'the weather or the pattern of demand'; 'cyclical unemployment', caused by 'the regular rhythm of rising and falling... international trade'; and 'casual unemployment', caused by skilled or unskilled workers being 'unable to work at their trade due to old age, illness or some other misfortune'.[37] Disabled people fell into the last category. The wish to render them employable, aroused by the heightened awareness of deficiencies in the labour market, was strengthened by the discovery of the accident in late Victorian Britain. Accidents – of course, a feature of pre-industrial society[38] – had achieved 'a public political presence' from the early nineteenth century. As Roger Cooter has argued:

> Children crippled through employment in mines and factories became a potent issue... in the 1830s and 1840s; revelations in the mid-1840s of the shocking conditions in which railway navvies sustained countless injuries and fatalities became a matter of public concern; and

cognizance of accidents in coal mines lead to the creation of a mines' inspectorate...in 1850. But factory reform, rather than the causes of the breaking of innocent bodies, was the object of the focus on children; the concern with railways labourers concentrated on their living conditions, rather than on their accidents; and the legendary injuries and fatalities of miners mostly provided social statisticians with a resource for moral exhortation.[39]

Therefore, the accident failed to trigger action in its own right.

Intervention was evaded because accidents – unlike cholera, which threatened public health across social and geographical divides – were heavily congregated in the industrial spaces of private industry that were occupied by the working class.[40] These employees were often held personally responsible for any impairment that they received, whether due to carelessness, recklessness or fatigue.[41] Furthermore, the very term 'accident' helped to excuse their middle-class bosses of culpability by acknowledging injuries, but insisting that they 'were unintended (in the sense of being both unforeseen and undesired)'.[42] When the accident finally emerged from obscurity, it was as part of a campaign to civilize the city by subjecting it to 'military-like unifying mechanisms... such as the...police and fire services, and...underground water, gas and sewer systems'. No longer regarded 'as more or less *private* (individualized) happenings', accidents became *public* events, 'affecting or concerning the whole of society'.[43]

The re-conceptualization of employment, acting in concert with the newly visible accident, stimulated additional segregated employment for disabled people. In 1904, soon after the charitable Sandlebridge Boarding Schools and Colony opened in Cheshire,[44] the Metropolitan Asylums Board commenced what became the Darenth Industrial Colony for 'higher-grade mental defectives';[45] and four years later the Lord Mayor Treloar Cripples' Hospital and College began offering 'crippled lads' a three-year technical training in 'trades suited to their limitations'.[46] Military initiatives accompanied these civilian ones. With the Boer War of 1899 to 1902, occupational rehabilitation had been left to the armed forces and charitable organizations like the Lord Roberts' Workshops.[47] However, the scale of the conflict between 1914 and 1918 led to greater state involvement, with instructional factories for disabled ex-servicemen and curative workshops in the military orthopaedic hospitals.

The curative workshop fulfilled a disciplinary function in ortho-paedic centres where many patients were mobile and easily bored by the routine of 'concerts, card-playing and smoking'.[48] Additionally, the workshops applied a scientific approach, parallel to the reappraisal of unemployment, which no longer envisaged work as simply virtuous, but understood it as 'valuable in social terms as a means to reconstitute...[the] sense of individual and communal worth'. Orthopaedic surgeons had experimented with these ideas before the War, adapting basic physiotherapy and simple craft-making to the rehabilitation of industrial workers as well as disabled children. In the curative workshop, however, they were fully implemented.[49] Patients contributed to the economy of the institution, saving limited resources by manufacturing splints and boots, undertaking carpentry and electrical work, and serving as clerical orderlies. The purposes were twofold. First, the jobs acted 'directly on the...recovery of the patient', giving 'exercise to the injured limb' and 'restoring co-ordinate movements'. Second, they conveyed the '[e]qually valuable...effect of being put to useful work' and fostered skills beneficial to future paid employment. In these ways, the wounded soldier was either rendered fit for military service or made 'an independent self-supporting citizen and not a crippled dependant'. Above all, the workshop was 'curative of his physical disability, and especially ke[pt] him from becoming an incurable idler'.[50] The same logic was applied to other impairments.[51] Integration into the labour market had thus become a precondition for social citizenship.

The era of mass unemployment

Unlike other European countries, Britain failed to implement 'statutory preferential employment arrangements' at the end of the First World War. Resistant to 'compulsion' and 'interference', and alert to the problems of enforcement, the government relied instead on the voluntary King's National Roll, which rewarded employers with at least 5 per cent of their workforce in receipt of a disability pension by inscribing their names on a list of honour.[52] The Blind Persons Act of 1920 did give local authorities a duty to provide segregated employment for those 'unable to perform any work for which eyesight is essential'. But the National League of the Blind and the TUC, reinforced by the independent support of the poor law authorities and a number of organizations for blind people, achieved this legislation only after a prolonged campaign dating back to the 1890s.[53] And when the Poor Law Act of 1930 addressed the employment of deaf people, local authorities were empowered but not required to help voluntary bodies place them in work.[54]

The *laissez-faire* outlook of central government left the job prospects of disabled people heavily dependent upon the charitable sector. Experiments continued. The National Institute for the Blind, which since 1904 had operated premises where qualified blind masseuses practised, started an Employment Bureau for blind piano tuners in 1916 and one for blind organists in 1929. In the following year, the first of a series of kiosks opened in London, selling newspapers, tobacco and cigarettes, confectionery and a range of wrapped goods; the blind kiosk holders were salaried employees of the Institute, whose 'interests are watched over by a sighted supervisor'.[55] The Central Council for the Care of Cripples was similarly active. Preoccupied at first with the national network of orthopaedic hospitals and after-care clinics for children,[56] the Council widened its brief in the early 1920s to include adults. Affiliated local associations were encouraged to form Employment Committees with representatives from the medical profession, the employment services, employers and trade unions.[57] Furthermore, the orthopaedic hospitals that enjoyed the Council's sponsorship carried forward the 'curative workshop' inherited from the First World War, using 'interesting labour' with employment potential to tackle the 'impatience or despondency of mind' that might otherwise frustrate recovery.[58]

In practice, funds were short and horizons limited. In 1924, however, facilities opened at the Wingfield Hospital in Oxford with training focused on carpentry, joinery and shoemaking that specialized in the production and alteration of surgical footwear. By the later 1930s, other hospitals had followed suite[59] and new training establishments – the Queen Elizabeth Foundation at Leatherhead, Surrey; St Loyes College, Exeter; the Stanmore Cripples Training College in Middlesex – were in operation where the course content was allegedly geared to the modern labour market rather than to traditional craft skills.[60] Vocational labour was also made available in the community with organizations like the Nottingham District Cripples' Guild employing six 'girls,' most of them former patients, in a workshop that made surgical instruments and appliances for in-house use.[61] By far the most vigorous player, however, was the British Legion. Founded in 1922 to further the welfare of ex-servicemen, the Legion made unemployment among its disabled constituency a particular priority. Not only did the manufacture of poppies for the annual Remembrance Days provide factory jobs for severely impaired workers, but employment exchanges and employment schemes were established and interest-free loans were advanced to enable members to take up new trades.[62]

The experiences of impaired people suggest that this patchwork of voluntary and statutory employment services was threadbare. Joanna Bourke has posited that 'the war exacerbated the low social and economic status of disabled civilians', shifting resources towards ex-servicemen. The resources on offer were not always popular. Contemporaries estimated that at least 50 per cent of those disabled by war would gain from retraining, but many were put off by the militarist institutional environment in which courses were mounted or the impractical nature of schemes which sought to turn bus conductors into farmers. Therefore, only 15 per cent were prepared to participate.[63] The men who did had contrasting encounters. Sidney Bell, a soldier with the Royal Scots Fusiliers, was impressed by the Local War Pensions Committee that considered his retraining after an arm had been amputated. A former apprentice joiner who had also 'passed some exams at night school before the war', he was surprised to be asked if he would like to train as a Sanitary Inspector. He could 'honestly say' that his new job was a change for the better. Others were less fortunate. Bill Thompson from Leeds was initially retrained as a hand tailor after the amputation of a leg, only to find that when he 'went for job interviews ... this work was out of date and firms needed machine tailors'.[64]

The statistical evidence demonstrates the extent to which the employment services were faltering. In September 1920, the Ministry of Labour conducted a sample survey of men receiving the out-of-work donation paid as an emergency benefit from 1918. The results were telling. 'In the United Kingdom as a whole the percentage of disabled men registered in their pre-service occupations was sixty-two as against seventy-seven per cent in the case of non-disabled men.' The London labour market revealed the degree to which their mobility was downward. The 'most notable increase was in porters, messengers, caretakers, etc., the number of whom increased by thirty-nine per cent; the number engaged in general light labouring work rose by twenty-eight per cent.'[65] In a society with a highly gendered division of labour, this denudation of job status threatened masculinity. The words of the character Harry Smith, in a play of 1923 called *The Unknown Warrior*, capture the dilemma: 'I'm fed up with making silly toys. It's not work for a man – but we're not men now, with half our insides and half our limbs gone; it's a good enough job for us, I suppose.'[66] Subjective experiences of work compounded the humiliation of deskilling.

Demoralization was also a concomitant of being without work. The Ministry of Labour's survey showed that across the United Kingdom 'the average number of weeks of unemployment was forty-four for disabled ex-servicemen as against twenty-six for non-disabled men.' Nor did the future look brighter: 'in the summer of 1920, just as the post-war boom burst, sixty-nine per cent of disabled ex-servicemen held extension out-of-work donation policies compared with forty-six per cent of the non-disabled.'[67] Unemployment among impaired people was not a new phenomenon. In 1911, for example, a study conducted by the City of Birmingham Education Committee reported that only 20 per cent of 'male cripples' were economically active, the position deteriorating with age.[68] Consequently, disabled ex-servicemen joined a coexisting body of work-poor citizens. The Great Depression of the inter-war period aggravated their situation. Whilst the gross domestic product (or the total flow of goods and services in the economy) continued to grow, it did so at a slackened pace, dropping from an average rate of 1.9 per cent per annum between 1870 and 1913 to 1.0 per cent between 1913 and 1938. Meanwhile, unemployment had by 1932 soared to 15.6 per cent of all workers, with catastrophic rates of over 60 per cent in some of the Northern and South Wales towns that had been at the heart of the Industrial Revolution.[69]

Faced with such an oversupply of labour, employers had little incentive to recruit impaired workers. Therefore, looking for a job in the open market was a dispiriting experience. Ron Moore, whose legs had been amputated after a road accident at the age of 10, began his search for a clerk's job in the late 1930s. He had no special training, no qualifications and no advice from his school or the labour exchange. After receiving rejections or no reply to his letters, he 'decided to go door-to-door looking for a job':

> For six months I went day after day to banks and insurance offices in the City....Sometimes I managed to get to see the manager but I wasn't in very good shape by the time I got to the interview. The artificial legs rubbed blisters where they joined the tops of my legs and they often bled. It was very painful walking around so when I got to the manager's office I had to ask to sit down. That didn't make a very good impression because in those days you were expected to stand to attention, cap in hand. Well, they always said the same thing, 'You've got no legs have you, I'm afraid we can't employ you.'

Fellow employees exhibited similar prejudices. When Bill Thompson, taught the redundant trade of a hand tailor, eventually obtained in-service training with a company manufacturing sanitary ware, he was subjected to discrimination by his workmates who 'wanted the bosses to cut my wage to make up for what they saw as my other income'[70] – in other words, his war pension.

The economic pressures, which underwrote these intolerant attitudes in the open labour market, also affected segregated employment. Throughout the inter-war period, the old institutions for people with sensory impairments marketed themselves in a language that patronized their workers. 'They want to work in their world of darkness,' opined the Swansea and South Wales Institution for the Blind. 'Will you assist them in their life's Work?'[71] The National League of the Blind called for better employment rights in these sheltered workshops, targeting low wages and poor conditions, and organizing national marches to London in 1920 and 1933.[72] The League has been accused of pressing for unrealistic rates of pay, which bore little resemblance to 'real earnings' or 'the need to preserve incentives' and hence threatened the financial viability of 'genuine employing agencies'.[73] But in the cold climate of the Great Depression, sheltered workshops were inevitably vulnerable. Take Swansea. At first the Institution weathered the economic storm; indeed, turnover actually increased in 1930/1, due partly to the introduction of a sales van which daily toured West Wales. Two years later, however, employees were laid off. Moreover, in the late 1930s the Joinery and Firewood Department was closed, along with the branch factory at Milford Haven that supplied the Pembrokeshire fishing industry.[74]

The retrenchment at Swansea was characteristic of Britain's inter-war employment services where statutory commitment was minimal and voluntary effort converged on traditional trades that were marginal to the economy. As a result, unemployment exceeded the overall rate, with 35,000 of the total blind population of 40,000 being without work in 1936.[75] During this decade, the National Institute for the Blind collaborated with the National Institute of Industrial Psychology in research that tried to identify new occupations that might be suitable for blind workers. The results were not 'immediately rewarding'.[76] For it took the crisis of the Second World War between 1939 and 1945 to expand the range of employment for all disabled people.

The legacy of the Second World War

A wartime employment service for disabled people got under way in 1941 when, after a sustained campaign by the TUC and the voluntary sector, the Ministry of Labour assumed responsibility for the vocational training of the war injured. Departmental rivalries thwarted the plan for a comprehensive programme covering service and civilian personnel, but the urgency of the manpower shortage generated by the conflict did enable the introduction of an 'interim scheme' and the appointment of an inter-departmental committee to investigate 'the wartime and the post-war aspects of rehabilitation'.[77] From the outset, the departure of key workers for the armed services had led to the recruitment and promotion of disabled people to fill the gaps in essential services at home. Ernest Williams, an inmate of the Birmingham Institution for the Blind during the 1920s, was working in a typing pool at Hereford when the War commenced:

> One morning the chief accountant called me in and said to me, 'You've been with us a fair time now haven't you Williams?...' I said 'Yes sir'. 'The only trouble with you is that you can't bloody well see.' Anyway he suggested promoting me to be in charge of one of the departments and getting me a secretary type person to help me with correspondence and such like.[78]

The 'Interim Scheme' built on this engagement of disabled people with the war economy. Applicable to all those over the age of 16 who could not return to work or obtain a job due to impairment of any cause, the Scheme linked hospitals, and hence medical advice, to employment exchanges and training centres.[79]

Traditional gender roles, temporarily suspended to allow non-disabled women to penetrate male employment,[80] proved more resilient for disabled women, as Jenny Waller found. A native of the Lake District, Jenny was born with cerebral palsy in 1920. She could

> remember reading a headline in the newspaper one Sunday, 'CRIPPLES CAN DO VITAL WAR WORK'. It seemed as though this would be the chance I'd been waiting for to work. So I sent off a letter straight away. The reply came back that it was for men only, they'd not thought of women.

Jenny sent endless letters seeking employment to no avail. Eventually, however, she was offered work at a Royal Ordinance factory in Staffordshire as one of over 300,000 disabled men and women who by 1945 had been interviewed under the Interim Scheme and placed in employment or training.[81]

Though this economic integration was celebrated by disability organizations as well as by impaired people themselves, there were concerns about whether long-term progress could be sustained in peacetime. In its 1944 *Annual Report*, for instance, the British Deaf and Dumb Association, whilst hoping that the 'satisfactory industrial position will be maintained after the War', observed that 'in the past' its members had 'always been amongst the first to be pushed to the wall in periods of depression'.[82] Official information films, all optimistically titled, sought to allay such anxieties: *Life Begins Again* (1942) told the story of how modern medicine was able to secure successful rehabilitation after industrial injury; *Back To Normal* (1945) portrayed how government training centres equipped disabled workers with the correct tools to resume employment.[83] Furthermore, the Minister of Labour was adamant that: 'This country will not be able for the next fifty years to afford an unemployed man or to allow a man to be kept away from industry because he is (un)fit or injured.'[84]

The debate was underscored by the linkage between work and citizenship, influential in statutory and voluntary services for disabled people since first articulated at the turn of the century. Emerging from the deliberations of the inter-departmental committee, the Disabled Persons (Employment) Act of 1944 Act was perceived as bestowing rights to engage in the labour market and hence win the status of a full citizen.[85] However, the committee concluded that 'the only satisfactory form of resettlement' was employment that disabled people took and kept on their own merits in a normal competitive environment. Whilst this was represented as being in their best interests, it was driven by employers who wished to avoid the cost of employing them and by trade unionists who wished to avoid the threat of their cheap labour. The effect was to polarize 'effective workers' – 'able to take their place in open employment' – from 'ineffective workers' – 'for whom sheltered employment would be provided'.[86]

The 1944 Act embodied this division between 'normal' and 'abnormal' workers. Catering for the disabled person who 'on account of injury, disease, or congenital deformity, is substantially handicapped in obtaining or keeping employment', it inaugurated an employment policy with three key elements that was overseen by Disablement Resettlement Officers (DROs) at the Ministry of Labour. First, training and resettlement schemes, which were usually based at government Employment Rehabilitation Centres, assessed work potential and offered work experience. Second, a quota scheme – linked to a voluntary register listing those disadvantaged in finding jobs commensurate with their impairments – required employers with more than 20 employees to recruit 3 per cent of their workforce from registered disabled people, unless exempt due to the nature of the work. And, third, segregated employment was developed, either in the workshops run by local authorities and voluntary bodies, or in the factories run by Remploy, a non-profit-making company created by the government in 1945. Since the Second World War, there have been changes of name as the Ministry of Labour became the Department of Employment and employment services were transferred to a new organization called the Manpower Services Commission. For more than 30 years, however, the policies framed in the 1940s survived virtually unaltered.[87]

The Piercy Committee, reporting on the resettlement services in 1956, was broadly content with their performance. Commenting on the quota scheme, the Committee concluded that 'its main value' had been to provide 'a sound basis for publicity among both employers and workpeople'.[88] The shift of emphasis from enforcement to persuasion sounded the death toll for employment rights because demand for disabled people's labour was no longer to be created by compliance with the quota. Therefore, evasion accelerated. In 1961, 61.4 per cent of firms were fulfilling their obligations; in 1978 the figure was down to 36.8 per cent; and by the later date, only nine prosecutions had been brought.[89] As well as acquiescing in the defiance of the quota, the Piercy Committee called for a sharper distinction between work and welfare. Sheltered workshops were 'intended to provide a livelihood' for their employees, and places were to be reserved for those 'able to make a significant contribution to production'. Separate therapeutic or diversionary facilities were desirable for disabled people capable of 'only a modicum of effort and industry'.[90] In practice, the social objectives of resettling workers in open employment were incompatible with the economic imperatives of the sheltered workshop. Therefore, staff with progressive impairments were retained and jobs preserved when inflation eroded profits and recession eroded demand.[91] Greater differentiation also denied work status to disabled people in jobs deemed recreational.

The shortcomings of employment policies were not confined to the quota scheme and sheltered workshops. Until the oil crisis struck in the early 1970s, the post-war British economy delivered economic growth, full employment and stable prices,[92] but positive attitudes to disabled people faded as the labour shortage abated. Therefore, Gerald Turner – a young man with cerebral palsy searching for a job in the late 1940s – found that when he 'went to the Labour Exchange...they just used to throw me out and say there wasn't any work for somebody like me. They didn't think I was any use to anyone.'[93] The dedicated Disablement Resettlement Service was likewise flawed over 20 years later when a Southampton study of physically impaired people of working age discovered that only 3 per cent of the sample as a whole, and 8 per cent of those in work, had been found a job by the DRO.[94] Moreover, though the 1944 Act was heralded as the first legislation to cater for all types of disabled people, its scope was narrow. Not only did the invidious designated employment scheme – restricted to lift operators and car park attendants –

associate disability with unskilled work, but both the Disablement Resettlement Officer and the Employment Rehabilitation Centre were orientated towards manual jobs and so failed to deliver rehabilitation across the full occupational range.[95]

People with mental impairments were also a low priority.[96] In the late 1970s, the majority of intellectually impaired school leavers were transferring to local authority adult training centres. Stereotyped craftwork had given way to sub-contract work that was boring, repetitive and of little educational value. In addition, DROs tended to regard the trainees as unemployable, leaving to family and friends the organization of any movement to open employment.[97] The failure of variations on the sheltered workshop encouraged the development of alternatives like the sheltered industrial group where a small number of employees – often former mental hospital patients – worked together within an ordinary employment environment. The idea, pioneered by the Industrial Therapy Organization in 1960, was absorbed into government policy, and by 1977 just over 100 places were available in between 20 and 30 schemes, most of which were managed by local authorities.[98] These sheltered industrial groups gestured towards an inclusive work environment. For the most part, however, policies concentrated on fitting individuals for jobs and compensating employers for taking them on. Therefore, workplaces were only belatedly added to the accessibility clauses of the 1976 Chronically Sick and Disabled Persons Act and when the Job Introduction Scheme was launched a year later, payments to employers for taking disabled workers on trial reduced them to economic liabilities unworthy of 'normal' employment.[99]

The bankruptcy of employment legislation after the Second World War was manifest in ongoing discrimination, low wages and unemployment. Joan Clarke opened her 1951 study of *Disabled Citizens* with the case of a 'lame girl [who] had a job in a store. One day the manager saw her walking across the floor. "Come here", he said. "You are lame. I can't have lame girls in this store." "I was lame when you engaged me!" "Maybe, but if I'd known I shouldn't have engaged you." So the girl lost her job.'[100] Employees as well as employers discriminated against disabled people with impunity in the immediate post-war period as David Swift experienced. At the age of 15, David – who had a hereditary muscular condition that caused him to walk with a limp – started work at a Nottingham bicycle factory. He was subjected to cruel insensitivity and ridicule:

> The foreman gave me a bad time, he didn't like me. He used to jibe me and walk behind me, I could actually feel what he was doing. He was trying to make the men laugh and taking it out of me and shouting 'Hoppy'. They thought it were funny to shout 'Hopalong Cassidy'.

David quit his job after a row in which he demanded the same wages as fellow workers and was told by the factory manager that 'you're very fortunate to be working here, you being crippled like you are.'[101]

Such low pay was not uncommon. Deprived of formal qualifications as a result of inadequate education, impaired people had few employment choices. Thus, in the OPCS survey carried out in the late 1960s, 72 per cent felt that their options had been limited by disability, while four out of ten said that they had been 'forced ... to take a job where their qualifications or skills ... were not used'. As a result, many were forced into unskilled manual employment.[102] Rates of pay at sheltered workshops were notorious. In September 1973, for example, the basic weekly wage at Remploy was only £18.12 per week or 47.6 per cent of manual male average earnings, whilst local authority workshops paid between £15.56 and £27.60. But low earnings were not confined to sheltered workshops. Alan Walker calculated from the OPCS survey that '[h]alf of the impaired single income units who were working had incomes below 42 per cent of average earnings', whilst '[o]ne in four had earnings below 32 per cent of the average.' Rising unemployment led to a deteriorating situation. By April 1978, 14.3 per cent of registered disabled people were out or work, compared with 6.1 per cent of the total UK workforce. Furthermore, in January of the same year, 54.0 per cent of the registered disabled population, but only 22.5 per cent of all the unemployed, had been without a job for more than 52 weeks.[103]

Conclusion

It has often been assumed that whereas institutional living was exclusionary, community living embraced disabled people in the concourse of everyday life. In Chapter 6, we have argued contrariwise that social inclusion was conditional upon fulfilling the requirements of economic rationality and participating effectively in the labour market. Deprived in education and exposed to job discrimination, disabled people of working age were marginal employees, vulnerable to low wages, to unemployment, and hence to poverty. In the nineteenth century, charitable services perpetuated this disadvantage by promoting divisive segregated training and sheltered workshops that traded in outdated, manual skills and associated impairment with poorly paid, low-status work. The Workmen's Unemployment Act of 1905 brought voluntary bodies into partnership with the state, but this mixed economy did not extend to disabled workers. The philanthropic initiatives on which they continued to rely were precarious in the face of economic depression. After 1939, however, a reversal of the inter-war labour surplus propelled many members of the impaired workforce into wartime jobs. Though the 1944 Disabled Persons (Employment) Act was represented as conferring the right to work, its quota system was never enforced and the focus on segregated workshops and manual labour was retained. Therefore, social citizenship was an empty promise for the many disabled people who were not properly integrated into the labour market.

7 Financial relief

The disabled people excluded from or marginal to the workforce negotiated financial relief within a mixed 'economy of makeshifts': combining 'earned income (of all sorts) with savings and loans, the support of family and neighbours, the claiming of welfare benefits and the help of charity'.[1] The informal elements of these 'strategies for survival'[2] are by their very nature difficult to reconstruct because they left few historical traces. Consequently, our examination of how disabled people 'made do'[3] of necessity neglects the deeds of relatives and local communities. The records that survive for the formal mechanisms of mutual aid, charitable assistance and the state demonstrate that the economic rationality so discriminatory in the labour market was also an ongoing influence in the dispensation of financial relief. Chapter 7 explores this theme. First, the role of self-help in the distribution of mutual aid and charitable assistance is investigated. Second, the administration of the poor laws is examined with particular reference to the displacement of customary rights by 'less eligibility' after 1834. Third, workmen's compensation, the old age pension, and health, unemployment and disablement benefits are evaluated as alternatives to discretionary means-tested help. And, finally, we ask to what extent the post-war social security settlement delivered social citizenship to disabled people.

Mutual aid

For much of the nineteenth century, self-help was the driving force behind mutual aid, charitable assistance and state support. Lecturing to artisans in the 1840s, its most famous exponent, Samuel Smiles, argued that whereas '[h]elp from without is often enfeebling... help from within invariably invigorates.' 'Whatever is done *for* men or classes,' he went on, 'to a certain extent takes away the stimulus and necessity of doing for themselves; and where men are subjected to over-guidance and over-government, the inevitable tendency is to render them comparatively helpless.'[4] Though this philosophy is often regarded as a product of the Victorian age, it was presaged in the later eighteenth century by the erosion of traditional paternalism and the rise of a more abrasive work ethic derived from the individualism of *laissez-faire* economics.[5] In adapting, however, the lower orders did not simply imitate middle-class notions of personal responsibility. Rather, they shaped their own collective version of self-help, in which risks were shared through systems of mutual aid.[6]

Friendly societies were the most common form of mutual aid. Numbers grew rapidly 'from an estimated 648,000 in 1793 to 704,350 in 1803, 925,429 in 1815, and over four million in 1872'.[7] Tracking the path of industrialization, this expansion has been attributed to the surplus incomes of better-paid workers, the increased chances of industrial injury, the destruction of family and community ties by geographical mobility, and the commodification of medical care.[8] Before the reform of the poor law in 1834, it was not unknown for local overseers to pay the friendly society fees or subscriptions for paupers, on the grounds that it was more cost-effective than outdoor relief. For others living in poverty, the financial criteria were a major impediment. But, in any event, the societies usually refused to accept new members over the age of 40 and imposed a disability test to avoid dependent members exhausting their resources. Like the Benevolent Brief in Wakefield, they welcomed '[n]o person... but such as shall be at the time of admission, of a sound constitution, as also his wife free from all lameness, sickness, and disorders whatforever'.[9]

If disabled people were prevented from joining mutual aid schemes, provision was made for members who later became impaired or elderly. Some societies catered specifically for industrial injury. Therefore, when the Monmouthshire and South Wales Miners' Permanent Provident Fund was established in 1881, it offered only accident benefit, covering half the miners on the coal field at the height of its popularity.[10] Other societies made arrangements within their general rules. In 1812, for example, the Female Friendly Society of Monmouth was granting a member who attained 'the age of 60 . . . 2/6 per week until she is 70 then paid 5/- per week thereforth during her life'. In the case of impairment, a sliding scale was applied which took account of the funds in reserve.[11] Gauging how many benefited from such regulations is impossible. However, the campaign against discrimination by the British Deaf and Dumb Association intimates that there were problems. The Association eventually persuaded the Church Benefit Society, founded in 1878, to accept deaf people on equal terms and by 1922 more than 20 of its lodges were for deaf members. This particular disabled group was said to make few insurance demands,[12] but the bill for long-term payments weakened the financial viability of friendly societies and led some to collapse under the weight of their ageing profiles.[13] The societies continued into the twentieth century. By 1900, however, they were in decline, to be superseded by statutory and commercial pension schemes.[14]

Charitable assistance

Whereas the friendly societies conferred rights in return for contributions, charitable assistance was discretionary and bestowed or withdrawn at the will of the donor.[15] The private gifts of benevolent individuals, like those of relatives and neighbours, are a largely inaccessible element within the 'economy of makeshifts', but disabled people's treatment at the hands of charitable organizations is more conspicuous. From the 1780s, a philanthropic bonanza swept across Britain in response to political unrest and moral disquiet.[16] These new foundations were evangelical proponents of the individualistic approach to poverty and used their funds to propel recipients towards self-help.[17] The first organization dedicated to countering mendacity was the Bath Society for the Suppression of Common Vagrants and Impostors. Set up in 1805, it sought to stamp out 'promiscuous donations to common beggars'. Tickets were issued to the nobility and gentry, who were asked to distribute these rather than alms when assistance was solicited. Recipients then reported to the Society, where they were subjected to 'strict investigation . . . to distinguish between fraud and real distress'. The resident poor were similarly examined, with visitors calling at the homes of applicants and enquiring into their means and character.[18] Only with such meticulous scrutiny was it possible to ensure that charitable aid was evincing the desired good conduct.[19]

The charities catering for disabled people tapped into such general relief. Therefore, a voluntary visitor calling on a Glasgow man with 'a shock paralysis' was 'glad' to hand out 'some of the Benevolent Society's tickets' on finding that he had not eaten for several days.[20] In 1869 the self-improvement ethos of the voluntary sector was energized and hardened by the establishment of the Charity Organization Society (COS). Encouraged by a crisis in statutory poor relief,[21] the Society believed that, in the words of a district committee report for 1876, the poor 'should meet all the ordinary contingencies of life, relying not upon private or public charity, but upon their own industry and thrift'.[22] Scathing of the 'Lady Bountifuls' who had scattered gifts casually, it blamed the proliferation of charitable organizations and their confused relationship with the state for multiplying indiscriminate relief and manufacturing pauperism.[23] For a solution, the COS proposed rational means to isolate 'those persons who are doing all they can to help themselves, and to whom temporary assistance is likely to prove a lasting benefit'. These 'deserving' poor were to be helped by charity, whilst the 'undeserving' were dispatched to the poor law. To achieve this separation, the Society created a network of local committees and affiliated societies, which then subjected each case to a detailed and systematic interrogation, which noted the employment record, patterns of income and expenditure, signs of thrift and recourse to state relief.[24]

Robert Humphreys has argued that the impact of these activities outside London has been exaggerated; there was, he says, a shortage of funds and volunteers, and the necessary collaboration with the poor law authorities and other charities failed to materialize.[25] Nevertheless, the power of the COS to release or withhold assistance on the basis of 'scientific' knowledge had serious consequences for the physical and psychological welfare of those falling under its gaze. Disabled people attracted the particular attention of the Society because their potential to reach economic independence through self-help despite impairment provided a potent endorsement of individualism. Influential reports were published on blindness, 'mental deficiency', and epilepsy and 'crippledom', and as late as the 1930s the chance to co-operate with the recently formed Council for the Promotion of Occupational Industries among the Physically Handicapped was welcomed.[26] The mentality embodied in these responses was displayed in the management of individual cases, impairment winning disabled people no moral concessions. An article published in a 1927 issue of the *Charity Organization Quarterly* is instructive:

> A man had been paralysed from the waist down since 1923. With his wife and one child he lived in one room in a slum, and, before his illness, had been a newsvendor. In 1925 application was made to provide him with an invalid . . . tricycle to enable him to escape from his prison cell of a room, and possibly to resume his work as newspaper seller and become once more independent of parish relief.

The request was turned down. One factor was medical evidence, indicating that 'the . . . illness was likely to get worse rather than better.' But personality weighed more heavily: 'The man – a rough sort of fellow – was unwilling or unable to give references as to character, got surly and complained of what he professed to consider the inquisitional methods of the Society . . . He said that he had been "crimed".'[27]

In theory, the criminalization of poverty had been under attack since the 1880s, when the discovery of unemployment ushered in a re-moralization of the poor[28] and a more sympathetic stance towards increased public intervention. The Charity Organization Society was at odds with this outlook. Sectors within the Society did recognize that the social system bore some responsibility for 'individual wrong-doing' and state support for the training of 'mental defectives' was even recommended. However, any extension of income maintenance outside the poor law was implacably opposed.[29] The public debate about old age pensions in the 1890s softened this attitude in respect of elderly people and other 'chronic cases'. Anxious to demonstrate that the voluntary sector could deliver, the COS relaxed its insistence that families should provide almost irrespective of their circumstances and 'district committees were encouraged to raise funds on an individual case-by-case basis after investigation.'[30] But as this position became increasingly untenable, other organizations within the voluntary sector began to recognize the inevitability of the state's advance and seek creative relationships.

The Guilds of Help that emerged from the turn of the century epitomized the 'new philanthropy'. Like the COS, they aimed to apply a 'scientific' casework methodology to process the poor. Mindful of the menace of socialism, however, they sought a partnership between charity, the community and the state that promoted responsible citizenship at local level and closed the gulf between donor and recipient. Working-class participation was much exaggerated, but the Guilds spread rapidly[31] and also spawned specialist charities for disabled people. In Nottingham, for example, the Cripples' Guild, founded in 1908, was the nodal point for local voluntary and statutory organizations. Adamant that 'if the desire and the willingness to make an effort towards improvement cannot be induced, the case is one for authority and not for charity,'[32] the Guild stringently imposed the work ethic. Therefore, the *Annual Report* for 1915 censured a 'young man of respectable appearance' who 'had never worked and could only suitably start as an apprentice and earn a small wage'. Begging was more 'profitable' and less 'troublesome', and so 'he preferred not to make any change to his mode of life.'[33] The demoralizing effects of discrimination and hardship, and the economics of inadequate wages, were absent from this interpretation. Instead, the voluntary sector policed disabled people's pursuit of financial relief, propelling those judged work-shy towards punitive state benefits.

Charitable relief was not abandoned as the twentieth-century state assumed more responsibility for the social security of its disabled citizens. In 1913, for instance, George Neve willed £100 to the incumbent and churchwardens of Sissinghurst in Kent with the instruction that they use the income to supply an annual Christmas dinner 'to such of the aged deserving poor of the district... without distinction of creed'.[34] In addition to this feudal philanthropy, the values represented by the Charity Organization Society and the Guilds of Help thrived. In 1895 the British Deaf and Dumb Association began a modest pension scheme. Payments were made to the 'old and poor' and to applicants under the age of 60 if they were 'by reason of inferiority, totally incapable of earning a livelihood'. But 'only the most deserving cases' were considered.[35] The Swansea and South Wales Institution for the Blind also offered material aid, weekly grants to the 'necessitous' of between two and five shillings amounting to £92 in 1922/3. By the turn of the decade, expenditure on 'weekly grants and gifts in kind' for the 'Unemployable Blind' had reached over £5600, not least because they 'outnumber[ed] those capable of useful work by about six to one'.[36]

Despite the expansion of this 'important service', the Institution remained anxious about mendacity. Therefore, the *Annual Report* for 1930/1 warned that though the 'natural desire to give help to the Blind Beggar standing at the street corner... indicates the true charitable spirit...the gift is ordered by the heart and not by the head.' Far from helping, 'indiscriminate giving' encouraged 'a means of obtaining a living that must be degrading'. Therefore, assistance was better given through the Institution, which had 'a knowledge of the circumstances in every case' and existed 'to provide well directed assistance – training and employment for the capable and support for those who cannot be employed'.[37] In the years up to 1979, voluntary organizations continued to hand out occasional gifts and small weekly aliments, calculated not to contravene the regulations for state benefits.[38] After 1945, however, the main burden of their activities focused on help in kind rather than help in cash and so it was in the institutional and community services that the collaborative relationship forged between the two World Wars was played out.[39]

The old poor law

Although the welfare state transformed the voluntary sector, public expenditure far outstripped philanthropic income throughout the modern period. Thus as early as 1788, charitable trusts were raising only 10 per cent of the sum collected from the poor rates: a gap that remained wide even after allowance has been made for other types of gift.[40] In England and Wales, and in Scotland, these poor rates fed into the 'economy of makeshifts' as outdoor relief to the 'deserving' or 'impotent' poor who were elderly, sick or infirm.[41] Under the Poor Law Act of 1601, however, parents, grandparents and children were to be assessed by the justices to maintain 'old, blind, lame and impotent' relatives 'not able to work'.[42] The ethic of self-help, executed through the family, drove statutory relief as well as mutual aid and charitable assistance.

The poor sought relief within a battery of 'customary rights' – 'regular doles, clothes, fuel, rent, medical relief, institutional provision' – that had 'solidified' from the second half of the seventeenth century.[43] Though rooted in paternalism rather than social citizenship,[44] these 'rights' imparted a confidence evident in the letters associated with non-resident relief whereby a 'host' parish, which was subsequently reimbursed, supported paupers living outside their place of settlement. Samuel Hearsum, aged 72, thus had no qualms about his due entitlement when in 1824 he wrote from St Marylebone in London to his 'home' parish in Chelmsford; indeed, he even chastised the overseers for their delay in contacting him and suggested that his preferred option of a weekly pension was cheaper than a costly removal back to Essex:

> According to promise I Expected a line from you before now to lit me Know Whether the Gent[lemen] of the Committee p[l]ease to allow me a small Trifle weekly, I think it very hard as I have pa[id] so much into the poor fund to be Forsed for the Triflon sum of 1s:6d per week, which I will endevour to make shift with, Gentalmen If not I hope you will be so good as to let me know wether you would pay Mr French to bring me Down or to Appley to Marylebone Parish to Pass me home which will be very Expenseiv as I Am not Able to Walk.[45]

In short, Hearsum was bargaining with the overseers in the knowledge that he had a customary right to assistance.

Revisionist historians have stressed the power that such negotiation bestowed upon the recipients of relief and disputed that the poor law was an instrument of social control, policing a deeply divided society. Lynn Hollen Lees, for instance, has argued that: 'Important elements of the welfare process were completely under the control of the poor', who 'decided when to ask for aid and when to refuse it'; 'need', she continued, did 'not trigger an automatic rush into the arms of welfare authorities' because there were other possibilities: asking relatives or neighbours, withholding rent or pawning household goods, applying for charity or seeking credit, leaving town and looking for work elsewhere. 'A few would [even] beg or steal in order to survive.' But if 'a choice between several unpalatable alternatives remains a choice', it is important not to romanticize the options. Life was harsh. Power was skewed inexorably towards the landed and middling classes. And, as a result, the room for manoeuvre was strictly limited.

Perhaps the relief system did reinforce 'social solidarity on the communal level'.[46] Perhaps it did confer 'rights ... and dignity as well as aid'.[47] Perhaps a high proportion of the population did claim poor relief at some point in their lives.[48] However, the relief received suggests that the material benefits enjoyed by the lower orders were parsimonious in the extreme.

Details of who received assistance under the old poor law were not regularly collected, but in 1802/3 Parliament commissioned an *Abstract of Returns Relative to the Expense and Maintenance of the Poor* in England and Wales, which included questions about pauper numbers. Though the response rate was high, there were problems with the replies. In particular, some parishes calculated an annual average, whilst others returned a total for the year as a whole. Separate figures were also given for 'adults and children outside, but not *inside*, local poorhouses'.[49] Flaws aside, these figures show that just over one million people, or 11.4 per cent of the total population, were paupers. Of these, 16 per cent 'were persons above sixty years of age or disabled from labour by permanent illness or other infirmity' – the best estimate of impairment that we have.[50] It is assumed that members of this 'deserving' group were the main recipients of the regular pension that was the dominant form of relief before 1834.[51] Since voluntary retirement was virtually unknown among the elderly poor, these pensions are more properly regarded as disability benefits, which were allocated only when ill health and impairment reduced the feasibility of permanent paid employment.[52]

The dispersal of pensions shows that rather than rigidly enforcing the kinship obligations of the 1601 Act, overseers operated 'in a close, complex, and shifting relationship with such support as families were able and willing to give'.

Nurse Chambers of Tonbridge lodged with her daughter and son-in-law for twenty-three years. Between 1771 and 1781 from the ages of 52 to 62 she followed her profession and the parish paid 6d. per week for her house-room. Then the payments slowly increased until her pension reached 1s. 6d. and her daughter received occasional extra sums for nursing her. This went on until her death in 1794 aged 75.[53]

Simple and convenient to administer, pensions were flexible in the case of changing circumstances, and popular with recipients who were able to exercise choice in their expenditure.[54] However, they were not generous. In west Kent, where Nurse Chambers lived, 'most old people even among the labouring poor did not receive regular relief or payments at subsistence level'.[55] Therefore, the elderly experienced acute poverty unless additional resources were available from elsewhere in the 'economy of makeshifts'.

Whereas old age was a chronologically-based category that was easily validated, disability was fluid, contestable, and open to abuse by the 'sturdy beggar' who faked impairment in order to obtain assistance.[56] This is not to condone a 'beggared' history that reduces all disabled people to isolated pariahs.[57] But the procedures for patrolling economic participation led some to meet with social disapprobation under the laws of settlement. In 1772 a Swansea JP examined Alexander Culbert. Of Irish extraction, he had been blinded during service in the Royal Navy:

> since his discharge at Portsmouth he has travell'd about, ... in Towns he is lead by a Dog & begs and his wife sells Laces, Garters & other trifling things without any License, and he has continued begging until he was taken up this day ... as he was begging in the street.

Neither his sensory impairment nor his military record was enough to prevent the justice from labelling Culbert as 'a Rogue and Vagabond'.[58] If the old poor law sheltered 'aged' and 'infirm' pensioners, it was liable to pillory younger disabled people who had difficulty integrating into the labour market.

Between 1784 and 1815, crude expenditure on poor relief rose almost threefold from approximately £2,000,000 to £6,000,000.[59] This growth was insufficient to cope with the rampant inflation of the Napoleonic Wars and the increased demand for support from younger families. Attitudes to the poor were also hardening due to the combined effects of *laissez-faire* economics and Evangelical religion, which construed man – in the words of the clerical economist, T. R. Malthus – as 'inert, sluggish and averse from labour, unless compelled from necessity'.[60] As a result, many elderly and 'impotent' claimants were said not to get the assistance that their past lives merited. A 'bare subsistence for the aged poor', wrote Sir Frederick Eden in the 1790s, 'is no more than the fair right of those who have spent their best days and exhausted their strength in the service of the public.'[61] This opinion was widely endorsed. Yet pensions did not keep pace with rising costs. 'The proportion of old people ... among recipients of regular relief fell faster than their share of the total population.' Existing pensions were replaced by irregular money doles and distributions of basic foodstuffs. And some parishes combined cuts in relief with the spectre of the workhouse. At Harrington in Cumberland, for example, a baker of 60, and his wife of a similar age, were said to 'prefer receiving thirty shillings annually for house-rent to going to Workington poorhouse'. In the previous year, the couple had received a weekly pension of 5s from the parish.[62]

From the end of the Napoleonic Wars, there were signs that austerity was abating. Between 1822 and 1825, for example, an elderly widow like Susannah Halls – living in Ipswich but with settlement in Chelmsford – was paid a regular pension of 2s 6d a week. Thomas Sokoll has argued that this sum – a common rate for a person in her circumstances – would have provided 'a moderate but relatively fair subsistence'. However, at only a quarter of what an agricultural worker in the region earned,[63] it locked elderly women into a life of relative deprivation and 'making do'. Elderly men may have been treated less generously. In the North Riding of Yorkshire, for instance, the parish of Coxwold required 'old men, partially disabled' to labour as road workers for a weekly allowance.[64] The lot of younger impaired people was especially insecure. For many years, the overseers at St Arvans in Monmouthshire bought wooden legs and single shoes for William Bridget. In October 1815, however, they decided to discontinue his weekly pay 'during the time that he will be tramping about'. Later granted £1 on a half-yearly basis, he was still in receipt of relief in 1833.[65] Thus neither the level nor the consistency of support warrants the conclusion that the old poor law supplied elderly or disabled people with a comprehensive system of financial relief.[66]

The new poor law

When the Poor Law Amendment Act set out to banish able-bodied pauperism in 1834, the workhouse test and the principle of less eligibility were decried as an assault on the customary rights of all the poor. David Thomson has contested this conclusion for elderly people by arguing that standard pensions of between 2s 6d and

3s a week were paid to single aged people, representing two-thirds of the incomes of younger working-class adults. Moreover, these payments were widespread. At 'any one moment' between 1840 and 1870, says Thomson, 'about 65–70% of all women in England and Wales who were aged 70 or more, along with 50–55% of all men so aged, were being given a regular Poor Law pension.'[67]

There is a broad consensus that the new poor law was most sympathetically inclined towards the 'aged and infirm',[68] but critics have challenged the detail of Thomson's analysis. The constant jockeying between the central authority and local guardians make it difficult to call any policy 'standard'. In addition, economy measures were attempted despite the privileged position of elderly people. First, assistant commissioners tried to compel the replacement of cash with foodstuffs; and the Out Relief Registration Order of 1852, requiring that 'one-third at least of such relief should be given in kind',[69] was only rescinded after widespread complaint from local guardians who resented any interference with their discretionary powers.[70] Second, some Unions reduced the level of pensions to the elderly. Keith Snell, for example, has estimated for rural areas that weekly rates of payment fell from between 2s 6d and 3s before 1834 to between 1s and 2s afterwards.[71] Such amounts were also typical of urban areas like Tynemouth in Devon and Preston in Lancashire, while under the Scottish poor law average pensions at mid-century were significantly less than half the figure calculated by Thomson. These sums suggest that working-class wages were in no way approximated.[72] Furthermore, pensions were not granted to a large majority of elderly people as the principal component of their income. On the contrary, they were allocated to a large minority, normally as one element within an 'economy of makeshifts'.[73]

Piecing together a subsistence lifestyle involved inputs from relatives as well as from employment, mutual aid, charity and the state. Though the Royal Commission on the Poor Laws berated the family for reneging on its responsibilities, the cause of any 'negligence' was often inability to pay and even when 'forced to contribute' relatives 'could afford very little'. It would be a mistake to imagine that all 'aged and infirm' applicants cowered before the new poor law because some were able to manipulate relief in order to achieve their own goals. In 1872, for example, an elderly mother from the Staffordshire Potteries refused to move in with any of her three sons, all of whom were willing to support her. Therefore, the magistrates ordered them to contribute to her maintenance via the guardians and she continued to live independently.[74] But moments of empowerment do not imply that all recipients controlled their fate. First, suitably deferential conduct was expected. In 1849, for instance, Elizabeth Keary was denied outdoor relief when she applied to the guardians at Atcham in Shropshire. The reason was not only her unwillingness to disclose details of her income, but also an impertinent attitude; indeed, the overseer recorded that her daughter 'had become so violent in her language that he had to turn her out of the house'.[75] A second constraint was the punitive stance towards the able-bodied poor. Whatever the official intentions, relief to disabled people was delivered through a system designed to stigmatize applicants without work and exclude them from the community. Customary rights may have retained some validity in some localities. But after 1834 the prospect of the workhouse became a palpable threat to the many struggling to exist with grudging relief from the poor law.

The crusade against outdoor relief from 1870 gave substance to this anxiety by increasing the institutionalization of paupers in the 'aged and infirm' category.[76] Six years later the average number of claimants on outdoor relief had collapsed from 843,000 to 567,000.[77] The vast majority decanted into the workhouse were the 'deserving' and not the able-bodied poor,[78] the proportion of the 'insane poor' on outdoor relief falling from 'roughly a quarter...at mid-century to only about 6 per cent in 1890'.[79] The mechanism used to exclude disabled people was a root-and-branch assessment of the sort advocated by the Charity Organization Society. Architect of the poor law version was Henry Longley, a member of the metropolitan inspectorate who in 1874 published an influential paper in the *Annual Report* of the Local Government Board. Longley deplored the policy of paying inadequate relief because it 'encouraged paupers to lie and beg', offered guardians 'a cheap, easy way to fob off applicants', and failed to give effective support to the genuinely destitute.[80] Only the institution was capable of providing adequate relief that was not excessive. Therefore, the workhouse test was to be extended from the able-bodied to all classes of pauper with the expectation that the applicant demonstrate 'why he should be excepted from the rule on indoor relief'.[81]

The purpose was to regulate the ramshackle administration of outdoor relief rather than ban it altogether. Whereas the Royal Commission of 1834 'had proposed negatively to deter able-bodied males via the workhouse', Longley 'proposed positively to educate the poor' through a series of codes that specified the qualifications for assistance, namely family responsibility and a provident lifestyle built on personal propriety.[82] On the ground, continuing decentralization ensured that the guardians' response was mixed. In the Merthyr Tydfil Union, the new policy was flaunted and elderly people remained in receipt of outdoor relief with supplements in severe weather; extra payments were even made to celebrate Queen Victoria's Jubilee in 1887.[83] Elsewhere, the screw was tightened. Family liability was thus relentlessly pursued. On 6 March 1874, for example, Richard and John Evans from Tredegar in Glamorganshire were called to court to explain why they were unable to contribute to the support of their parents, who were chargeable to the Aberystwyth Union in Cardiganshire. When they failed to appear an order was made, but no payment was forthcoming and a second summons was also ignored. Therefore, a policeman was dispatched to Tredegar. Richard capitulated when his house was possessed. John capitulated at Merthyr, en route for Aberystwyth and a likely prison sentence.[84] Restrictions were imposed on applicants as well as their relatives. In the Northamptonshire Union of Brixworth, only 'deprivation of limbs, or eyesight, or extreme old age' qualified the 'partially disabled' for outdoor relief because they were deemed prone to idleness.[85] Similarly, in the Nottinghamshire Union of Basford, wage subsidies for elderly workers were abandoned, whilst 'far fewer people classified as non-able-bodied . . . got outdoor relief'.[86]

The crusade against outdoor relief persisted until the 1890s, when the Local Government Board began slowly to rethink its policy. Prompted by the report of the Royal Commission on the Aged Poor, the Board asked local guardians to look carefully at 'the antecedents of destitute persons whose physical faculties have failed by reason of age and infirmity' and to grant outdoor relief where they had 'been of good character, thrifty according to their opportunities, and generally independent in early life' – unless their 'health or surrounding circumstances' made indoor relief advisable.[87] The Board reiterated this message in 1900. The *Relief Regulation Order* of 1911 added a medical test to the moral injunctions. One of the few legacies of the Royal Commission on the Poor Laws,[88] the medical test was a product of the Minority Report's commitment to specialist treatment for each category of pauper. Dropped for elderly applicants due to their weight of numbers, the test was retained for younger age groups. The medical officer 'declare[d] the existence of a particular disability and its degree'; the relieving officer supplied the guardians with the information necessary to determine entitlement.[89] Medical opinion was subordinate to lay opinion, but its very presence in a service dedicated to the mere relief of destitution was indicative of the increasing medicalization of impairment.

In 1911 there were 3,686,000 'aged and infirm' adults receiving indoor *and* outdoor relief. Plummeting with the introduction of old age pensions from 1909, the figure had fallen to 2,359000 by 1922. The inter-war recession inflated the numbers once more, so that by 1931 they had climbed to 3,458,000.[90] Serious unemployment created tensions between the disabled and the non-disabled. Short of funds, some poor law authorities resented the demands of ex-servicemen. In West Ham, for example, the Union complained in 1929 that 'too often the pensioner, instead of regarding his allowance as compensation for his disability and loss of earning power, consider[ed] it a reason why he should in addition receive assistance from the rates'.[91] Disabled civilians also encountered cheeseparing attitudes. Ted Williams, who was blind, came close to destitution during the 1930s due to short-time working at his sheltered workshop:

> The favourite was to give food tickets, not money. I myself used to go down to the Board of Guardians Relief place . . . and they would give me some of these tickets and with those I would go and get my week's groceries at a certain shop. And we were given the bare minimum to pay the rent as well.[92]

From 1929 Public Assistance Committees replaced the Boards of Guardians in an attempt at rationalization. This process was extended in 1934 when a new Unemployment Assistance Board assumed responsibility for a national system of means-tested benefits that extricated the jobless from outdoor relief.[93] Finally wound up in 1948, the poor law continued to cast a shadow over late twentieth-century state welfare.[94]

The birth of national insurance

Despite the claims that poor relief amounted to social citizenship before 1834, there was no personal entitlement but only a paternalist obligation to supply assistance to 'deserving' cases. Even these customary rights were scuttled with the advent of the new poor law, which if gentler to disabled people by the end of its lifespan still required that they demonstrate legitimate need. From the end of the nineteenth century, however, poor relief was increasingly by-passed by alternative types of financial relief or social security, most notably workmen's compensation, old age pensions, national insurance benefits and war pensions. In common with the early unemployment legislation,[95] all four schemes embodied the late nineteenth-century reappraisal of poverty as a social problem demanding collective action, rather than a moral defect for which the individual was personally responsible.[96] Furthermore, disabled or elderly people who fulfilled the qualification criteria claimed as citizens with a social right to assistance.

The Workmen's Compensation Act of 1897 established 'the right to some measure of financial security in the event of injury at work'.[97] The outcome of trade union pressure at a time when poor relief was also under scrutiny,[98] the Act developed from the tradition of factory legislation to replace the compensation 'lottery', which varied 'from industry to industry, from employer to employer, even from accident to accident'.[99] Companies were thus obliged to insure against industrial injury and compensate their workers, almost irrespective of any direct culpability.[100] There were flaws. To avoid liability, employers like the Barrow Steel Works immediately decided not to take on men over 50 or those who were 'known to have any defects, such as the loss of a limb, defective sight or hearing'.[101] Company doctors were accused of sending men back to work before they were fit, hence denying them the right to compensation.[102] Cover was not extended to all employments until 1906. And the state played only a regulatory role. Nevertheless, a scheme that 'entailed some redistribution of income' as well as 'the sharing of risks' was 'a first instalment' of the reforms that laid the foundations for the welfare state.[103]

When the Workmen's Compensation Bill was discussed in Parliament, the Liberal opposition regretted that this Conservative measure did not make reimbursement the duty of the community as a whole.[104] In the case of the old age pension, introduced in 1908, the responsibility was shared via the taxation system. Charles Booth had recommended this solution since the early 1890s, persuaded by the extensive destitution that his survey of London poverty revealed among elderly people and by the advocacy of Samuel Barnett, founder of the Toynbee Hall settlement in East London, who had been calling for state pensions since 1883. Booth was a member of the Royal Commission on the Aged Poor, which sat between 1893 and 1895 to consider alternatives to the poor law amidst growing public concern that some guardians were withdrawing support from elderly people. The Royal Commission concurred with Booth that whilst accepting relief did not normally stigmatize 'the old [who] claimed [it] very much as a right', the payments made were wholly inadequate. Instead of proposing a radical way forward, however, the Commission simply reiterated the principles of 1871, hanging on to the distinction between the 'deserving' and the 'undeserving' poor. Therefore, all that emerged was an ameliorative circular in which the Local Government Board urged the sensitive assessment of elderly people.[105]

The debate rumbled on. As the support of the trade unions increased, however, and the opposition of the friendly societies declined, pressure for change mounted. It was a force that the Liberal government, taking office after a landslide victory in 1906, would have found hard to resist, particularly since 59 per cent of its own MPs had endorsed pensions in their election addresses.[106] The scheme put in place was a non-contributory one funded by the Exchequer. British citizens over the age of 70 were entitled to a pension of 5s a week if they passed a test of character and if their annual income was less than £21. Autobiographical accounts told euphoric tales of the first payments. In *Larkrise to Candleford*, for example, Flora Thompson recalled how life was 'transformed' for the rural elderly poor, who 'suddenly rich' and '[i]ndependent for life', went to draw their first payment with 'tears of gratitude' running down their cheeks.[107] Robert Roberts described similar scenes in urban Salford.[108] Even the *Manchester Guardian* reported on 2 January 1909 that 'many of the recipients expressed heartfelt thanks to the willing instruments of the State's bounty – the post-office clerks who handed them their money.' Moreover, these clerks were said 'to have taken great trouble to make the necessary routine as easy as possible to the old people, very many of whom were infirm, deaf, nearly blind, and otherwise afflicted in body as well as estate'.[109]

For all the euphoria, it is important not to overestimate the impact of the old age pension. First, there was not a mass exodus from the labour market. Though the number of men over 65 in retirement was gradually increasing, the pension was too small to lure those still capable of full-time employment. Not until the inter-war period did long-term changes in the organization of work combine with recession to shrink the job opportunities of older workers.[110] Second, applicants did not escape the mentality of poor relief because they were visited at home by a pension officer, who then submitted his report to the decision-making committees, appointed by local councils. This procedure, in itself reminiscent of the poor law, embodied tests that were also resonant. In addition to qualifying on the basis of nationality, residency and age, claimants had to undergo a means test that included not just income in the preceding year but also furniture and effects above a minimum value and regular gifts in cash or kind from children who were still expected to contribute to their parents' maintenance. Over and above these economic criteria were four moral tests. Elderly people were excluded from the pension scheme if they were admitted to a lunatic asylum, if they had been imprisoned within the last ten years, if they had been convicted of drunkenness, or if they had habitually failed to work. Between 1908 and 1920, almost three million claims were made. Moral factors came into play in comparatively few of the one-in-five cases that were rejected. Symbolically, however, they served to perpetuate the demeaning ethos of poor relief.[111]

The prolonged deliberations over old age pensions raised the question of financial support for younger people whose impairments were not covered by the Workmen's Compensation Act. In 1899, for instance, the Women's Trade Union League informed the Select Committee on the Aged Deserving Poor that 'in the dangerous trades very often a woman is unable to earn her own living when she is still quite young.' Similarly, the Bradford Textile Workers Association argued that 'old age pensions should be granted to all persons making application...and that the only test to be applied should be incapacity by physical disablement to work.'[112] Provision for such situations arrived in 1911. Conscious of the cost of their non-contributory old age pension, the Liberal government opted for the insurance alternative to poor relief when tackling unemployment and illness. Like workmen's compensation, the section of the National Insurance Act that dealt with unemployment was largely the outcome of working-class pressure. That dealing with health insurance, on the other hand, was motivated more by worries about national economic and military efficiency.[113]

The insurance principle ran contrary to a number of vested interests. Workers resented the compulsory deductions; employers complained that implementing the scheme would be costly and time consuming; and friendly societies and insurance companies feared that it would deprive them of business.[114] To appease the latter, health – but not unemployment – insurance was administered through friendly societies and insurance companies that had been approved to pay benefits and organize a 'panel' of doctors to treat members – though not their wives and children.[115] As well as this medical care, sickness benefit 'was available for up to 26 weeks a year to all workers earning less than £250 per annum, in return for a joint contribution from employer and employed'. It was after this first six months that disablement benefit became operational, paid at half the rate for sickness benefit. Though the number of claimants stabilized during the 1930s, the proportion receiving long-term disablement benefit grew. Increased diagnosis and early detection, and financial preferences created by the social security regulations, partly explain this trend, but a major factor was the effect of the economic depression for impaired workers marginal to the workforce.[116] Therefore, the growing constituency who received disablement benefit in inter-war Britain was not composed of scroungers.

This was the conclusion of a survey of long-term claimants conducted by the Ministry of Health in 1938 with the express purpose of rooting out abuse; 60 per cent of the sample was considered unsuitable for referral, mainly because they were bedridden or institutionalized. Of the remainder, 29 per cent were unfit for work and 2 per cent had died. Only the 9 per cent left were either capable of light employment or ineligible for benefit. Included among the recipients of disablement benefit were former veterans who had re-entered the labour market and hence lost the right to a war pension.[117] In the early stages of the First World War, disabled ex-servicemen had to fall back on the charitable assistance provided by organizations like the Prince of Wales's National Relief Fund and the Soldiers' and Sailors' Help Society. In 1915, however, the Naval and Military War Pensions Act made public funds available; and when the Ministry of Pensions was set up two years later, degree of disablement was used to determine the levels of payment made to ex-servicemen; as a Ministry official told the Departmental Committee on Workmen's Compensation in 1919, disability was to be measured crudely 'in relation to a theoretically perfect physical machine'. Consequently, 'men who had lost two or more limbs or suffered severe facial disfigurement were said to have a 100 per cent disability (worth a pension of 27s. 6d.), whilst men who had lost two fingers of either hand were said to have a 20 per cent disability (worth 5s. 6d.).'[118]

Those campaigning for a unified system of social security deplored the emergence of differential benefits for military and civilian claimants. The right of war pensioners to preferential treatment was justified in terms of the heavy demand for volunteers and compulsory conscription from 1916, which had compelled them to make sacrifices to defend the national interest. Even before the War was out, the Ministry of Pensions was being accused of reneging on its duty to the disabled ex-serviceman by cutting costs and appealing to charity.[119] However, trade unionists in particular resented the fact that industrial workers were compensated not for their degree of disablement but only for their loss of earning capacity. The war pension was also widely feared as a mechanism for suppressing wages. 'Already', wrote Bernard Shaw to the Fabian reformer, Sidney Webb, in September 1918, 'employers openly ask what pension a man has and make him an offer accordingly.'[120] But the most severely disadvantaged were not industrial or military casualties, but the disabled people who had no rights to financial benefit and continued to scrape a living from incidental employment or meagre state relief. As one anonymous 'peace cripple' complained in an autobiographical essay, 'in these days of reforms, pensions, and National Insurance, somebody might have thought of us'.[121]

The preoccupation of social security policy with mass unemployment left the financial deprivation of disabled people in inter-war Britain largely untouched. In 1920, however, the non-contributory old age pension was extended to blind people from the age of 50. Ongoing concern about this costly yet inadequate benefit led to the 1925 Old Age and Widows and Orphans Contributory Pensions Act. The Act augmented the health insurance scheme. An extra payment was required. In return, contributors and their wives were entitled to a pension between the ages of 65 and 70, and to a non-contributory pension thereafter without test of means. As a result of this new legislation, almost eight out of ten elderly people over 70 became eligible for a pension. For the remaining 20 per cent, there was only the prospect of means-tested assistance from the Public Assistance Committee. This retained the taint of the poor law. Therefore, when in 1940 a supplementary pension was introduced to deal with exceptional hardship and administered through the Assistance Board that had previously only handled unemployment, the number of applications far exceeded expectations.[122] Younger disabled people with no rights to national insurance had no such benefit. Therefore, we can assume that on the eve of the welfare state, poverty and impairment were still intertwined.

The Beveridge settlement

Financial want was one of the 'five giants on the road to reconstruction' that William Beveridge sought to demolish in his Plan for Social Security. Beveridge made bold claims for the proposals, published in 1942 at the height of the Second World War. 'A revolutionary moment in the world's history' was, he insisted, 'a time for revolutions, not for patching.'[123] In reality, the scheme of national insurance and national assistance that he put forward relied on precedent, consolidating prior contributory initiatives and seeking to dispense with the hated means test. Furthermore, the motor behind the creation of the welfare state was the achievement of social solidarity in the context of a total war that had battered morale and devastated infrastructures. For Beveridge, therefore, 'the project began from the needs of society rather than from the needs of the individual.' It follows that 'the over-riding preoccupation was not with raising the living standards of those experiencing "Want" most acutely... and still less with reducing inequality.' Rather, the 'central emphasis was on guaranteeing a basic minimum income... which would... enhance a sense of collective belonging.'[124] Therefore, the concept of social citizenship associated with the new welfare state was a modest one unlikely to engineer the end of financial exclusion.

The rights of disabled people were a low priority within this agenda for rebuilding post-war Britain. Though disability – defined as the 'inability of a person of working age, through illness or accident, to pursue a gainful occupation' – was one of Beveridge's 'primary causes of need', the ways in which benefits mapped out perpetuated the relationship between poverty and impairment. The Beveridge Plan assumed family allowances, a wide-ranging health and rehabilitation service, and full employment. It then recommended a universal, inclusive system of social security, administered by one body, to which all contributors made the same payments and drew the same benefits that were fixed at adequate rates.[125] These 'fundamental principles' were translated almost intact into legislation by the Labour government. War pensions were largely unaffected. However, the National Insurance Act of 1946 introduced a universal retirement pension for men over 65 and women over 60, replaced workmen's compensation with an industrial disablement benefit now paid according to degree of 'incapacity', and allowed those who became permanently disabled for employment to claim sickness benefit indefinitely. Unemployment was also covered. Two years later the National Assistance Act added a means-tested payment for those without the right to national insurance or whose benefits fell below its own minimum standard.

There were three main problems with this post-war social security package. First, the range of benefits available to disabled people was paid at rates that varied according to the cause and not the effects of impairment. War pensions, for example, were more generous than industrial disablement and retirement pensions or sickness benefit. In addition, war pensions were affected by the rank of the claimant, whilst both they and industrial disablement pensions were dependent upon medical assessments that imposed crude percentage measurements of impairment. The list of industrial diseases was also arbitrary; occupational deafness, for example, was not included until 1975.[126] Compounding all these anomalies was the messy business of compensation, which involved the state and the courts, insurance companies and employers. Though civil liability for personal injury was reviewed by the Pearson Commission that reported in 1978, its recommendations were 'almost entirely concerned with the cause and not with the effect of disablement' and preserved the 'preference' given to accident victims.[127] For impaired people, therefore, the issues remained unresolved.

The second problem with the post-war package was the low level of national insurance and national assistance payments. Conscious of the deprivation that many elderly people had suffered during the War and alert to public support for their proper care, the government abandoned Beveridge's recommendation to phase in retirement pensions over a 20-year period.[128] The victim of this 'costly deviation'[129] was his principle of adequacy. Already, there was little room for manoeuvre because, faced with a flat-rate contribution that had to be affordable by the poorest paid worker, Beveridge was using Rowntree's austere subsistence threshold that left little space to accommodate regional variations in the price of essentials. In a 1944 White Paper on social insurance, however, the wartime Coalition government argued for benefit rates that provided only 'a *reasonable* insurance against want'. As Rodney Lowe has concluded:

> The effect of this compromise was to destroy the whole logic of the [Beveridge] Report because the payment of insurance contributions would no longer automatically guarantee freedom from poverty. If claimants had no other source of income, they would have to apply for means-tested national assistance in order to supplement their inadequate insurance benefits.[130]

For the many disabled who did, benefit levels trailed far behind the standard of living. In June 1969, for example, the scale rate of basic means-tested assistance for a single pensioner was only 38 per cent of take-home pay for a manual worker with average earnings.[131]

The third problem with the post-war package was its inability to reach many entitled to help but deterred by the confusing jungle of benefits and the stigma still associated with them. The bugbear was means-tested national assistance. Though Beveridge had envisaged this scheme as a safety net of diminishing relevance, the decision to peg national insurance benefits below the rates for national assistance ensured a large and growing clientele. Between 1948 and 1965, the total number of claimants and their dependants climbed from 1,465,000 to 2,840,000: a rise from 3.0 per cent to 5.4 per cent of the total population. Moreover, the vast majority of these claimants were either elderly or 'sick and disabled'.[132] At the time, it was taken for granted that most disabled people were receiving their entitlements. The Phillips Committee, for instance, investigating the economic and financial difficulties of providing for old age, conceded that a 'few people may fail to apply for help simply through ignorance that they are eligible.' However, there was 'no evidence to suggest that the present arrangements for national assistance are not fully capable of playing their essential part of preventing distress among the old by securing a basic minimum'.[133]

This optimism overlooked the ambivalence at the heart of social security in an economically rational society where the work ethic was paramount. Despite pressing for a unified structure, Beveridge believed that national assistance 'must be felt to be something less desirable than insurance benefit; otherwise the insured persons get nothing for their contributions'.[134] Claimants, particularly those with memories of the poor law, picked up the message and opted to forego benefit rather than endure the stigma of means testing. On the basis of Rowntree's final survey of York, Atkinson, Maynard and Trinder have calculated a take-up rate for national assistance of no more than 51 per cent.[135] The rediscovery of poverty in the 1960s led to a stronger emphasis on the right to social security, irrespective of any contribution record. Hence, national assistance was renamed supplementary benefit and there was pressure to reduce the reliance on means testing.[136] By 1979 the estimated take-up rate for supplementary benefit as a whole was 70 per cent. For pensioners, and sick and disabled claimants, however, the proportions were slightly lower at 65 per cent and 63 per cent respectively. The sums lost were considerable. Pensioners left unclaimed £145,000,000 per annum, worth an average of £3.10 per week; sick and disabled people left unclaimed £90,000 worth an average of £15.40 per week.[137]

As its limitations became increasingly apparent, the social security system underwent a process of reform in which national insurance was elaborated and new benefits were invented to deal with circumstances previously unmet. First in line for a makeover was the retirement pension. By the 1950s the financial health of elderly people was dependent upon what Richard Titmuss called a 'social division of welfare'.[138] Though tax allowances were of minimal importance, there had been a major expansion in occupational or superannuated pensions. In the mid-1930s, approximately three million employees were members of such schemes, half in the public sector and half in the private sector. Twenty years later, the number of public employees who were covered had doubled, whilst the number in industry and commerce had grown fourfold.[139] The combination of these occupational pensions with a state pension, which for the first time in 1946 required withdrawal from full-time employment, consolidated the sharper demarcation between economic activity and economic inactivity that had been evident with unemployment as well as retirement since the early twentieth century. Immediately after the Second World War, a labour shortage, and demographic anxieties about the costs of supporting an ageing population, led elderly people to stay at work. Only in the following decade did it become the norm for the 'culture of retirement'[140] to extend beyond the prosperous middle class.

By 1981 less than 10 per cent of men over 65 were active in the labour force.[141] This withdrawal from employment created problems for the state old age pension that was seen as both expensive and increasingly inadequate. The National Insurance Act of 1959 was a tepid attempt by the Conservative government to address these difficulties. Beveridge's flat-rate scheme was dropped for a graduated scheme in which an additional earnings-related contribution was paid in return for an enhanced pension. The cost criterion was satisfied because the extra contributions were diverted to the national insurance fund that was in deficit. However, poorly paid workers were excluded and without index linking the real value of benefits was seriously eroded by inflation. Despite this ineffective legislation, the complexities of pension reform were such that no major changes were implemented until the Social Security Pensions Act of 1975. A Labour measure attracting all-party support, this Act introduced the State Earnings Related Pension Scheme or SERPS. Those with private cover adjudged to be sufficient were permitted to opt out, but all other working people gained access to enhanced state provision with inflation proofing, including women whose employment record was disrupted by family responsibilities. The catch was the assumption that future contributors would bear higher deductions than current contributors who would by then be netting better pensions. It was this dilemma that caused SERPS to be scaled down by the Thatcher government in 1986.[142]

Though the right to a retirement pension was an important development for the majority of disabled people who were elderly, the Beveridge Plan largely ignored the special requirements associated with impairment. In 1962 an annual tax allowance of £100 was introduced for blind (but not deaf) people who were at work and sufficiently well paid to gain.[143] Otherwise, only discretionary additions to national assistance or supplementary benefit were available.[144] The formulation of new benefits dedicated to disability thus addressed a major omission. Emerging with cross-party support from the reappraisal of social security in the later 1960s, these benefits tried to tackle both income maintenance and the extra costs generated by impairment. In 1971 the Conservative government put in place an invalidity pension for members of the national insurance scheme who were unable to return to work after 28 weeks. Payment was made at the level of the sickness benefit available for the first six months, but there were higher allowances for dependent children and for those impaired early in their working lives. Four years later the Labour government introduced a non-contributory invalidity pension for people of working age who had no right to national insurance. Paid at just 60 per cent of the contributory invalidity pension, NCIP was guilty of gender discrimination in requiring married and cohabiting women to prove that they were incapable of not only paid employment but also normal household duties. By June 1978 this extra test had denied the pension to 9400 women, or 15 per cent of applicants who were 'unfit' for paid work.[145]

The same gendered assumptions afflicted the invalid care allowance that commenced in 1976. Claimants other than married women had a right to assistance if they were of working age and looking after a severely disabled relative for at least 35 hours a week. Severe disability for the purposes of this benefit was defined as being in receipt of the attendance allowance or the constant attendance allowance payable under the war pensions scheme. The attendance allowance was the first new benefit designed to meet the extra costs of impairment. Introduced in 1971, it was a non-contributory, non-means-tested payment for people with major physical and/or mental impairments who required substantial, long-term care during the daytime, at night, or continuously. Adults were eligible and so were children over the age of 2 if the attention that they needed was 'in excess of that normally required by a child of the same age and sex'. Children over 5 were also included in the mobility allowance, which targeted people who were either unable or virtually unable to walk, or unable to walk without the exertion seriously endangering their health. Phased in from 1976, the allowance sought to achieve equal status for disabled drivers and passengers by replacing with a single payment the piecemeal arrangements for tricycles and cars that dated back to the First World War. The transfer from hardware to cash was followed by an exemption from road tax, the relaxation of hire purchase controls, and the establishment of Motability – a company with charitable status set up by the government to organize car leasing and car purchase schemes.[146]

The measures that augmented post-war social security from the 1970s not only increased the anomalies within the system but also failed to resolve low benefits and non-take-up. Both the attendance allowance and the mobility allowance were too meagre to offset the full costs incurred,[147] whilst in 1972 the invalidity pension for a single person was a mere 19 per cent of male gross earnings and just 53 per cent of final household income per head. The subsequent decision to link such long-term benefits to prices or earnings – whichever rose faster – did little to erode these differentials.[148] Therefore, 'the number of "sick and disabled" who...had to rely on supplementary benefit...declined only from 323,000 in 1970 to 223,000 in 1978.'[149] The multiplication of benefits intended as a way of removing disabled people from supplementary benefit increased rather than diminished the anomalies that existed under the Beveridge Plan. Invalidity pensions were paid at different rates according to whether they were contributory or non-contributory; elderly people were barred from claiming the mobility allowance; and gender discrimination curtailed the benefit rights of married and cohabiting women.

The development of benefits that were selective by need but not means added a class dimension to take-up, giving disabled people from more affluent middle-class backgrounds rights to non-contributory social security. A South Wales study of 37 families who had children with Down's Syndrome suggests that they pursued their entitlements effectively. All parents in social classes I and II were aware of the attendance allowance, all claimed it and all were successful. Conversely, only two of the six applications from social classes IV and V were granted benefit. 'Need' – measured with reference to toilet training, freedom of movement and sleeping arrangements – did not distinguish the successful from the unsuccessful cases; what mattered was the ability to compile a convincing application.[150] But if the middle class was active in seeking out selective benefits, they were not taken up with universal enthusiasm. Thus, in a small North Yorkshire study, 20 disabled people of working age 'were failing to receive a total of 51 benefits for which they appeared to be eligible. The value of these unclaimed benefits, at 1979 benefit rates, amounted to approximately £17,456 a year – an average of £872.80 per person.'[151]

The reasons for this non-take-up were more complex than a simple lack of knowledge. Though the new selective benefits were social rights, their allocation was conditional upon satisfying criteria of need and hence they were smeared with the stigma of the means test and rendered less legitimate than the contributory national insurance scheme. '[O]rganisational and regulatory procedures', and the attitudes of professional and administrative staff who assessed eligibility, reinforced this perception. Therefore, the social security system was unable to override 'dominant social values' that tied citizenship to work and 'paying your way'.[152]

Conclusion

In this chapter, we have looked at the types of financial relief from which disabled people assembled their mixed and makeshift domestic economies. Family and community support, largely invisible to the historical eye, was a major part of their survival strategies, but these inputs were complemented by the voluntary and statutory sectors. Mutual aid and charitable organizations aimed to restrict their assistance to those who helped themselves, concurring with the state that economic activity was the desirable outcome of assistance. The new poor law sounded this message with vigour, removing the paternalist customary rights that had informed the distribution of benefits before 1834. From the late nineteenth century, the reconstitution of poverty as a social problem rather than a moral defect not only mellowed the administration of poor relief but also encouraged new benefits outside its parameters – workmen's compensation, old age and war pensions, the national insurance initiatives – that conferred social rights. Implementation of the Beveridge Plan after 1945 absorbed these developments into a model system of social citizenship. But for disabled people marginal to the workforce, benefit levels were low and take-up stigmatizing. Therefore, the welfare state failed to guarantee them against poverty and financial exclusion.

8 Community care

Although the Royal Commission on Mental Illness and Mental Deficiency coined the term 'community care' in 1957,[1] the idea of supporting disabled people in their own homes or localities was evident in the medieval almshouse, developed in the boarding out schemes run by nineteenth-century poor law authorities, and honed into a system of guardianship and supervision under the Mental Deficiency Act of 1913. Chapter 8 unpicks the mixed economy of community care of which these initiatives were a part. First, special housing, hostels and group homes are evaluated as loci for inclusive community living. Second, the dynamics of family care are examined in relation to the inputs from friends, neighbours and the state. Third, the influence of economic rationality in the development and allocation of community medical and support services is explored. And, finally, how far the Chronically Sick and Disabled Persons Act of 1970 delivered social citizenship is considered. As with financial benefits that were selective and divisive rather than universal and inclusive, sustaining social rights was difficult where loss of autonomy was a precondition for the receipt of a service.

Special housing

Disabled people's financial deprivation disadvantaged them in the housing market, exposing them to accommodation of poor standard. In the late 1960s, for example, 35 per cent of those placed in the two most serious categories of impairment were without the exclusive use of hot water, a fixed bath and an inside WC, compared to 23 per cent of the population of Great Britain as a whole.[2] The social right to adequate accommodation was shared by all citizens. But for disabled people special housing requirements were identified over and above this necessity. With mental impairments, it was the venue for delivering social support; with physical impairments, architectural modifications were recommended to avoid the needless restrictions. Steps were a particular problem, not just for wheelchair users but also for ambulant people with walking aids. However, narrow corridors and doorways, poorly designed kitchens and bathrooms, and wrongly positioned plugs and switches were also impediments to independence.[3]

The earliest manifestation of special housing was the almshouse. Originating in the medieval period, almshouses were derived from the generic institution that also gave rise to the modern hospital.[4] Though many had monarchical or religious patrons, others were 'the spontaneous gifts of private benefactors', and some were founded by municipal corporations, London companies or trade union bodies.[5] Strict rules, replicating aspects of the institutional regime, were imposed to control behaviour. Thus Thomas Powis's Hospital in Chepstow was not unusual in requiring almspersons 'to keep their respective rooms clean and in neat order', to obtain written permission before being absent for more than 24 hours, and to face expulsion if 'guilty of insobriety, insubordination, breach of regulations, or immoral or unbecoming conduct'.[6] Nor was satisfactory accommodation guaranteed. In 1909, the medical officer of health had already condemned the Welshpool Almshouse as unfit for human habitation when the last resident died and it was demolished after the trustees failed to amass the funds for repair.[7]

David Thomson has estimated that '[i]n many advantaged older urban centres, such as Cambridge, Bedford, Lincoln or Hereford, 10 per cent or more of mid-nineteenth-century elderly women lived at community expense in . . . charity housing,' whilst nationwide the proportion was 'perhaps 5 per cent'.[8] Immediately after the Second World War, the National Association of Almshouses was launched to expand as well as modernize the stock of dwellings, and 30 years later it claimed that there were over 22,000 almshouses in existence.[9] Voluntary housing associations, a Victorian invention whose role was expanded under the 1974 Housing Act to increase the range of rented accommodation,[10] supplied over 100,000 homes for elderly people.[11] But by far the most important elements within the mixed economy of special accommodation were the local authorities that managed the 420,000 'sheltered' units in the public sector.[12]

Although the Royal Commission on the Poor Laws had approved the development of 'cottage homes' in its Report of 1909,[13] the housing requirements of elderly people were not a priority and they were placed at the end of the queue for slum clearance.[14] The *Housing Manual*, published jointly by the Ministry of Health and the Ministry of Works in 1944, signalled a shift in attitude with its recognition that thermal insulation and handrails to the bath and stairs, plus some outside support to live independently, would be beneficial to older council tenants.[15] The first scheme incorporating these design and welfare features was built in 1948 in the Dorset town of Sturminster Newton. Subsequently, single-person units, many of them occupied by elderly people, proved popular, but administrative complications and the lack of financial incentives meant that fully fledged sheltered accommodation was slow to materialize.[16] In 1969, however, the concept of sheltered accommodation was refined with the introduction of Category 1 housing for the more active elderly and Category 2 housing for the less active who were offered additional facilities like laundries and refectories.[17] The ageing process made it difficult to sustain the two categories.[18] Furthermore, the construction of elderly 'ghettoes' was a 'dividing practice' that excluded their occupants from mainstream community life and represented old age as a stigmatized phase of the life cycle.

Hostels and group homes, and purpose-built accommodation for physically disabled people, also attracted stigma. Blind and deaf hostels dated from the later nineteenth century. In 1899, for instance, the Swansea and South Wales Institute for the Blind rented a house in the town for its residential trainees, adding two new wings to give 20 extra beds. This particular hostel closed in 1938 due to lack of demand,[19] but the charitable sector continued to manage such facilities and in 1946 the National Association for Mental Health was running '11 agricultural hostels for mentally handicapped men'.[20] The physical destruction and social dislocation of the Second World War led the government to promote hostels for elderly people displaced into squalid air-raid shelters by the conflict.[21] Reporting *On the State of the Public Health, 1939–45*, the Chief Medical Officer concluded that 'a similar provision has a definite place in the care of this type of patient after the War.'[22] Local authorities, however, were slow to complement voluntary effort by activating their responsibilities under the new National Health Service and the first hostels for intellectually impaired tenants did not open until 1955. Moreover, despite the endorsement of the 1957 Royal Commission on Mental Illness and Mental Deficiency, there were by 1962 only 30 hostels with a total of approximately 600 places 'to cover the needs of the entire mental disorder and mental handicap service'.[23]

The statutory and voluntary hostels that emerged in the post-war period were conceived as either short-stay, halfway houses designed to rehabilitate their residents for independent living, or long-stay permanent homes for those perceived to need ongoing care and support to survive outside the mental hospital. By the mid-1960s, short-term hostels were being denounced as inappropriate for many long-term patients who, though not employable following the remission of their symptoms, 'were fully capable, with sufficient preparation, of looking after themselves with the minimum of staff support'. What emerged to meet this criticism were '"artificial families" for a group of people who had lost contact with their own'. The group homes that ensued grew rapidly and by the late 1970s local Associations of Mental Health managed more than 150. Networks of homes were also developed by psychiatric hospitals. As well as offering sustained care, the more familial ethos of the group home addressed worries that the hostel replicated the restrictive conditions of the institution. A 1976 study did suggest that group homes permitted greater autonomy, residents reporting that 'just over half of all decisions about which they were asked were taken on their own personal responsibility, compared with just over one-third for hostel residents.' However, neither hostels nor group homes were effectively integrated into their localities and social contacts in both settings were 'not very close', 53 per cent being 'limited to brief formal conversations with staff or fellow residents'.[24] Community living did not necessarily bring community inclusion.

Domestic housing was likewise problematic. In the aftermath of the Second World War, the needs of disabled ex-servicemen were vociferously articulated,[25] but the enormity of slum clearance, overcrowding and the dire shortage of ordinary family dwellings quickly swamped this commitment.[26] In 1951 there was a rekindling of interest when a supplement to the *Housing Manual*, with a chapter given over to disabled people in general and the wheelchair user in particular, drew attention to a number of potentially helpful design features, notably ramps, broad doorways, wide halls, roomy bathrooms, fitments at wheelchair height and strategically located handgrips.[27] Nevertheless, the voluntary sector was left to take the initiative. In 1960, for instance, the Central Council for the Care of Cripples combined with the National Federation of Housing Societies to convert a property into self-contained units for wheelchair users; whilst three years later the National Deaf-Blind League completed specially designed flats. Simultaneously, the Royal Institute of British Architects published their seminal guide to *Designing for the Disabled*, which was based on investigations partly financed by the Polio Research Fund.[28]

Government involvement finally flowered under the auspices of the elderly when in 1961 a circular noted that 'in designing special housing accommodation for less active old people, it is useful to bear in mind that a number of features provided are also those needed by the disabled.'[29] Three years later a second circular pointed to the potential of ground-floor flats.[30] But even after the 1970 Chronically Sick and Disabled Persons (CSPD) Act required that local housing authorities have 'regard to the special needs' associated with impairment, the specifications were indeterminate. Clarification came in 1974 when 'wheelchair housing' and 'mobility housing' were born. Wheelchair housing, intended for full-time wheelchair users and for housewives who used a wheelchair indoors, had specially designed kitchens and bathrooms, additional space to ease circulation through doorways and along passages, and no steps inside or in the immediate vicinity. Mobility housing, intended for the able-bodied as well as disabled people who were ambulant rather than full-time wheelchair users, had to meet only two conditions: the approach had to be level or ramped, and the door sets to principal living areas and bedrooms had to be wide enough to admit most wheelchairs. No extra space was allowed beyond the standard fixed for local authority dwellings of the same size.[31]

Mobility housing proved more popular than wheelchair housing. By 1979 local authorities in England had completed 10,195 mobility but only 3514 wheelchair units, whilst the figures for housing associations were 1912 and 580 units respectively.[32] However, a number of housing departments were reluctant to build because they were sceptical of the 'need' for special dwellings or unsure of how many were required. Instead, they advocated the adaptation of disabled people's existing homes. Adaptation had been permissible since the 1948 National Assistance Act empowered but did not oblige local authorities 'to make arrangements for promoting the welfare of the blind, the deaf or dumb, or other persons who are permanently and substantially handicapped'. This assistance – which by 1960 had become a statutory duty for the 'general classes' as well as for blind, and deaf and dumb people[33] – was consolidated in the Chronically Sick and Disabled Persons Act, which mandated local authorities to help with arranging 'works of adaptation...or the provision of any additional facilities designed to secure...greater safety, comfort or convenience'. Furthermore, after the 1974 Housing Act, disabled people were able to apply for discretionary house improvement grants to make a dwelling more suitable for their accommodation or welfare. For those who fulfilled the qualifying conditions, intermediate grants were also available as of right to install basic amenities even where these existed but were not readily accessible due to impairment.

During 1979 over 68,000 adaptations were carried out under the Chronically Sick and Disabled Persons Act, about half in the private sector and half in the public sector. In addition, private owners obtained 1017 improvement grants and 629 intermediate grants.[34] These routes to adaptation were often tortuous. Funding and good technical advice were scarce. Communication across departmental and professional boundaries was essential but difficult. And, as a result, delay and bureaucracy were rampant.[35] 'Very disappointed' was the verdict one mother of a disabled child passed on her engagement with the application process in 1976; 'The system is so big and complicated you feel lost in it.'[36] But even when adaptations were implemented, a comparison of two surveys from the Department of the Environment in the late 1970s suggests – albeit tentatively – that they were less successful than special housing. In the first survey of 249 occupants of purpose-built units, 83 per cent used wheelchairs; in the second survey of 180 occupants of houses that had been substantially adapted, 68 per cent used wheelchairs. If special and adapted accommodation were equally suitable, we would expect the disabled people in purpose-built dwellings to have more difficulty because of their greater reliance on wheelchairs. Yet the reverse was true. A half coped with the WC easily alone in special units in contrast to only 35 per cent in adapted homes, whilst the proportions able to bath or shower in the conventional way were three-quarters and a half respectively.[37]

The implication is not that purpose building was the ideal solution. Mobility housing was an opportunity to make the public sector stock more inclusive for at least some disabled people, rather than fitting them to standardized architectural conventions. Wheelchair units, on the other hand, were often provided on a segregated or divisive basis that jeopardized the community integration of their occupants. All special accommodation assumed a willingness to move that elderly people in particular were reluctant to undertake because of deep attachments to their local neighbourhoods and social networks. Moreover, the heavy concentration of purpose-built housing in a contracting public sector not only reduced the expansion of provision but also rendered it largely 'out of bounds' to the growing contingent of owner-occupiers for whom changing tenure was neither an attractive nor a realistic option. Therefore, housing policies failed to supply disabled people with the suitable homes that were pivotal to their participation as equal citizens.[38]

Families, friends and neighbours

Defective accommodation had far-reaching ramifications, on occasions leading to unnecessary hospitalization and unemployment.[39] However, it also increased the level of support that was required to maintain disabled people at home. The statutory services were one ingredient within a mixed economy of care that also embodied the voluntary sector, the commercial sector, and the informal sector of relatives, friends and neighbours. Classical sociology nurtured the view that industrialization had so eroded the capacity for informal care that families were forced to abandon their disabled members to the formal services of the state.[40] More recent historiography has undercut this myth of family decline, pointing to the creative role of relatives in the processes of institutionalization and to their continuing responsibility for care in the community.

The institutionalization of disabled people was until recently associated with family deficiency. When Grace W. was admitted to the Devon Asylum at Exminster in 1848, the medical superintendent noted that she had been 'under the protection of a son and his wife who are now committed for trial for their ill usage of her and depriving her of all the necessities of life'. How widespread such abuse and neglect were it is impossible to measure, but the prevalence of individual cases, and the unwillingness of local juries to prosecute relatives committing even extreme acts of cruelty against defenceless 'lunatics', suggest that they may not have been uncommon.[41] Under the Children's Act of 1908, a parent or legal guardian was deemed guilty of neglect if he treated any child 'in a way likely to cause injury to his health, [and] if he fail[ed] to provide adequate food, clothing, medical aid or lodging'.[42] Nevertheless, mental welfare officers alleged that disabled children were still concealed at home.[43] For all families, the inter-war professionalization of childcare extended the definition of good parenting well beyond the avoidance of such extreme neglect to absorb the material, psychological and moral preoccupations of the middle class. And for poorer families with disabled children, institutionalization was the price to be paid for failing to employ the approved methods of discipline and encouragement, to police moral – and especially sexual – behaviour, and to demonstrate a sound understanding of both the impairment and the needs that it generated.[44]

But if the perceived shortcomings of some families led to imposed confinement, others played an active role in 'initiating the identification of mental disability, participating in the certification process,... and facilitating discharge back into the community'.[45] This involvement 'depended to a large degree on the capacity of family and kinship households to accommodate the behaviour of the individual within the cycle of life events that shaped [their]...resources'. If a mentally disabled adult committed or threatened violence, the family might seek admission to protect themselves and the wider community.[46] And in 'idiot' children too aggression was a factor in certification, along with emotional disengagement, inarticulate speech and difficulties with 'feeding, dressing, toileting and self-care'.[47] From the carers' perspective, 'the ageing, retirement, or death of parents, the arrival of new siblings, and the ageing of defectives, all tended to make...request for institutional aid more likely.' And a worsening of the family's economic or housing situation could lead them to petition for an asylum place or resist the discharge of a patient. These decisions were not 'an abdication of responsibility' but a pragmatic response to 'economic need'. Families did not believe that they had a social right to be relieved of their burden of care by the state.[48] Rather, they tried to access institutional services strategically as their circumstances changed.[49]

The micro-politics of family care were located within the broader framework of social relations. In an important article on admission to the Lancashire asylums, John Walton demonstrated that the Industrial Revolution was not uniformly destructive but variable in its impact. Admission rates relative to population were highest in the big conurbations of Liverpool and Manchester, but they were lowest in the new textile centres like Bury and Rochdale and not in established small towns and traditional agricultural areas. The reasons were both material and ideological. Far from destroying family-based employment, the factory system preserved working patterns that were capable of absorbing employees whose productivity was poor. With wage levels above the working-class average, there were more financial resources to retain disabled relatives at home. And the textile towns – compact enough to sustain family ties – also generated new social networks – around work and leisure as well as the neighbourhood – that protected against incarceration. Furthermore, these raw industrial communities were remote from the traditional structures of authority that policed insanity in the countryside and – as seedbeds of religious Dissent and political radicalism – they were tolerant when other social norms were breached. Therefore, particular material and ideological configurations perpetuated a willingness to care that post-dated industrialization.[50]

The family's continuing commitment is thrown into sharpest relief by the resistance of relatives to incarceration. After finally deciding to institutionalize her intellectually impaired son in 1958, one mother described how for 18 months she 'cried myself to sleep'. 'I felt like a murderess', she said. 'I really felt I had condemned him to death.'[51] Other families fought off confinement, one sister of a woman with Down's Syndrome remembering an incident in the 1930s when her father had 'ordered...out' the district nurse, 'shouting and swearing, telling her to go away and mind her own business'.[52] The family structures through which this commitment was delivered therefore survived the Industrial Revolution. More specifically, the multi-generational extended family was not broken up and replaced with an isolated nuclear family of parents and dependent children. On the contrary, average household size in England remained almost static at 4.75 persons from the sixteenth to the nineteenth century,[53] and it has been estimated that during the same period 'only 5.8 per cent of all households...contained more than two generations.' But of greater significance than family structure was proximity. In Michael Anderson's words, 'kinship does not stop at the front door. There are few functions which can be performed by a co-residing kinsman which he cannot perform equally well if he instead lives next door or even up the street.'[54]

Though proximity is difficult to measure for the distant past, there is evidence that elderly people in pre-industrial England were enmeshed in geographically close family relationships. Studies of Preston, the Staffordshire Potteries and Bethnal Green in London show that during the nineteenth century relatives continued to strive for residential adjacency. Moreover, J. H. Sheldon, investigating Wolverhampton in the later 1940s, found that 30 per cent of his elderly sample had relatives living 'not more than five minutes walking distance' away. A similar picture emerged from subsequent surveys in East London. Therefore, reviewing the post-war sociological literature in 1959, Peter Townsend concluded that 'most old people have children living nearby even when they live alone.' By the end of the twentieth century, geographical mobility was undermining this nearness, particularly for middle-class families who were 'more widely dispersed than working-class ones, but also less constrained by distance due to readier access to transport and telephones'.[55] For most of the modern era, however, family structures were predisposed towards supporting disabled people in the community.

The state began to engage with these structures under the old poor law where families as well as 'non-related individuals' were 'hired' to accommodate disabled people within their households.[56] This unsupervised system of 'boarding out', often used when mental impairments were deemed innocuous, not only failed to protect against mistreatment but also jarred with the deterrent principles of 1834.[57] It survived in the impoverished agricultural economies of rural Wales, primarily because 'the lack of alternative employment opportunities, and the low standard of living, made the small cash payments offered [by parishes] for the care of a lunatic or idiot an inducement' for potential carers.[58] Elsewhere, however, it was largely eclipsed by the rise of the asylum. Only in Scotland did the Board of Lunacy – 'unwavering' in its support of community care – introduce supervised arrangements for boarding out that removed 'the accumulation of chronic cases from asylums', whilst offering a 'domestic life' to patients who were 'apparently incurable, harmless and not suffering from any bodily or mental disorder requiring specialised treatment.' Therefore, at the turn of the century, 'over 20 per cent of registered pauper insane were boarded out.'[59] Though only common in Victorian Scotland, the concept of boarding out gradually spread as local education authorities and voluntary organizations lodged disabled children with foster parents. In 1910/11, for instance, the Shropshire Convalescent and Surgical Home announced that children who 'were quite able to go to school and yet required surgical supervision and care' had been put 'in the charge of competent cottage women at a slightly lower cost'.[60]

The 1913 Mental Deficiency Act developed these initiatives. Though infamous for its policy of incarceration, this legislation also created a system of community care and control. If the family home was deemed adequate, statutory supervision was exercised through regular visits by social workers. Less frequently, if this condition was not met, the 'defective' was either placed with a legal guardian or granted extended leave on license from an institution.[61] Post-war social policy extended the principle of care in the community to other disabled client groups. The 'welfare services should...ensure that all handicapped persons...have the maximum opportunity of sharing in and contributing to the life of the community', maintained the circular that accompanied the 1948 National Assistance Act, 'so that their capacities are realized to the full, their self-confidence developed, and their social contacts strengthened.'[62] The 1959 Mental Health Act likewise stressed the importance of reserving hospitals for psychiatric treatment that required an in-patient stay.[63] However, community care was construed as care outside the big institutions and included residential as well as family homes. Not until the 1970s was it reinterpreted as care by the community of relatives, friends and neighbours.[64]

Quantifying the incidence of such informal care is problematic, at least until it gained visibility from the social survey. In 1962 Peter Townsend and Dorothy Wedderburn carried out the first national investigation of *The Aged in the Welfare State*. Their findings reiterated the conclusion of previous community studies in London's East End, flagging up the minimal role of friends and neighbours in comparison to the heavy reliance on relatives. Of those needing assistance with bathing, 50 per cent were helped by a household member, 7 per cent by another relation, and 2 per cent by a friend. For those having difficulty with heavy housework, the proportions were 51 per cent, 13 per cent, and 3 per cent respectively. When the Office of Population Censuses and Surveys conducted similar research in 1976, the proportion being assisted with bathing by a household member had dropped to 33 per cent. Relatives from outside grew by only 2 per cent and friends by 1 per cent whilst other helpers beyond the household – who did not register at all in 1962 – were of assistance in 4 per cent of cases. Elderly people increasingly lived alone, but none of these groups offset the resulting deficit of personal care. Furthermore, their input for heavy housework actually contracted slightly, leaving 'the immediate family…as important as ever in meeting needs'.[65]

The centrality of relatives, no less pronounced in physical and mental impairment than in old age,[66] was enveloped in a high idealism that fused the 'natural' and moral.[67] In practice, reciprocity played a major role in family care. Just as elderly parents became more welcome co-residents once the old age pension enabled a contribution to household expenses, so those with the ability to offer 'services' – childcare, for instance – were more likely to receive assistance themselves.[68] Nor was the quality of support guaranteed. In some families, impairment was a source of disappointment, guilt or shame, and disabled people were condemned to a marginal existence, isolated by 'feelings of insecurity and inferiority'. 'My grandma used to say that I'd been cursed and that I was being punished by God for what I'd done in a past life', explained David Swift, born with a hereditary muscular condition in 1936. 'That was why I was disabled she said, and when I'd served out this punishment everything would be all right.'[69] Even where attitudes were less negative, the provision of care generated ambivalence. During the 1920s, Tom Atkins spent more than six years in an orthopaedic hospital after contracting polio at the age of 3. He sensed that his parents were 'not happy' with the decision to release him because of 'certain problems at home'. The 'problems' were his sister with Down's Syndrome and 'an invalid grandmother', who lived upstairs permanently bedridden until she was eventually admitted to a poor law institution 'because the situation became intolerable for my mother'.[70]

Tom's mother was not unusual in shouldering principal responsibility for care. Using lunacy returns for nineteenth-century north Wales, David Hirst and Pamela Michael have demonstrated 'a preponderance of female carers'. Of the 25 'lunatics' identified as living at home or with relatives between 1828 and 1858, six mothers and five wives were main carers compared with three fathers and one husband. Only one of the 98 'idiots' resided with his wife, but there were 33 mothers serving as the main carer in contrast to 24 fathers.[71] This gendered division of care in rural Wales was replicated among admissions to the Earlswood Asylum in urban Surrey.[72] It embodied the notion that women were genetically equipped for domesticity by virtue of their reproductive biology.[73] Twentieth-century social change taxed the viability of these mores. A falling birth rate, allied to geographical mobility, produced a shrinking pool of carers. Family networks were disrupted by divorce and remarriage. And from the Second World War women increasingly re-entered paid employment when their children went to school.[74] Yet from the 1970s, a series of studies were demonstrating that female carers outnumbered male carers by as many as three to one[75] and spent up to ten hours each day on 'purely caring activities' without the 'associated household tasks'.[76]

Whether performed by men or women, family caring on such a scale exacted a heavy price. It restricted employment opportunities and induced financial hardship;[77] it damaged physical and mental health;[78] it upset relationships with spouses, children, siblings and friends.[79] But family care was also too readily construed as preferable for disabled people. Help from relatives was permeated by taboos. Martha Loane, in her account of district nursing at the start of the twentieth century, observed how an elderly mother 'cooks and cleans and scrubs' for her paralysed daughter's family, 'but the idea of washing her daughter now that she is helpless never enters her mind'. Anticipating a visit from the vicar, the daughter observed that 'Mother's set the room straight, but it didn't seem as if she could bring herself to touch *me*.'[80] Children found it equally difficult to touch their parents.[81] These sensitivities undermined the material quality of family care, but the relentless pressure of delivering assistance also undermined its interpersonal dimension.[82] Such socio-psychological tensions upset the assumptions that governed family interaction and hence alienated disabled people from the conventions that ordered family life. Therefore, depending on relatives was capable of compounding the social discrimination experienced beyond the home.

Community medical services

Although 'the family...constituted the first line of responsibility when individuals had their self-maintaining capacities impaired or threatened', its role was complemented by medical and support services that were of commercial, voluntary and statutory origin.[83] Medical practice in eighteenth-century Britain was not the subject of state regulation. On the contrary, 'regular' physicians, surgeons and apothecaries or chemists – who had followed the 'orthodox' training prescribed by their professional bodies – competed for patients in a commercial marketplace, and not only with 'irregular' practitioners but also with lay and proprietary remedies.[84] Therefore, disabled people purchased what health care they could afford, no doubt attracted to cheaper concoctions such as Scots Pills and Daffy's Elixir that included rheumatism and deafness among the multitude of ailments for which a cure was promised.[85] The Medical Act of 1858 moved the medical profession towards greater integration by establishing a single register of all qualified practitioners and banning those who were not listed from government posts.[86] Nevertheless, 'unorthodox' treatments still flourished, prompting the National Institute for the Deaf in 1929 to warn against the false claims of 'cunning' advertisements and travelling 'specialists'.[87] According to Marie Hagger, herself deaf, poverty was to blame: 'So whether you were deaf or you'd got a bad arm, bad leg or whatever, a home cure was the only result. All sorts of things, except the right thing, that was get the correct treatment. No, they never did because they couldn't afford to.'[88]

Disabled people in poverty had experienced some free access to basic health care since the days of the old poor law. The 1601 Act ignored treating as opposed to maintaining the sick, but parishes began to pay medical practitioners to tend not only paupers but also other local people unable to meet the cost of assistance.[89] Despite the regular appointment of medical officers from the second half of the eighteenth century, health care remained an omission when the poor law was overhauled in 1834. Eight years later, however, the medical service was 'formalized' and by 1844 'there were over 2800 district medical officers in England and Wales.' In Scotland, government grants were made available to promote medical relief. There was, of course, no right to treatment. Furthermore, the poor law medical service was weakened by the heavy emphasis on economy and deterrence; medical officers were usually paid a meagre annual stipend that was indifferent to their caseload, whilst relieving officers acted as gatekeepers to health care. Yet disabled people used the service.[90] In one week during 1868, for instance, the medical officer for Colyton in Devon treated an amputated finger, four serious fractures, and a man paralysed by a spinal injury who had fallen from a ladder whilst thatching a rick.[91] Elderly and chronically sick patients were also given yearly 'tickets' that sanctioned ongoing medical relief without repeated recourse to the relieving officer.[92]

From the 1850s, a number of poor law unions began to complement medical officers with funding for public dispensaries.[93] A charitable dispensary movement had emerged in the late eighteenth century, prompted by complaints that the new voluntary hospitals not only exposed their patients to the risk of fever but also through institutionalization encouraged an unhealthy dependency.[94] Imitating the system of associated philanthropy adopted by voluntary hospitals,[95] these dispensaries typically offered an outdoor medical service to the deserving poor, perhaps charging a small *ad hoc* or weekly fee for the advice and medicines prescribed by their physicians and surgeons; home visits were a possibility for those too ill to attend the 'clinic' in person. The poor law guardians on occasions subscribed to pre-existing voluntary dispensaries. At other times, they set up their own establishments or promoted new foundations, claiming that the cost was offset by the lesser burden on medical officers.[96] Following the Metropolitan Poor Act of 1867, an extensive outdoor service was set up to reduce overcrowding in the London infirmaries and 20 years later a total of 44 dispensaries were managing over 100,000 consultations, half of them home visits.[97] Outside the capital, however, their 'contribution was never more than marginal'.[98]

By the turn of the twentieth century, the increasing proportion of subscriptions from organizations of employers and of employees, and also from working men's clubs, was changing the role of dispensaries. Still more significant was the exodus of these corporate members brought about by the National Insurance Act of 1911,[99] which 'deprived' dispensaries of many patients by providing free access to a 'panel' doctor for insured men. In theory, the scheme covered all those aged between 16 and 65 who earned less than £160 per annum. But, in practice, there was no mechanism for ensuring full participation and so many in the poorest paid jobs that disabled men were prone to occupy were probably left out, along with the women, children and elderly people whom the Act explicitly overlooked.[100] The effect was to focus the attention of dispensaries on these excluded groups, and at the York Dispensary chronic conditions – along were infectious diseases – accounted for most patients during the 1930s.[101] The increased employment of disabled men and women during the Second World War may have improved their access to 'panel' doctors.[102] However, not until the emergence of the NHS did they become entitled to free medical care that was comprehensive and universal.

If health services were patchy before 1948, the government did become increasingly involved with the supply of aids. At the end of the First World War, the Ministry of Pensions assumed responsibility for issuing appliances to disabled ex-servicemen. A 'little known' industry prior to the war, limb making expanded rapidly after 1914, 'necessitated' by the 'mass bodily destruction' of the conflict.[103] By the mid-1920s 'more than three-fifths of artificial limbs provided...were made of light metals' rather than of cheaper and less effective wood,[104] their technology acting as 'the supreme icon of modernity'.[105] Oral testimonies reveal that where the appliance was not of high quality long-term suffering was the outcome. Doing voluntary work in Leeds for BLESMA,[106] Bill Thompson found that as late as 1936 a lot of men had stumps that 'kept coming out in abscesses...[because they] had been given poor legs in the first place'.[107] Improvisation was the fate of the civilian disabled population to whom the state offered no assistance. Alice Maguire – who as a child had polio during the First World War – used a calliper manufactured by her great-grandfather, the village blacksmith, whilst Elsie Cooper – also with polio – wore callipers and boots paid for by money that her mother had begged from a string of charities.[108] For adults injured at work, few employers were willing to finance artificial limbs and so trade unions struggled to raise the necessary funds, the Miners' Federation collecting at concerts and football matches.[109]

In 1939 the Ministry of Pensions' Limb Service for disabled ex-servicemen was extended to casualties in wartime employment directed by the Ministry of Labour. Children of school age were added under the Education Act of 1944. Therefore, the NHS inherited 30,000 civilian amputees when it took over the service in 1948. No fewer than '5960 war pensioners and 8106 civilian patients were fitted with artificial limbs and arms' in the first year.[110] Appliances of other types also became more easily available. Between 1948 and 1957, for example, 580,000 hearing aids were allocated, releasing from what Aneurin Bevan called a 'kind of twilight life' those who were neither profoundly nor totally deaf, but unable to afford a commercial appliance.[111] During the 1950s, interest in aids grew, encouraged by exhibitions mounted by organizations like the Central Council for the Disabled and dedicated to 'Outwitting Handicaps'.[112] This belief in the ability of ingenuity to triumph was captured most forcefully by POSSUM (the Patient Operator Selector Mechanism), which harnessed the residual movements of severely disabled people to perform a variety of everyday tasks. By the early 1970s, however, only 200 POSSUM units were in operation; the British Medical Association was rebuking the artificial limb and appliance industry for its 'monopoly, centralized supply and technical backwardness';[113] and the NHS had yet to replace its old-fashioned body-wore hearing aids with modern behind-the-ear devices.[114] Provision had improved relative to the pre-war situation, but disabled people reliant on the state were excluded from the most up-to-date technology.

Though the NHS provided hospitals as well as aids and appliances, its lynch pin was the primary care delivered through general practice. There was a forerunner in the shape of the School

Medical Service. Only medical inspection became a statutory duty in 1907, but local education authorities increasingly used their permissive powers to establish school clinics and to waive their fees until free treatment was finally authorized in 1918. The Service was an early manifestation of surveillance medicine in which the doctor moved beyond control of the sick person towards the establishment of standards for society as a whole.[115] Disabled children were thus calibrated against able-bodied norms, being poked and prodded in a state of undress with no respect for their privacy. The process traumatized them, inducing 'pain', 'anguish' and 'humiliation'. As Marie Hagger recalled of being diagnosed deaf in 1935 when she was 10: 'I went to my room and I think I cried for about three days. The tears just wouldn't stop.'[116] General practice did not absorb the functions of the School Medical Service, but from 1948 it was the pivot of medical care for disabled people, gatekeeping the hospital and community services.

Despite epitomizing social citizenship, the universal framework of the NHS gave patients a conditional right of access but no automatic right to treatment.[117] Consequently, professional judgement controlled the distribution of resources. General practitioners had a comprehensive mandate to address the social circumstances as well as the physical and mental health of patients, but their approach to impairment was distorted by a therapeutic or medical model of health, which – inspired by the diktats of economic rationality – stressed cure rather than care and hence regarded non-clinical matters as trivial. There is some evidence to suggest that in the early 1970s disabled people consulted their GPs more frequently than other patients. Diseases of the circulatory system, for instance, together with long-term respiratory complaints and 'disorders of the bones and organs of movement' generated an 'attendance ratio' that was above 'the overall mean of 2.6 attendances'. However, prone to be dismissive of chronic conditions that medicine could do little to alleviate, GPs spent less time with these patients. Interpreting the length as opposed to the frequency of appointments is complicated by the fact that 'in most disease groups the mean time per consultation is higher for new-patient-initiated consultations' than for consultations initiated by the doctor or an 'old' patient. Nevertheless, once a person was confirmed as a chronically impaired case, for whom 'curative treatment was unavailable and medical care...mainly supportive', the average consultation time slumped below the average for other 'return' consultations.[118] Of this older patients were seemingly conscious, complaining that the doctor was 'always in a hurry'.[119] On these grounds, it would seem that disabled people's social right to equitable GP services was undermined.

Community support services

Although the concept of community care long predated the welfare state, community support services in the period to 1979 remained highly fragmented. Help of a rudimentary nature was made available under the poor law, the authorities exercising discretion where assistance was required due to apparent impairment. In 1814, for example, overseers at Chepstow paid 1s. 6d. 'for shaving Charles Fisher 6 weeks',[120] whilst in 1830 the vestry of Great Ayton in the North Riding of Yorkshire hired nurses for a 'chronic invalid'.[121] When responsibility for poor relief passed to local authorities in 1929, some developed 'a home nursing service for the domiciliary treatment of the adult sick'.[122] However, the main root for the post-war mixed economy of community support services – home nursing, health visiting, home help, meals-on-wheels and social work – was not these scattered statutory initiatives but the charitable or voluntary sector.

William Rathbone is often credited with appointing the first home nurse in 1859, but his scheme for ministering to the sick in the poorest areas of Liverpool shared much with the work of religious bodies in operation for more than 20 years. A 'Jill-of-all-trades' drawn from the local working-class community yet supervised by a lady inspector, the district nurse initially performed a variety of tasks that were subsequently differentiated and devolved as a result of professionalization. Health visitors thus took over education in disease and hygiene, home helps dealt with domestic duties,[123] and the advice and counselling functions of district nurses became the particular preserve of voluntary or 'social' workers whom charities for disabled people were recruiting in growing numbers from the later nineteenth century.[124] It was through forging financial partnerships with this network that local authorities met their expanding corpus of statutory obligations in the early twentieth century. Therefore, during the inter-war years, their fees became an increasing important source of income for voluntary organizations.[125]

In 1920 blind people became the first disabled group to win a social right to community support, following a campaign going back to the 1890s that had the endorsement of the National League for the Blind and the Parliamentary Committee of the TUC as well as the Central Poor Law Commission.[126] The Blind Persons Act required local authorities to both register blind people and arrange schemes for their welfare. Designed to remove them from the clutches of the poor law, the Act enabled co-operation with voluntary bodies to provide workshops and home teaching but also visiting and leisure activities. In 1929 the Local Government Act permitted domiciliary assistance, a power that became a statutory duty in 1938.[127] Though Geoffrey Finlayson was exaggerating when he lauded the 'comprehensive statutory system' that emerged for blind people in conjunction with local voluntary organizations,[128] the legislative framework did mean that community support was better resourced for visual than for other categories of impairment where only charities were involved. Nevertheless, disabled people were not empowered to arrange services that met their own needs, being forced instead to rely on standardized assistance that was conditional upon assessment.

The welfare state, needless to say, altered the relationship between the statutory and voluntary sectors. Employment, social security and health care policies – all regarded as essential to economic efficiency – were 'nationalized' under the control of central government. Community care, on the other hand, remained with local authorities, which had new statutory powers but no statutory duty to deliver support. The new powers stemmed from two pieces of legislation. First, the National Health Service Act of 1946 conferred a general power to 'make arrangements for...the care of persons suffering from illness or mental defectiveness' and a specific power to organize domestic assistance not only in maternity cases – which had been permissible since 1918 – but also 'for households where such help is required owing to the presence of any person who is ill,...mentally defective, [or] aged'. Second, the National Assistance Act of 1948 permitted local authorities 'to promote the welfare of persons who are blind, deaf or dumb and others, who are substantially and permanently handicapped by illness, injury or congenital deformity'.

This package of measures was extremely constricted. Like the Blind Persons Act, it was assumed that local authorities rather than disabled people themselves were best placed to determine services. But even within their own slim parameters, the Acts were unambitious, prompting Means and Smith to observe that 'it remained *ultra vires* for local authorities to...develop their own meals-on-wheels services, chiropody facilities, laundry services, visiting schemes or counselling services.'[129] Furthermore, community care did not feature among the areas flagged up for future development, namely information about the facilities available; advice about managing with impairments; workshops and employment at home; recreational amenities; and a classified register of 'handicapped persons'. In the circular spelling out the implications of the 1948 Act, the Minister seized his option to turn the welfare of blind people from a permissive power into a statutory duty. Therefore, most initial activity was confined to visual impairment, other facilities being sidelined to evolve later 'along the lines of the existing blind welfare services if the Minister decides to give local authorities further guidance'.[130] This guidance – not forthcoming until 1951 – encouraged schemes for both deaf people and other impaired groups. In the promotion of all these initiatives, however, the emphasis was on partnership with the voluntary sector. Local authorities were to make funds available, but there was no requirement of public provision.[131]

The persistence of this alliance – underwritten by a general reluctance on the part of central government to meddle with local autonomy – primed the Ministry of Health to limit its advice to 'matters of detail...[that] failed to specify the...overall direction' of policy.[132] At first the Ministry was confident that services were adequate and co-ordinated. From the early 1950s, however, doubts set in about the capacity of the voluntary sector to finance the necessary range of health and welfare services. Some local authorities decided to run their own domiciliary services.[133] Leicester's Health Committee, for example, took over the District Nursing Association in 1954, having operated a home help scheme since the end of the Second World War.[134] Nevertheless, '[b]y 1956 92 per cent of authorities in England and Wales with schemes for the welfare of the deaf still relied on the staffs of voluntary organizations to carry them out', whilst only 28 per cent of those with 'schemes for the generally handicapped' themselves provided the services.[135]

The outcome was geographical disparity. In 1960 variation in the supply of home nurses ranged from 0.16 to 0.25 per 1000 population. 'Diversity was even greater in the home help service... [t]he better areas provid[ing] as many as 2 home helps per 1000 population, the worst as few as 0.07 per 1000.'[136]

The Mental Health Act of 1959 intensified the pressure on local authorities because activities in this area were minimal. Though the first community psychiatric nurse had been appointed in 1954, the service did not flourish until the early 1970s.[137] Social work was similarly immature, being concentrated on mentally ill patients in the psychiatric hospitals and 'mentally defective' clients in the community. The Act sought to avoid unnecessary institutional admissions by expanding community options, but existing powers were simply defined more clearly and local authorities instructed to exercise them without prevarication. At the same time, their other responsibilities for community support were extending. In 1959 chiropody services were authorized. In 1960 schemes for disabled people who were not blind or deaf became a statutory duty rather than merely a permissive power. And in 1962 local authority meals-on-wheels services were permitted. However, it was not until 1968 that the provision of home help became mandatory,[138] finally reversing the residential thrust of the National Assistance Act that had subordinated the community services.[139]

As well as stiffening the obligations of local authorities, central government also tried to plan the more rational deployment of their limited funds. Since 1955 a virtual embargo had been imposed on capital expenditure, despite 'mounting public indignation over the plight of the elderly, the disabled, the mentally ill and the mentally handicapped'.[140] During 1959, however, local authorities were asked to submit a programme of capital projects in community care for which they were seeking future loan sanction.[141] There was a more ambitious stab at planning in 1962 when, in an attempt to capture the potential released by the Hospital Plan and its anticipated reduction in psychiatric beds,[142] local authorities were invited to plot how their community services would develop over the next ten years. Considerable expansion was envisaged, home nurses increasing by 2086 in England and Wales, home helps by 11,605, and social workers by 1936.[143] But the spatial variation evident at the beginning of the decade did not disappear.[144]

For, with no rationale for community care and no 'positive lead from central Government',[145] there was no systematic relationship between demand and resources. Consequently, the social citizenship that attached to the 'nationalized' components of the welfare state in its first 20 years was attenuated with community care because geographical access to local authority provision, initially permissive, was highly variable.

The Chronically Sick and Disabled Persons Act

From the late 1960s, community care was caught up in a series of reforms. Social services in Scotland were overhauled with the creation of new social work departments. Administrative change followed in England and Wales. First, unified social services departments (SSDs) replaced the former health, welfare and children's departments in compliance with the recommendations of the Seebohm Report. Second, local authorities were stripped of responsibility for community health services with the reorganization of the NHS. The outcome was a bifurcation between home help and meals-on-wheels that stayed with the new SSDs, and health visiting and home nursing that were transferred to the NHS. Superimposed upon these changes was the Chronically Sick and Disabled Persons Act of 1970. Under Section 1, local authorities were obliged both to inform themselves of the number of persons requiring help and to publicize broadly the facilities on offer. Under Section 2, they were required to provide a number of community support services, including practical assistance at home and meals at home or elsewhere.

In the aftermath of this legislation, White Papers were published on improving services in respect of intellectual impairment, mental illness and old age.[146] The planning system also rolled on. In 1972 development proposals for the next decade were requested from the new social services departments, though without a firm estimate of future resources or a radical assessment of alternatives to existing services.[147] *Priorities for Health and Personal Social Services* adopted a more sophisticated procedure. Published in 1976 as part of a comprehensive consultation process, the document was based on an application of cost-effectiveness analysis.[148] The results were far from trouble free. Of course, all quantitative methodologies brush aside the subtle, qualitative policy outputs that defy measurement. But that aside, the analysis was flawed. Community care was trotted out as a 'slogan' with no effort to build it into 'a coherent policy'. Co-ordination across central government departments was left to local authorities and local health authorities. And there were incongruities between stated priorities and recommended growth rates.[149] Nevertheless, at a time when economic problems were dictating savage cuts, the proportion of public expenditure devoted to the health and personal social services stayed virtually constant,[150] suggesting that the planning exercise may have protected the budget from predatory rivals.

It is not surprising that a faulty planning process working in a financial crisis failed to deliver inclusive community care. Evaluating the performance of the CSDP Act is difficult because there are no national statistics for disabled people's use of social work, and the breakdown by client and age groups for home nursing, home help and meals-on-wheels does not allow their call on these services to be reliably identified. Between 1972 and 1979, however, the total number of persons who received home nursing rose from 1,841,400 to 3,248,500; the total number of cases attended by home helps from 473,900 to 730,300; and the total number of meals supplied in recipients' homes from 15,833,000 to 26,181,000.[151] But spatial divergence continued. Topliss and Gould have calculated that in 1977/8 the all-England average for the provision of home help, expressed as a rate per 1000 population over the age of 65, was 90.8 clients, but the highest provider was supporting 193.6 clients compared with 37.8 clients for the lowest provider.[152] Even before the *Priorities* document, the budget negotiated centrally was distributed in block grants, which were based on formulae that tried to estimate local circumstances. The problem was that health authorities and local authorities were left to determine their own priorities, enlightened only if they so pleased by guidelines from central government.[153]

Geographical variation is a crude measure of exclusion from community support because 'territorial justice' insists not on equality between localities but a distribution of resources that matches their population characteristics.[154] Disabled people's take-up of services, on the other hand, is a better indicator of the extent to which their requirements were met. For the decade following the Chronically Sick and Disabled Persons Act, there is no research commensurate with the national survey of physical impairment that charted take-up for Britain as a whole in the late 1960s. We do know from the 1976 study of elderly (but not necessarily disabled) people living in English communities that 33.3 per cent had been visited by a doctor during the past six months; 4.4 per cent by a health visitor; 7.8 per cent by a district nurse; 8.9 per cent by a home help; 2.6 per cent by the meals-on-wheels service; and 3.9 per cent by a local authority welfare officer.[155] The CSDP Act itself led to a string of local surveys, designed to fulfil Section 1 but often of poor quality.[156] In 1974, however, the house-to-house census carried out by Southampton City Council was the starting point for an academic study of disabled people under retirement age and living locally in private households. All elderly and mentally impaired people were omitted on the grounds that their 'needs... might be very different', but physically impaired adults and children were included. Their receipt of statutory services was miniscule. Home helps, for instance, supported just 4 per cent of those requiring assistance in self-care, whilst district nurses aided less than one per cent. And in the sample as a whole, 'only a third... received any social service support at all.'[157]

This limited impact is partially explained by the dilution that occurred when the CSDP Act was interpreted for local authorities. First, the government argued that a full enumeration of the population – identifying every disabled person – was not necessary under Section 1, which in any event did not apply to Scotland.[158] Second, the definition of 'need' was linked to financial exigency, tempting hard-up departments to ignore the circumstances of those for whom they could not afford services.[159] But the flaws went beyond a single piece of legislation. Section 2 perpetuated the narrow menu of the Blind Persons Act and the National Assistance Act with their needs-based culture that envisaged disabled people as passive recipients.[160] The upshot was provision insensitively dispatched and unimaginatively constructed. For though attitude scales threw up 'a generalized orientation of goodwill' towards social services,[161] digging beneath the surface revealed a raft of procedural and substantive dissatisfactions.

On the procedural front, disabled people objected to long delays, terse consultations, and irregular or unreliable delivery.[162] On the substantive front, both the timing and the content of services failed to match their self-defined requirements. The domestic services were typically timed for once or twice a week during office hours and disabled people complained that more frequent provision with evening and weekend coverage was only exceptionally offered.[163] Furthermore, since home help and meals-on-wheels were interpreted as substitutes for the family, precedence was given to social qualifications like household status and gender when allocations were made and people living alone or without access to a female carer were more likely to receive assistance.[164] The content of the domestic services similarly raised concerns. Client evaluations of home help recorded low standards of cleanliness,[165] whilst meals-on-wheels were described as 'badly cooked and tasteless'.[166] In addition, though home helps were marketed as versatile, clients criticized them for undertaking an inflexible repertoire of tasks.[167] With the professional services, it was their therapeutic aspirations that caused dissonance. Home nurses shared with general practitioners the medical model of health care in which acute but curable illnesses were privileged over long-term, chronic and disabling conditions that demanded personal hygiene more than clinical skills. Nurses were thus reluctant to relieve relatives of their caring function and clinical factors determined regular visits even among those with a higher degree of impairment.[168]

Home nurses were seemingly well received amongst those patients who met their narrow criteria.[169] Conversely, social workers – whose professional credentials were more contested – were subject to greater flack. Until 1971, those based in local authority departments essentially offered disabled people a down-to-earth advice and support service more concentrated on severe impairment and single-person households.[170] Since the 1920s, however, 'the new psychological and psychiatric knowledge that so bedazzled the American social worker' had been a minority interest in Britain.[171] This socio-psychiatric version of the therapeutic or individual model understood impairment as a personal tragedy; in the words of the 1956 Younghusband Report, 'the individual has to learn how to accept it and, in so far as it cannot be overcome, how to live with it.'[172] The unified social services departments that combined care for all client groups also fostered greater professionalization, which in promoting the therapeutic model downgraded 'practical' social work tasks with clients who had little economic potential. Mental illness, with its legal directives, fitted the new template. But other disabled people, whose circumstances held out little prospect of 'cure', found themselves competing less successfully against children and families for qualified social workers and their time.[173] As a result, the response to social work was far from positive, especially among blind people for whom previous provision had been most developed. The competence of social workers as multi-purpose practitioners was questioned.[174] In addition, clients like Mrs Hewson, the mother of a disabled child, queried the relevance of psychological insight: 'When you talk to other people – I mean my husband's mum, she gets grants for clothes and all sorts, and yet it's different when I ask her about it... I still don't know what the social worker's here to do for me.'[175]

The defects in community support services help to explain why requests for (extra) provision were modest. Therefore, in the Southampton study domiciliary chiropody was most sought after with 15 per cent wanting, but not receiving treatment. The mainstream support services, however, had less appeai: 6 per cent wishing for home help; 2 per cent for meals-on-wheels; one per cent for home nursing; and 6 per cent for social work.[176] During the 1970s, both voluntary and statutory organizations attempted to escape from uniform provisions that imposed a 'false homogeneity' upon disabled people.[177] In 1974, for instance, the Crossroads Care Attendant Scheme Trust began to send paid, but unqualified care attendants into the homes of severely disabled people, the aim being to 'bridge the gaps that are left by the existing statutory services... without in any way duplicating the help provided'.[178] Local authorities from Coventry to East Sussex experimented with more intensive home help input. And Kent Social Services Department allowed a small group of social workers to recruit and pay local helpers with a view to preventing the admission of elderly people to residential care.[179] Whilst these schemes diversified previously standardized services, it was only from the early 1980s that the independent living movement demonstrated how disabled people might be empowered to shape their own support mechanisms.[180] The Chronically Sick and Disabled Persons Act thus failed to liberate disabled people from inadequate, needs-based services that compromised their status as citizens.

Conclusion

In this chapter, we have examined the mixed economy of community care. Contrary to claims that the family was broken apart by industrialization, relatives emerged as key players, negotiating institutional admissions and supplying the vast majority of support at home with minimal assistance from neighbours, friends and the voluntary and statutory sectors. Economic priorities ensured that the state was slow to take on responsibility for services, leaving disabled people and their families exposed to stressful caring relationships. Medical relief and boarding out were organized by the poor law authorities, 'panel' doctors and school doctors came into being at the beginning of the twentieth century, and the Ministry of Pensions arranged aids and appliances for disabled ex-servicemen from the end of the First World War. However, it was voluntary societies that experimented with special housing, and they were also heavily involved in administering the 1913 Mental Deficiency Act, the 1920 Blind Persons Act, and the 1948 National Assistance Act. The 1970 Chronically Sick and Disabled Persons Act did increase the availability of statutory services, but they continued to be geographically variable and reached only a small proportion of disabled people who met the narrow, economically rational allocation criteria. Moreover, recipients were dissatisfied with the decision-making procedures and with the timing and content of assistance, which was distributed not as a right but according to professional assessments of need. Therefore, the community care policies in the late 1970s fell short of conveying social citizenship.

9 Conclusion

Disability has been a neglected area of historical enquiry in Britain. Disability studies, whilst recognizing the contemporary significance of the past, have oversimplified the impact of the Industrial Revolution. And though mental impairments have generated a rich historical literature, old age has stimulated relatively little interest, and physical and sensory impairments almost none. *Disability and Social Policy in Britain since 1750* has attempted to construct a history that acknowledges the differences between types of impairment, but explores the common exclusion of disabled people from the full rights of citizenship brought about by their marginality to the labour market. In this conclusion, we summarize the main strands of the argument, consider how policies have developed since 1979, and ask whether disability histories may contribute to the personal and political identities of disabled people.

Institutional living

Recent research in history and the social sciences has attacked the dualism of institutional versus community care. Raymond Jack, for example, has argued for a 'systemic view' that includes 'the family as well as a variety of caring services', and 'conceives of an integrated network of institutions that are interdependent and complementary, rather than more and less desirable or just plain good and bad'.[1] Though institutional living was positively experienced by some disabled people as a safe haven from poverty and discrimination, sequestration was the ultimate form of exclusion. Foucault's 'great confinement' seriously exaggerated the British situation post-1660, but the rise of workhouses, hospitals, asylums and schools did create carceral settings into which disabled people were deposited. Originating in the commercial or voluntary sectors, these new institutions were not primarily the product of an increasingly powerful state; and if after 1800 central government made more strenuous efforts to control the management of workhouses and asylums, their writs were dependent upon agencies of local government. Towards the end of the nineteenth century, a smattering of poor law infirmaries joined the voluntary hospitals that had been in existence from the early eighteenth century and these public hospitals were later relocated with the local authorities that became responsible for special education and the mental deficiency institutions. The voluntary sector continued to supply school places for disabled children. In 1948, however, all medical – but not residential – institutions were transferred to central government with the establishment of the National Health Service.

Economic rationality was so culturally ingrained from before the Industrial Revolution that the mixed economy of institutional provision was no impediment to its application. Schools, whilst articulating their humanitarian goals, placed heavy emphasis on equipping disabled children for economic independence. The workhouse was designed for the able-bodied who failed this test, but its regime of 'less eligibility' extended to all inmates, turning disabled people into 'visible monuments to the fate of others who might no longer chose to subjugate themselves to the disciplinary requirements' of the labour market.[2] Medicine was also harnessed to the pursuit of economic rationality. Like schools, voluntary hospitals stressed their altruistic motives; but well before doctors went into partnership with the nineteenth-century state, hospital treatment was concentrated on patients with the greatest employment potential. Psychiatric medicine was frustrated in its therapeutic aspirations until the drug revolution of the 1950s. From the late Victorian period, however, orthopaedic (and later rehabilitation) medicine began to defend in economic terms its endeavour to return the disabled body to 'normal', pioneering surveillance of the total population for traces of deviancy. Geriatrics, conversely, emerged to free up medical resources for the younger, productive population by diverting elderly people into social rather than health services.

The prominence of economic rationality in justifications for institutional living shaped the citizenship of disabled people. Paternalist obligation did little to protect the civil liberties of asylum patients who were compulsorily detained, and yielded only the most rudimentary mechanisms to regulate institutional conditions. The extension of the franchise in 1867 and 1884–5 ushered in a new era of political citizenship in which a larger segment of the male working class was entitled to exercise the parliamentary vote. But despite assuming that 'all members of society deserve equal inclusion,' liberal democracy also expected its participants to be rational and self-sufficient[3] and so asylum patients and recipients of poor relief were excluded. These electoral changes broadly coincided with a relative decline in Britain's economic performance, an intensification of international rivalries, and growing unease about the social consequences of urbanization. The resulting loss of confidence helped to reconfigure poverty and unemployment. The 'respectable' poor were now regarded as victims of a volatile economy. However, they were sharply differentiated from an underclass or 'residuum' that was regarded as physically and mentally degenerate rather than morally responsible for its social deprivation.[4]

This eugenic emphasis on the hereditary nature of impairment was a major factor in the institutionalization of disabled people in the late nineteenth and early twentieth centuries. Workhouses accommodated an increasing proportion of non-able-bodied paupers, often ignoring calls to relax the harsh regime that applied to 'delinquent' inmates. Asylums expanded in number and size, the patriarchal ethos of the smaller, early institutions giving way to mass living with humiliating practices that on occasions deteriorated into abuse. And special schools multiplied, segregating disabled children in punitive environments that typically offered a substandard education. The eugenic legacy of confinement survived into the post-war period, thus compromising the social rights of the welfare state. Disabled people resisted. However, their isolated acts of rebellion were no match for modern government, which – with assistance from the professions – retained institutional living as a 'dividing practice' for those deemed in breach of the criteria for citizenship.

Community living

Community living was not immune to the forces of exclusion that incarcerated disabled people because their social integration was also conditional upon participation in the labour market. Since the mid-nineteenth century, blind institutions had sought to make their inmates economically active through workshops as well as educational programmes; and the late Victorian reconstitution of poverty and unemployment encouraged the translation of the workshop to physical and mental impairment. Under the influence of the First World War, it matured into a curative centre with jobs geared to physical recovery and economic independence. Prior to 1939, however, most employment initiatives were charitable, segregated and limited to manual craft skills that left disabled people exposed to low wages and unemployment, particularly when the economy sank into recession. Labour shortages during the Second World War briefly sucked them into work, but though the 1944 Act was anticipated as conferring the right to employment, the non-enforcement of its provisions preserved the economic marginality of disabled people and hence undermined their status as citizens of the welfare state.

The intransigence of economic marginality perpetuated the financial exclusion of community living experienced from before the Industrial Revolution. Faced with poor wages, joblessness and the extra costs of impairment, disabled people cobbled together a makeshift domestic economy of support from family and community as well as from mutual aid, charitable assistance and state relief. After the new poor law had dismantled the customary right to assistance that paternalism had endorsed, self-help was the driving force behind all these sources of income. But the lack of entitlement to poor relief was incompatible with political citizenship.[5] Therefore, from the late nineteenth century a series of benefits came into being that were understood as social rights where the qualifying conditions – industrial injury, sickness, old age – were satisfied. Though the Beveridge Report continued in this tradition, the system of social security that it authored was inconsistent with social citizenship. All benefit levels were low. Peripheral to the labour market, however, disabled people were often excluded from national insurance schemes that were available as of right and hence more reliant on means-tested national assistance benefits that were felt to be stigmatizing. Selective benefits later introduced as conditional social rights to meet the special circumstances of impairment failed to suppress this attitude. Therefore, social security was unable to escape the work ethic.

Community care was equally embroiled with economic rationality. The vast majority of disabled people had always lived beyond the walls of the institution with the support of relatives who relieved the state of the costs of caring. Rudimentary health care became available through the poor law, the school medical service, the national insurance 'panel', and the Ministry of Pension's Limb Service. Social care, however, was predominantly the preserve of the charitable sector, which after 1900 forged partnerships with local authorities. This mixed economy persisted into the post-war period with voluntary agencies pioneering facilities like purpose-built accommodation as well as continuing to supply the health and social services that they had organized since the nineteenth century. Over time the statutory duties imposed upon local authorities were extended until the 1970 Chronically Sick and Disabled Persons Act required them to provide a range of support services. Yet the right to community care was an entitlement to access rather than delivery.[6] Therefore, services were allocated according to needs-based criteria that reinforced socio-economic norms, professional personnel giving priority to patients or clients with therapeutic potential. In community as in institutional living, social policies were 'divisive practices' that contrived to make disabled people excluded citizens by implementing the conditions of economic rationality.

Social policies since 1979

In 1979 Margaret Thatcher stormed into office to begin almost 20 years of Conservative rule. Though the public services had been under siege since the economic crisis at the beginning of the decade, her victory marked the final demise of the 'citizenship of entitlement' that had been the emblem of the post-war welfare state. The transition to a 'citizenship of contribution' that privileged obligations over rights was accompanied by an attempt to promote the virtues of self-help and rekindle the *laissez-faire* principles of the mid-nineteenth century. In driving back the frontiers of the state, the Thatcher government envisaged reverting to a mixed economy of welfare in which the commercial, voluntary and informal sectors played an enhanced role. New Labour broadly endorsed this agenda from 1997. Consequently, at the opening of the twenty-first century, there is a party political consensus as to the essential features of disability policy.

In 2000 all disabled people were finally enfranchised when patients detained in mental hospitals became entitled to vote if they were not guilty of a criminal offence.[7] Exercising that formal right is more difficult given the physical inaccessibility of polling stations, the complexities of postal or proxy voting, and the continuing omission of institutionalized disabled people from the electoral register.[8] Yet even voting is no guarantee of political inclusion. Though an ageing population ensures that an increasing proportion of voters are impaired, the electorate as a whole gives priority to the economy and the mainstream health and education services, and favours means-tested provision for the selective services directed towards minority groups. Moreover, the policy-making process between elections is dominated by the interests of professional groups, with occasional reference to the voluntary bodies that traditionally provided services *for* disabled people but failed to involve them in their management structures.[9] Since 1981, however, the British Council of Organizations of Disabled People has co-ordinated a coalition of groups that disabled people themselves control; and it is through this social movement, rather than the formal political system, that the case for an inclusive society based on the extension of rights has been most vigorously articulated.[10]

The social policies put in place during the last quarter-century have done little to advance this cause. In 1983 a new Mental Health Act reconfigured civil rights in relation to mental impairment, replacing the 1959 legislation after a long period of consultation. Three changes were of particular significance. First, the duration of compulsory orders for admission was reduced. Second, definitions were narrowed to remove 'mental handicap' unless there was also 'abnormally aggressive or seriously irresponsible conduct', and sexual deviance, alcoholism and drug abuse unless there was demonstrable evidence of 'mental disorder'. Finally, the consent of patients, and its confirmation by three appointees of the new Mental Health Act Commission, was required before psychosurgery and other 'irreversible or hazardous' treatments were carried out. However, consent to treatment was not demanded for the first three months after admission, and excluded the vast majority of patients who were not compulsorily detained.[11] The 1983 Act is currently under protracted review.[12]

The mental hospitals that accommodated compulsory patients continued to empty in line with the policy of decarceration that had been applied to all institutions for disabled people since the 1960s. Developing effective mechanisms for community living proved more intractable. Social security was in the vanguard of the Thatcher government's reform programme, the ideological significance of financial dependency for individual responsibility singling it out for priority treatment. Following a series of minor amendments, the 1986 Social Security Act scaled down the State Earnings Related Pensions Scheme, replaced supplementary benefit with income support, and inaugurated a discretionary social fund that offered grants and loans to meet exceptional circumstances.[13] For disabled people, the loss of additional payments under the supplementary benefit scheme was devastating because the standardized disability premiums that superseded them were insufficient to compensate for the extra costs of impairment. From the early 1990s, these costs were addressed by a non-contributory, non-means-tested disability living allowance for those under 65 who, though not entitled to the mobility or attendance allowances, were unlikely to find paid employment. The means-tested disability working allowance was designed to offset low wages.[14]

The new allowances did nothing to guarantee disabled people a social right to income maintenance. On the contrary, the continuing use of medical evidence to police assistance, and the ongoing obsession with the preservation of work incentives, perpetuated a labyrinth of benefits that stigmatized claimants and left financial exclusion unresolved.[15] Social security changes in the 1980s also had the unintended effect of increasing institutionalization by footing the bill for the private residential homes that families selected for their elderly relatives. The 1990 NHS and Community Care Act rectified this anomaly.[16] In addition, the Act revolutionized the organization of health and social services, importing market principles from the commercial sector in a bid to improve efficiency. Processes of opting out were set in motion whereby hospitals became self-governing trusts that negotiated contracts for their facilities, and general practitioners became independent fund-holders who met the costs of prescribing and hospital visits for their patients.[17] As a group marginal to the economic rationale for health care, disabled people's right to treatment is a likely victim amidst concern that financial criteria are increasing inequalities by distorting the allocation of resources.[18]

As well as recasting the NHS, the 1990 Act transformed the administration of community care. Care by as opposed to merely in the community had been strenuously promoted for more than a decade, eroding any prior notion of a partnership between the family and the state. Under the new legislation, however, local authority care managers – now responsible for assessing individual need and devising health and social care packages – were instructed to use voluntary and commercial organizations wherever possible.[19] In 1996 the prohibition against local authorities making direct payments to disabled people for the purchase of services was lifted. For those below retirement age who are able to plug into schemes for independent living, the right to funds that enable personalized support without recourse to relatives and friends is empowering.[20] But for the majority of disabled people who rely on the local authority to co-ordinate their services, there is no such autonomy. First, the compassion generated by their 'special needs' compromises the right to assistance. Second, though the mixed economy is justified in terms of consumer power, mean- ingful choices are illusive and narrow profit margins for the companies that trade in social care may produce rigid services of dubious quality.

The housing environment in which community care is conducted underwent similar privatization through the exaltation of home ownership. The rampant inflation of house prices has stretched the finances of lower income groups to breaking point. Yet completions by the voluntary housing associations in no way match the collapse of public sector building and the sale of council dwellings. Therefore, disabled people who are already economically disadvantaged may gravitate towards the shrinking private rented market where amenities are poor.[21] Though govern- ments remain largely indifferent to barrier-free housing in any sector, commercial developers have moved into sheltered accom- modation, taking care to ensure the contractual ejection of owner-occupiers whose welfare requirements become too excessive. Moreover, whilst the contraction of the public sector slowed the construction of special housing, sheltered and purpose-built accommodation was not up for sale.[22] What has to be questioned is the legitimacy of 'ghettos' that in resembling residential care brand their occupants as excluded citizens.

The expanding role of commercial and voluntary provision in housing and community care has reduced the public sector to a safety net that catches the special needs of residual groups. Therefore, in contrast to the social citizenship of the early post-war period, claiming state assistance is no longer 'a guarantee of inclusion' but 'a badge of exclusion'.[23] Only through integration into education and the labour market is full membership of society conferred. Policies in both areas have been wanting. First, the 1988 Education Reform Act, which introduced the National Curriculum, permitted modifications for disabled children at the discretion of head teachers, thus opening the door to inferior teaching that limited life chances.[24] Indeed, implementation of the education clauses of the Disability Discrimination Act were delayed until 2002.[25] Second, with the abolition of the quota in 1994 support for jobs in 'sheltered workshops and reserved occupations gave way to "supported placements" with mainstream employers', signalling a preference for subsidized working that was endorsed by the Disability Working Allowance.[26] Before 1995, disability was a legitimate reason for excluding an employee, even if the impairment had no effect on job performance.[27] Furthermore, the National Minimum Wage, introduced in 1999, has failed to overcome the income inequalities of disabled people at work.[28]

Backing labour market integration represents 'an important paradigm shift in thinking about the welfare state' because it abandons the pursuit of equality for the lesser benchmark of equal opportunity.[29] But under this scenario, integration is executed through paid work that is 'fundamentally unequal'. Therefore, even if 'disabled people achieve equal opportunities within the labour market, it will still be the case that what "integration" means is participation in a capitalist economy driven by profit and based upon exploitation'.[30] In addition, social exclusion is more than financial inequality. Disabled people are also marginalized by the broader 'organization and ethos of society's political, educational, cultural and welfare institutions'.[31] Extending civil, political and social rights is vital in combating this discrimination. The European Convention on Human Rights, absorbed into British law from 1 October 2000,[32] may help to nurture the necessary changes. By focusing on the individual, however, rights run the risk of creating 'the ideological veneer of equality, equity, fairness and justice' that deflects attention from the structural reasons for social exclusion.[33] If social policies are to advance an inclusive society, they must confront the economic rationality that has underpinned these constraints since before the Industrial Revolution and cultivate a model of citizenship for which paid employment is not a qualifying condition.

The relevance of history

When G. R. Elton penned his definitive account of *The Practice of History* in 1969, he urged the discipline to ignore 'the necessarily ignorant demands of "society" ... for immediate applicability'.[34] Historians of social policy are among the many who have discarded this advice and declared that the past does have lessons to teach. It is true that 'on a broader front, certain policy issues, dilemmas, problems and choices do recur in social welfare.' The legacy of the workhouse, for instance, highlights the corrosive effects of selective measures in a society that valorizes individualism and self-help.[35] In practice, however, there are few contemporary problems for which blueprint solutions can be extracted because the old adage that history never repeats itself is a sound one.[36] Therefore, the contemporary relevance of historical enquiry is not confined to policy troubleshooting. Exploring the past is also a cultural practice that enhances how we understand the present and contributes to the reflexivity around which personal and collective identities are woven.

Identities are rooted in the past because unless people know 'where they have been, it is difficult to know where they are going.'[37] Whilst memory was a key factor in structuring fixed identities, it assumes even greater significance as these have become more fluid. With reminiscence, often used as a therapy for elderly people, personal narratives occupy a private space of little relevance beyond the settings in which they are told. History, on the other hand, offers a public space for reflexive interaction with the past, having proved its worth as a 'pedagogical political culture' that helps individuals and social groups to comprehend their 'place in local, national and international realities'.[38] In a recent study of the disabled people's movement, Jane Campbell and Mike Oliver argue that a history of disability is 'not yet feasible' due to 'the neglect of the lives and experiences of disabled people'.[39] Though past exclusion does mean that the historical sources that relate to social policy are heavily skewed towards service providers, their interpretation is open to critical analysis. Just as important, disabled people are themselves contributing personal testimonies of their lives in the twentieth century.

Of course, there is a risk that these narratives are privileged over other accounts, whilst their '"confessional stance"' may affirm 'a fixed "disabled" identity' that either represents all disabled people as '"triumphing over adversity" or...as...pathological objects available for voyeuristic gaze'.[40] Nevertheless, these stories – rich in detail and telling in their condemnation of past practices – may be acts of liberation for those whose self-esteem has been battered by discrimination. In the words of one former patient of a mental deficiency institution: 'I'd just like people to know so they can realize what it was we'd had to go through. It's not true what was written down! They did it just to keep us locked up, so that people would think we're mental!'[41] In placing such experiences within their wider historical context, and searching for their antecedents in previous centuries, this book has aimed to supply the story, or 'chain of events', with a 'discourse' or 'plot' that explains what happened.[42]

Conclusion

Far from being a nostalgic quest for a cosy, comforting past, histories that reveal exploitation have the potential to raise personal and political consciousness. First, they may undermine the passive, tragic assumptions of the medicalized, individual model and shift the burden of responsibility to the economic, social and political organization of society. Second, they may demonstrate that attitudes and policies towards disability are culturally constructed and, consequently, open to change. Third, they may reach disabled people – for example, those with learning difficulties or the impairments of old age – who are not currently active in the disability movement. And, finally, as the record of labour history and women's history testifies, they may encourage the inclusiveness necessary for effective political action, breaking down the artificial divisions between different types of disability.[43] As a non-disabled person, I am a 'positional' rather than an 'organic' observer.[44] It is for disabled people themselves to decide whether this particular study can be put to use in their personal or political emancipation.

Notes

Introduction

1 *Equal Opportunities Review*, 65 (January/February 1996) 31.
2 C. Woodhams and S. Corby, 'Defining Disability in Theory and Practice: A Critique of the British Disability Discrimination Act 1995', *Journal of Social Policy*, 32 (2003) 162–3, 172–4. See also C. Gooding, 'Disability Discrimination Act: From Statute to Practice', *Critical Social Policy*, 20 (2000) 533–6; A. Roulstone, 'The Legal Road to Rights?: Disabling Premises, *Obiter Dicta* and the Disability Discrimination Act 1995', *Disability and Society*, 18 (2003) 122–4.
3 K. Blakemore and R. Drake, *Understanding Equal Opportunity Policies* (Hemel Hempstead: Prentice Hall Europe, 1996) pp. 9–10.
4 C. Barnes, G. Mercer and T. Shakespeare, *Exploring Disability: A Sociological Introduction* (Cambridge: Polity, 1999) p. 220; M. Oliver, *Understanding Disability: From Theory to Practice* (Basingstoke: Macmillan – now Palgrave Macmillan, 1996) pp. 46–9, 52; M. Oliver and C. Barnes, *Disabled People and Social Policy: From Exclusion to Inclusion* (London: Longman, 1998) p. 90.
5 The nature of the Enlightenment, modernity and postmodernity is rehearsed in H. Dunthorne, *The Enlightenment* (London: Historical Association, 1991); R. Porter, *The Enlightenment* (Basingstoke: Macmillan – now Palgrave Macmillan, 1990); K. Kumar, *From Post-Industrial to Post-Modern Society: New Theories of the Contemporary World* (Oxford: Blackwell, 1995); P. Leonard, *Postmodern Welfare: Reconstructing an Emancipatory Project* (London: Sage, 1997); D. Lyon, *Postmodernity* (Buckingham: Open University Press, 1994); M. O'Brien and S. Penna, *Theorizing Welfare: Enlightenment and Modern Society* (London: Sage, 1998) ch. 7; M. Sarup, *Identity, Culture and the Postmodern World* (Edinburgh: Edinburgh University Press, 1996).

6 M. J. Wiener, 'The Unloved State: Twentieth-Century Politics in the Writing of Nineteenth-Century History', *Journal of British Studies*, 33 (1994) 284–90.

7 G. Finlayson, 'A Moving Frontier: Voluntarism and the State in British Social Welfare, 1911–1949', *Twentieth Century British History*, 1 (1990) 183–5.

8 L. Stone, 'Introduction', in L. Stone (ed.), *An Imperial State At War: Britain from 1689 to 1815* (London: Routledge, 1994), pp. 1–2.

9 J. Brewer, *The Sinews of Power: War, Money and the English State, 1688–1783* (London: Unwin Hyman, 1989), pp. xiii–xviii; Stone, 'Introduction', pp. 1–9.

10 P. Harling and P. Mandler, 'From "Fiscal-Military" State to Laissez-Faire State, 1760–1850', *Journal of British Studies*, 32 (1993) 66–70.

11 J. Innes, 'The Domestic Face of the Fiscal-Military State', in Stone (ed.), *Imperial State*, pp. 97–108.

12 M. J. Daunton, 'Payment and Participation: Welfare and State Formation in Britain, 1900–1951', *Past and Present*, 150 (1996) 171.

13 J. Harris, 'Political Thought and the Welfare State, 1870–1940: An Intellectual Framework for British Social Policy', *Past and Present*, 135 (1992) 134–5; J. Lewis, 'Family Provision of Health and Welfare in the Mixed Economy of Care', *Social History of Medicine*, 8 (1995) 3; J. Lewis, 'The Boundary Between Voluntary and Statutory Social Service in the Late Nineteenth and Early Twentieth Centuries', *Historical Journal*, 39 (1996) 176.

14 R. Lowe, 'Welfare's Moving Frontier', *Twentieth Century British History*, 6 (1995) 374.

15 I. Barns, J. Dudley, P. Harris and A. Petersen, 'Introduction: Themes, Context and Perspectives', in A. Petersen, I. Barns, J. Dudley and P. Harris *Poststructuralism, Citizenship and Social Policy* (London: Routledge, 1999) p. 17; M. Bulmer and A. M. Rees, 'Conclusion: Citizenship in the Twenty-first Century', in M. Bulmer and A. M. Rees (eds), *Citizenship Today: The Contemporary Relevance of T. H. Marshall* (London: UCL Press, 1996) pp. 273–4; P. Higgs, 'Risk, Governmentality and the Reconceptualization of Citizenship', in G. Scrambler and P. Higgs (eds), *Modernity, Medicine and Health: Medical Sociology Towards 2000* (London: Routledge, 1998) pp. 186–8; D. King, *In the Name of Liberalism: Illiberal Social Policy in the United States and Britain* (Oxford: Oxford University Press, 1999) pp. 19–21.

16 G. Finlayson, *Citizen, State, and Social Welfare in Britain, 1830–1990* (Oxford: Clarendon Press, 1994) pp. 12–13. See also R. H. Cox, 'The Consequences of Welfare Reform: How Conceptions of Social Rights Are Changing', *Journal of Social Policy*, 27 (1998) 3.

17 United Nations, http://www.un.org/Overview/rights.html, accessed 18 December 2003.

18 Oliver and Barnes, *Disabled People*, pp. 119–22.

19 J. Parker, *Citizenship, Work and Welfare: Searching for the Good Society* (Basingstoke: Macmillan – now Palgrave Macmillan, 1998) p. 8.

20 T. H. Marshall, *Class, Citizenship, and Social Development* (Chicago: University of Chicago Press, 1964) pp. 78–81, 92.

21 W. G. Runciman, 'Why Social Inequalities Are Generated by Social Rights', in Bulmer and Rees (eds), *Citizenship Today*, p. 54.

22 R. Pinker, 'T. H. Marshall', in V. George and R. Page (eds) *Modern Thinkers on Welfare* (Hemel Hempstead: Prentice Hall, 1995) p. 104. See also A. M. Rees, 'T. H. Marshall and the Progress of Citizenship', in Bulmer and Rees (eds), *Citizenship Today*, p. 18.

23 Marshall, *Class*, p. 96.

24 T. Bottomore, 'Citizenship and Social Class, Forty Years On', in T. H. Marshall and T. Bottomore, *Citizenship and Social Class* (London: Pluto, 1992) pp. 90–1; V. George and P. Wilding, *The Impact of Social Policy* (London: Routledge & Kegan Paul, 1984) pp. 66–117; J. Le Grand, *The Strategy of Inequality: Redistribution and the Social Services* (London: Allen & Unwin, 1982) chs 3, 4 and 5; R. Mishra, *Society and Social Policy: Theoretical Perspectives on Welfare* (London: Macmillan, 1977) p. 31; J. Parker, *Social Policy and Citizenship* (London: Macmillan, 1975) pp. 29–50.

25 L. Hollen Lees, *The Solidarities of Strangers: The English Poor Laws and the People, 1700–1948* (Cambridge: Cambridge University Press, 1998) pp. 11, 73–81. Poor relief is discussed more fully in Chapter 2, pp. 20–2 and Chapter 7, pp. 146–50.

26 S. Webb and B. Webb, *English Poor Law History: Part 1. The Old Poor Law* (London: Longman, Green, 1927) p. 406.

27 Marshall, *Class*, pp. 86–8. See also A. Borsay, *Medicine and Charity in Georgian Bath: A Social History of the General Infirmary, c.1739–1830* (Aldershot: Ashgate, 1999), pp. 181–6, 233–7; Rees, 'T. H. Marshall', pp. 7–8; Mishra, *Society*, pp. 27–8.

28 D. Marks, *Disability: Controversial Debates and Psychosocial Perspectives* (London: Routledge, 1999) p. 75. See also Bottomore, 'Citizenship', p. 91; B. Brook, *Feminist Perspectives on the Body* (London: Longman, 1999) p. 97; B. Fawcett, *Feminist Perspectives on Disability* (London: Longman, 2000) pp. 86–7.

29 Bulmer and Rees, 'Conclusion', p. 276.

30 C. L. Bacchi and C. Beasley, 'Citizen Bodies: Is Embodied Citizenship a Contradiction in Terms?', *Critical Social Policy*, 22 (2002) 324–7.

31 B. Grant, *The Deaf Advance: A History of the British Deaf Association* (Edinburgh: Pentland Press, 1990) p. 92.

32 M. Ignatieff, 'Citizenship and Moral Narcissism', *Political Quarterly*, 60 (1989) 71.

33 Oliver, *Understanding Disability*, pp. 67–75.

34 J. Clarke and M. Langan, 'Introduction', in M. Langan (ed.) *Welfare: Needs, Rights and Risks* (London: Routledge, 1998) p.1.

35 C. Barnes, 'Disability Studies: New or Not So New Directions', *Disability and Society*, 14 (1999) 578.

36 P. Beresford, 'What Have Madness and Psychiatric System Survivors Got to Do with Disability and Disability Studies?', *Disability and Society*, 15 (2000) 167–72.

37 B. Gleeson, *Geographies of Disability* (London: Routledge, 1999) p. 201; P. Stastny, 'From Exploitation to Self-Reflection: Representing Persons with Psychiatric Disabilities in Documentary Film', *Literature and Medicine*, 17 (1998) 68–9.

38 M. Priestley, 'Adults Only: Disability, Social Policy and the Life Course', *Journal of Social Policy*, 29 (2000) 431.

39 D. Armstrong, *Political Anatomy of the Body: Medical Knowledge in Britain in the Twentieth Century* (Cambridge: Cambridge University Press, 1983) p. 42; Oliver and Barnes, *Disabled People*, p. 19.

40 A. I. Harris with E. Cox and C. R. W. Smith, *Handicapped and Impaired in Great Britain* (London: HMSO, 1971) pp. 2, 4.

41 P. Abberley, *Handicapped By Numbers: A Critique of the OPCS Disability Surveys*, (Bristol: Bristol Polytechnic, no date) p. 8.

42 P. Townsend, *Poverty in the United Kingdom: A Survey of Household Resources and Standards of Living* (Harmondsworth: Penguin, 1979) p. 691.

43 C. Wright Mills, *The Sociological Imagination*, (Harmondsworth: Penguin, 1970) pp. 14–5; M. Oliver, *Social Work with Disabled People* (Basingstoke: Macmillan, 1983) pp. 15–27.

44 UPIAS, *Fundamental Principles of Disability* (London: Union of the Physically Impaired Against Segregation, 1976) pp. 3–4.

45 M. Oliver, *The Politics of Disablement* (Basingstoke: Macmillan – now Palgrave Macmillan, 1990) pp. 7–8.

46 Oliver and Barnes, *Social Policy*, pp. 15–21. See also Barnes, Mercer and Shakespeare, *Exploring Disability*, pp. 24–6.

47 J. Walmsley and D. Atkinson, 'Oral History and the History of Learning Disability', in J. Bornat, R. Perks, P. Thompson and J. Walmsley (eds), *Oral History, Health and Welfare* (London: Routledge, 2000) pp. 181–5.

48 P. Townsend, 'The Structured Dependency of the Elderly: A Creation of Social Policy in the Twentieth Century', *Ageing and Society*, 1 (1981) 5–6, 9.

49 V. Finkelstein, *Attitudes and Disabled People: Issues for Discussion* (New York: World Rehabilitation Fund, 1980) pp. 8–11.

50 Finkelstein, *Attitudes*, p. 8.

51 D. Stone, *The Disabled State* (Basingstoke: Macmillan, 1984) pp. 15, 21–8, 51.

52 Oliver, *Politics*, pp. 27–30.

53 Gleeson, *Geographies*, pp. 33, 34, 95–7, 100–3, 106–10.

54 Gleeson, *Geographies*, p. 59.

55 These issues are discussed fully in C. Barnes and G. Mercer (eds), *Exploring the Divide: Illness and Disability* (Leeds: Disability Press, 1996). See also C. Tregaskis, 'Social Model Theory: The Story So Far...', *Disability and Society*, 17 (2002) 464–5.

56 Barnes, Mercer and Shakespeare, *Exploring Disability*, pp. 86–91; Fawcett, *Feminist Perspectives*, p. 37; K. Patterson and B. Hughes, 'Disability Studies and Phenomenology: The Carnal Politics of Everyday Life', *Disability and Society*, 14 (1999) 599; C. Phillipson, *Reconstructing Old Age: New Agendas in Social Theory and Practice* (London: Sage, 1998), pp. 13–14, 21–3.

57 Oliver and Barnes, *Disabled People*, p. xv.

58 C. Barnes, *Disabled People in Britain and Discrimination: A Case for Anti-Discrimination Legislation* (London: Hurst, 1991) pp. 11–15; C. Barnes, 'Theories of Disability and the Origins of the Oppression of Disabled People in Western Society', in L. Barton (ed.), *Disability and Society: Emerging Issues and Insights* (London: Longman, 1996) pp. 49, 51–6.

59 E. J. Evans, *The Forging of the Modern State: Early Industrial Britain, 1783–1870* (London: Longman, 1983) p. 103.

60 A. Borsay, *Disabled People People in the Community: A Study of Housing, Health and Welfare Services* (London: Bedford Square Press, 1986) pp. 4–6.

61 A. P. Donajgrodzki, 'Introduction', in A. P. Donajgrodzki (ed.), *Social Control in Nineteenth Century Britain* (London: Croom Helm, 1977) p. 9.

62 C. Shore and S. Wright, 'Policy: A New Field of Anthropology', in C. Shore and S. Wright (eds) *Anthropology of Policy: Critical Perspectives on Governance and Power* (London: Routledge, 1997) p. 5.

63 P. Burke, *History and Social Theory* (Cambridge: Polity, 1992) pp. 85–6.

64 M. Foucault, *Discipline and Punish: The Birth of the Prison* (Harmondsworth: Penguin, 1979) pp. 198–9.

65 M. Foucault, 'Two Lectures', in C. Gordon (ed.), *Michel Foucault Power/Knowledge: Selected Interviews and Other Writings, 1972–1977* (Brighton: Harvester Press, 1980) pp. 98, 142. See also M. Foucault,

The History of Sexuality: Volume 1. An Introduction (Harmondsworth: Penguin, 1981) p. 94.

66 Foucault, 'Two Lectures', p. 65. See also Leonard, *Postmodern Welfare*, pp. 16–17.

67 Armstrong, *Political Anatomy*, pp. 9, 11, 42, 51, 64, 66–7, 86–7. See also V. Berridge, *Health and Society in Britain Since 1939* (Cambridge: Cambridge University Press, 1999) pp. 48–52; M. Bury, 'Postmodernity and Health', in Scrambler and Higgs (eds), *Modernity*, pp. 10–11; Higgs, 'Risk', pp. 189–90; King, *In the Name*, p. 10.

68 B. S. Turner, *Medical Power and Social Knowledge* (London: Sage, 1987) p. 217.

69 D. Gladstone, *The Twentieth-Century Welfare State* (Basingstoke: Macmillan – now Palgrave Macmillan, 1999) p. 113; Leonard, *Postmodern Welfare*, pp. 96–100.

70 Bury, 'Postmodernity', p. 23.

71 Shore and Wright, 'Policy', p. 29.

72 D. Taylor, 'Social Identity and Social Policy', *Journal of Social Policy*, 27 (1998) 333.

73 L. H. Martin, H. Gutman and P. H. Hutton (eds), *Technologies of the Self: A Seminar with Michel Foucault* (London: Tavistock, 1988) p. 18.

74 A. Giddens, *Modernity and Self-Identity: Self and Society in the Late Modern Age* (Cambridge: Polity, 1991) p. 5. See also Leonard, *Postmodern Welfare*, pp. 32–60; Sarup, *Identity*, pp. 14, 47–8, 88.

75 Foucault, 'Two Lectures', p. 98; Foucault, *History*, p. 94.

2 Workhouses

1 M. Foucault, *Madness and Civilization: A History of Insanity in the Age of Reason* (London: Tavistock, 1965) pp. 35–60.

2 W. Higgins, 'To Him That Hath…: The Welfare State', in R. Kennedy (ed.), *Australian Welfare History: Critical Essays* (Melbourne: Macmillan, 1982) p. 105.

3 R. Porter, *Mind-Forg'd Manacles: A History of Madness in England from the Restoration to the Regency* (Harmondsworth: Penguin, 1987) pp. 5–9.

4 Commission of the European Communities, *Background Report: Social Exclusion – Poverty and Other Social Problems in the European Community* (Luxembourg: Office for Official Publications of the European Communities, 1993) p. 1.

5 J. Keithley, 'Review of M. Purdy and D. Banks (eds), *Health and Exclusion: Policy and Practice in Health Provision*, London: Routledge, 1999', in *Journal of Social Policy*, 29 (2000) 154.

6   P. Dwyer, *Welfare Rights and Responsibilities: Contesting Social Citizenship* (Bristol: Policy Press, 2000) pp. 7–8; R. Levitas, 'The Concept of Social Exclusion and the New Durkheimian Hegemony', *Critical Social Policy*, 16 (1996) 8; J. Percy-Smith, 'Introduction: The Contours of Social Exclusion', in J. Percy-Smith (ed.), *Policy Responses to Social Exclusion: Towards Inclusion?* (Buckingham: Open University Press, 2000) p. 2

7   Keithley, 'Review', 154.

8   M. Daunton, *Progress and Poverty: An Economic and Social History of Britain 1700–1850* (Oxford: Oxford University Press, 1995) pp. 463–7.

9   S. King, *Poverty and Welfare in England: A Regional Perspective* (Manchester: Manchester University Press, 2000) p. 20; P. Murray, *Poverty and Welfare, 1830–1914* (London: Hodder & Stoughton, 1999) pp. 16–18.

10   Daunton, *Progress*, pp. 453–4; T. V. Hitchcock, 'The English Workhouse: A Study in Institutional Poor Relief in Selected Counties, 1696–1750', (University of Oxford, D.Phil. thesis, 1985) p. 250; King, *Poverty*, pp. 24–5; P. Slack, *The English Poor Law, 1531–1782* (Basingstoke: Macmillan – now Palgrave Macmillan, 1990) pp. 41–4; P. Slack, *Poverty and Policy in Tudor and Stuart England* (London: Longman, 1988) pp. 195–200.

11   E. G. Thomas, 'The Old Poor Law and Medicine', *Medical History*, 24 (1980) 6.

12   Porter, *Mind-Forg'd Manacles*, p. 117.

13   J. Crowley and A. Reid (eds), *The Poor Law in Norfolk, 1700–1850: A Collection of Source Material* (Ely: EARO, Resource and Technology Centre, 1983) p. 42.

14   Inscription over the entrance, in K. Morrison, *The Workhouse: A Study of Poor-Law Buildings in England* (Swindon: English Heritage, 1999) p. 21.

15   G. W. Oxley, *Poor Relief in England and Wales, 1601–1834* (Newton Abbot: David and Charles, 1974) pp. 90–2. See also Hitchcock, 'English Workhouse', ch. 7.

16   Daunton, *Progress*, p. 455.

17   Crowley and Reid (eds), *Poor Law*, pp. 50, 64; R. P. Hastings, *Poverty and the Poor Law in the North Riding of Yorkshire, c.1780–1837* (York: Borthwick Institute of Historical Research, 1982) pp. 22–3; Morrison, *Workhouse*, p. 16.

18   P. Thane, *Old Age in English History: Past Experiences, Present Issues* (Oxford: Oxford University Press, 2000) pp. 116–17, 157–8.

19   S. G. Checkland and E. O. A. Checkland (eds) *The Poor Law Report of 1834* (Harmondsworth: Penguin, 1974) p. 57. See also D. Englander,

Poverty and Poor Law Reform in Nineteenth-Century Britain, 1834–1914 (Harlow: Longman, 1998) pp. 13–15; A. Kidd, *State, Society and the Poor in Nineteenth-Century England* (Basingstoke: Macmillan – now Palgrave Macmillan, 1999) pp. 26–8; D. King, *In the Name of Liberalism: Illiberal Social Policy in the United States and Britain* (Oxford: Oxford University Press) p. 302; D. King, *Poverty*, pp. 27–9.

20 A. Paterson, 'The Poor Law in Nineteenth-Century Scotland', in D. Fraser (ed.) *The New Poor Law in the Nineteenth Century* (London: Macmillan, 1976) pp. 171–93.

21 D. Ashforth, 'The Urban Poor Law', in Fraser (ed.) *New Poor Law*, pp. 131–2; A. Digby, 'The Labour Market and the Continuity of Social Policy After 1834: The Case of the Eastern Counties', *Economic History Review*, XXVIII (1975) 69–83; M. E. Rose, *The Relief of Poverty, 1834–1914* (London: Macmillan, 1972) p. 12.

22 King, *Poverty*, pp. 10, 234–6, 249–51, 256–9.

23 Englander, *Poverty*, p. 16; D. G. Wright, *Popular Radicalism: The Working-Class Experience 1780–1880* (London: Longman, 1988) pp. 106–10.

24 King, *In the Name*, p. 302; L. Hollen Lees, *The Solidarities of Strangers: The English Poor Laws and the People, 1700–1948* (Cambridge: Cambridge University Press) p. 41; M. Thomson, *The Problem of Mental Deficiency: Eugenics, Democracy, and Social Policy in Britain, c.1870–1959* (Oxford: Clarendon Press, 1998) pp. 6, 37, 51–4, 304.

25 Lees, *Solidarities*, pp. 154–65.

26 K. Williams, *From Pauperism to Poverty* (London: Routledge & Kegan Paul, 1981) pp. 53, 57. See also King, *Poverty*, pp. 21, 29; Lees, *Solidarities*, p. 141; Rose, *Relief*, p. 12.

27 Lees, *Solidarities*, pp. 121–6.

28 Rose, *Relief*, p. 14.

29 Williams, *From Pauperism*, pp. 158–62 Table 4.5, pp. 204–5 Table 4.23, p. 231 Table 4.39.

30 A. Savidge, *Royal Tunbridge Wells* (Tunbridge Wells: Midas, 1975) p. 121.

31 Crowley and Reid (eds), *Poor Law*, pp. 129, 134; F. Driver, *Power and Pauperism: The Workhouse System, 1834–1884* (Cambridge: Cambridge University Press, 1993) p. 59; P. Hembry, *British Spas from 1815 to the Present: A Social History* (London: Athlone, 1997) p. 106; T. A. Markus, *Buildings and Power: Freedom and Control in the Origin of Modern Building Types* (London: Routledge, 1993) pp. 141–2; Morrison, *Workhouse*, pp. 43–5; H. Richardson, *English Hospitals, 1660–1948* (Swindon: English Heritage, 1998) pp. 55–6.

32 Markus, *Buildings*, pp. 142, 144; Morrison, *Workhouse*, pp. 87–8, 113; Williams, *From Pauperism*, p. 116.

33 Morris, *Workhouse*, p. 194.

34 I. Anstruther, *The Scandal of the Andover Workhouse* (London: Geoffrey Bles, 1973) pp. 93–5. See also A. Crowther, *The Workhouse System, 1834–1929: The History of an English Social Institution* (London: Methuen, 1981) p. 44; Englander, *Poverty*, pp. 38–9.

35 Anstruther, *Scandal*, pp. 75–6. See also A. Brundage, *The Making of the New Poor Law 1832–1839* (London: Hutchinson, 1978) p. 157.

36 A. Digby, *Pauper Palaces* (London: Routledge & Kegan Paul, 1978) pp. 163–5. See also Crowther, *Workhouse System*, p. 44; R. G. Hodgkinson, *The Origins of the National Health Service: Medical Services of the New Poor Law, 1834–1871* (London: Wellcome Historical Medical Library, 1967) pp. 547–9; Murray, *Poverty*, p. 52.

37 Digby, *Pauper Palaces*, p. 163; Hodgkinson, *Origins*, p. 546; A. Reid, *The Union Workhouse: A Study Guide for Teachers and Local Historians* (Chichester: Phillemore, 1994) p. 6.

38 Englander, *Poverty*, p. 39; Hodgkinson, *Origins*, p. 152.

39 Crowther, *Workhouse System*, p. 198.

40 Anstruther, *Scandal*, pp. 87, 88, 133.

41 Driver, *Power*, pp. 105–11; Hodgkinson, *Origins*, p. 184; Morrison, *Workhouse*, pp. 161–3; Williams, *From Pauperism*, p. 215 Table 4.31; D. Wright, 'Learning Disability and the New Poor Law in England, 1834–1867', *Disability and Society*, 15 (2000) 735, 737.

42 P. Bartlett, *The Poor Law of Lunacy: The Administration of Pauper Lunatics in Mid-Nineteenth-Century England* (London: Leicester University Press, 1999) p. 47.

43 Hodgkinson, *Origins*, p. 172.

44 H. Taine, *Notes on England* (1874) pp. 300–2, in M. E. Rose (ed.), *The English Poor Law* (Newton Abbot: David and Charles, 1971) pp. 169–71.

45 Hodgkinson, *Origins*, p. 172.

46 Ashforth, 'Urban Poor Law', p. 139.

47 C. Dickens, 'A Walk in a Workhouse', *Household Words* (25 May 1850), in C. Dickens, *Selected Journalism 1850–1870* (Harmondsworth: Penguin, 1997) p. 239.

48 Hodgkinson, *Origins*, p. 474.

49 Wright, 'Learning Disability', 740.

50 Hodgkinson, *Origins*, p. 469.

51 S. Webb and B. Webb, *English Poor Law History: Part 2. The Last Hundred Years* (London: Longmans, Green, 1929) p. 140.

52 Hodgkinson, *Origins*, p. 507.

53 Williams, *From Pauperism*, pp. 158–62 Table 4.5, 169–72 Table 4.6.

54 M. E. Rose, 'The Crisis of Poor Relief in England, 1860–1890', in W. J. Mommsen (ed.), *The Emergence of the Welfare State in Britain and Germany, 1850–1950* (London: Croom Helm, 1981) pp. 54–8.

55 Englander, *Poverty*, p. 106.

56 Williams, *From Pauperism*, p. 97.

57 R. Humphreys, *Sin, Organized Charity and the Poor Law in Victorian England* (Basingstoke: Macmillan – now Palgrave Macmillan, 1995) pp. 22, 31, 171.

58 Thane, *Old Age*, p. 172–3.

59 Humphreys, *Sin*, p. 32.

60 Crowther, *Workhouse System*, pp. 89–90. See also Hodgkinson, *Origins*, pp. 508, 513–4; Morrison, *Workhouse*, pp. 106–8, 110, 119; Richardson, *English Hospitals*, p. 66.

61 L. M. Edwards, 'Hubert von Herkomer: "Sympathy for the Old and for Suffering Mankind"', in J. Treuherz (ed.), *Hard Times: Social Realism in Victorian Art* (London: Lund Humphries, 1987) pp. 90, 93–5.

62 J. Treuherz, 'Introduction', in Treuherz (ed.), *Hard Times*, p. 9.

63 Edwards, 'Hubert von Herkomer', pp. 93–4.

64 Edwards, 'Hubert von Herkomer', pp. 90, 95; Treuherz, 'Introduction', p. 13.

65 B. Abel-Smith, *The Hospitals, 1800–1948: A Study in Social Administration in England and Wales* (London: Heinemann, 1964) p. 212.

66 H. Gough, 'The Blean Union Workhouse: The Medical Officer's Report Book (Part Two)', *Bygone Kent*, 14 (1993) 277–8.

67 Lees, *Solidarities*, p. 295.

68 See Chapter 7, pp. 156–7.

69 Local Government Board, *Thirtieth Annual Report*, no. 11 (1900–01), Appendix A, in Rose, *English Poor Law*, pp. 252–4. See also Englander, *Poverty*, p. 26; Williams, *From Pauperism*, p. 119.

70 See Chapter 5, pp. 101–3.

71 Morrison, *Workhouse*, pp. 173–4.

72 A. Digby, 'The Rural Poor Law', in Fraser (ed.), *New Poor Law*, p. 169.

73 P. Townsend, *The Last Refuge: A Survey of Residential Institutions and Homes for the Aged in England and Wales* (London: Routledge & Kegan Paul, 1964) p. 16.

74 Rose, *Relief*, pp. 44–5.

75 Crowther, *Workhouse System*, pp. 90–1; Thomson, *Problem*, p. 102.

76 Lees, *Solidarities*, p. 335; R. Means and R. Smith, 'From Public Assistance Institutions to "Sunshine Hotels": Changing State Perceptions About Residential Care for Elderly People, 1939–1948', *Ageing and Society*, 3 (1983) 160–1.

77   *The Problem of the Deaf: A Handbook of Information on Deafness, the Deaf and Dumb and the Deafened Through Disease or Accident* (London: National Institute for the Deaf, 1939) pp. 20–1.

78   See, for example, H. Dunbar, *History of the Society for the Blind in Glasgow and the West of Scotland, 1859–1989* (Glasgow: Glasgow and West of Scotland Society for the Blind, 1989) p. 64.

79   Lord Fraser of Lonsdale, *My Story of St Dunstan's* (London: Harrap, 1961) pp. 184–5.

80   See, for example, Royal National Institution for Deaf People, www.rnid.org.uk/whatis/history.html, accessed 30 April 2000.

81   Means and Smith, 'From Public Assistance Institutions', 162–71; J. Parker, *Local Health and Welfare Services* (London: Allen & Unwin, 1965) pp. 106–7.

82   Means and Smith, 'From Public Assistance Institutions', 173–4.

83   Townsend, *Last Refuge*, p. 21.

84   Townsend, *Last Refuge*, pp. 21, 29–34, 39, 82–3, 84–5.

85   J. Adams, 'The Last Years of the Workhouse, 1930–1965', in J. Bornat, R. Perks, P. Thompson and J. Walmsley (eds), *Oral History, Health and Welfare* (London: Routledge, 2000) p. 109.

86   Townsend, *Last Refuge*, p. 22 Table 1.

87   J. Campbell and M. Oliver, *Disability Politics: Understanding Our Past, Changing Our Future* (London: Routledge, 1996) p. 29; R. Means and R. Smith, *Community Care: Policy and Practice* (Basingstoke: Macmillan, 1994) p. 27.

88   C. Barnes, G. Mercer and T. Shakespeare, *Exploring Disability: A Sociological Introduction* (Cambridge: Polity, 1999) pp. 213–14.

89   E. J. Miller and G. V. Gwynne, *A Life Apart: A Pilot Study of Residential Institutions for the Physically Handicapped and the Young Chronic Sick* (London: Tavistock, 1972) p. 161.

90   Barnes, Mercer and Shakespeare, *Exploring Disability*, pp. 148–9.

91   D. Thomson, 'Workhouse to Nursing Home: Residential Care of Elderly People in England Since 1840', *Ageing and Society*, 3 (1983) 54, 60.

92   Crowther, *Workhouse System*, pp. 225–6.

93   Englander, *Poverty*, p. 34.

94   Williams, *From Pauperism*, p. 208 Table 4.27.

95   M. Pelling and R. M. Smith, 'Introduction', in M. Pelling and R. M. Smith (eds), *Life, Death and the Elderly: Historical Perspectives* (London: Routledge, 1991) pp. 17–9.

96   See, for example, E. J. Evans, *The Forging of the Modern State: Early Industrial Britain, 1783–1870* (London: Longman, 1983) pp. 148–56.

97   M. Loane, *The Queen's Poor: Life As They Find It in Town and Country* (London: Middlesex University Press, 1998) p. 95.

98 Crowther, *Workhouse System*, p. 240. See also P. Horn (ed.), *Oxfordshire Village Life: The Diaries of George James Dew (1846–1928), Relieving Officer* (Abingdon: Beacon, 1983) pp. 20, 76, 81–2; F. Thompson, *Larkrise to Candleford* (Harmondsworth: Penguin, 1973) pp. 89–90.

99 A. Reid, *Gressenhall Workhouse: An Historical Introduction* (Norwich: Norfolk Museums Service, 1988) p. 4.

100 Crowther, *Workhouse System*, p. 221; Englander, *Poverty*, pp. 41–4.

101 Reid, *Union Workhouse*, p. 59.

102 A. Robbins, *The Workhouses of Purton and the Cricklade and Wootton Bassett Union* (Purton, Wiltshire: Purton Historical Society, 1992) p. 110.

103 S. Humphries and P. Gordon, *Out of Sight: The Experience of Disability, 1900–1950* (Plymouth: Northcote House, 1992) p. 87.

104 For appraisals of oral testimony as a methodology, see S. Caunce, *Oral History and the Local Historian* (London: Longman, 1994); P. Thompson, *The Voice of the Past* (Oxford: Oxford University Press, 1978); E. Tonkin, *Narrating Our Pasts: The Social Construction of Oral History* (Cambridge: Cambridge University Press, 1992).

3 Hospitals

1 N. D. Jewson, 'The Disappearance of the Sick Man from Medical Cosmology', *Sociology*, 10 (1976) 225–44. See also N. D. Jewson, 'Medical Knowledge and the Patronage System in Eighteenth-Century England', *Sociology*, 8 (1974) 370–3; C. Lawrence, *Medicine in the Making of Modern Britain, 1700–1920* (London: Routledge, 1994) pp. 11–12, 29–32, 72–3; R. Porter, *The Greatest Benefit to Mankind: A Medical History of Humanity From Antiquity to the Present* (London: HarperCollins, 1997) ch. XI.

2 R. Porter, 'The Gift Relation', in L. Granshaw and R. Porter (eds), *The Hospital in History* (London: Routledge, 1989) pp. 156–7.

3 J. Woodward, *To Do the Sick No Harm: A Study of the British Voluntary Hospital System to 1875* (London: Routledge & Kegan Paul, 1974) pp. 147–8 Appendix 1.

4 R. Pinker, *English Hospital Statistics, 1861–1938* (London: Heinemann, 1966) p. 57 Table 7.

5 S. Cherry, *Medical Services and the Hospitals, 1860–1939* (Cambridge: Cambridge University Press, 1996) pp. 71–4; J. Mohan, *Planning, Markets and Hospitals* (London: Routledge, 2002) pp. 21–37.

6 Robert Jones and Agnes Hunt Orthopaedic Hospital, Oswestry, *Annual Report* (1945) p. 19.

7   B. Abel-Smith, *The Hospitals, 1800–1948: A Study in Social Adminis-tration in England and Wales* (London: Heinemann, 1964) pp. 83, 94–6, 202–4, 207–9; A. Crowther, *The Workhouse System, 1834–1929: The History of an English Social Institution* (London: Methuen, 1981) p. 183; M. W. Flinn, 'Medical Services under the New Poor Law', in D. Fraser (ed.), *The New Poor Law in the Nineteenth Century* (London: Macmillan, 1976) pp. 47–8, 55–6, 65; R. Means and R. Smith, *From Poor Law to Community Care: The Development of Welfare Services for Elderly People, 1939–1971* (Bristol: Policy Press, 1998) p. 19; J. Parker, *Local Health and Welfare Services* (London: Allen & Unwin, 1965) p. 31; C. Webster, 'The Elderly and the Early National Health Service', in M. Pelling and R. Smith (eds), *Life, Death and the Elderly: Historical Perspectives* (London: Routledge, 1999) p. 167.

8   National Health Service Act 1946, para. 1.

9   H. Dean, *Welfare Rights and Social Policy* (Harlow: Pearson Education, 2002) p. 147.

10 V. Berridge, *Health and Society in Britain Since 1939* (Cambridge: Cambridge University Press, 1999) pp. 27–8.

11 A. Walker, *Social Planning: A Strategy for Socialist Welfare* (Oxford: Blackwell, 1984) pp. 166–8.

12 M. Foucault, *Discipline and Punish: The Birth of the Prison* (Harmonsworth: Penguin, 1979) p. 27.

13 A. Borsay, *Medicine and Charity in Georgian Bath: A Social History of the General Infirmary, c.1739–1830* (Aldershot: Ashgate, 1999); Porter, 'Gift Relation', pp. 149–72.

14 I. Loudon, *Medical Care and the General Practitioner, 1750–1850* (Oxford: Clarendon Press, 1986) p. 19.

15 Woodward, *To Do the Sick No Harm*, pp. 7, 9.

16 'Rules and Orders of the Public Infirmary at Liverpool', in G. McLoughlin, *A Short History of the First Liverpool Infirmary, 1749–1824* (Chichester: Phillimore, 1978) p. 74.

17 M. E. Fissell, *Patients, Power and the Poor in Eighteenth-Century Bristol* (Cambridge: Cambridge University Press, 1991) p. 103 Table 5.1. See also C. Edwards, 'Age-Based Rationing of Medical Care in Nineteenth-Century England', *Continuity and Change*, 14 (1999) 227–51.

18 J. Wood, *A Description of Bath 1765* (Bath: Kingsmead Reprints, 1969) p. 279.

19 Borsay, *Medicine*, pp. 225–8.

20 Royal National Hospital for Rheumatic Diseases, Minute Book, 16 Feb. 1738.

21 Borsay, *Medicine*, p. 216–22 Tables 7.1, 7.2, 7.3 and 7.4. Colica pictonum or lead poisoning was a form of paralysis accompanied by

gastro-intestinal pain and fever, vomiting and costiveness. Patients at the near-contemporary Bristol Infirmary clocked up an average stay of 43 days and those at Northampton 105 days. The Salop Infirmary in Shrewsbury normally reported a minimum success rate of 50 per cent, whilst at Liverpool eight out of ten patients were regularly described as 'cured' at least until the second decade of the nineteenth century.

22 Fissell, *Patients*, p. 108; Jewson, 'Medical knowledge', 370–3; Lawrence, *Medicine*, pp. 11–2.

23 A. Borsay, 'Returning Patients to the Community: Disability, Medicine and Economic Rationality Before the Industrial Revolution', *Disability and Society*, 13 (1998) 656–7.

24 Borsay, *Medicine*, pp. 360–2.

25 W. B. Howie, 'Consumer Reaction: A Patient's View of Hospital Life in 1809', *British Medical Journal* (8 September 1973) 534–6.

26 M. E. Fissell, 'The Disappearance of the Patient's Narrative and the Invention of Hospital Medicine', in R. French and A. Wear (eds), *British Medicine in an Age of Reform* (London: Routledge, 1991) pp. 92–4, 100–6.

27 S. Hogarth, ' Joseph Townend and the Manchester Infirmary: A Plebeian Patient at the End of the Long Eighteenth Century', in A. Borsay and P. Shapely (eds), *Medicine, Charity and Mutual Aid: The Consumption of Health and Welfare, c.1550–1950* (Aldershot: Ashgate, forthcoming).

28 L. Granshaw, '"Fame and Fortune by Means of Bricks and Mortar": The Medical Profession and Specialist Hospitals in Britain, 1800–1948', in Granshaw and Porter (eds), *Hospital*, pp. 199–200, 202–4.

29 N. R. Smith, *Elements of Orthopaedic Surgery* (Bristol and London: John Wright and Simpkin Marshall, 1937) p. 1.

30 H.-J. Stiker, *A History of Disability*, (Ann Arbor: University of Michigan Press, 1999) p. 114.

31 M. W. White, *Years of Caring: The Royal Orthopaedic Hospital* (Studley: Brewin, 1997) pp. 15, 18–9.

32 J. A. Cholmeley, *History of the Royal National Orthopaedic Hospital* (London: Chapman & Hall, 1985) pp. 1–3.

33 R. Cooter, *Surgery and Society in Peace and War: Orthopaedics and the Organization of Modern Medicine, 1880–1948* (Basingstoke: Macmillan – now Palgrave Macmillan, 1993) pp. 15–17.

34 Cooter, *Surgery*, pp. 18–24.

35 See Chapter 5 pp. 105–6.

36 Report of the Inter-Departmental Committee on Physical Deterioration, Cmnd 2175 (London: HMSO, 1904) pp. 13–14, in E. J. Evans (ed.), *Social Policy, 1830–1914: Individualism, Collectivism*

and the Origins of the Welfare State (London: Routledge & Kegan Paul, 1978) pp. 227–8.

37 Cooter, *Surgery*, pp. 53–64.

38 A. G. Hunt, 'Baschurch and After: 1. The Birth of a Pioneer Hospital', *The Cripples' Journal*, 1 (1924) 18–23; A. G. Hunt, 'Baschurch and After: 2. Fourteen Years On', *The Cripples' Journal*, 1 (1924) 86–94; A. G. Hunt, 'Baschurch and After: 3. During the War', *The Cripples' Journal*, 1 (1924) 180–5.

39 Cooter, *Surgery*, pp. 105–6, 164; R. Jones, *An Address on the Orthopaedic Outlook in Military Surgery* (London: British Medical Association, 1918) pp. 3–4.

40 J. S. Reznick, 'Work-Therapy and the Disabled British Soldier in Great Britain in the First World War: The Case of Shepherd's Bush Military Hospital, London', in D. A. Gerber (ed.), *Disabled Veterans in History* (Ann Arbor: University of Michigan Press, 2000) pp. 198–9.

41 J. Lynn-Thomas, 'Crippledom in Wales', *The Cripples' Journal*, 1 (1924) 61.

42 Cooter, *Surgery*, pp. 152, 153, 157–9, 166. See also D. Cantor, 'The Aches of Industry: Philanthropy and Rheumatism in Inter-War Britain', in J. Barry and C. Jones (eds), *Medicine and Charity Before the Welfare State* (London: Routledge, 1991) pp. 225–45.

43 G. R. Girdlestone, *The Care and Cure of Crippled Children* (Bristol and London: J. Wright and S. Marshall, 1924) p. 3.

44 J. Anderson. *A Record of Fifty Years Service to the Disabled by the Central Council for the Disabled* (London: Central Council for the Disabled, 1969) pp. 8–9, 29.

45 D. Armstrong, *Political Anatomy of the Body: Medical Knowledge in Britain in the Twentieth Century* (Cambridge: Cambridge University Press, 1983) p. 9.

46 Nottingham District Cripples' Guild, *Annual Report* (1915) p. 8; Nottingham District Cripples' Guild, *Annual Report* (1939) pp. 5–7.

47 J. Bourke, *Dismembering the Male: Men's Bodies, Britain and the Great War* (London: Reaktion Books, 1996) pp. 52–3.

48 Girdlestone, *Care*, pp. 21, 30.

49 Princess Elizabeth Orthopaedic Hospital, Exeter, House Visitors Report Book (1928–54) 16 June 1937. See also 15 June 1935; 28 Dec. 1942; 13 Nov. 1945.

50 S. Humphries and P. Gordon, *Out of Sight: The Experience of Disability, 1900–1950* (Plymouth: Northcote House, 1992) pp. 16–19; White, *Years*, p. 196.

51 Princess Elizabeth Orthopaedic Hospital, Exeter, Hospital Management and Other Committee Minutes, 19 Mar. 1931.

52 Princess Elizabeth Orthopaedic Hospital, Exeter, Hospital Management and Other Committee Minutes, 16 May 1929.

53 White, *Years*, pp. 196–7, 205.

54 Humphries and Gordon, *Out of Sight*, pp. 80–1, 92–6.

55 J. Stevenson, *Social Conditions in Britain Between the Wars* (Harmondsworth: Penguin, 1977) p. 157.

56 T. Gould, *A Summer Plague: Polio and Its Survivors* (New Haven, CT, and London: Yale University Press, 1995) pp. 229–39.

57 M. Oswin, *The Empty Hours: A Study of the Week-End Life of Handicapped Children in Institutions* (London: Allen Lane, 1971) pp. 63, 80–3.

58 See, for example, 'Rules and Orders of the Public Infirmary at Manchester, 1752', in W. Brockbank, *Portrait of a Hospital, 1752–1948 to Commemorate the Bi-Centenary of the Royal Infirmary, Manchester* (London: William Heinemann, 1952) p. 206; 'Rules and Orders of the Public Infirmary at Liverpool', p. 71.

59 J. Kirkup, 'A Pioneer Accident Service: Bath Casualty Hospital, 1788–1826', in R. Rolls, J. Guy and J. R. Guy (eds), *A Pox on the Provinces: Proceedings of the Twelfth Congress of the British Society for the History of Medicine* (Bath: Bath University Press, 1990) pp. 51–7.

60 Cooter, *Surgery*, pp. 100–4.

61 S. J. Woodall, *The Manor House Hospital: A Personal Record* (London: Routledge & Kegan Paul, 1966) pp. 12, 14, 17, 23, 46–7, 70–1, 117–18.

62 R. Cooter, 'The Moment of the Accident: Culture, Militarism and Modernity in Late-Victorian Britain', in R. Cooter and B. Luckin (eds) *Accidents in History: Injuries, Fatalities and Social Relations* (Amsterdam: Rodopi, 1997) p. 114.

63 F. Honigsbaum, *The Division in British Medicine: A History of the Separation of General Practice from Hospital Care, 1911–1968* (London: Kogan Page, 1979) p. 240.

64 L. Duncombe, D. Page, M. Price, D. Stokes and S. Willcox (eds) *Under the Doctor* (Pontypool: Village Publishing, 1995) p. 32. Unfortunately, this oral testimony is undated, but in all probability it relates to the inter-war period.

65 Cooter, *Surgery*, pp. 184–5.

66 Cooter, *Surgery*, pp. 141–2; Honigsbaum, *Division*, pp. 239–41. Workmen's compensation is also discussed in Chapter 7, pp. 155–6.

67 R. M. Titmuss, *Problems of Social Policy* (London: HMSO, 1950) pp. 476–7.

68 K. Jones, *The Making of Social Policy in Britain 1830–1990* (London: Athlone, 1991) p. 120.

69 Titmuss, *Problems*, pp. 466–7, 469–70, 477–8.

70   Titmuss, *Problems*, pp. 478–9.

71   Cooter, *Surgery*, p. 228.

72   P. Rotha, *Documentary Film*, (London: Faber & Faber, 1952) p. 88. For general discussions of the documentary movement, see J. Baxendale and C. Pawling, *Narrating the Thirties: A Decade in the Making: 1930s to the Present* (Basingstoke: Macmillan – now Palgrave Macmillan, 1996) ch. 2.

73   A. Borsay, '"Fit to Work": Representing Rehabilitation on the South Wales Coalfield during the Second World War', in A. Borsay (ed.), *Medicine in Wales, c.1800–2000: Public Service or Private Commodity?* (Cardiff: University of Wales Press, 2003) pp. 128–53.

74   Cooter, *Surgery*, pp. 218–19, 229–33, 248.

75   C. Webster, *The National Health Service: A Political History* (Oxford: Oxford University Press, 1998) p. 114.

76   Cooter, *Surgery*, pp. 218–20, 229; L. Guttmann, 'History of the National Spinal Injuries Centre, Stoke Mandeville Hospital, Aylesbury', *Paraplegia*, 34 (1967) 115; M. Tremblay, 'Lieutenant John Counsell and the Development of Medical Rehabilitation and Disability Policy in Canada', in Gerber (ed.) *Disabled Veterans*, pp. 323–4.

77   Guttmann, 'History', p. 116–18.

78   M. Oliver, *Understanding Disability: From Theory to Practice* (Basingstoke: Macmillan – now Palgrave Macmillan, 1996) p. 105. See also Gould, *Summer Plague*, p. 240.

79   Webster, *National Health Service*, p. 117.

80   D. Law and B. Paterson, *Living After A Stroke* (London: Souvenir, 1980) pp. 42, 59, 62–75.

81   A. Morris and A. Butler, *No Feet to Drag: Report on the Disabled* (London: Sidgwick & Jackson, 1972) p. 73.

82   D. Marks, *Disability: Controversial Debates and Psychosocial Perspectives* (London: Routledge, 1999) p. 98.

83   Flinn, 'Medical Services', p. 65.

84   T. Thomas, *Poor Relief in Merthyr Tydfil Union in Victorian Times* (Cardiff: Glamorgan Archive Service, 1992) p. 108.

85   Abel-Smith, *Hospitals*, pp. 83, 94–6, 202–4, 207–9; Crowther, *Workhouse System*, p. 183.

86   Crowther, *Workhouse System*, p. 176.

87   Means and Smith, *From Poor Law*, p. 20.

88   P. Thane, *Old Age in English History: Past Experiences, Present Issues* (Oxford: Oxford University Press, 2000) pp. 436–7. See also M. Jefferys, 'Recollections of the Pioneers of the Geriatrics Specialty', in J. Bornat, R. Perks, P. Thompson and J. Walmsley (eds), *Oral History, Health and Welfare* (London: Routledge, 2000) p. 82.

89   Crowther, *Workhouse System*, p. 188.
90   Parker, *Local Health and Welfare Services*, p. 31.
91   R. Means and R. Smith, 'From Public Assistance Institutions to "Sunshine Hotels": Changing State Perceptions About Residential Care for Elderly People, 1939–1948', *Ageing and Society*, 3 (1983) 163.
92   Webster, *National Health Service*, p. 6.
93   Thane, *Old Age*, p. 443; Webster, 'Elderly', p. 177.
94   P. Townsend, *The Last Refuge: A Survey of Residential Institutions and Homes for the Aged in England and Wales* (London: Routledge & Keegan Paul, 1964) pp. 21–2.
95   Thane, *Old Age*, pp. 447–8.
96   'A Hospital Plan for England and Wales, 1962', in B. Watkin (ed.), *Documents on Health and Social Services 1834 to the Present Day* (London: Methuen, 1975) p. 154.
97   Thane, *Old Age*, pp. 450, 452.
98   Webster, 'Elderly', p. 170.
99   P. Bridgen, 'Hospitals, Geriatric Medicine, and the Long-Term Care of Elderly People, 1946–1976', *Social History of Medicine*, 14 (2001) 507–23.
100 M. Martin, 'Medical Knowledge and Medical Practice: Geriatric Medicine in the 1950s', *Social History of Medicine*, 8 (1995) 453–4.

4   Asylums

1   A. Digby, 'Contexts and Perspectives', in D. Wright and A. Digby (eds), *From Idiocy to Mental Deficiency: Historical Perspectives on People with Learning Difficulties* (London: Routledge, 1996) p. 2.
2   D. Wright, *Mental Disability in Victorian England: The Earlswood Asylum, 1847–1901* (Oxford: Clarendon Press, 2001) p. 16.
3   S. Humphries and P. Gordon, *Out of Sight: The Experience of Disability, 1900–1950* (Plymouth: Northcote House, 1992) pp. 87–90.
4   R. Porter, *Mind-Forg'd Manacles: A History of Madness in England from the Reformation to the Regency* (Harmondsworth: Penguin, 1987) pp. 39–48.
5   Porphyria is a periodic, unpredictable and hereditary physical disease that affects the nervous system.
6   C. MacKenzie, *Psychiatry for the Rich: A History of Ticehurst Private Asylum, 1792–1917* (London: Routledge, 1992) p. 6.

7   W. F. Bynum, 'Rationales for Therapy in British Psychiatry, 1780–
    1835', *Medical History*, 18 (1974) 319; A. Scull, *The Most Solitary
    of Afflictions: Madness and Society in Britain, 1700–1900* (New
    Haven, CT: Yale University Press, 1993) pp. 56–67.
8   A. Digby, *Madness, Morality and Medicine: A Study of the York
    Retreat, 1796–1914* (Cambridge: Cambridge University Press,
    1985) p. 34.
9   Porter, *Mind-Forg'd*, pp. 108, 158.
10 MacKenzie, *Psychiatry*, p. 7.
11 Porter, *Mind-Forg'd*, p. 109.
12 S. Tuke, *Description of the Retreat, An Institution Near York* (London:
    Dawsons, 1964) pp. 141–2.
13 Porter, *Mind-Forg'd*, pp. 206, 276–7. See also Digby, *Madness*, p. 34.
14 J. M. Cox, *Practical Observations on Insanity* (London: Baldwin
    and Murray, 1804) pp. 168–9.
15 A. Borsay, *Medicine and Charity in Georgian Bath: A Social History
    of the General Infirmary, c.1739–1830* (Aldershot: Ashgate, 1999)
    p. 21; M. Donnelly, *Managing the Mind: A Study of Medical Psychology
    in Early Nineteenth-Century Britain* (London: Tavistock, 1983)
    pp. 6–10; MacKenzie, *Psychiatry*, pp. 90–1, 204–6; W. L. Parry-Jones,
    *The Trade in Lunacy: A Study of Private Madhouses in England in
    the Eighteenth and Nineteenth Centuries* (London: Routledge &
    Kegan Paul, 1972) pp. 282–3, 289; Porter, *Mind-Forg'd*, pp. 122,
    164–5.
16 K. Jones, *A History of the Mental Health Services* (London:
    Routledge & Kegan Paul, 1972) pp. 42–3; Porter, *Mind-
    Forg'd*, pp. 130–4; L. D. Smith, *'Cure, Comfort and Safe Custody':
    Public Lunatic Asylums in Early Nineteenth-Century England*
    (London: Leicester University Press, 1999) p. 17; L. D. Smith,
    'The County Asylum in the Mixed Economy of Care', in J. Melling
    and B. Forsythe (eds), *Insanity, Institutions and Society: A Social
    History of Madness in Comparative Perspective* (London: Routledge,
    1999) p. 34.
17 Smith, *'Cure'*, pp. 12, 18.
18 Digby, *Madness*, p. 12.
19 Digby, *Madness*, pp. 34, 37–9, 49–52.
20 Jones, *History*, pp. 129, 143; Smith, *'Cure'*, p. 23.
21 Parry-Jones, *Trade*, p. 287. See also H. G. Orme and W. H. Brock,
    *Leicestershire's Lunatics: The Institutional Care of Leicestershire's
    Lunatics during the Nineteenth Century* (Leicester: Leicestershire's
    Museums, Art Galleries and Records Service, 1987) pp. 38–9.
22 Scull, *Most Solitary*, pp. 55–6.

23 P. Bartlett, *The Poor Law of Lunacy: The Administration of Pauper Lunatics in Mid-Nineteenth-Century England* (London: Leicester University Press, 1999) p. 36.

24 L. Walsh, '"The Property of the Whole Community": Charity and Insanity in Urban Scotland: the Dundee Royal Lunatic Asylum, 1805–1850', in Melling and Forsythe (eds), *Insanity*, p. 181.

25 Donnelly, *Managing*, pp. 22–3, 27;

26 Smith, '*Cure*', p. 25.

27 Bartlett, *Poor Law*, pp. 2, 32, 47–51.

28 Jones, *History*, p. 357 Table 2.

29 MacKenzie, *Psychiatry*, pp. 204–6.

30 D. Wright, 'Learning Disability and the New Poor Law in England, 1834–1867', *Disability and Society*, 15 (2000) 738–41.

31 See Chapter 5, pp. 101–2.

32 Jones, *History*, pp. 204–8; N. Malin, D. Race and G. Jones, *Services for the Mentally Handicapped in Britain* (London: Croom Helm, 1980) p. 41.

33 J. Walmsley, D. Atkinson and S. Rolph, 'Community Care and Mental Deficiency, 1913 to 1945', in P. Bartlett and D. Wright (eds), *Outside the Walls of the Asylum: A History of Care in the Community, 1750–2000* (London: Athlone, 1999) p. 186 Table 9.1.

34 Jones, *History*, p. 358 Table 3.

35 J. Walmsley, '"Talking to Top People": Some Issues Relating to the Citizenship of People with Learning Difficulties', in J. Swain, V. Finkelstein, S. French and M. Oliver (eds), *Disabling Barriers – Enabling Environments* (London: Sage, 1993) p. 260.

36 M. Thomson, *The Problem of Mental Deficiency: Eugenics, Democracy and Social Policy in Britain, c.1870–1959* (Oxford: Clarendon Press, 1998) pp. 6, 51–4.

37 Jones, *History*, pp. 31–3.

38 E. Murphy, 'The Mad-House Keepers of East London', *History Today* (September 2001) 33.

39 V. Skultans, *English Madness: Ideas on Insanity, 1580–1890* (London: Routledge & Kegan Paul, 1979) pp. 112–13.

40 Jones, *History*, pp. 108–10.

41 J. Lane, *A Social History of Medicine: Health, Healing and Disease in England 1750–1950* (London: Routledge, 2001) pp. 104–5.

42 Jones, *History*, pp. 145–7.

43 D. J. Mellett, 'Bureaucracy and Mental Illness: The Commissioners in Lunacy, 1845–90', *Medical History*, 25 (1981) 221–47.

44 B. Forsythe, J. Melling and R. Adair, 'Politics of Lunacy: Central State Regulation and the Devon Pauper Lunatic Asylum, 1845–1914', in Melling and Forsythe (eds), *Insanity*, p. 69.

45 Parry-Jones, *Trade*, p. 282.
46 C. N. French, *The Story of St Luke's Hospital, 1750–1948* (London: Heinemann, 1951) p. 70.
47 J. Crammer, *Asylum History: Buckinghamshire County Pauper Lunatic Asylum – St John's* (London: Royal College of Psychiatrists, 1990) p. 47; J. Rogers (ed.), *In the Course of Time: A History of Herrison Hospital and of Mental Health Care in Dorset 1863–1992* (Dorchester: West Dorset Mental Health NHS Trust, 1992) pp. 19, 26.
48 Digby, *Madness*, pp. 85–6, 105–35.
49 M. Foucault, *Madness and Civilization: A History of Insanity in the Age of Reason* (London: Tavistock, 1965) p. 234.
50 Digby, *Madness*, pp. 86, 199.
51 Digby, *Madness*, pp. 199–200.
52 Crammer, *Asylum History*, pp. 58, 63–6.
53 Jones, *History*, p. 357, Appendix 1, Table 2.
54 R. Hunter and I. Macalpine, *Psychiatry for the Poor: 1851 Colney Hatch Asylum – Friern Hospital 1973: A Medical and Social History* (London: W. Dawson, 1974) p. 11.
55 A. Scull, *Museums of Madness: The Social Organization of Insanity in Nineteenth-Century England* (Harmondsworth: Penguin, 1982), pp. 194–5.
56 Hunter and Macalpine, *Psychiatry*, pp. 86–7, 132, 134, 136, 150.
57 Scull, *Museums*, p. 252.
58 Scull, *Museums*, chs 4 and 5. For a revised version of this argument, see Scull, *Most Solitary*, ch. 4.
59 P. Michael and D. Hirst, 'Establishing the "Rule of Kindness": The Foundation of the North Wales Lunatic Asylum, Denbigh', in Melling and Forsythe (eds), *Insanity*, pp. 159–76. See also Walsh, 'Dundee', p. 183.
60 D. Wright, 'Getting Out of the Asylum: Understanding the Confinement of the Insane in the Nineteenth Century', *Social History of Medicine*, 10 (1997) 139–41, 143–5, 148.
61 L. D. Smith, 'Eighteenth-Century Madhouse Practice: The Prouds of Bilston', *History of Psychiatry*, iii (1992) 47–51.
62 D. Wright, 'The Discharge of Pauper Lunatics from County Asylums in Mid-Victorian England: The Case of Buckinghamshire, 1853–1872', in Melling and Forsythe (eds), *Insanity*, p. 95.
63 Wright, 'Getting Out', 142, 152.
64 R. Adair, B. Forsythe and J. Melling, 'A Danger to the Public?: Disposing of Pauper Lunatics in Late-Victorian and Edwardian England: Plympton St Mary Union and the Devon County Asylum, 1867–1914', *Medical History*, 42 (1998) 24. See also B. Forsythe,

J. Melling and R. Adair, 'The New Poor Law and the County Pauper Lunatic Asylum: The Devon Experience, 1834–1884', *Social History of Medicine*, 9 (1996) 335–355; P. Horn (ed.), *Oxfordshire Village Life: The Diaries of George James Dew (1846–1928), Relieving Officer* (Abingdon: Beacon, 1983) pp. 64, 80–1.

65 Wright, 'Getting Out', 145.
66 Scull, *Museums*, p. 163.
67 Digby, *Madness*, p. 231 Table 9.11.
68 Skultans, *English Madness*, pp. 120–1 Table 2.
69 Crammer, *Asylum History*, p. 61.
70 Skultans, *English Madness*, p. 125 Table 4.
71 Wright, 'Learning Disability', 740.
72 Scull, *Museums*, p. 252.
73 Wright, 'Discharge', 99–103, 108.
74 Digby, *Madness*, p. 219.
75 M. Finnane, 'Asylums, Families and the State', *History Workshop Journal*, 20 (1985) 141.
76 Jones, *History*, p. 153.
77 Jones, *History*, pp. 26–7, 29–30, 33, 61, 108–9, 147–8; Wright, *Mental Disability*, pp. 47–8.
78 Jones, *History*, pp. 161–4, 167–70.
79 Mellett, 'Bureaucracy', 239, 241.
80 P. Noble, 'Mental Health Services: An Historical Review', *Medicine, Science and the Law*, 21 (1981) 19.
81 Jones, *History*, pp. 176–8.
82 The Ministry of Health took over responsibility for the Board of Control from the Home Office when it was established in 1919.
83 Malin, Race and Jones *Services*, pp. 41–2.
84 Wright, 'Discharge', 94–5, 104–5.
85 Thomson, *Problem*, pp. 267–8.
86 A. Suzuki, 'Framing Psychiatric Subjectivity: Doctor, Patient and Record-Keeping at Bethlem in the Nineteenth Century', in Melling and Forsythe (eds). *Insanity*, pp. 117, 131–2.
87 P. Fennell, *Treatment Without Consent: Law, Psychiatry and the Treatment of Mentally Disordered People Since 1845* (London: Routledge, 1996) pp. 23, 35–6, 47. See also Digby, *Madness*, pp. 122–30.
88 D. Armstrong, *Political Anatomy of the Body: Medical Knowledge in Britain in the Twentieth Century* (Cambridge: Cambridge University Press) pp. 19–20. See also Digby, *Madness*, pp. 138–9.
89 A. Hardy, *Health and Medicine in Britain Since 1860* (Basingstoke: Palgrave – now Palgrave Macmillan, 2001) pp. 71–4.
90 Fennell, *Treatment*, pp. 63–4; Noble, 'Mental Health Services', 19.

91   Jones, *History*, p. 181.
92   Armstrong, *Political Anatomy*, pp. 30–1; G. Baruch and A. Treacher, *Psychiatry Observed* (London: Routledge & Kegan Paul, 1978) pp. 60–2.
93   Crammer, *Asylum History*, p. 135.
94   Noble, 'Mental Health Services', 19–20.
95   J. M. L. Eyden, 'The Mentally Disordered', in D. C. Marsh (ed.), *An Introduction to the Study of Social Administration* (London: Routledge & Kegan Paul, 1965) pp. 178–9; Rogers, *Herrison Hospital*, p. 43; Thomson, *Problem*, p. 97.
96   Fennell, *Treatment*, p. 64.
97   Fennell, *Treatment*, pp. 64–5, 76–7, 118–19.
98   Fennell, *Treatment*, pp. 122–6, 129–37.
99   D. Gittins, *Madness in its Place: Narratives of Severalls Hospital, 1913–1997* (London: Routledge, 1998) pp. 198, 200.
100 Baruch and Treacher, *Psychiatry Observed*, p. 40.
101 J. Parker, *Local Health and Welfare Services* (London: George Allen & Unwin) p. 102.
102 Fennell, *Treatment*, pp. 138–49.
103 Jones, *History*, p. 291.
104 Eyden, 'Mentally Disordered', p. 179.
105 Jones, *History*, p. 289.
106 Noble, 'Mental Health Services', 21–2.
107 Jones, *History*, p. 292.
108 Rogers (ed.), *Herrison Hospital*, p. 45; Armstrong, *Political Anatomy*, pp. 70–1; Malin, Race and Jones, *Services*, p. 46.
109 J. Walmsley and D. Atkinson, 'Oral History and the History of Learning Disability', in J. Bornat, R. Perks, P. Thompson and J. Walmsley (eds), *Oral History, Health and Welfare* (London: Routledge, 2000) p. 189.
110 Parker, *Local Health and Welfare Services*, p. 104.
111 Jones, *History*, p. 358 Table 4, p. 362 Table 11.
112 N. Timmins, *The Five Giants: A Biography of the Welfare State* (London: HarperCollins, 1995) p. 211.
113 J. Hoenig and M. W. Hamilton, *The Desegregation of the Mentally Ill* (London: Routledge & Kegan Paul, 1969) p. 2.
114 Baruch and Treacher, *Psychiatry Observed*, pp. viii, 76, 84.
115 Noble, 'Mental Health Services', p. 22.
116 L. O. Gostin, *The Mental Health Act 1959: Is It Fair?* (London: MIND, 1978); L. O. Gostin, 'Time to Act', *Mind Out* (January 1981), 22–3; R. Levitt, *The Reorganized National Health* Service (London: Croom Helm, 1977) p. 205.
117 See, for example, Donnelly, *Managing*, ch. 3.

118 Smith, '*Cure*', p. 34.
119 C. Philo, '"Enough to Drive One Mad": The Organization of Space in Nineteenth-Century Lunatic Asylums', in J. Wolch and M. Dear (eds), *The Power of Geography: How Territory Shapes Social Life* (Boston, MA: Unwin Hyman, 1989) pp. 266–70.
120 H. Richardson, *English Hospitals, 1660–1948* (Swindon: English Heritage, 1998) pp. 173, 177.
121 T. A. Markus, *Buildings and Power: Freedom and Control in the Origin of Modern Building Types* (London: Routledge, 1993) pp. xix–xx, 5, 130–41.
122 'Mabel Cooper's Life Story', in D. Atkinson, M. Jackson and J. Walmsley (eds), *Forgotten Lives: Exploring the History of Learning Disability* (Kidderminster: British Institute of Learning Disabilities, 1997) p. 29; H. Parr and C. Philo, 'Mapping "Mad" Identities', in S. Pile and N. Thrift (eds), *Mapping the Subject: Geographies of Cultural Transformation* (London: Routledge, 1995) p. 204.
123 A. Ingram, *The Madhouse of Language: Writing and Reading Madness in the Eighteenth Century* (London: Routledge, 1991) pp. 153–5.
124 K. Davies, '"Silent and Censured Travellers"?: Patients' Narratives and Patients' Voices: Perspectives on the History of Mental Illness Since 1948', *Social History of Medicine*, 14 (2001) 272, 286–7.
125 Gittins, *Madness*, pp. 17, 19, 21–2, 59, 98–101; Wright, *Mental Disability*, 141–2.
126 Digby, *Madness*, pp. 58–61, 86, 192–3, 199–200. See also Gittins, *Madness*, p. 154; Wright, *Mental Disability*, pp. 97–8.
127 Herefordshire MIND, *Boots On! Out!* (Little Logaston: Logaston Press, 1995) pp. vii–viii.
128 Hunter and Macalpine, *Psychiatry*, p. 136. See also Wright, *Mental Disability*, p. 143.
129 R. Fido and M. Potts, 'Using Oral Histories', in Atkinson, Jackson and Walmsley (eds), *Forgotten Lives*, p. 43.
130 'Mabel Cooper's Life Story', p. 24.
131 J. Walmsley, 'Telling the History of Learning Disability from Local Sources', in Atkinson, Jackson and Walmsley (eds), *Forgotten Lives*, p. 90.
132 Gittins, *Madness*, pp. 137–8.
133 See, for example, Digby, *Madness*, pp. 197–8.
134 Walmsley and Atkinson, 'Oral History', pp. 195, 198.
135 *Testimony: Telling the Stories of those who Survived the Old Victorian Asylums* (London: Mental Health Media, 2000) video.
136 Fido and Potts, 'Using Oral Histories', p. 43. See also Herefordshire MIND, *Boots On!* p. 14.

137 Gittins, *Madness*, p. 171. See also A. Stevens, 'Recording the History of an Institution: The Royal Eastern Counties Institution at Colchester', in Atkinson, Jackson and Walmsley (eds), *Forgotten Lives*, p. 62.

138 See, for example, J. Ryan with F. Thomas, *The Politics of Mental Handicap* (Harmondsworth: Penguin, 1980); Gittins, *Madness*, pp. 140, 142.

139 See, for example, *Allegations of Ill-treatment of Patients and Other Irregularities at the Ely Hospital, Cardiff*, Cmnd 3795 (London: HMSO, 1971); *Whittingham Hospital*, Report of a Committee of Enquiry, Cmnd 4861 (London: HMSO, 1972).

140 See, for example, P. Morris, *Put Away: A Sociological Study of Institutions for the Mentally Retarded* (London: Routledge & Kegan Paul, 1969); B. Robb, *Sans Everything: A Case to Answer* (London: Nelson, 1967).

141 V. Berridge, *Health and Society in Britain Since 1939* (Cambridge: Cambridge University Press, 1999) p. 36.

142 Gittins, *Madness*, pp. 67–70, 143–4.

143 K. Jones, *Asylums and After: A Revised History of the Mental Health Services: From the Early 18th Century to the 1990s* (London: Athlone, 1993) pp. 164–5, 180.

5 Schools

1 J. Rée, *I See A Voice: Language, Deafness and the Senses – A Philosophical History* (London: HarperCollins, 1999) pp. 137–9.

2 P. Beaver, *A Tower of Strength: Two Hundred Years of the Royal School for Deaf Children, Margate* (Lewes: The Book Guild, 1992) pp. 23, 28–9; G. Phillips, 'Scottish and English Institutions for the Blind, 1792–1860', *Scottish Historical Review*, LXXIV (1995) 181, 183; M. G. Thomas, *The Royal National Institute for the Blind, 1868–1956* (London: Royal National Institute for the Blind, 1957) p. 11.

3 See, for example, Brighton Institution for the Instruction of Deaf and Dumb Children, *Seventh Report* (Brighton: R. Sicklemore, 1848) p. 15; *Twenty-Fifth Report of the General Institution for the Instruction of Deaf and Dumb Children at Edgbaston, near Birmingham* (Birmingham: Wrightson and Webb, 1838) pp. 12–4.

4 Beaver, *Tower*, p. 62; A. J. Boyce, *The History of the Yorkshire Residential School for the Deaf* (Doncaster: Doncaster Municipal Borough Council Museums and Arts Services, 1996) p. 8.

5 J. S. Hurt, *Outside the Mainstream: A History of Special Education* (London: Batsford, 1988) p. 92.

6 D. O. Haswell, *The Social Condition of the Blind* (Published by the author, 1876) p. 10; D. E. Woodford, *Touch, Touch and Touch Again* (Feltham, Middlesex: British Deaf History Society, 2000) pp. 84–7 Appendix 2.

7 *Nineteenth Annual Report of the Midland Institution for the Blind, Nottingham* (Nottingham: T. Forman, 1862) p. 6. See also Midland Institution for the Blind, *Sixth Report* (Nottingham: A. Staveley, 1849) p. 7.

8 Brighton Institution, *Seventh Report*, p. 27, Appendix, 'Opening of the New Asylum, June 27 1848. From the *Brighton Gazette.*'

9 *Account of the General Institution Established in Birmingham for the Instruction of Deaf and Dumb Children* (Birmingham: James Belcher and Son, 1814) p. 12.

10 W. C. Fenton, *A Brief View of the Institutions for the Deaf and Dumb in Europe and America with Some Remarks Relative to the Yorkshire Institution for the Deaf and Dumb* (Doncaster: Charles White, 1833) p. 18.

11 Beaver, *Tower*, p. 46

12 *The Welshman* (5 February 1847). See also Midland Institution for the Blind, *Eighth Report* (Nottingham: Staveley, 1851) p. 8; *Second Report of the West of England Institution for the Instruction of Deaf and Dumb Children of the Counties of Devon, Cornwall, Somerset, and Dorset* (Exeter: W. C. Pollard, 1828) pp. 5, 14.

13 West of England Institution for the Instruction of Deaf and Dumb Children of the Counties of Devon, Cornwall, Somerset, and Dorset, *Report for the Year 1865: Fortieth Report* (Exeter: William Pollard, 1866) p. 8. See also W. Sleigh, *A Voice from the Dumb: A Memoir of John William Lashford, Late a Pupil in the Brighton and Sussex Institution for the Deaf and Dumb* (London: Hamilton, Adams; Brighton: Charles A. Johnson, 1849) p. ii.

14 *Nineteenth Annual Report of the Midland Institution*, p. 6. See also Swansea and South Wales Institution for the Blind, *Fifty-Seventh Annual Report* (No place of publication or publisher, 1923) frontispiece.

15 Hurt, *Outside*, pp. 97–9.

16 A. F. Dimmock, *Cruel Legacy: An Introduction to the Record of Deaf People in History* (Edinburgh: Scottish Workshop Publications, 1993) p. 20; Rée, *I See*, p. 139.

17 Beaver, *Tower*, pp. 47–8.

18 Boyce, *History*, p. 43; Rée, *I See*, pp. 225–6.

19 H. Lane, *The Mask of Benevolence: Disabling the Deaf Community* (New York: Vintage, 1993) p. 113–14.

20 J. Branson and D. Miller, 'From Myth to History: Maginn, Gallaudet and the Destruction of BSL-Based Manualism in Deaf Education in Britain', *Deaf History Journal*, 4 (August 2000) 15–25.

21 Lane, *Mask*, pp. 116–18, 125; Rée, *I See*, p. 230

22 *The Education of a Deaf Child* (Birmingham: Royal School for Deaf Children, no date) p. 15. See also Royal Cambrian Institution for the Deaf and Dumb, *Annual Report* (Swansea: Alexandra Printing, 1930) p. 32; Swansea and South Wales Institution, *Fifty-Seventh Annual Report*, p. 12.

23 *A Report of the Purposes, Progress, and Present State of the Asylum for the Support and Education of Indigent Deaf and Dumb Children, Situated in the Kent Road, Surrey, London* (London: Gilbert and Rivington, 1859) pp. 12–13. See also Fenton, *Brief View*, p. 17.

24 *Education of a Deaf Child*, p. 15. See also *Asylum for the Support and Education of Indigent Deaf and Dumb Children*, pp. 12–13; Fenton, *Brief View*, p. 17.

25 For a succinct summary of this debate, see K. Gleadle, *British Women in the Nineteenth Century* (Basingstoke: Palgrave – now Palgrave Macmillan, 2001) pp. 4–5; S. Bruley, *Women in Britain Since 1900* (Basingstoke: Macmillan – now Palgrave Macmillan, 1999) pp. 15–23, 38–46, 60–70, 78–91, 93–105, 119–28, 163–72.

26 Haswell, *Social Condition*, pp. 10, 12, 13, 16–17.

27 *Education of a Deaf Child*, p. 9.

28 M. Oliver, 'Disability and Dependency: A Creation of Industrial Societies?', in J. Swain, V. Finkelstein, S. French and M. Oliver (eds), *Disabling Barriers – Enabling Environments* (London: Sage, 1993) p. 55.

29 See Chapter 3, pp. 50–1.

30 S. Humphries and P. Gordon, *Out of Sight: The Experience of Disability, 1900–1950* (Plymouth: Northcote House, 1992) p. 61.

31 Royal Institution for the Instruction of Deaf and Dumb Children, *Annual Report*, pp. 12, 32, 34. See also *Education of a Deaf Child*, p. 17

32 D. Wright, *Mental Disability in Victorian England: The Earlswood Asylum, 1847–1901* (Oxford: Clarendon Press, 2001) pp. 33–4, 36, 40, 69, 130, 137, 144, 153.

33 Wright, *Mental Disability*, pp. 144–50.

34 D. Gladstone, 'The Changing Dynamic of Institutional Care: The Western Counties Idiot Asylum, 1864–1914', in D. Wright and A. Digby (eds), *From Idiocy to Mental Deficiency: Historical*

Perspectives on People with Learning Disabilities (London: Routledge, 1996) p. 137.

35 Wright, *Mental Disability*, p. 170.

36 Gladstone, 'Changing Dynamic of Institutional Care', pp. 149, 151–5.

37 Gladstone, 'Changing Dynamic of Institutional Care', pp. 139–40.

38 J. Alston, *The Royal Albert: Chronicles of an Era* (Lancaster: Centre for North-West Regional Studies, 1992) pp. 20–1. See also pp. 40, 50–1, 66, 77.

39 Wright, *Mental Disability*, pp. 91, 153.

40 Alston, *Royal Albert*, pp. 9, 47.

41 Wright, *Mental Disability*, pp. 129, 154, 162–4, 173–6.

42 C. Darwin, *The Descent of Man* (Harmondsworth: Penguin, 2004) p. 159.

43 D. King, *In the Name of Liberalism: Illiberal Social Policy in the United States and Britain* (Oxford: Oxford University Press, 1999) pp. 51–2, 54–6, 68;

44 R. A. Soloway, *Democracy and Degeneration: Eugenics and the Declining Birthrate in Twentieth-Century Britain* (Chapel Hill: University of North Carolina Press, 1995) pp. xvii, xxiv. See also M. Freeden, 'Eugenics and Progressive Thought: A Study in Ideological Affinity', *Historical Journal*, 22 (1979) 658–9.

45 G. Jones, 'Eugenics and Social Policy between the Wars', *Historical Journal*, 25 (1982) 726.

46 D. Marks, *Disability: Controversial Debates and Psychosocial Perspectives* (London: Routledge, 1999) p. 35.

47 M. Jackson, *The Borderland of Imbecility: Medicine, Society and the Fabrication of the Feeble Mind in Late Victorian and Edwardian England* (Manchester: Manchester University Press, 2000) pp. 28–30.

48 C. Barnes, *Disabled People in Britain and Discrimination: A Case for Anti-Discrimination Legislation* (London: Hurst, 1991) pp. 18–19.

49 M. Jackson, 'Institutional Provision for the Feeble-Minded in Edwardian England: Sandlebridge and the Scientific Morality of Permanent Care', in Wright and Digby, *From Idiocy*, pp. 161–2, 169–71.

50 Jackson, 'Institutional Provision', pp. 171–2.

51 Jackson, *Borderland*, pp. 172–3, 177–81; Jackson, 'Institutional Provision', pp. 173–4.

52 Jackson, *Borderland*, pp. 70–2.

53 Haswell, *Social Condition*, pp. 12, 31.

54 See, for example, Midland Institution, *Eighth Report*, p. 8.

55 Haswell, *Social Condition*, p. 31.

56 M. Sanderson, *Education, Economic Change and Society in England, 1780–1870* (Basingstoke: Macmillan, 1983) pp. 9–22; W. B. Stephens, *Education in Britain, 1750–1914* (Basingstoke: Macmillan – now Palgrave Macmillan, 1998) pp. 1–5.

57 D. Fraser, *The Evolution of the British Welfare State* (London: Macmillan, 1973) pp. 72–5.

58 U. Henriques, *Before the Welfare State: Social Administration in Early Industrial Britain* (London: Longman, 1979) pp. 227, 229; Stephens, *Education*, pp. 83–7.

59 L. McCoy, 'Education for Labour: Social Problems of Nationhood', in G. Lewis (ed.), *Forming Nation, Framing Welfare* (London: Routledge, 1998) pp. 111–12.

60 E. Topliss, *Provision for the Disabled* (Oxford and London: B. Blackwell and M. Robertson, 1975) pp. 5–6.

61 Fraser, *Evolution*, pp. 80–1; Stephens, *Education*, pp. 79–80.

62 S. Tomlinson, *The Sociology of Special Education* (London: Routledge & Kegan Paul, 1982) pp. 36–7.

63 McCoy, 'Education', p. 121.

64 Tomlinson, *Sociology*, p. 38.

65 Hurt, *Outside*, p. 134.

66 Thomas, *Royal National Institute*, pp. 76–8, 85–8, 89–90.

67 M. Thomson, *The Problem of Mental Deficiency: Eugenics, Democracy, and Social Policy in Britain, c.1870–1959* (Oxford: Clarendon Press, 1998) pp.14–15.

68 See Chapter 4, p. 71.

69 D. Armstrong, *Political Anatomy of the Body: Medical Knowledge in Britain in the Twentieth Century* (Cambridge, Cambridge University Press, 1983) p. 64; Hurt, *Outside*, pp. 148–50; Jackson, *Borderland*, p. 221–3.

70 J. Anderson, *A Record of Fifty Years Service to the Disabled by the Central Council for the Disabled* (London: Central Council for the Disabled, 1969) p. 59; Topliss, *Provision*, p. 33; F. Watson, *Civilization and the Cripple* (London: J. Bale, 1930) p. 32.

71 Hurt, *Outside*, pp. 104–5.

72 Tomlinson, *Sociology*, p. 38.

73 S. Koven, 'Remembering and Dismemberment: Crippled Children, Wounded Soldiers, and the Great War in Great Britain', *American Historical Review*, 99 (1994) 1172, 1175.

74 R. Cooter, *Surgery and Society in Peace and War: Orthopaedics and the Organization of Modern Medicine, 1880–1948* (Basingstoke: Macmillan – now Palgrave Macmillan, 1993) p. 65.

75 G. R. Girdlestone, *The Care and Cure of Crippled Children*, (Bristol and London: J. Wright and S. Marshall, 1924) p. 10.

76   Humphries and Gordon, *Out of Sight*, p. 66.
77   D. G. Pritchard, *Education and the Handicapped, 1760–1960* (London: Routledge & Kegan Paul, 1963) pp. 220–1.
78   Tomlinson, *Sociology*, pp. 42–3.
79   Pritchard, *Education*, p. 138.
80   Thomson, *Problem*, pp. 33–4. The school medical service is discussed in Chapter 8, pp. 185–6.
81   Tomlinson, *Sociology*, pp. 43–8.
82   Hurt, *Outside*, p. 103; Jackson, *Borderland*, p. 221.
83   Hurt, *Outside*, pp. 144–5.
84   G. Sutherland, *Ability, Merit and Measurement: Mental Testing and English Education, 1880–1940* (Oxford: Clarendon Press, 1984) pp. 57–8, 68–9.
85   Hurt, *Outside*, p. 155.
86   Sutherland, *Ability*, pp. 70, 85–96, 128.
87   Hurt, *Outside*, pp. 161–2; Tomlinson, *Sociology*, p. 49.
88   J. Walmsley and S. Rolphe, 'Development of Community Care for People with Learning Difficulties, 1913–1945', *Critical Social Policy*, 21 (2001) p. 200.
89   Hurt, *Outside*, p. 164.
90   *Report of the Inter-Departmental Committee on Physical Deterioration*, Cmnd 2175 (London: HMSO, 1904) pp. 13–14, in E. J. Evans (ed.), *British Social Policy, 1830–1914: Individualism, Collectivism and the Origins of the Welfare State* (London: Routledge & Kegan Paul, 1978) p. 228.
91   Thomson, *Problem*, p. 51.
92   Royal Institution, *Annual Report*, p. 5.
93   Girdlestone, *Care*, p. 10.
94   Jones, 'Eugenics', 723.
95   Koven, 'Remembering', 1173.
96   J. Barnes, 'Education: The Changing Balance of Power', in D. Gladstone (ed.), *British Social Welfare: Past, Present and Future* (London: UCL Press, 1995) p. 35.
97   P. Henderson, *Disability in Childhood and Youth* (Oxford: Oxford University Press, 1974) p. 13.
98   J. S. Clarke, *Disabled Citizens* (London: Allen & Unwin, 1951) pp. 127–8.
99   Thomson, *Problem*, p. 285.
100 Sutherland, *Ability*, pp. 112–24.
101 M. Sanderson, 'Education', in R. M. Page and R. Silburn, *British Social Welfare in the Twentieth Century* (Basingstoke: Macmillan – now Palgrave Macmillan, 1998) pp. 136–8, 141.
102 Tomlinson, *Sociology*, pp. 49–52; Topliss, *Provision*, p. 30 Table II.
103 C. Barnes, G. Mercer and T. Shakespeare, *Exploring Disability: A Sociological Introduction* (Cambridge: Polity, 1999) p. 106.

104 Clarke, *Disabled Citizens*, pp. 130–1.

105 Barnes, Mercer and Shakespeare, *Exploring Disability*, pp. 107–8; J. R. Buckle, *Work and Housing of Impaired Persons in Great Britain* (London: HMSO, 1971) pp. 4–9; National Federation of the Blind of the United Kingdom and the Association of Blind and Partially Sighted Teachers and Students, 'Education Provision for the Visually Handicapped', in D. M. Boswell and J. M. Wingrove (eds), *The Handicapped Person in the Community: A Reader and Sourcebook* (London: Tavistock, 1974) pp. 274–5.

106 Barnes, 'Education', pp. 37–42.

107 N. Malin, D. Race and G. Jones, *Services for the Mentally Handicapped in Britain* (London: Croom Helm, 1980) pp. 51, 61.

108 M. Oliver, *Understanding Disability: From Theory to Practice* (Basingstoke: Macmillan – now Palgrave Macmillan, 1996) p. 80. See also Barnes, Mercer and Shakespeare, *Exploring Disability*, pp. 105–6; Hurt, *Outside*, pp. 187–8.

109 J. M. Davies and N. Watson, 'Where Are the Children's Experiences?: Analysing Social and Cultural Exclusion in "Special" and "Mainstream" Schools', *Disability and Society*, 16 (2001) 672.

110 Humphries and Gordon, *Out of Sight*, pp. 45–56. See also F. Perry, *Living in Darkness* (Oswestry: Sherbourne Publications, 1999) pp. 3–5.

111 Tomlinson, *Sociology*, p. 28.

112 A. Stevens, 'Recording the History of an Institution: The Royal Eastern Counties Institution at Colchester', in D. Atkinson, M. Jackson and J. Walmsley (eds), *Forgotten Lives: Exploring the History of Learning Disability* (Kidderminster: British Institute of Learning Disabilities, 1997) pp. 60–1.

113 Royal Cambrian Institution, *Annual Report*, p. 30.

114 'Rules for the Teachers', in Institution for the Deaf and Dumb, Birmingham, Minutes of the House Committee, 1889–1901.

115 M. Jackson, 'Images of Deviance: Visual Representations of Mental Defectives in Early Twentieth-Century Medical Texts,' *British Journal for the History of Science*, 28 (1995), p. 319; M. Jackson, 'Images from the Past: Using Photographs', in Atkinson, Jackson and Walmsley (eds), *Forgotten Lives*, pp. 68–70.

116 Humphries and Gordon, *Out of Sight*, p. 84

117 S. French with J. Swain, 'Institutional Abuse: Memories of a "Special" School for Visually Impaired Girls – A Personal Account', in J. Bornat, R. Perks, P. Thompson and J. Walmsley (eds) *Oral History, Health and Welfare* (London, Routledge, 2000) p. 172.

118 T. Cook, J. Swain and S. French, 'Voices from Segregated Schooling: Towards an Inclusive Education System', *Disability and Society*, 16 (2001) 296–7.

119 Boyce, *History*, pp. 10, 46, 77; Humphries and Gordon, *Out of Sight*, pp. 66, 79–80; Dimmock, *Cruel Legacy*, p. 26; *Living Heritage of the Deaf Community*, (Carlisle: British Deaf Association, 1993) video.

120 French with Swain, 'Institutional Abuse', pp. 163–4, 171–2.

121 Humphries and Gordon, *Out of Sight*, p. 68.

122 French with Swain, 'Institutional Abuse', pp. 164–6, 169–70. See also J. Campbell and M. Oliver, *Disability Politics: Understanding our Past, Changing our Future* (London: Routledge, 1996) p. 106; Cook, Swain and French, 'Voices', p. 297–8; Humphries and Gordon, *Out of Sight*, p. 92

123 Cook, Swain and French, 'Voices', pp. 297–8.

124 French with Swain, 'Institutional Abuse', p. 165.

125 Cook, Swain and French, 'Voices', p. 297; Humphries and Gordon, *Out of Sight*, pp. 75–6.

126 French with Swain, 'Institutional Abuse', pp. 169–70, 176. See also Campbell and Oliver, *Disability Politics*, p. 32.

127 French with Swain, 'Institutional Abuse', p. 175; Humphries and Gordon, *Out of Sight*, pp. 80–1; Jackson, *Borderland*, pp. 182–3.

6 Work

1 J. Walmsley and S. Rolph, 'Development of Community Care for People with Learning Difficulties, 1913–1945', *Critical Social Policy*, 21 (2001) 61.

2 A. Giddens, 'T. H. Marshall, the State and Democracy', in M. Bulmer and A. M. Rees (eds), *Citizenship Today: The Contemporary Relevance of T. H. Marshall* (London: UCL Press, 1996) pp. 65–7.

3 R. Levitas, 'The Concept of Social Exclusion and the New Durkheimian Hegemony', *Critical Social Policy*, 16 (1996) 8–9, 11.

4 P. Colquhoun, *A Treatise on Indigence* (London: J. Hatchard, 1806) p. 7.

5 A. Briggs, *The Age of Improvement 1783–1867* (London: Longmans, 1959) p. 294. See also E. J. Evans, *The Forging of the Modern State: Early Industrial Britain, 1783–1870* (London: Longman, 1983) pp. 101–9, 148–56, 255–62.

6 J. M. Guy, *The Victorian Social-Problem Novel* (Basingstoke: Macmillan – now Palgrave Macmillan, 1996).

7 O. R. McGregor, 'Social Research and Social Policy in the Nineteenth Century', *British Journal of Sociology*, 8 (1957) 147–50, 152–3; L. Goldman, 'The Social Science Association, 1857–1886: A Context for Mid-Victorian Liberalism', *English Historical Review*, CI (1986) 132; L. Goldman, 'A Peculiarity of the English? The Social

Science Association and the Absence of Sociology in Nineteenth-Century Britain', *Past and Present*, 114 (1987) 169–71; L. Goldman, 'Statistics and the Science of Society in Early Victorian Britain: An Intellectual Context for the General Register Office', *Social History of Medicine*, 4 (1991) 415.

8   D. Englander, 'Comparisons and Contrasts: Henry Mayhew and Charles Booth as Social Investigators', in D. Englander and R. O'Day (eds), *Retrieved Riches: Social Investigation in Britain, 1840–1914* (Aldershot: Scolar Press, 1995) pp. 109, 119.

9   H. Mayhew, *London Labour and the London Poor* (Harmondsworth: Penguin, 1985) pp. 260, 262.

10   Englander, 'Comparisons', pp. 105–23; P. Murray, *Poverty and Welfare, 1830–1914* (London: Hodder & Stoughton, 1999) pp. 81–4; K. Williams, *From Pauperism to Poverty* (London: Routledge & Kegan Paul, 1981) pp. 263–4.

11   Englander, 'Comparisons', pp. 122–4, 132–3; Williams, *From Pauperism*, pp. 309–11, 345–7.

12   K. Coates and R. Silburn, *Poverty: The Forgotten Englishmen* (Harmondsworth: Penguin, 1970) p. 46.

13   B. Abel-Smith and P. Townsend, *The Poor and the Poorest* (London: Bell, 1965) pp. 39–40.

14   P. Clarke, *Hope and Glory: Britain, 1900–1990* (London: Penguin, 1996) pp. 302–9; A. Deacon, 'Spending More to Achieve Less?: Social Security Since 1945', in D. Gladstone (ed.), *British Social Welfare: Past, Present and Future* (London: UCL Press, 1995) pp. 77–9; R. Lowe, *The Welfare State in Britain Since 1945* (Basingstoke: Macmillan – now Palgrave Macmillan, 1993) pp. 135–41; A. Marwick, *British Society Since 1945* (Harmondsworth: Penguin, 1982) chs 7 and 8; M. Oliver and C. Barnes, *Disabled People and Social Policy: From Exclusion to Inclusion* (London: Longman, 1998) p. 79.

15   A. I. Harris, *Income and Entitlement to Supplementary Benefit* (London: HMSO, 1970) pp. 11–13.

16   P. Townsend, *Poverty in the United Kingdom: A Survey of Household Resources and Standards of Living* (Harmondsworth: Penguin, 1979) pp. 738, 787.

17   See Chapter 1, p. 9.

18   See, for example, S. Baldwin, *Disabled Children – Counting the Costs: The Results of a Special Survey in the North and Midlands of Families with a Handicapped Child* (London: Disability Alliance, 1977); M. Hyman, *The Extra Costs of Disabled Living* (Horsham: National Fund for Research into Crippling Diseases, 1977); I. Loach, *The Price of Deafness: A Review of the Financial and Employment Problems of the Deaf and Hard of Hearing* (London: Disability Alliance, 1976).

19 Social security is discussed in Chapter 7, pp. 161–7.

20 P. Townsend, 'The Structured Dependency of the Elderly: A Creation of Social Policy in the Twentieth Century', *Ageing and Society*, 1 (1981) 10–13.

21 S. Koven, 'Remembering and Dismemberment: Crippled Children, Wounded Soldiers, and the Great War in Britain', *American Historical Review*, 99 (1994) 1193.

22 R. Lee, *John William Lowe 1804–1876* (Feltham, Middlesex: British Deaf History Society Publications, 1995) pp. 18–21.

23 See Chapter 5, p. 97.

24 J. S. Hurt, *Outside the Mainstream: A History of Special Education* (London: Batsford, 1988) p. 144.

25 *A Report of the Purposes, Progress, and Present State of the Asylum for the Support and Education of Indigent Deaf and Dumb Children Situated in the Kent Road, Surrey, London* (London: Gilbert and Rivington, 1859) pp. 13–14; Derbyshire Association in Aid of the Deaf and Dumb, *Annual Report for January 1st, 1881* (Derby: Bemrose and Sons, 1881) p. 2; Royal Cambrian Institution for the Deaf and Dumb, *Annual Report* (Swansea: Alexander Printing, 1930) p. 7.

26 Swansea and South Wales Institution for the Blind, *65th Annual Report* (Swansea: Alexandra Printing, 1930/1) p. 9.

27 M. and J. Wymer, *Another Door Opens* (London: Souvenir Press, 1980) p. 79.

28 Department of Employment, *Sheltered Employment for Disabled People: A Consultative Document* (London: Department of Employment, 1973) pp. 3, 6, 9.

29 Department of Employment, *Sheltered Employment*, pp. 13–14.

30 G. Phillips, 'Scottish and English Institutions for the Blind, 1792–1860', *Scottish Historical Review*, LXXIV (1995) pp. 186–9, 194, 207–9.

31 'Facsimile of First Annual Report and Balance Sheet, Swansea Auxiliary of the Society for Teaching the Blind to Read', in Swansea and South Wales Institution for the Blind, *Annual Report* (No place of publication or publisher, 1935) p. 8.

32 Swansea and South Wales Institution for the Blind, *A Souvenir* (No place of publication or publisher, 1935); Swansea and South Wales Institution for the Blind, *Fifty-Seventh Annual Report* (No place of publication or publisher, 1923) p. 4.

33 See Chapter 3, p. 51, and Chapter 5, pp. 102–3.

34 I. Gazeley and P. Thane, 'Patterns of Visibility: Unemployment in Britain during the Nineteenth and Twentieth Centuries', in G. Lewis (ed.), *Forming Nation, Framing Welfare* (London: Routledge, 1998) p. 184. See also S. Glynn, 'Employment, Unemployment and the Labour Market', in R. M. Page and R. Silburn

(eds), *British Social Welfare in the Twentieth Century* (Basingstoke: Macmillan – now Palgrave Macmillan, 1998) pp. 179–80; L. Hollen Lees, *The Solidarities of Strangers: The English Poor Laws and the People, 1700–1948* (Cambridge: Cambridge University Press, 1998) pp. 287–9.

35 'Circular Addressed by the President of the Local Government Board to the Several Boards of Guardians' (1886), in R. Pope, A. Pratt and B. Hoyle (eds), *Social Welfare in Britain, 1885–1985* (London: Croom Helm, 1986) pp. 78–80. See also M. E. Rose, *The Relief of Poverty, 1834–1914* (London: Macmillan, 1972) pp. 42–3.

36 M. Bruce, *The Coming of the Welfare State* (London: Batsford, 1968) p. 23.

37 J. Harris, *Unemployment and Politics: A Study in English Social Policy 1886–1914* (Oxford: Clarendon Press, 1972) p. 12.

38 R. Porter, 'Accidents in the Eighteenth Century', in R. Cooter and B. Luckin (eds), *Accidents in History: Injuries, Fatalities and Social Relations* (Amsterdam: Rodopi, 1997) pp. 90–9.

39 R. Cooter, 'The Moment of the Accident: Culture, Militarism and Modernity in Late-Victorian Britain', in Cooter and Luckin (eds), *Accidents*, pp. 107–8.

40 Cooter, 'Moment', p. 114.

41 R. Cooter and B. Luckin, 'Accidents in History: An Introduction', in Cooter and Luckin (eds), *Accidents*, pp. 3–4.

42 M. Sanders, 'Accidents of Production: Industrialism and the Worker's Body in Early Victorian Fiction', in H. G. Klaus and S. Knight (eds), *British Industrial Fictions* (Cardiff: University of Wales Press, 2000) pp. 24–6, 33–4.

43 Cooter, 'Moment', pp. 121, 123.

44 See Chapter 5, pp. 103–5.

45 G. M. Ayers, *England's First State Hospitals and the Metropolitan Asylums Board, 1867–1930* (London: Wellcome Institute of the History of Medicine, 1971) p. 171.

46 H. Gauvain, 'The Lord Mayor Treloar Cripples' Hospital and College', *The Cripples' Journal*, 1 (1924) 65, 66, 68.

47 Department of Employment, *Sheltered Employment*, p. 3; E. Topliss, *Provision for the Disabled* (Oxford and London: B. Blackwell and M. Robertson, 1975) pp. 11, 49.

48 R. Jones, *An Address on the Orthopaedic Outlook in Military Surgery* (London: British Medical Association, 1918) p. 5.

49 J. S. Reznick, 'Work-Therapy and the Disabled British Soldier in Great Britain in the First World War: The Case of Shepherd's Bush Military Hospital, London', in D. A. Gerber (ed.) *Disabled Veterans*

in History (Ann Arbor: University of Michigan Press, 2000) pp. 187–9.

50 Jones, *Address*, pp. 3, 5–6.

51 See, for example, M. G. Thomas, *The Royal National Institute for the Blind, 1868–1956* (London: Royal National Institute for the Blind, 1957) p. 35.

52 H. Bolderson, 'The Origins of the Disabled Persons Employment Quota and its Symbolic Significance', *Journal of Social Policy*, 9 (1980) 172–3.

53 'The National League of the Blind' (Unpublished typescript, 19 December 1947) p. 1.

54 J. M. L. Eyden, 'The Physically Handicapped', in D. C. Marsh (ed.), *An Introduction to the Study of Social Administration* (London: Routledge & Kegan Paul, 1965) p. 164.

55 Thomas, *Royal National Institute*, pp. 59, 93–8, 101–2.

56 See Chapter 3, pp. 52–3.

57 J. Anderson, *A Record of Fifty Years Service to the Disabled by the Central Council for the Disabled* (London: Central Council for the Disabled, 1969) p. 14.

58 F. Watson, *Civilization and the Cripple* (London: J. Bale, 1930) p. 20.

59 Watson, *Civilization*, pp. 31, 36–7, 88.

60 Anderson, *Record*, pp. 15, 27; E. T. Atkins, *One Door Closes, Another Opens: A Personal Experience of Polio* (Walthamstow, London: Waltham Forest Oral History Workshop, 1994) p. 71; Department of Employment, *Sheltered Employment*, p. 3.

61 Nottingham District Cripples' Guild, *Annual Report* (1939) p. 6.

62 G. Finlayson, *Citizen, State and Social Welfare in Britain, 1830–1990* (Oxford: Clarendon Press, 1994) pp. 222–3.

63 J. Bourke, *Dismembering the Male: Men's Bodies, Britain and the Great War* (London: Reaktion Books, 1996) pp. 44, 71.

64 E. Elsey, 'Disabled Ex-Servicemen's Experiences of Rehabilitation and Employment after the First World War', *Oral History*, 25 (1997) 56.

65 D. Englander, 'Soldiers and Social Reform in the First and Second World Wars', *Historical Research*, LXVII (1994) 320.

66 Bourke, *Dismembering*, p. 75.

67 Englander, 'Soldiers', 320.

68 Bourke, *Dismembering*, pp. 44, 265.

69 D. H. Aldcroft, *The British Economy between the Wars* (Oxford: Philip Allan, 1983) p. 6 Table 1; C. More, *The Industrial Age: Economy and Society in Britain 1750–1986* (London: Longman, 1989) p. 238 Table 25.1; J. Stevenson, *Social Conditions in Britain between the Wars* (Harmondsworth: Penguin, 1977) p. 231.

70 Elsey, 'Disabled Ex-Servicemen's Experiences', 56.

71 Swansea and South Wales Institution for the Blind, *72nd Annual Report* (Swansea: E. Davies, 1938) back cover.

72 S. Humphries and P. Gordon, *Out of Sight: The Experience of Disability, 1900–1950* (Plymouth: Northcote House, 1992) pp. 115, 124–5.

73 'National League of the Blind', p. 3.

74 Swansea and South Wales Institution, *65th Annual Report*, pp. 8–9; Swansea and South Wales Institution, *72nd Annual Report*, p. 6.

75 Humphries and Gordon, *Out of Sight*, p. 126.

76 Thomas, *Royal National Institute*, p. 107.

77 Bolderson, 'Origins', 175–7.

78 Humphries and Gordon, *Out of Sight*, pp. 129–32.

79 Bolderson, 'Origins', 176; R. M. Titmuss, *Problems of Social Policy* (London: HMSO, 1950) p. 478.

80 G. Braybon and P. Summerfield, *Out of the Cage: Women's Experiences in Two World Wars* (London: Pandora, 1987) pp. 158, 167–8.

81 Humphries and Gordon, *Out of Sight*, pp. 132–3.

82 B. Grant, *The Deaf Advance: A History of the British Deaf Association* (Edinburgh: Pentland Press, 1990) p. 60.

83 A. Borsay, '"Fit to Work": Representing Rehabilitation in the South Wales Coalfield during the Second World War', in A. Borsay (ed.), *Medicine in Wales, c. 1800–2000: Public Service or Private Commodity?* (Cardiff: University of Wales Press, 2003) p. 145.

84 D. E. Gladstone, 'Disabled People and Employment', *Social Policy and Administration*, 19 (1985) 101.

85 M. Oliver and C. Barnes, *Disabled People and Social Policy: From Exclusion to Inclusion* (London: Longman, 1998) p. 43.

86 Bolderson, 'Origins', 177–81. See also Englander, 'Soldiers', 323.

87 S. Lonsdale, *Work and Inequality* (London: Longman, 1985) pp. 120–41; Topliss, *Provision*, pp. 49–61.

88 *The Rehabilitation and Training of Disabled Persons* (Piercy Report), Cmnd 9883 (London: HMSO, 1956) para. 169.

89 Employment Service Division, *The Quota Scheme for the Employment of Disabled People: A Discussion Document* (London: Manpower Services Commission, 1979) p. 10 Table 2; D. Jordan, *A New Employment Programme Wanted for Disabled People* (London: Disability Alliance, March 1979) pp. 28–31; S. Lonsdale, *Job Protection for the Disabled* (London: Low Pay Unit, April 1981) pp. 6, 8–10; J. Melville, 'Able to Work', *New Society* (29 April 1976) 235.

90 *Rehabilitation and Training of Disabled Persons*, para. 202.

91 Jordan, *New Employment Programme*, p. 32; K. Harper, 'The Do-Good Business That's Fallen on Hard Times', *Guardian* (17 November 1976).

92 See, for example, B. W. E. Alford, *British Economic Performance, 1945–1975* (Basingstoke: Macmillan, 1988).

93 Humphries and Gordon, *Out of Sight*, p. 136.

94 E. Topliss, *Survey of Physically Disabled People under Retirement Age Living in Private Households in Southampton* (Southampton: Department of Sociology and Social Administration, University of Southampton, 1976) p.17.

95 Melville, 'Able to Work', 236.

96 Thomson, *Problem*, pp. 288–9.

97 D. Lane, *The Work Needs of Mentally Handicapped Adults* (London: Disability Alliance, December 1980) pp. 11–2; Lonsdale, *Work and Inequality*, pp. 131–2.

98 C. Barnes, G. Mercer and T. Shakespeare *Exploring Disability: A Sociological Introduction* (Cambridge: Polity, 1999) p. 144. See also Department of Employment, *Sheltered Employment*, p. 8; Employment Service Agency, *Rehabilitation, Retraining, Resettlement* (London: HMSO, 1976) pp. 19–20; Lonsdale, *Work and Inequality*, pp. 140–1; N. Wanbrough, 'Up the Enclaves', *New Society* (27 February 1975) 522–3.

99 B. Bagilhole, *Equal Opportunities and Social Policy: Issues of Gender, Race and Disability* (London: Longman, 1997) p. 117; Barnes, Mercer and Shakespeare, *Exploring Disability*, pp. 113–14; K. Blakemore and R. Drake, *Understanding Equal Opportunity Policies* (London: Prentice Hall, 1996) pp. 15–16, 155–7; Oliver and Barnes, *Disabled People*, p. 43; A. Sinfield, *What Unemployment Means* (Oxford: Martin Robertson, 1981) pp. 126–7.

100 J. S. Clarke, *Disabled Citizens* (London: Allen & Unwin, 1951) p. 15.

101 Humphries and Gordon, *Out of Sight*, p. 137. See also T. Gould, *A Summer Plague: Polio and its Survivors* (New Haven, CT, and London: Yale University Press, 1995) pp. 257–8; A. Morris and A. Butler, *No Feet to Drag: Report on the Disabled* (London: Sidgewick and Jackson, 1972) pp. 53, 60–1.

102 J. R. Buckle, *Work and Housing of Impaired Persons in Great Britain* (London: HMSO, 1971) pp. 22, 28, Table 13 (facing p. 20).

103 Jordan, *New Employment Programme*, pp. 13–6, 22–4. See also I. Loach, *The Price of Deafness: A Review of the Financial and Employment Problems of the Deaf and Hard of Hearing* (London: Disability Alliance, 1976) pp. 19–20.

7 Financial relief

1 A. Kidd, *State, Society and the Poor in Nineteenth-Century England* (Basingstoke: Macmillan – now Palgrave Macmillan, 1999) p. 2.

2   D. Vincent, *Poor Citizens: The State and the Poor in Twentieth-Century Britain* (London: Longman, 1991) p. 3.

3   S. King, *Poverty and Welfare in England: A Regional Perspective* (Manchester: Manchester University Press, 2000) p. 258.

4   S. Smiles, *Self-Help* (London: Institute of Economic Affairs, 1996) p. 1.

5   A. Borsay, *Medicine and Charity in Georgian Bath: A Social History of the General Infirmary, c.1739–1830* (Aldershot: Ashgate, 1999) pp. 181–6, 233–7.

6   S. Cordery, 'Friendly Societies and the Discourse of Respectability in Britain, 1825–1875', *Journal of British Studies*, 34 (1995) 35–6.

7   H. Marland, *Medicine and Society in Wakefield and Huddersfield, 1780–1870* (Cambridge: Cambridge University Press, 1987) p. 177.

8   M. Gorsky, 'The Growth and Distribution of English Friendly Societies in the Early Nineteenth Century', *Economic History Review*, LI (1998) 507.

9   Marland, *Medicine*, pp. 183–4, 188–9.

10 D. Jones, 'Did Friendly Societies Matter?: A Study of Friendly Society Membership, 1794–1910', *Welsh History Review*, 12 (1984–5), 332.

11 E. T. Davies and K. E. Kissack, *The Inns and Friendly Societies of Monmouth* (Monmouth: Monmouth Historical and Educational Trust, 1981) pp. 45–7 Appendix C.

12 B. Grant, *The Deaf Advance: A History of the British Deaf Association* (Edinburgh: Pentland Press, 1990) p. 57.

13 P. H. J. H. Gosden, *Self-Help: Voluntary Associations in the Nineteenth Century* (London: Batsford, 1973) pp. 20–21, 97–8, 260–4.

14 A. M. Carr-Saunders, D. Caradog Jones and C. A. Moser, *A Survey of Social Conditions in England and Wales* (Oxford: Clarendon Press, 1958) p. 201; R. Lowe, 'Welfare's Moving Frontier', *Twentieth Century British History*, 6 (1995) 371–2.

15 G. Finlayson, *Citizen, State and Social Welfare in Britain, 1830–1990* (Oxford: Clarendon Press, 1994) p. 209.

16 F. K. Prochaska, 'Women in English Philanthropy, 1790–1830', *International Review of Social History*, 19 (1974) 426–7.

17 D. Andrew, *Philanthropy and Police: London Charity in the Eighteenth Century* (Princeton: Princeton University Press, 1989) pp. 169, 174, 200.

18 P. V. Turner, *'Charity for a Hundred Years': History of the Monmouth Street Society, Bath, from 1805 to 1904* (No place of publication, publisher or date) p. 25. See also Kidd, *State*, pp. 77–9.

19 *First Report of the Society for Bettering the Conditions and Increasing the Comforts of the Poor* (London: 1797) pp. i, ii, 3.

20 H. Dunbar, *History of the Society for the Blind in Glasgow and the West of Scotland, 1859–1989* (Glasgow: Glasgow and West of Scotland Society for the Blind, 1989) p. 29.

21 See Chapter 2, pp. 31–2.

22 J. Parker, *Social Policy and Citizenship* (London: Macmillan, 1975) p. 8.

23 J. Fido, 'The Charity Organization and Social Casework in London, 1869–1900', in A. P. Donajgrodzki (ed.), *Social Control in Nineteenth Century Britain* (London: Croom Helm, 1977) pp. 208–13.

24 Kidd, *State*, p. 99; G. Mooney, '"Remoralizing" the Poor?: Gender, Class and Philanthropy in Victorian Britain', in G. Lewis (ed.), *Forming Nation, Framing Welfare* (London: Routledge 1998) pp. 68–76; K. Woodroofe, *From Charity to Social Work in England and the United States* (London: Routledge & Kegan Paul, 1962) pp. 25–55.

25 R. Humphreys, *Sin, Organized Charity and the Poor Law in Victorian England* (Basingstoke: Macmillan – now Palgrave Macmillan, 1995) pp. 7–10, 105, 107, 173–4.

26 R. Cooter, *Surgery and Society in Peace and War: Orthopaedics and the Organization of Modern Medicine* (Basingstoke: Macmillan – now Palgrave Macmillan, 1993) pp. 56, 59; D. Owen, *English Philanthropy, 1660–1960* (Cambridge, MA: Harvard University Press, 1964) pp. 235–6; M. Rooff, *A Hundred Years of Family Welfare: A Study of the Family Welfare Association (formerly Charity Organization Society) 1869–1969* (London: Michael Joseph, 1972) p. 129.

27 Rooff, *Hundred Years*, pp. 333–7. See also L. Hollen Lees, *The Solidarities of Strangers: The English Poor Laws and the People, 1700–1948* (Cambridge: Cambridge University Press, 1998) p. 273; F. B. Smith, *The People's Health 1830–1910* (London: Weidenfeld & Nicolson, 1979) pp. 397–9.

28 See Chapter 6, pp. 126–7.

29 Woodroofe, *From Charity*, pp. 191–2. See also J. Lewis, *The Voluntary Sector, the State and Social Work in Britain* (Aldershot: Edward Elgar, 1995) p. 62; Owen, *English Philanthropy*, p. 236.

30 Lewis, *Voluntary Sector*, pp. 58–9. See also Fido, 'Charity Organization Society', pp. 225–6; Humphreys, *Sin*, pp. 123–5.

31 M. Cahill and T. Jowitt, 'The New Philanthropy: The Emergence of the Bradford City Guild of Help', *Journal of Social Policy*, 9 (1980) 359, 377–8, 381–2; F. Cushlow, 'Guilded Help?', in K. Laybourn (ed.) *Social Conditions, Status and Community, 1860–c.1920* (Stroud: Alan Sutton, 1997) pp 33–43; G. Finlayson, 'A Moving Frontier: Voluntarism and the State in British Social Welfare, 1911–1949', *Twentieth Century British History*, 1 (1990) 202; K. Laybourn, 'The Guild of Help and the Community Response to Poverty, 1904–c.1914', in Laybourn (ed.) *Social Conditions*, pp. 9–11, 13–15, 19, 28.

32 Nottingham District Cripples' Guild, *Annual Report* (1914) p. 10.

33 Nottingham District Cripples' Guild, *Annual Report* (1915) p. 7.

34 C. C. R. Pile, *The Charities of Cranbrook* (Cranbrook and District Local History Society, no place of publication or date) p. 14.

35 Grant, *Deaf Advance*, p. 37.

36 Swansea and South Wales Institution for the Blind, *Fifty-Seventh Annual Report* (No place of publication or publisher, 1923) p. 5; Swansea and South Wales Institution for the Blind, *65th Annual Report* (Swansea: Alexander Printing, 1930/1) p. 7.

37 Swansea and South Wales Institution, *65th Annual Report*, p. 12.

38 Dunbar, *History*, pp. 30–1.

39 See Chapter 2, p. 38, and Chapter 8, pp. 188–90.

40 P. Slack, *The English Poor Law, 1531–1782* (Basingstoke: Macmillan – now Palgrave Macmillan, 1990) p. 52.

41 See Chapter 2, 31–2.

42 D. Thomson, '"I am not my father's keeper": Families and the Elderly in Nineteenth-Century England', *Law and History Review*, 2 (1984) 266.

43 T. Hitchcock, P. King and P. Sharpe, 'Introduction: Chronicling Poverty – The Voices and Strategies of the English Poor, 1640–1840', in T. Hitchcock, P. King and P. Sharpe (eds), *Chronicling Poverty: The Voices and Strategies of the English Poor, 1640–1840* (Basingstoke: Macmillan – now Palgrave Macmillan, 1997) p. 10. See also King, *Poverty*, pp. 31, 98–9.

44 See Chapter 1, pp. 6–7.

45 T. Sokoll, 'Old Age in Poverty: The Record of Essex Pauper Letters, 1780–1834', in Hitchcock, King and Sharpe (eds) *Chronicling Poverty*, pp. 129, 139–40.

46 Lees, *Solidarities*, pp. 7, 37.

47 R. Mitchison, *Coping with Destitution: Poverty and Relief in Western Europe* (Toronto: Toronto University Press, 1991) pp. 33, 48.

48 M. Daunton, *Progress and Poverty: An Economic and Social History of Britain, 1700–1850* (Oxford: Oxford University Press, 1995) p. 452; King, *Poverty*, p. 116.

49 J. D. Marshall, *The Old Poor Law 1795–1834* (London: Macmillan, 1968) p. 31. See also Lees, *Solidarities*, p. 117; K. Williams, *From Pauperism to Poverty* (London: Routledge & Kegan Paul, 1981) p. 147.

50 Lees, *Solidarities*, pp. 44–6; Marshall, *Old Poor Law*, p. 34; P. Thane, *Old Age in English History: Past Experiences, Present Issues* (Oxford: Oxford University Press, 2000) p. 150.

51 G. W. Oxley, *Poor Relief in England and Wales, 1601–1834* (Newton Abbot: David and Charles, 1974) p. 62.

52 E. H. Hunt, 'Paupers and Pensioners: Past and Present', *Ageing and Society*, 9 (1990) 413.
53 Thane, *Old Age*, pp. 141, 145.
54 Oxley, *Poor Relief*, pp. 62–3.
55 Thane, *Old Age*, pp. 114.
56 D. Stone, *The Disabled State* (Basingstoke: Macmillan, 1984) pp. 15, 22, 29, 51.
57 B. J. Gleeson, 'Disability Studies: A Historical Materialist View', *Disability and Society*, 12 (1997) 191.
58 R. K. J. Grant, *On the Parish: An Illustrated Source Book on the Care of the Poor under the Old Poor Law* (Cardiff: Glamorgan Archive Service, 1988) pp. 48–9.
59 Marshall, *Old Poor Law*, p. 23.
60 T. R. Malthus, *An Essay on the Principle of Population* (Harmondsworth: Penguin, 1970) pp. 71, 93–4, 97–8, 101–2, 105.
61 F. M. Eden, *The State of the Poor: Volume 1* (London: 1797) p. 411.
62 Thane, *Old Age*, pp. 117–18, 147–8.
63 Sokoll, 'Old Age', p. 132. See also Hunt, 'Paupers', 410.
64 R. P. Hastings, *Poverty and the Poor Law in the North Riding of Yorkshire, c. 1780–1837* (York: Borthwick Institute of Historical Research, 1982) p. 17.
65 I. Waters, *Poor People* (Chepstow: Moss Rose Press, 1984) pp. 9–10.
66 Thane, *Old Age*, p. 150. See also Marshall, *Old Poor Law*, pp. 39, 45.
67 D. Thomson, 'The Decline of Social Welfare: Falling State Support for the Elderly since Early Victorian Times', *Ageing and Society*, 4 (1984) 451, 453,455–6, 468.
68 King, *Poverty*, pp. 231.
69 Thane, *Old Age*, p. 170.
70 T. Thomas, *Poor Relief in Merthyr Tydfil Union in Victorian Times* (Cardiff: Glamorgan Archive Service, 1992) pp. 25, 148–9.
71 K. D. M. Snell, *Annals of the Labouring Poor: Social Change and Agrarian England, 1660–1900* (Cambridge: Cambridge University Press, 1985) pp. 131–5.
72 Hunt, 'Paupers', 417–9, 422.
73 Thane, *Old Age*, p. 171.
74 Thane, *Old Age*, pp. 6, 168–9.
75 Lees, *Solidarities*, p. 168.
76 See Chapter 2, pp. 31–2.
77 Williams, *From Pauperism*, pp. 158–62 Table 4.5.
78 Humphreys, *Sin*, pp. 22, 31, 171.
79 P. Bartlett, *The Poor Law of Lunacy: The Administration of Pauper Lunatics in Mid-Nineteenth-Century England* (London: Leicester University Press, 1999) p. 47.

80 Lees, *Solidarities*, p. 261.

81 Williams, *From Pauperism*, p. 97.

82 Williams, *From Pauperism*, pp. 98–9.

83 Thomas, *Poor Relief*, p. 149.

84 W. J. Lewis, *Born on a Perilous Rock: Aberystwyth Past and Present* (Aberystwyth: Cambrian News, 1980) p. 150. See also P. Horn (ed.), *Oxfordshire Village Life: The Diaries of George James Dew (1846–1928) Relieving Officer* (Abingdon: Beacon, 1983) p. 46.

85 Humphreys, *Sin*, p. 32.

86 Lees, *Solidarities*, p. 264.

87 Lees, *Solidarities*, p. 277.

88 See Chapter 2, pp. 35–7.

89 Williams, *From Pauperism*, pp. 133–4.

90 Williams, *From Pauperism*, p. 231, Table 4.39.

91 J. Bourke, *Dismembering the Male: Men's Bodies, Britain and the Great War* (London: Reaktion Books, 1996) p. 72.

92 S. Humphries and P. Gordon, *Out of Sight: The Experience of Disability, 1900–1950* (Plymouth: Northcote House, 1992) p. 129.

93 M. Hill, *Social Security Policy in Britain* (Aldershot: Edward Elgar, 1990) pp. 23–5.

94 P. Thane, 'Histories of the Welfare State', in W. Lamont (ed.) *Historical Controversies and Historians* (London: UCL Press, 1998) p. 59.

95 See Chapter 6, p. 126.

96 Lees, *Solidarities*, pp. 233, 242.

97 P. W. J. Bartrip and S. B. Burman, *The Wounded Soldiers of Industry: Industrial Compensation Policy, 1833–1897* (Oxford: Clarendon Press, 1983) p. 1.

98 P. W. J. Bartrip and P. T. Fenn, 'The Measurement of Safety: Factory Accident Statistics in Victorian and Edwardian Britain', *Historical Research*, 63 (1990) 69.

99 Bartrip and Burman, *Wounded Soldiers*, p. 34.

100 P. Thane, *Foundations of the Welfare State* (London: Longman, 1982) p. 44.

101 Thane, *Old Age*, pp. 275–6.

102 N. Gray, *The Worst of Times: An Oral History of the Great Depression in Britain* (London: Wildwood House, 1985) p. 46; N. Whiteside, 'Counting the Cost: Sickness and Disability Among Working People in an Era of Industrial Recession, 1920–1939', *Economic History Review*, XL (1987) 241.

103 Bartrip and Burman, *Wounded Soldiers*, pp. 2–3, 205–6, 211, 214–15.

104 Lees, *Solidarities*, p. 315.

105 Thane, *Old Age*, pp. 73–93.

106 Thane, *Old Age*, pp. 194–216.

107 F. Thompson, *Larkrise to Candleford* (Harmondsworth: Penguin, 1973) pp. 96–7.

108 R. Roberts, *The Classic Slum* (Harmondsworth: Penguin, 1973) p. 84.

109 *Manchester Guardian*, 2 January 1909, in E. J. Evans (ed.), *Social Policy, 1830–1914: Individualism, Collectivism and the Origins of the Welfare State* (London: Routledge & Kegan Paul, 1978) pp. 275–6.

110 M. Anderson, 'The Impact on the Family Relationships of the Elderly of Changes Since Victorian Times in Governmental Income-Maintenance Provision', in E. Shanas and M. B. Sussman (eds) *Family, Bureaucracy and the Elderly* (Durham, NC: Duke University Press, 1977) p. 40; P. Johnson, 'The Employment and Retirement of Older Men in England and Wales, 1881–1981', *Economic History Review*, XLVII (1994) 126; Thane, *Old Age*, pp. 279–86, 308.

111 M. Jones, 'The 1908 Old Age Pensions Act: The Poor Law in New Disguise?', in Laybourn (ed.) *Social Conditions*, pp. 83–97.

112 Thane, *Old Age*, pp. 208–9.

113 J. R. Hay, *The Origins of the Liberal Welfare Reforms 1906–1914* (Basingstoke: Macmillan, 1975, p. 54.

114 P. Murray, *Poverty and Welfare, 1830–1914* (London: Hodder & Stoughton, 1999) pp. 111–12.

115 For a discussion of medical care for disabled people under the 1911 National Insurance Act, see Chapter 8, p. 184.

116 Whiteside, 'Counting', 230, 233.

117 Whiteside, 'Counting', 235, 238–41.

118 Bourke, *Dismembering*, pp. 43, 61–3, 65–7.

119 Bourke, *Dismembering*, p. 43, 60–2.

120 Englander, 'Soldiers', 320–2.

121 S. Koven, 'Remembering and Dismemberment: Crippled Children, Wounded Soldiers, and the Great War in Great Britain', *American Historical Review*, 99 (1994) 1200.

122 R. Means and R. Smith, *From Poor Law to Community Care: The Development of Welfare Services for Elderly People, 1939–1971* (Bristol: Policy Press, 1998) pp. 14–6; Thane, *Foundations*, pp. 130, 142–3, 245; Thane, *Old Age*, pp. 318, 332, 355–7.

123 *Social Insurance and Allied Services*, Cmd 6404 (London: HMSO, 1942) paras 7 and 8.

124 M. Langan, 'The Contested Concept of Need', in M. Langan (ed.), *Welfare: Needs, Rights and Risks* (London: Routledge, 1998) p. 8.

125 *Social Insurance*, para. 311. See also para. 17.

126   B. Bagilhole, *Equal Opportunities and Social Policy: Issues of Gender, Race and Disability* (London: Longman, 1997) p. 127; I. Loach, *The Price of Deafness: A Review of the Financial and Employment Problems of the Deaf and Hard of Hearing* (London: Disability Alliance, 1976) p. 9; E. Topliss, *Provision for the Disabled* (Oxford and London: B. Blackwell and M. Robertson, 1975) pp. 64–9.

127   Royal Association for Disability and Rehabilitation, *Comment by the Legal and Parliamentary Committee on the Report of the Royal Commission on Civil Liability and Compensation for Personal Injury* (London: RADAR, August 1978) p. 1. See also J. G. Fleming, 'The Pearson Report: Its "Strategy"', *New Law Review*, 42 (1979) 249–69; N. S. Marsh, 'The Pearson Report on Civil Liability and Compensation for Death or Personal Injury', *Law Quarterly Review*, 95 (1979) 513–35.

128   Means and Smith, *From Poor Law*, pp. 113–16.

129   Hill, *Social Security Policy*, p. 31.

130   R. Lowe, *The Welfare State in Britain Since 1945* (Basingstoke: Macmillan – now Palgrave Macmillan, 1993) pp. 131–2.

131   A. B. Atkinson, *Poverty in Britain and the Reform of Social Security* (Cambridge: Cambridge University Press, 1969) p. 19 Table 1.2.

132   Lowe, *Welfare State*, p. 144 Table 6.3.

133   *Report of the Committee on the Economic and Financial Problems of the Provision for Old Age*, Cmd 9333 (London: HMSO, 1954) para. 262.

134   *Social Insurance*, para. 369.

135   A. B. Atkinson, A. K. Maynard and C. G. Trinder, 'National Assistance and Low Incomes in 1950', *Social Policy and Administration*, 15 (1981) 30.

136   Hill, *Social Security Policy*, pp. 43–4; H. Phillips and C. Glendinning, *Who Benefits?: Report of a Welfare Rights Project with People with Disabilities in North Yorkshire* (London: Disability Alliance, March 1981) p. 3.

137   A. Deacon and J. Bradshaw, *Reserved for the Poor: The Means Test in British Social Policy* (Oxford and London: Basil Blackwell and Martin Robertson, 1983) p. 124 Table 1, p. 131 Table 2.

138   R. M. Titmuss, 'The Social Division of Welfare: Some Reflections on the Search for Equity', in R. M. Titmuss, *Essays on 'The Welfare State'* (London: Unwin University Books, 1963) p. 42.

139   Carr-Saunders, Jones and Moser, *Social Conditions*, p. 197.

140   A. Blaikie, *Ageing and Popular Culture* (Cambridge: Cambridge University Press, 1999) pp. 51, 62–3.

141   Johnson, 'Employment', p. 106.

142   A. Deacon, 'Spending More to Achieve Less?: Social Security Since 1945', in D. Gladstone (ed.), *British Social Welfare: Past,*

Present and Future (London: UCL Press, 1995) pp. 83–4; D. Gladstone, *The Twentieth-Century Welfare State* (Basingstoke: Macmillan – now Palgrave Macmillan, 1999) p. 64; Hill, *Social Security Policy*, pp. 36, 39; F. McGlone, 'Away from the Dependency Culture?: Social Security Policy', in S. P. Savage and L. Robins (eds) *Public Policy Under Thatcher* (Basingstoke: Macmillan – now Palgrave Macmillan, 1990) pp. 163, 165, 167; Thane, *Old Age*, pp. 376–8.

143 Loach, *Price of Deafness*, p. 9.

144 Deacon, 'Spending More', p. 86; Lowe, *Welfare State*, p. 155.

145 C. Glendinning, *'After Working All These Years': A Response to the Report of the National Insurance Advisory Committee on the 'Household Duties' Test for Non-Contributory Invalidity Pension for Married Women* (London: Disability Alliance, November 1980); I. Loach and R. Lister, *Second Class Disabled: A Report on the Non-Contributory Invalidity Pension for Married Women* (London: Equal Rights for Disabled Women Campaign, July 1978) pp. 5–7; J. Tunnard and N. Warren (eds) *The National Welfare Benefits Handbook* (London: Child Poverty Action Group, 1979), pp. 106–7.

146 S. Large, 'Mobility for the Physically Disabled', in K. Jones (ed.) *Year Book of Social Policy in Britain 1976* (London: Routledge & Kegan Paul, 1977) pp. 189–93; Tunnard and Warren (eds) *National Welfare Benefits Handbook*, pp. 104–5, 108–9, 111–12.

147 See, for example, S. Baldwin, 'Mobility Allowance', *New Society* (1 January 1976) 18.

148 Disability Alliance, *Poverty and Low Incomes Amongst Disabled People* (London: Disability Alliance, February 1977) p. 12 Table 3; N. Timmins, *The Five Giants: A Biography of the Welfare State* (London: HarperCollins, 1995) p. 344.

149 R. Stowell, *Disabled People on Supplementary Benefit* (London: Disablement Income Group, July 1980) p. 3.

150 B. Shepperdson, 'Attending to Need', *New Society* (28 June 1973) 754.

151 Phillips and Glendinning, *Who Benefits?*, pp. 17–22.

152 Phillips and Glendinning, *Who Benefits?*, pp. 4, 23–37.

8 Community care

1 J. Jones, J. Brown and J. Bradshaw, *Issues in Social Policy* (London: Routledge & Kegan Paul, 1978) pp. 114–15.

2 J. R. Buckle, *Work and Housing of Impaired Persons in Great Britain* (London: HMSO, 1971) p. 75 Extract from Table 70, p. 79 Extract from Table 75.

3   S. Sainsbury, *Registered As Disabled* (London: Bell, 1970) pp. 91, 95–100.

4   See Chapter 3, p. 43.

5   W. H. Godfrey, *The English Alms-House* (London: Faber & Faber, 1955) pp. 15, 17.

6   I. Waters, *Poor People* (Chepstow: Moss Rose Press, 1984) p. 36. See also N. Orme and M. Webster, *The English Hospital, 1070–1570* (New Haven, CT: Yale University Press, 1995) pp. 121–6; *Schemes for the Future Management and Regulation of the Hospital of William Browne, in the Borough of Stamford in the County of Lincoln* (London: W. M. Clowes, 1890) pp. 18–23.

7   R. L. Brown, 'A House of Noble Poverty?: A History of the Welshpool Almshouse', *Sayce Papers*, 1 (1995) 30–1.

8   D. Thomson, 'The Welfare of the Elderly in the Past: A Family or Community Responsibility?', in M. Pelling and R. M. Smith (eds), *Life, Death and the Elderly: Historical Perspectives* (London: Routledge, 1991) p. 207.

9   A. Butler, C. Oldman and J. Greve, *Sheltered Housing for the Elderly: Policy, Practice and the Consumer* (London: George Allen & Unwin, 1983) p. 74.

10   A. Murie, P. Niner and C. Watson, *Housing Policy and the Housing System* (London: Allen & Unwin, 1976) pp. 205–8.

11   *Housing Association Tenants* (London: National Federation of Housing Associations, April 1979) pp. 1–3.

12   J. Mintel, 'Property Prospects and Government Policy', *New Age* (Summer 1980) 10–1.

13   Butler, Oldman and Greve, *Sheltered Housing*, p. 22.

14   A. Blaikie, *Ageing and Popular Culture* (Cambridge: Cambridge University Press, 1999) p. 48.

15   Ministry of Health and Ministry of Works, *Housing Manual, 1944* (London: HMSO, 1944) p. 22.

16   J. Parker, *Local Health and Welfare Services* (London: George Allen & Unwin, 1965) pp. 128–9.

17   Butler, Oldman and Greve, *Sheltered Housing*, pp. 70–1, 97.

18   L. James and B. Bytheway, 'Is Sheltered Housing an Alternative to Part III Accommodation?' *Housing* (February 1979) 24; D. Fox and J. Casemore, 'Sheltered Housing: A National Policy, Locally Executed', *Housing* (December 1979) 18 Table 2.

19   Swansea and South Wales Institution for the Blind, *A Souvenir* (No place of publication or publisher, 1935); Swansea and South Wales Institution for the Blind, *72nd Annual Report* (Swansea: E. Davies, 1938), p. 7.

20   National Association for Mental Health, http://www.mind.org.uk/information/factsheets/H/HistoryofMind2.asp, accessed 10 December 2000.

21 R. M. Titmuss, *Problems of Social Policy* (London: HMSO, 1950) pp. 450–2.

22 J. Welshman, 'Growing Old in the City: Public Health and the Elderly in Leicester, 1948–74', *Medical History*, 40 (1996) 75.

23 C. Webster, *The Health Services Since the War: Volume 1 – Problems of Health Care: The National Health Service Before 1957* (London: HMSO, 1988) pp. 376–7.

24 P. Ryan, 'Residential Care for the Mentally Disabled', in J. K. Wing and R. Olsen (eds), *Community Care for the Mentally Disabled* (Oxford: Oxford University Press, 1979) pp. 60–4, 71–4, 81–2.

25 *Hansard*, 21 June 1948, 1098.

26 When the Ministry of Health had the brief for housing, these emphases were clear in their *Annual Reports* and after a specialist housing ministry was formed in 1951, the same priorities applied.

27 Ministry of Local Government and Planning, *Housing for Special Purposes: Supplement to the Housing Manual, 1949* (London: HMSO, 1951) p. 16.

28 J. Anderson, *A Record of Fifty Years Service to the Disabled by the Central Council for the Disabled* (London: Central Council for the Disabled, 1969) pp. 48–52; *Report of the Ministry of Health for the Year Ended 31 December 1962* (Health and Welfare Services), Cmnd 2062 (London: HMSO, 1963) p. 81; *Report of the Ministry of Health for the Year Ended 31 December 1963* (Health and Welfare Services), Cmnd 2389 (London: HMSO, 1963) p. 24.

29 Ministry of Housing and Local Government and Ministry of Health, *Services for Old People*, Circular 10/61 (London: HMSO, 17 March 1961) para. 22.

30 Ministry of Housing and Local Government, *Flats for the Disabled*, Circular 54/64 (London: HMSO, 18 September 1964) paras 2–3.

31 Department of the Environment, *Housing for People who are Physically Handicapped*, Circular 74/74 (London: HMSO, 7 May 1974) paras 8, 10, 12; *Towards a Housing Policy for Disabled People*, Report of the Working Party on Housing (London: Central Council for the Disabled, 1976) p. 20. The specifications of wheelchair and mobility housing were amplified in S. Goldsmith, *Wheelchair Housing*, (London: Department of the Environment, 1975), and S. Goldsmith, *Mobility Housing*, (London: Department of the Environment, 1974).

32 Department of the Environment and Welsh Office, *Local Housing Statistics: England and Wales*, No. 44 (London: HMSO, February 1978) Table 10; Department of the Environment and Welsh Office, *Local Housing Statistics: England and Wales*, No. 47 (London: HMSO, November 1978) Table 12; Department of the Environment and Welsh Office, *Local Housing Statistics: England*

and Wales, No. 50 (London: HMSO, August 1979) Table 12; Department of the Environment and Welsh Office, *Local Housing Statistics: England and Wales*, No. 54 (London: HMSO, August 1980) Table 12.

33 Ministry of Health, *Welfare Services for Mentally Disordered Persons and for Handicapped Persons*, Circular 16/60 (London: HMSO, 18 July 1960) para. 2.

34 Department of Health and Social Security, 'Aids to Households: England' Unpublished Statistical Series, 1979) Table N. 1.

35 Department of the Environment, *Adaptations of Housing for People who are Physically Handicapped*, Circular 59/78 (London: HMSO, 29 August 1978) para. 18; A. Borsay, 'An Uneasy Alliance: The Relationship Between Occupational Therapists and Housing Officials, *Housing Review*, 31 (1982) 175–7; U. Keeble, *Aids and Adaptations* (London: Bedford Square Press, 1979) chs 4, 11, 12, 13.

36 D. Pomeroy, J. Fewtrell, N. Butler and R. Gill, *Handicapped Children: Their Homes and Life-Styles*, (London: Department of the Environment, 1978) p. 29.

37 S. Goldsmith and K. Kirby, 'Purpose-Built or Adapted: The Neighbourhood Counts', *Municipal and Public Services Journal* (9 December 1977) 1241–2; J. Morton, *Wheelchair Housing: A Survey of Purpose-Designed Dwellings for Disabled People*, (London: Department of the Environment, no date) p. 31 Table 28, p. 33 Table 30.

38 B. Bagilhole, *Equal Opportunities and Social Policy: Issues of Gender, Race and Disability* (London: Longman, 1997) pp. 166–7; Buckle, *Work*, p. 106; E. Topliss and B. Gould, *A Charter for the Disabled* (Oxford: B. Blackwell and M. Robertson, 1981) pp. 123–5.

39 A. Morris and A. Butler, *No Feet to Drag: Report on the Disabled* (London: Sidgwick & Jackson, 1972) pp. 70–3; J. S. Clarke, *Disabled Citizens* (London: Allen & Unwin, 1951) p. 168.

40 G. Fennell, C. Phillipson and H. Evers, *The Sociology of Old Age* (Milton Keynes: Open University Press, 1988) pp. 27–8; A. Scull, *Museums of Madness: The Social Organization of Insanity in Nineteenth-Century England* (Harmondsworth: Penguin, 1982) p. 220.

41 J. Melling, B. Forsythe and R. Adair, 'Families, Communities and the Legal Regulation of Lunacy in Victorian England: Assessments of Violence, Crime and Welfare in Admissions to the Devon Asylum, 1845–1914', in P. Bartlett and D. Wright (eds), *Outside the Walls of the Asylum: A History of Care in the Community, 1750–2000* (London: Athlone, 1999) pp. 164–71, 179. See also D. Wright, *Mental Disability in Victorian England: The Earlswood Asylum, 1847–1901* (Oxford: Clarendon Press, 2001) pp. 56–8.

42 M. Thomson, *The Problem of Mental Deficiency: Eugenics, Democracy, and Social Policy in Britain, c. 1870–1959* (Oxford: Clarendon Press, 1998) p. 258.

43 J. Walmsley and D. Atkinson, 'Oral History and the History of Learning Disability', in J. Bornat, R. Perks, P. Thompson and J. Walmsley, *Oral History, Health and Welfare* (London: Routledge, 2000) 189.

44 Thomson, *Problem*, pp. 258–9. See also J. Walmsley and S. Rolph, 'Development of Community Care for People with Learning Difficulties, 1913–1945', *Critical Social Policy*, 21 (2001) 63–4, 67–70.

45 Wright, *Mental Disability*, p. 6.

46 Melling, Forsythe and Adair, 'Families', pp. 172–3.

47 D. Wright, '"Childlike in His Innocence": Lay Attitudes to "Idiots" and "Imbeciles" in Victorian England', in D. Wright and A. Digby (eds), *From Idiocy to Mental Deficiency: Historical Perspectives on People with Learning Difficulties* (London: Routledge 1996) pp. 123–5.

48 Thomson, *Problem*, pp. 261–4.

49 Wright, *Mental Disability*, p. 82.

50 J. K. Walton, 'Lunacy in the Industrial Revolution', *Journal of Social History*, 14 (1980) 1–18.

51 J. Walmsley, 'Telling the History of Learning Disability from Local Sources', in D. Atkinson, M. Jackson and J. Walmsley (eds), *Forgotton Lives: Exploring the History of Learning Disability* (Kidderminster: British Institute of Learning Disabilities, 1997) p. 90.

52 Walmsley and Rolph, 'Development', pp. 71–2.

53 For an appraisal of these figures, see M. Anderson, *Approaches to the History of the Western Family 1500–1914* (London: Macmillan, 1980) pp. 22–7.

54 P. Thane, *Old Age in English History: Past Experiences, Present Issues* (Oxford: Oxford University Press, 2000) pp. 130, 298–9.

55 Thane, *Old Age*, pp. 122, 299, 408–9, 412, 418, 420–1, 430.

56 D. Wright, 'Learning Disability and the New Poor Law in England, 1834–1867', *Disability and Society*, 15 (2000) 733.

57 M. Horsburgh, '"No Sufficient Security": The Reaction of the Poor Law Authorities to Boarding-Out', *Journal of Social Policy*, 12 (1983) 51–70. See also R. G. Hodgkinson, *The Origins of the National Health Service* (London: Wellcome Historical Medical Library, 1967) p. 177; R. Mitchison, *The Old Poor Law in Scotland: The Experience of Poverty, 1574–1845* (Edinburgh: Edinburgh University Press, 2000) pp. 172–3, 218.

58 D. Hirst and P. Michael, 'Family, Community and the Lunatic in Mid-Nineteenth-Century North Wales', in Bartlett and Wright (eds), *Outside*, pp. 84–5.

59 H. Sturdy and W. Parry-Jones, 'Boarding-out Insane Patients: The Significance of the Scottish System, 1857–1913', in Bartlett and Wright (eds), *Outside*, pp. 86–114.

60 Shropshire Convalescent and Surgical Home for Women and Children, Baschurch, *Eleventh Annual Report* (October 1910/11) p. 2. See also G. J. Eagling, *A History of a London School for the Deaf: Ackmar Road, 1898–1983* (Doncaster: British Deaf History Society, 1998) pp. 4–5.

61 Thomson, *Problem*, pp. 156–9.

62 Ministry of Health, *National Assistance Act, 1948*, Circular 87/48 (London: HMSO, 7 June 1948) para. 60.

63 Parker, *Local Health and Welfare Services*, p. 100.

64 V. Berridge, *Health and Society in Britain Since 1939* (Cambridge: Cambridge University Press, 1999) p. 34.

65 A. C. Bebbington, 'Changes in the Provision of Services to the Elderly in the Community over Fourteen Years', *Social Policy and Administration*, 13 (1979) 111, 117–9.

66 See, for example, A. Borsay, *Disabled People in the Community: A Study of Housing, Health and Welfare Services* (London: Bedford Square Press, 1986) pp. 139–40 Tables 14 and 15; M. Bayley, *Mental Handicap and Community Care: A Study of Mentally Handicapped People in Sheffield* (London: Routledge & Kegan Paul, 1973) pp. 91–7.

67 M. Barrett and M. McIntosh, *The Anti-Social Family* (London: Verso, 1982) p. 26.

68 M. Anderson, 'The Impact on the Family Relationships of the Elderly of Changes Since Victorian Times in Govermental Income-Maintenance Provision', in E. Shanas and M. B. Sussman (eds), *Family, Bureaucracy and the Elderly* (Durham, NC: Duke University Press, 1977) pp. 50–3, 58–9; Thane, *Old Age*, pp. 414–16.

69 S. Humphries and P. Gordon, *Out of Sight: The Experience of Disability, 1900–1950* (Plymouth: Northcote House, 1992) pp. 11, 25–33.

70 E. T. Atkins, *One Door Closes, Another Opens: A Personal Experience of Polio* (Walthamstow: Waltham Forest Oral History Workshop, 1994) pp. 51, 54–5, 87–9.

71 Hirst and Michael, 'Family', pp. 75–7.

72 Wright, *Mental Disability*, pp. 51–2.

73 H. Land, 'Who Cares for the Family?' *Journal of Social Policy*, 7 (1978) 258; J. Lewis, *Women in England, 1870–1950* (Brighton: Wheatsheaf Books, 1984) pp. 145–53.

74 R. M. Moroney, *The Family and the State: Considerations for Social Policy* (London: Longman, 1976) pp. 15–23; L. Rimmer, *Families in Focus: Marriage, Divorce and Family Patterns* (London: Study Commission on the Family, October 1980) p. 65; G. Braybon and

P. Summerfield, *Out of the Cage: Women's Experiences in Two World Wars* (London: Pandora, 1987) p. 146; E. Roberts, *Women's Work, 1840–1940* (Basingstoke: Macmillan, 1988) p. 22.

75 *The Experience of Caring for Elderly and Handicapped Dependants: Survey Report* (Manchester: Equal Opportunities Commission, March 1980) pp. 9–10. See also A. Hunt, *The Elderly At Home: A Study of People Aged Sixty Five and Over Living in the Community in England in 1976* (London: HMSO, 1978) p. 78 Table 10.9.8, p. 83 Table 10.13.2, p. 84 Table 10.13.3.

76 *Caring for the Elderly and Handicapped: Community Care Policies and Women's Lives* (Manchester: Equal Opportunities Commission, March 1982) pp. 13–16. See also M. Nissel and L. Bonnerjea, *Family Care of the Handicapped Elderly: Who Pays?* (London: Policy Studies Institute, January 1982) pp. 15–22.

77 See, for example, *Who Cares for the Carers?: Opportunities for Those Caring for the Elderly and Handicapped* (Equal Opportunities Commission, March 1982) p. 7; *Experience of Caring*, pp. 18–19; H. Land, *Parity Begins At Home: Women's and Men's Work in the Home and its Effect on their Paid Employment* (Manchester: Equal Opportunities Commission and Social Science Research Council, September 1981) pp. 4–5

78 See, for example, J. Bradshaw and D. Lawton, 'Tracing the Causes of Stress in Families with Handicapped Children', *British Journal of Social Work*, 8 (1978) 183; *Experience of Caring*, pp. 28–9; Nissel and Bonnerjea, *Family Care*, pp. 42–5.

79 See, for example, Bayley, *Mental Handicap*, pp. 36–48; *Experience of Caring*, pp. 23–8; Pomeroy, Fewtrell, Butler and Gill, *Handicapped Children*, pp. 18–9, 51, 54–6; Nissel and Bonnerjea, *Family Care*, pp. 30–6.

80 M. Loane, *The Queen's Poor: Life as They Find it in Town and Country* (London: Middlesex University Press, 1998) pp, 177–8.

81 R. Blythe, *The View in Winter: Reflections on Old Age* (Harmondsworth: Penguin, 1979) p. 59.

82 *Caring for the Elderly*, p. 13.

83 Moroney, *Family*, pp. 4, 9–10.

84 D. Porter and R. Porter, *Patient's Progress: Doctors and Doctoring in Eighteenth-Century England* (Cambridge: Polity Press, 1989) pp. 96–114.

85 P. S. Brown, 'Medicines Advertised in Eighteenth-Century Bath Newspapers', *Medical History*, 20 (1976) 153–4.

86 W. F. Bynum, *Science and the Practice of Medicine in the Nineteenth Century* (Cambridge: Cambridge University Press, 1994) pp. 179–80;

C. Lawrence, *Medicine in the Making of Modern Britain, 1700–1920* (London: Routledge, 1994) pp. 55–7.

87 *The Problem of the Deaf: A Handbook of Information on Deafness, the Deaf and Dumb and the Deafened through Disease or Accident,* (London: National Institute for the Deaf, 1929) pp. 79–80.

88 Humphries and Gordon, *Out of Sight,* p. 22.

89 G. W. Oxley, *Poor Relief in England and Wales, 1601–1834* (Newton Abbot: David & Charles, 1974) pp. 65, 67, 72.

90 W. Flinn, 'Medical Services under the New Poor Law', in D. Fraser (ed.), *The New Poor Law in the Nineteenth Century* (London: Macmillan, 1976) pp. 47–50, 53–5; A. Paterson, 'The Poor Law in Nineteenth-Century Scotland', in Fraser (ed.) *New Poor Law,* p. 189.

91 J. Robin, *The Way We Lived Then* (Aldershot: Ashgate, 2000) p. 115.

92 Flinn, 'Medical Services', pp. 49–50.

93 Flinn, 'Medical Services', p. 50.

94 D. Andrew, *Philanthropy and Police: London Charity in the Eighteenth Century* (Princeton, NJ: Princeton University Press, 1989) pp. 132–3, 155–6; B. Croxon, 'The Public and Private Faces of Eighteenth-Century London Dispensary Charity', *Medical History,* 41 (1997) 127, 135–9; J. V. Pickstone, *Medicine and Industrial Society: A History of Hospital Development in Manchester and its Region, 1752–1946* (Manchester: Manchester University Press, 1985) pp. 16–17.

95 See Chapter 3, p. 44.

96 Flinn, 'Medical Services', pp. 50–1; Hodgkinson, *Origins,* p. 205; K. A. Webb, *'One of the Most Useful Charities in the City': York Dispensary, 1788–1988* (York: Borthwick Institute of Historical Research, 1988) p. 2.

97 Abel-Smith, *The Hospitals, 1800–1948: A Study in Social Administration in England and Wales* (London: Heinemann, 1964) p. 90; K. Morrison, *The Workhouse: A Study of Poor Law Buildings in England* (Swindon: English Heritage, 1999) p. 165.

98 Flinn, 'Medical Services', p. 51.

99 Webb, 'One of the Most Useful Charities', pp. 28–9.

100 P. Thane, *Foundations of the Welfare State* (London: Longman, 1982) p. 86.

101 Webb, 'One of the Most Useful Charities', p. 30.

102 See Chapter 6, pp. 133–4.

103 M. Guyatt, 'Better Legs: Artificial Limbs for British Veterans of the First World War', *Journal of Design History,* 14 (2001) 307, 311–12.

104 J. Bourke, *Dismembering the Male: Men's Bodies, Britain and the Great War* (London: Reaktion Books, 1996) p. 46.

105 Guyatt, 'Better Legs', 318.
106 The British Limbless Ex-Servicemen's Association.
107 E. Elsey, 'Disabled Ex-Servicemen's Experience of Reliabilitation and Employment after the First World War', *Oral History*, 25 (1997) 55.
108 Humphries and Gordon, *Out of Sight*, pp. 20, 23.
109 Bourke, *Dismembering*, pp. 47–8.
110 Bourke, *Dismembering*, p. 266 footnote 90.
111 Webster, *Health Services*, p. 398.
112 Anderson, *Record*, pp. 39, 43.
113 Morris and Butler, *No Feet*, pp. 87–9, 119.
114 J. Ashley, *Acts of Defiance* (Harmondsworth: Penguin, 1992) pp. 344–5. This decision was taken in 1973.
115 J. D. Hirst, 'The Growth of Treatment Through the School Medical Service', *Medical History*, 33 (1989) 318–42.
116 Humphries and Gordon, *Out of Sight*, pp. 57, 59.
117 H. Dean, *Welfare Rights and Social Policy* (Harlow: Pearson Education, 2002) pp. 146–7.
118 D. C. Morrell, 'Expressions of Morbidity in General Practice', *British Medical Journal*, 262 (22 May 1971) 455, 457 Table VI. See also C. Webster, 'The Elderly and the Early National Health Service', in Pelling and Smith (eds), *Life*, pp. 180–1.
119 P. Wood and K. Jones, 'Getting Primary Care on the National Health Service', *Journal of Consumer Studies and Home Economics*, 3 (1979) 145.
120 Waters, *Poor People*, pp. 9–10.
121 R. P. Hastings, *Poverty and the Poor Law in the North Riding of Yorkshire, c. 1780–1837* (York: Borthwick Institute of Historical Research, 1982) p. 14.
122 Parker, *Local Health and Welfare Services*, p. 29.
123 M. Dexter and W. Harbert, *The Home Help Service* (London: Tavistock Publications, 1983) pp. 4–7. See also R. Dingwall, A.-M. Rafferty and C. Webster, *An Introduction to the Social History of Nursing* (London: Routledge, 1988) pp. 173–80.
124 A. F. Young and E. T. Ashton, *British Social Work in the Nineteenth Century* (London: Routledge & Kegan Paul, 1956) pp. 188–90, 196–7, 204–5.
125 D. Gladstone, *The Twentieth-Century Welfare State* (Basingstoke: Macmillan – now Palgrave Macmillan, 1999) pp. 108–9.
126 'The National League of the Blind' (unpublished typescript, 19 December 1947) p. 1.
127 Parker, *Local Health and Welfare Services*, pp. 35–6.

128 G. Finlayson, *Citizen, State and Social Welfare in Britain, 1830–1990* (Oxford: Clarendon Press, 1994) p. 280.

129 R. Means and R. Smith, *Community Care: Policy and Practice* (Basingstoke: Macmillan – now Palgrave Macmillan, 1994) p. 24.

130 Ministry of Health, *Report of the Ministry of Health for the Year Ended 31 March 1950*, Part I, Cmnd 8342 (London: HMSO, 1951) pp. 152–3. See also Ministry of Health, *National Assistance Act*, paras 58–9, 71.

131 R. Means and R. Smith, *From Poor Law to Community Care: The Development of Welfare Services for Elderly People, 1939–1971* (Bristol: Policy Press, 1998) p. 248.

132 Means and Smith, *From Poor Law*, p. 156.

133 Parker, *Local Health and Welfare Services*, p. 125, 157.

134 Welshman, 'Growing Old', p. 84.

135 Parker, *Local Health and Welfare Services*, p. 155.

136 Webster, *Health Services*, pp. 374–5.

137 *National Survey of Community Psychiatric Nursing Services* (Wigan: Community Psychiatric Nurses' Association, 1980) p. 1.

138 A. Forder (ed.), *Penelope Hall's Social Services of England and Wales* (London: Routledge & Kegan Paul, 1969) p. 270; Means and Smith, *From Poor Law*, p. 232; Parker, *Local Health and Welfare Services*, pp. 100, 102–5, 135.

139 Welshman, 'Growing Old', p. 76.

140 Webster, *Health Services*, pp. 221–2.

141 G. Sumner and R. Smith, *Planning Local Authority Services for the Elderly* (London: Allen & Unwin, 1969) p. 253.

142 See Chapter 3, pp. 45, 63.

143 *Health and Welfare: The Development of Community Care – Plans for the Health and Welfare Services of the Local Authorities in England and Wales*, Cmnd 1973 (London: HMSO, 1963) p. 366 Table II.

144 See, for example, L. G. Moseley, 'Variations in Socio-Medical Services for the Aged', *Social and Economic Administration*, 2 (1968) 169–83.

145 K. Jones, *Asylums and After: A Revised History of the Mental Health Services: From the Early Eighteenth Century to the 1990s* (London: Athlone, 1993) p. 183.

146 C. Webster, *The National Health Service: A Political History* (Oxford: Oxford University Press, 1998) pp. 79–80.

147 A. Webb and N. Falk, 'Planning the Social Services: The Local Authority Ten Year Plans', *Policy and Politics*, 3 (1974) 40–1. See also T. A. Booth, 'Forward Planning of Local Authority Social

Services', in T. A. Booth (ed.), *Planning for Welfare: Social Policy and the Expenditure Process* (Oxford: Basil Blackwell and Martin Robertson, 1979) p. 138.

148 Department of Health and Social Security, *Priorities for Health and Personal Social Services in England: A Consultative Document* (London: HMSO, 1976). Whereas cost-benefit analysis attaches money costs and benefits to each component of alternative decisions and selects the option with the highest total benefit or the lowest total cost, cost-effectiveness analysis 'compares the social costs of attaining a particular objective and hence . . . does not have to concern itself with benefit valuation'. See A. J. Culyer, *The Economics of Social Policy* (Oxford: Martin Robertson, 1973) pp. 156–7.

149 M. Brown, 'Priorities for Health and Personal Social Services', in K. Jones (ed.), *Year Book of Social Policy in Britain 1976* (London: Routledge & Kegan Paul, 1977) pp. 30–1. See also G. T. Banks, 'Programme Budgeting in the DHSS', in Booth (ed.), *Planning*, p. 162.

150 Central Statistical Office, *National Income and Expenditure: 1980 Edition*, (London: HMSO, 1980) pp. 64–5 Table 9.4.

151 Department of Health and Social Security, *Health and Personal Social Services Statistics for England, 1978* (London: HMSO, 1980) p. 141 Table 6.6, p. 158 Tables 7.7 and 7.8; Department of Health and Social Security, *Health and Personal Social Services Statistics for England 1982* (London: HMSO, 1982) p. 94 Table 6.6, p. 104 Table 7.7.

152 Topliss and Gould, *Charter*, p. 105 Table III.

153 Banks, 'Programme Budgeting', pp. 155–72.

154 B. Davies, *Social Needs and Resources in Local Services* (London: Michael Joseph, 1968) p. 16.

155 Hunt, *Elderly*, p. 87 Table 11.2.1. The term 'council welfare officer' was not defined and so may have included social services, housing and other local authority personnel.

156 M. J. Brown and R. Bowl, *Study of Local Authority Chronic Sick and Disabled Persons Surveys* (Birmingham: University of Birmingham Social Services Unit, 1976).

157 E. Topliss, *Survey of Physically Disabled People under Retirement Age Living in Private Households in Southampton* (Southampton: Dept of Sociology and Social Policy, University of Southampton, 1976) pp. 1, 2, 26–7.

158 Department of Health and Social Security, *The Chronically Sick and Disabled Persons Act 1970*, Circular 12/70 (17 August 1970) para. 7.

159   J. Cook and P. Mitchell, *Putting Teeth in the Act: A History of Attempts to Enforce the Provisions of Section 2 of the Chronically Sick and Disabled Persons Act 1970* (London: Royal Association for Disability and Rehabilitation, no date) pp. 1–7, 31–2; Topliss and Gould, *Charter*, pp. 111–2.

160   M. Oliver, *Understanding Disability: From Theory to Practice* (Basingstoke: Macmillan – now Palgrave Macmillan, 1996) pp. 69–70.

161   T. Robinson, *In Worlds Apart: Professionals and their Clients in the Welfare State* (London: Bedford Square Press, 1978) pp. 6–7.

162   A. Glampson and E. M. Goldberg, 'Post-Seebohm Social Services: (2) The Consumer's View – A Comparison Between 1972 and 1975', *Social Work Today*, 8 (9 November 1976) 9–10.

163   *Caring for the Elderly*, p. 28.

164   Hunt, *Elderly*, p. 87 Table 11.2.1; Land, 'Who Cares?' 268.

165   Borsay, *Disabled People*, p. 113.

166   J. Kemm, 'When the Face Behind the Food Is Needed More', *Health and Social Services Journal* (9 January 1981) 20.

167   M. Blaxter, *The Meaning of Disability: A Sociological Study of Impairment* (London: Heinemann, 1976) pp. 66–7; *Experience of Caring*, p. 31.

168   E. Topliss, *Social Responses to Handicap* (London: Longman, 1982) p. 100.

169   Blaxter, *Meaning*, p. 63.

170   A. I. Harris, with E. Cox and C. R. W. Smith, *Handicapped and Impaired in Great Britain* (London: HMSO, 1971) p. 50 Tables 38 and 39.

171   K. Woodroofe, *From Charity to Social Work in England and the United States* (London: Routledge & Kegan Paul, 1962) pp. 136–41.

172   Parker, *Health and Welfare Services*, p. 137.

173   For a fuller discussion of these issues, see A. Borsay, '"First Child Care, Second Mental Health, Third the Elderly": Professional Education and the Development of Social Work Priorities', *Research, Policy and Planning*, 7 (1989) 22–6.

174   Glampson and Goldberg, 'Post-Seebohm Social Services', 9.

175   C. Glendinning, *Unshared Care: Parents and their Disabled Children* (London: Routledge & Kegan Paul, 1983) pp. 157–62.

176   E. Topliss, *Provision for the Disabled* (Oxford and London: B. Blackwell and M. Robertson, 1975) p. 130 Table VII.

177   A. Purkis and P. Hodson, *Housing and Community Care* (London: Bedford Square Press, 1982) p. 26. See also Blaxter, *Meaning*, p. 13.

178 G. Weightman, *Crossroads Care Attendant Scheme Trust* (London: Royal Association for Disability and Rehabilitation, 1977).
179 S. Latto and B. Healey, *An Approach to Care in the Community* (Coventry: Coventry Social Services Department, no date); A. M. Brunner, *An Evaluation of the Hove Intensive Domiciliary Care Project* (Lewes: East Sussex Social Services Department, March 1979); Personal Social Services Research Unit, *The Kent Community Care Project: An Interim Report* (Canterbury: University of Kent at Canterbury, March 1979) pp. 9–11.
180 M. Oliver and C. Barnes, *Disabled People and Social Policy: From Exclusion to Inclusion* (London: Longman, 1998) p. 85.

9 Conclusion

1 R. Jack, 'Institutions in Community Care', in R. Jack (ed.) *Residential Versus Community Care: The Role of Institutions in Welfare Provision* (Basingstoke: Macmillan – now Palgrave Macmillan, 1998) pp. 12, 17–18. See also J. Walmsley and S. Rolph, 'Development of Community Care for People with Learning Difficuties, 1913–1945', *Critical Social Policy*, 21 (2001) p. 181.
2 M. Oliver, 'Disability and Participation in the Labour Market', in P. Brown and R. Scase (eds), *Poor Work: Disadvantage and the Division of Labour* (Milton Keynes: Open University Press, 1991) p. 139.
3 D. King, *In the Name of Liberalism: Illiberal Social Policy in the United States and Britain* (Oxford: Oxford University Press, 1999) pp. 11–12.
4 M. Jackson, *The Borderland of Imbecility: Medicine, Society and the Fabrication of the Feeble Mind in Late Victorian and Early Edwardian England* (Manchester: Manchester University Press, 2000) pp. 35–8; L. Hollen Lees, *The Solidarities of Strangers: The English Poor Laws and the People, 1700–1948* (Cambridge: Cambridge University Press, 1998) p. 245; M. Thomson, *The Problem of Mental Deficiency: Eugenics, Democracy, and Social Policy in Britain, c.1870–1959* (Oxford: Clarendon Press, 1998) pp. 6, 304.
5 Lees, *Solidarities*, pp. 294–305.
6 H. Dean, *Welfare Rights and Social Policy* (Harlow: Pearson Education, 2002) p. 146.
7 Department of Health, http://www.doh.gov.uk/mentalhealth/weeklybull.htm, accessed 6 December 2003.

8   C. Barnes, *Disabled People in Britain and Discrimination: A Case for Anti-Discrimination Legislation* (London: Hurst, 1991) pp. 208–14.

9   A. Borsay, *Disabled People in the Community: A Study of Housing, Health and Welfare Services* (London: Bedford Square Press, 1986) pp. 11–19.

10 M. Oliver and C. Barnes, *Disabled People and Social Policy: From Exclusion to Inclusion* (London: Longman, 1998) pp. 17, 72.

11 K. Jones, *Asylums and After: A Revised History of the Mental Health Services: From the Early Eighteenth Century to the 1990s* (London: Athlone, 1993) pp. 208–10.

12 Department of Health, http://www.doh.gov.uk/menhlthref.htm, accessed 6 December 2003.

13 N. Deakin, *The Politics of Welfare* (London: Methuen, 1987) pp. 127–9, 141–6.

14 C. Barnes, G. Mercer and T. Shakespeare, *Exploring Disability: A Sociological Introduction* (Cambridge: Polity, 1999) pp. 136–7.

15 Barnes, Mercer and Shakes peare, *Exploring Disability*, pp. 137–9.

16 V. Berridge, *Health and Society in Britain Since 1939* (Cambridge: Cambridge University Press, 1999) pp. 69–70.

17 H. Jones, 'Health', in R. M. Page and R. Silburn (eds), *British Social Welfare in the Twentieth Century* (Basingstoke: Macmillan – now Palgrave Macmillan, 1998) pp. 172–4.

18 E. J. Evans, *Thatcher and Thatcherism* (London: Routledge, 1997) p. 69.

19 Oliver and Barnes, *Disabled People*, pp. 40, 140–3.

20 Barnes, Mercer and Shakespeare, *Exploring Disability*, pp. 148–50.

21 N. Ginsburg, 'Housing', in Page and Silburn (eds), *British Social Welfare*, pp. 237–43; S. Monk and M. Kleinman, 'Housing', in P. Brown and R. Sparks (eds), *Beyond Thatcherism: Social Policy, Politics and Society* (Milton Keynes: Open University Press, 1989) pp. 126–30.

22 Barnes, Mercer and Shakespeare, *Exploring Disability*, pp. 119–20.

23 L. Morris, 'Legitimate Membership of the Welfare Community', in M. Langan (ed.), *Welfare: Needs, Rights and Risks* (London: Routledge, 1998) p. 221.

24 M. Oliver, *Understanding Disability: From Theory to Practice* (Basingstoke: Macmillan – now Palgrave Macmillan, 1996) p. 81.

25 Disability Rights Commission, http://www.drc-gb.org/law/dda.asp, accessed 6 December 2003.

26 Barnes, Mercer and Shakespeare, *Exploring Disability*, pp. 113–14.

27 B. Bagilhole, *Equal Opportunities and Social Policy: Issues of Gender, Race and Disability* (London: Longman, 1997) p. 116.

28 J. Schneider, K. Simons and G. Everatt, 'Impact of the National Minimum Wage on Disabled People', *Disability and Society*, 16 (2001) 723–47.

29 R. Lister, 'From Equality to Social Inclusion: New Labour and the Welfare State', *Critical Social Policy*, 18 (1998) 215.

30 R. Levitas, 'The Concept of Social Exclusion and the New Durkheimian Hegemony', *Critical Social Policy*, 16 (1996) 18.

31 F. Bowring, 'Social Exclusion: Limitations of the Debate', *Critical Social Policy*, 20 (2000) 319–20.

32 Department for Constitutional Affairs, http://www.dca.gov.uk/hract/hramenu.htm, accessed 6 December 2003.

33 M. Adler and S. Asquith, 'Discretion and Power', in M. Adler and S. Asquith (eds), *Discretion and Welfare* (London: Heinemann, 1981) pp. 17, 21. See also Borsay, *Disabled People*, pp. 191–2.

34 G. R. Elton, 'Some Thoughts on History at the Universities', *History*, LIV (1969) 66.

35 A. Digby, *British Welfare Policy: Workhouse to Workfare* (London: Faber & Faber, 1989) pp. 1, 30, 35. See also J. Brown, *The British Welfare State: A Critical History* (Oxford: Blackwell, 1995) p. vi; D. Fraser, *The Evolution of the British Welfare State* (London: Macmillan, 1973) p. 232; K. Jones, *The Making of Social Policy in Britain, 1830–1990* (London: Athlone, 1991) p. xi; R. Means and R. Smith, *From Poor Law to Community Care: The Development of Welfare Services for Elderly People, 1939–1971* (Bristol: Policy Press, 1998) pp. 1–2, ch. 8.

36 J. Tosh, *The Pursuit of History: Aims, Methods and New Directions in the Study of Modern History*, (London: Longman, 1991) pp. 10–20.

37 M. Sarup, *Identity, Culture and the Postmodern World* (Edinburgh: Edinburgh University Press, 1996) pp. 96–8. See also K. Jenkins, *Re-Thinking History* (London: Routledge, 1991) pp. 18–9.

38 M. Sarup, *An Introductory Guide to Post-Structuralism and Post-modernism* (London: Harvester Wheatsheaf, 1993) pp. 186–7.

39 J. Campbell and M. Oliver, *Disability Politics: Understanding our Past, Changing our Future* (London: Routledge, 1996) p. 17.

40 D. Marks, *Disability: Controversial Debates and Psychosocial Perspectives* (London: Routledge, 1999) p. 183.

41 R. Fido and M. Potts, 'Using Oral Histories' in D. Atkinson, M. Jackson and J. Walmsley (eds), *Forgotten Lives: Exploring the History of Learning Disability* (Kidderminster: British Institute of Learning Disabilities, 1997) p. 45. See also S. French with J. Swain, 'Institutional Abuse: Memories of a "Special School" for Visually Impaired Girls – A Personal Account', in J. Bornat, R. Perks, P. Thompson and

J. Walmesley (eds), *Oral History, Health and Welfare* (London: Routledge, 2000) p. 178.

42 Sarup, *Identity*, p. 17.

43 Barnes, Mercer and Shakespeare, *Exploring Disability*, pp. 213–20; B. Gleeson, *Geographies of Disability* (London: Routledge, 1999) pp. 203–5; Tosh, *Pursuit*, pp. 6–9, 21.

44 Oliver, *Understanding Disability*, pp. 167. See also R. Drake, 'What Am I Doing Here?: "Non-Disabled" People and the Disability Movement', *Disability and Society*, 12 (1997) 643–4.

Chronology of events

This chronology offers an overview of the development of social policies for disabled people and serves as a guide to the key events referred to in the text. It is divided into four parts: (1) Before 1750; (2) The Era of the Industrial Revolution, 1750–1850; (3) The Growth of Collectivism, 1850–1939; and (4) The Development of the Welfare State Since 1939.

Part 1 Before 1750

1247   The London priory dedicated to St Mary of Bethlehem, which became the Bethlem Lunatic Asylum, was founded.

1597   Poor law legislation in Scotland enabled voluntary contributions via the kirk to support the 'aged' and 'impotent' but not the able-bodied.

1601   Poor law legislation in England and Wales required each parish to: (1) support the 'aged' and 'impotent'; (2) bring up orphaned children; and (3) provide work for those capable of employment but without a job.

1714   The Vagrancy Act specifically permitted the detention of 'lunatics' for the first time in English law.

1720   The Westminster Hospital opened to become the first voluntary subscription infirmary in London.

1723   Knatchbull's Act allowed parishes in England and Wales to build workhouses without obtaining a local Act of Parliament.

1736   The Winchester County Hospital opened to become the first voluntary subscription infirmary in the provinces.

1742   The General Infirmary at Bath opened, giving 'cripples' and other poor but worthy visitors access to the spa waters.

1744   Vagrancy legislation required two magistrates, rather than the usual one, to authorize the detention of a 'mad person'.

Part 2 The era of the Industrial Revolution, 1750–1850

1751   St Luke's Hospital for Lunatics was established in London on a subscription basis.

1764   The first British 'special' school for deaf children opened in Edinburgh under the commercial proprietorship of Thomas Braidwood.

1774   The Madhouses Act set up a commission from the Royal College of Physicians to license and visit private madhouses in London.

1782   Gilbert's Act authorized the combination of adjacent parishes in England and Wales to construct workhouses for 'sick', 'aged' and 'infirm' inmates.

1791   The first British charity school for blind children opened in Liverpool.

1792   The first British charity school for deaf children opened in Bermondsey, London.

1796   The Quaker Retreat, one of the pioneers of moral management for 'insane' patients, opened in York.

1808   The County Asylum Act permitted, but did not require counties in England and Wales to build asylums for pauper and criminal 'lunatics'.

1813   *A Description of the Retreat, An Institution Near York* was published by Samuel Tuke, explaining the philosophy of moral management.

1817   The General Institution for the Relief of Persons labouring under Bodily Deformity was founded in Birmingham, the first hospital in Britain dedicated to orthopaedics.

1828   The Madhouses Act tightened the inspection of private asylums and introduced the power to revoke licences.

1832   The Reform Act extended the parliamentary franchise, adding 217,000 voters to an electorate of 435,000 and enabling the urban middle classes to share power with traditional rural elites.

        The Royal Commission on the Poor Laws was established.

1833   The state began to offer modest grants to two religious societies, one Anglican and the other Nonconformist, which were developing charitable schools.

1834   The Poor Law Amendment Act: (1) set up a central Poor Law Commission; (2) merged parishes into a smaller number of unions managed by Boards of Guardians; (3) restricted relief for able-bodied applicants (and their families) to the work-house where conditions were 'less eligible' (or worse) than those of independent labourers; and (4) removed the vote from any paupers who were enfranchised under the 1832 Reform Act.

1838   The Chartist movement published a People's Charter which among its six demands included universal male suffrage.

1843   The Midland Institution for the Blind was founded in Nottingham.

1845   The Lunacy Acts: (1) distinguished within the general cate-gory of 'insanity' the 'idiot', incapable since birth of thought or judgement, from the 'lunatic' and the person of 'unsound mind'; (2) required all counties and boroughs in England and Wales to construct asylums for the treatment of their pauper lunatics, either singly or in combination with neighbouring authorities; and (3) replaced the Metropolitan Commissioners with Lunacy Commissioners who had authority nationwide to monitor the construction and operation of public asylums, over-see private asylums and co-operate with the poor law commis-sioners in scrutinizing the workhouse 'lunatic' pauper population.

The Scottish Poor Law Amendment Act created a central board of supervisors and parochial boards with the authority to raise and distribute local funds.

The Luke James Hansard's Alleged Lunatic's Friend Society was founded, the first pressure group to defend the liberty of the subject.

1847   The Poor Law Commission became the Poor Law Board.

The Cambrian Institution for the Deaf and Dumb was founded in Aberystwyth, later moving south to Swansea.

1848   The National Asylum for Idiots opened in temporary premises in London.

Part 3 The growth of collectivism, 1850–1939

1851   The first attempt was made to identify sensory impairments in the decennial Census.

1851   The Colney Hatch Asylum opened with 1250 beds.

The first edition of Henry Mayhew's *London Labour and the London Poor* was published serially with empirical pen portraits that included disabled people.

1853   The Poor Law Commission banned the use of chains, manacles and other mechanical restraints in workhouses.

1857   The construction of public asylums in Scotland became a statutory obligation.

1858   The Medical Act established a single register of all qualified practitioners and banned those who were not listed from government posts.

1859   The first home nurse was appointed in Liverpool as part of a charitable initiative by William Rathbone.

1863   The National Asylum for Idiots moved to purpose-built premises at Earlswood in Surrey.

1866   The *Lancet*, a leading medical journal, published a series of articles that were highly critical of London workhouse medicine.

        P. Martin Duncan and William Millard published *A Manual for the Classification, Training and Education of the Feeble-Minded, Imbecile and Idiotic.*

1867   Franchise reform doubled the parliamentary electorate to almost 2,000,000, bringing in many men from the urban working class.

        The Metropolitan Poor Act created the Metropolitan Asylums Board with a common fund to encourage the development of hospitals in London.

1868   The Second Poor Law Amendment Act encouraged separate infirmaries in the provinces but without the inducement of a central board and a common fund.

        The British and Foreign Blind Association, later the National Institute for the Blind, was founded.

1869   The Goschen Minute, drafted by the president of the Poor Law Board, restated the centrality of the workhouse and 'less eligibility', which had informed the Poor Law Amendment Act of 1834.

        The Charity Organization Society was founded to foster self-help in the administration of philanthropic assistance.

1870   The Education Act required elected School Boards to set up elementary schools for children aged between 5 and 12 in areas where the voluntary sector was delivering too few places.

        Institutions for the 'harmless insane' were opened by the Metropolitan Asylums Board at Caterham and Leavesden on the outskirts of London.

1871   The Poor Law Board was replaced by the Local Government Board, whose functions also included those formerly managed by the Medical Department of the Privy Council.

1874   Henry Longley published an influential paper in the *Annual Report* of the Local Government Board, which advocated a crusade against outdoor relief by extending the workhouse test to all classes of pauper.

1879   The Lunacy Commissioners circulated guidelines recommending the limited use of restraint, exclusion and bathing as modes of punishment.

1880   The First World Congress to Improve the Welfare of the Deaf and Blind decided at its meeting in Milan to promote the oral instruction of deaf people at the expense of sign language and the combined method.

Education became compulsory for pupils aged between 5 and 10.

1884/5   Franchise reform tripled the parliamentary electorate, granting the vote to most male agricultural labourers.

1885   The Medical Relief (Disqualification Removal) Act restored the vote to patients receiving medical relief under the poor law.

1886   The Idiots Act enabled local authorities to build separate asylums for intellectually impaired patients.

1888   The local management of asylums was transferred from magistrates to county councils.

1889   The *Report of the Royal Commission on the Blind, the Deaf and the Dumb* was published.

Charles Booth began publishing his surveys on the *Life and Labour of the People of London*, the seventeenth and final volume of which appeared in 1903.

1890   The Lunacy Act introduced a complex system of legal orders and medical certificates to prevent wrongful asylum admission.

The British Deaf and Dumb Association was founded.

1892   The first special school for intellectually impaired children opened in Leicester.

1893   The Elementary Education (Blind and Deaf Children) Act transferred responsibility for the education of blind and deaf children from the poor law authorities to local education authorities, which were given a duty to develop their own 'special' schools or grant-aid schools in the voluntary sector. Parents were obliged to send children who were blind or deaf.

1894   A series of reports on provincial workhouses by a special commission were published in the *British Medical Journal*.

1895   The *Report of the Royal Commission on the Aged Poor* was published.

1896 The National Association for Promoting the Welfare of the Feeble-Minded was founded.

1897 The Workmen's Compensation Act established the right to financial security if injured at work.

1899 Start of the Boer War.

   The Elementary Education (Defective and Epileptic Children) Act empowered local education authorities to provide schools for intellectually impaired children who were not in existing facilities.

   Seebohm Rowntree's first survey of York, *Poverty: A Study in Town Life*, was published.

1900 Agnes Hunt's Salop Convalescent Home for Women and Children opened at Baschurch near Oswestry, later becoming a pioneer of orthopaedic surgery, open-air therapy and post-operative after-care clinics.

1902 End of the Boer War.

   The Sandlebridge Boarding Schools and Colony for 'mentally defective' residents opened at Great Warford in Cheshire.

1903 The Heritage Craft Schools and Hospital opened at Chailey in Sussex.

1904 The *Report of the Inter-Departmental Committee on Physical Deterioration* was published.

   The Metropolitan Asylums Board began what became the Darenth Industrial Colony for 'higher-grade mental defectives'.

1905 The Workmens' Unemployment Act: (1) encouraged local authorities to provide non-stigmatizing jobs for claimants who had previously avoided poor law assistance; and (2) empowered local distress committees to organize labour exchanges, maintain unemployment registers and facilitate migration or emigration.

   The first local authority residential school for 'crippled' children opened in Manchester.

1907 A school medical service was introduced with a duty to inspect but no requirement to treat children.

   The Eugenics Education Society was founded to promote public awareness of positive and negative hereditary qualities and social responsibility towards them.

1908 The Old Age Pensions Act introduced a non-contributory benefit funded by the state for elderly people over the age of 70 who had relatively low incomes and passed a character test.

Lord Mayor Treloar Cripples Hospital and College opened offering a three-year technical training in trades considered suitable for disabled men.

Alfred Tredgold's *Textbook of Mental Deficiency* was published.

1909   The Majority and Minority Reports of the Royal Commission on the Poor Laws were published, the former recommending the replacement of boards of guardians with local government public assistance committees and the latter recommending the break-up of the poor law with the transfer of its functions to relevant local government departments.

1911   The National Insurance Act used contributions from employees, employers and the state to support both unemployment benefit, and sickness benefit that after six months was reduced and paid as disablement benefit. Members of the national insurance scheme, but not their families, also had access to medical care through a panel of doctors.

The Relief Regulation Order added a medical test to the assessment of non-elderly applicants for relief outside the workhouse.

1913   The Mental Deficiency Act: (1) established the Board of Control in place of the lunacy commissioners; (2) introduced a four-way classification of intellectual impairment; (3) required local authorities to maintain mental deficiency institutions; and (4) set up a system of supervised community care and control.

The workhouse was renamed the poor law institution.

1914   Start of the First World War.

The Elementary Education (Defective and Epileptic Children) Act required local education authorities: (1) to provide special schools or classes to which parents were obliged to send their 'feeble-minded' children; and (2) to ascertain 'defective' children and identify those incapable of being taught in special schools.

1915   A special Act of Parliament permitted the Maudsley Hospital in London to admit voluntary patients.

1916   The Shepherd's Bush Military Hospital, which became a showcase for wartime orthopaedic medicine, opened at a former London workhouse infirmary.

1918   End of the First World War.

Paupers regained the right to vote in the Representation of the People Act, which enfranchised men over 21 and women over 30.

The Education Act made schools for mentally and physically 'defective' children mandatory on the terms that had applied to blind and deaf children since 1893.

1919   The Central Council for the Care of Cripples was founded, later being known as the Central Council for the Disabled and RADAR, the Royal Association for Disability and Rehabilitation.

1920   The Blind Persons Act required local authorities to: (1) compile registers of blind people; and (2) make arrangements for their welfare, which might include home teaching, workshops, voluntary visitors and social activities. The old age pension was also extended to blind people from the age of 50.

1921   Questions about sensory impairments were dropped from the decennial Census.

1922   The British Legion for ex-servicemen was founded.

1925   In return for an extra payment to the national insurance scheme, the Old Age and Widows and Orphans Contributory Pensions Act entitled contributors and their wives to a contributory pension between the ages of 65 and 70, and to a non-contributory pension without means testing at 70 plus.

1926   The *Report of the Royal Commission on Lunacy and Mental Disorder* was published.

1929   The Wall Street Crash compounded Britain's existing economic problems to produce the Great Depression of the 1930s.

The Local Government Act replaced boards of guardians with public assistance committees. Domiciliary assistance for blind people became permissible.

The *Report of the Interdepartmental Committee on Mental Deficiency, 1925–1929* (the Wood Report) was published.

1930   The Mental Treatment Act introduced the concept of the voluntary patient, and recommended out-patient clinics and observation wards.

The Poor law Act empowered, but did not require local authorities to help voluntary organizations find deaf people jobs.

1937   A report from Political and Economic Planning concluding that the poor treatment of chronically sick patients in former workhouses caused permanent disability.

The Stanmore Cripples Training College was founded at the county branch of the Royal National Orthopaedic Hospital at Brockley Hill in Middlesex.

Part 4 The development of the welfare state since 1939

1939   Start of the Second World War.

1940   The Committee for the Welfare of the Aged was founded which, after several name changes, became Age Concern in 1971.

1941   An Interim Scheme for engaging disabled people in the war industries was announced.

        Seebohm Rowntree's second survey of York, *Poverty and Progress*, was published.

1942   *Social Insurance and Allied Services* (the Beveridge Report) was published.

        The Ministry of Information film, *Life Begins Again*, was released to promote industrial rehabilitation.

1943   The *Report of the Interdepartmental Committee on the Rehabilitation and Resettlement of Disabled Persons* (the Tomlinson Report) was published.

1944   Disabled Persons (Employment) Act introduced: (1) training and resettlement programmes; (2) a scheme that required larger employers to recruit 3 per cent of their workforces from registered disabled people; and (3) segregated sheltered workshops.

        The Education Act: (1) required local authorities to provide children with a schooling suited to their 'age, ability and aptitude'; and (2) conceded that where possible mainstream schools were the most appropriate environment in which to teach disabled children.

        The spinal injuries unit opened at Stoke Mandeville Hospital in Aylesbury, Buckinghamshire.

1945   End of the Second World War.

        The Handicapped Pupils and Medical Services Regulations replaced the term 'mental deficiency' with 'educational subnormality' and 'maladjustment', and identified special provisions to assist disabled children studying in mainstream schools.

        The Ministry of Information film, *Back to Normal*, was released, showing how government training equipped disabled workers to resume employment.

1946   The National Health Service Act promoted a system of physical and mental health care that was comprehensive, collective, universally available to the population as a whole, and free of charge at the point of receipt.

The National Insurance Act introduced: (1) a universal retirement pension; (2) replaced workmen's compensation with industrial disablement benefit; and (3) permitted permanently disabled workers to claim sickness benefit indefinitely.

The National Association for Mental Health, from 1972 MIND, was established from the merger of three mental health organizations: the Central Association for Mental Health (1913); the National Council for Mental Hygiene (1922); and the Child Guidance Council (1927).

1948   The United Nations Declaration of Human Rights was ratified.

The National Health Service was launched.

The National Assistance Act: (1) required local authorities to provide accommodation for all 'who by reason of age, infirmity or any other circumstances are in need of care or attention which is not otherwise available'; (2) provided a means-tested payment for claimants who either had no right to national insurance or whose benefits fell below its own minimum standard; and (3) permitted local authorities 'to promote the welfare of persons who are blind, deaf or dumb and others, who are substantially and permanently handicapped by illness, injury or congenital deformity'.

1951   Seebohm Rowntree's third survey of York, *Poverty and the Welfare State*, was published.

1956   The *Report of the Committee of Inquiry on the Rehabilitation, Training and Resettlement of Disabled Persons* (the Piercy Report) was published.

1957   The *Report of the Royal Commission on the Law Relating to Mental Illness and Mental Deficiency, 1954–7* was published.

1959   The Mental Health Act: (1) abolished the Board of Control; (2) removed controls on the admission and treatment of voluntary patients; (3) revised the procedures for compulsory admission; (4) established a right of appeal to Mental Health Review Tribunals; and (5) encouraged local authorities to make arrangements for the social care of people who did not need hospital treatment.

The National Insurance Act introduced a graduated pension scheme where enhanced benefits were received in return for an additional earnings-related contribution.

1960   *The Last Refuge* was published by Peter Townsend, surveying conditions in residential accommodation for elderly people.

1961   Enoch Powell as Minister of Health announced the rundown of mental hospitals as policies for community care developed.

1962   *A Hospital Plan for England and Wales* was published, which introduced the concept of the district general hospital with between 600 and 800 beds.

The first national study of elderly people, *The Aged in the Welfare State* by Peter Townsend and Dorothy Wedderburn, was published.

Ken Kesey's novel, *One Flew Over the Cuckoos Nest*, depicted the devastating effects of brain surgery.

1963   *Health and Welfare: The Development of Community Care* was published, containing the embryonic plans of local authorities for growing their social services.

Designing for the Disabled was published by the Royal Institution of British Architects.

1964   Poverty was rediscovered by Brian Abel-Smith and Peter Townsend in their path-breaking book, *The Poor and the Poorest.*

1965   The Disablement Income Group was founded to reform social security for disabled people.

1968   New social work departments were created in Scotland.

The *Report of the Committee on Local Authority and Allied Personal Social Services* (the Seebohm Report) recommended: (1) unified social services departments (in place of the former health, welfare and children's departments); and (2) the transfer of responsibility for community health services to the reorganized NHS.

1970   The Local Authority Social Services Act created unified social services departments in England and Wales along the lines recommended by the Seebohm Report.

The Chronically Sick and Disabled Persons Act required local authorities to: (1) inform themselves of the number of disabled people requiring assistance; (2) publicize the services on offer; (3) provide community support services; and (4) have regard to the needs of disabled people when framing housing policies.

Junior training centres were transferred from the NHS to local education authorities.

1971   The United Nations Declaration on the Rights of Mentally Retarded Persons was ratified.

The invalidity pension was introduced for members of the national insurance scheme who were unable to return to work after 28 weeks.

The non-contributory, non-means-tested attendance allowance was introduced for people with major physical and/or mental impairments who required substantial long-term care during the daytime, at night or continuously.

Handicapped and Impaired in Great Britain was published, the first of three disability reports commissioned by the Department of Health and Social Security, and its relevant Welsh and Scottish counterparts, from the government's Office of Population Censuses and Surveys.

1973   Britain joined the European Economic Community, now the European Union.

1974   Two concepts of special housing for disabled people were identified: (1) wheelchair housing for full-time wheelchair users and housewives who used a wheelchair indoors; and (2) mobility housing for able-bodied as well as disabled occupants who were ambulant rather than full-time wheelchair users.

1975   The United Nations Declaration on the Rights of Disabled Persons was ratified.

The Social Security Pensions Act introduced the State Earnings Related Pension Scheme (or SERPS) as a safety net for those who had no or insufficient private pension cover.

The non-contributory invalidity pension was introduced for people of working age who had no right to national insurance. Married and cohabiting women had to demonstrate that they were incapable of normal household duties as well as paid employment.

1976   The Chronically Sick and Disabled Persons Act added workplaces to the clauses in the 1970 Chronically Sick and Disabled Persons Act that related to the accessibility of premises.

The invalid care allowance was introduced for claimants other than married women who were of working age and looking after a seriously disabled relative for at least 35 hours a week.

The mobility allowance was phased in for claimants over 5 years old and under retirement age who were unable or virtually unable to walk.

The Union of the Physically Impaired Against Segregation published its definitions of impairment and disability.

1978   The *Report of the Committee of Enquiry into the Education of Children and Young People* (the Warnock Report) was published.

The *Report of the Royal Commission on Civil Liberty and Compensation for Personal Injury* (the Pearson Commission) was published.

1979   The Conservative government led by Margaret Thatcher was elected.

Peter Townsend's monumental study of *Poverty in the United Kingdom* was published.

1980   The World Health Organization published an expanded version of the International Classification of Impairment, Disability and Handicap.

1981   The Education Act required local authorities to assess or 'statement' disabled children and mainstream schools to offer a range of special provision.

The British Council of Organizations of Disabled People was set up.

1983   The Mental Health Act: (1) reduced the length of compulsory orders; (2) narrowed the legal definitions of mental impairments; and (3) required consent to treatment three months after admission.

1985   The Hampshire Centre for Independent Living was established to secure facilities and support that allowed disabled people choice and control.

1986   The Social Security Act replaced supplementary benefit with income support and set up a discretionary social fund to meet exceptional circumstances.

1988   The Education Reform Act introduced the National Curriculum but allowed modifications for disabled children at the discretion of the headteacher.

1990   The NHS and Community Care Act: (1) reduced the flow of state subsidies to private residential homes; (2) allowed hospitals and general practitioners to opt out of state control; and (3) applied market principles to the organization of health and social services.

1995   The Disability Discrimination Act made it illegal to discriminate against disabled people 'in connection with employment, the provision of goods, facilities and services or the disposal or management of premises'.

2000   Patients in mental hospitals became entitled to vote if they were not guilty of a criminal offence.

Select bibliography

Adair, R., Forsythe, B. and Melling, J. 'A Danger to the Public?: Disposing of Pauper Lunatics in Late-Victorian and Edwardian England: Plympton St Mary Union and the Devon County Asylum, 1867–1914', *Medical History*, 42 (1998).

Alston, J. *The Royal Albert: Chronicles of an Era* (Lancaster: Centre for North-West Regional Studies, 1992).

Anderson, J. *A Record of Fifty Years Service to the Disabled from 1919 to 1969 by the Central Council for the Disabled* (London: Central Council for the Disabled, 1969).

Armstrong, D. *Political Anatomy of the Body: Medical Knowledge in Britain in the Twentieth Century* (Cambridge: Cambridge University Press, 1983).

Atkins, E. T. *One Door Closes, Another Opens: A Personal Experience of Polio* (Walthamstow, London: Waltham Forest Oral History Workshop, 1994).

Atkinson, D., Jackson, M. and Walmsley, J. (eds) *Forgotten Lives: Exploring the History of Learning Disability* (Kidderminster: British Institute of Learning Disabilities, 1997).

Bacchi, C. L. and Beasley, C. 'Citizen Bodies: Is Embodied Citizenship a Contradiction in Terms?', *Critical Social Policy*, 22 (2002).

Bagilhole, B. *Equal Opportunities and Social Policy: Issues of Gender, Race and Disability* (London: Longman, 1997).

Baldwin, S. *Disabled Children – Counting the Costs: The Results of a Special Survey in the North and Midlands of Families with a Handicapped Child* (London: Disability Alliance, 1977).

Barnes, C. *Disabled People in Britain and Discrimination: A Case for Anti-Discrimination Legislation* (London: Hurst, 1991).

Barnes, C., Mercer, G. and Shakespeare, T. *Exploring Disability: A Sociological Introduction* (Cambridge: Polity, 1999).

Bartlett, P. *The Poor Law of Lunacy: The Administration of Pauper Lunatics in Mid-Nineteenth-Century England* (London: Leicester University Press, 1999).

Bartlett, P. and Wright, D. (eds) *Outside the Walls of the Asylum: A History of Care in the Community, 1750–2000* (London: Athlone, 1999).

Barton, L. (ed.) *Disability and Society: Emerging Issues and Insights* (London: Longman, 1996).

Bartrip, P. W. J. and Burman, S. B. *The Wounded Soldiers of Industry: Industrial Compensation Policy, 1833–1897* (Oxford: Clarendon Press, 1983).

Bartrip, P. W. J. and Fenn, P. T. 'The Measurement of Safety: Factory Accident Statistics in Victorian and Edwardian Britain', *Historical Research*, 63 (1990).

Bayley, M. *Mental Handicap and Community Care: A Study of Mentally Handicapped People in Sheffield* (London: Routledge & Kegan Paul, 1973).

Beaver, P. *A Tower of Strength: Two Hundred Years of the Royal School for Deaf Children, Margate* (Lewes: The Book Guild, 1992).

Bebbington, A. C. 'Changes in the Provision of Services to the Elderly in the Community over Fourteen Years', *Social Policy and Administration*, 13 (1979).

Beresford, P. 'What Have Madness and Psychiatric System Survivors Got to Do with Disability and Disability Studies?', *Disability and Society*, 15 (2000).

Blaikie, A. *Ageing and Popular Culture* (Cambridge: Cambridge University Press, 1999).

Blakemore, K. and Drake, R. *Understanding Equal Opportunity Policies* (London: Prentice Hall, 1996).

Bolderson, H. 'The Origins of the Disabled Persons Employment Quota and its Symbolic Significance', *Journal of Social Policy*, 9 (1980).

Bornat, J., Perks, R., Thompson, P. and Walmsley, J. (eds) *Oral History, Health and Welfare* (London: Routledge, 2000).

Borsay, A. *Disabled People in the Community: A Study of Housing, Health and Welfare Services* (London: Bedford Square Press, 1986).

Borsay, A. '"First Child Care, Second Mental Health, Third the Elderly": Professional Education and the Development of Social Work Priorities', *Research, Policy and Planning*, 7 (1989).

Borsay, A. 'Returning Patients to the Community: Disability, Medicine and Economic Rationality Before the Industrial Revolution', *Disability and Society*, 13, 1998).

Borsay, A. *Medicine and Charity in Georgian Bath: A Social History of the General Infirmary, c.1739–1830* (Aldershot: Ashgate, 1999).

Borsay, A. (ed.) *Medicine in Wales, c.1800–2000: Public Service or Private Commodity?* (Cardiff: University of Wales Press, 2003).

Bourke, J. *Dismembering the Male: Men's Bodies, Britain and the Great War* (London: Reaktion Books, 1996).

Bowring, F. 'Social Exclusion: Limitations of the Debate', *Critical Social Policy*, 20 (2000).

Bridgen, P. 'Hospitals, Geriatric Medicine, and the Long-Term Care of Elderly People, 1946–1976', *Social History of Medicine*, 14 (2001).

Brown, M. J. and Bowl, R. *Study of Local Authority Chronic Sick and Disabled Persons Surveys* (Birmingham: University of Birmingham Social Services Unit, 1976).

Buckle, J. R. *Work and Housing of Impaired Persons in Great Britain* (London: HMSO, 1971).

Bulmer, M. and Rees, A. M. (eds) *Citizenship Today: The Contemporary Relevance of T. H. Marshall* (London: UCL Press, 1996).

Butler, A., Oldman, C. and Greve, J. *Sheltered Housing for the Elderly: Policy, Practice and the Consumer* (London: George Allen & Unwin, 1983).

Campbell, J. and Oliver, M. *Disability Politics: Understanding Our Past, Changing Our Future* (London: Routledge, 1996).

Caring for the Elderly and Handicapped: Community Care Policies and Women's Lives (Manchester: Equal Opportunities Commission, March 1982).

Clarke, J. S. *Disabled Citizens* (London: Allen & Unwin, 1951).

Cook, J. and Mitchell, P. *Putting Teeth in the Act: A History of Attempts to Enforce the Provisions of Section 2 of the Chronically Sick and Disabled Persons Act 1970* (London: Royal Association for Disability and Rehabilitation, no date).

Cook, T., Swain, J. and French, S. 'Voices from Segregated Schooling: Towards an Inclusive Education System', *Disability and Society*, 16 (2001).

Cooter, R. *Surgery and Society in Peace and War: Orthopaedics and the Organization of Modern Medicine, 1880–1948* (Basingstoke: Macmillan – now Palgrave Macmillan, 1993).

Cooter, R. and Luckin, B. (eds) *Accidents in History: Injuries, Fatalities and Social Relations* (Amsterdam: Rodopi, 1997).

Cox, R. H. 'The Consequences of Welfare Reform: How Conceptions of Social Rights Are Changing', *Journal of Social Policy*, 27 (1998).

Crammer, J. *Asylum History: Buckingham County Pauper Lunatic Asylum – St John's* (London: Royal College of Psychiatrists, 1990).

Davies, J. M. and Watson, M. 'Where Are the Children's Experiences?: Analysing Social and Cultural Exclusion in "Special" and "Mainstream" Schools', *Disability and Society*, 16 (2001).

Davies, K. '"Silent and Censured Travellers"?: Patients' Narratives and Patients' Voices: Perspectives on the History of Mental Illness Since 1948', *Social History of Medicine*, 14 (2001).

Dean, H. *Welfare Rights and Social Policy* (Harlow: Pearson Education, 2002).

Digby, A. *Madness, Morality and Medicine: A Study of the York Retreat, 1796–1914* (Cambridge: Cambridge University Press, 1985).

Dimmock, A. F. *Cruel Legacy: An Introduction to the Record of Deaf People in History* (Edinburgh: Scottish Workshop Publications, 1993).

Donnelly, M. *Managing the Mind: A Study of Medical Psychology in Early Nineteenth-Century Britain* (London: Tavistock, 1983).

Drake, R. 'What Am I Doing Here?: "Non-Disabled" People and the Disability Movement', *Disability and Society*, 12 (1997).

Dunbar, H. *History of the Society for the Blind in Glasgow and the West of Scotland, 1859–1989* (Glasgow: Glasgow and West of Scotland Society for the Blind, 1989).

Dwyer, P. *Welfare Rights and Responsibilities: Contesting Social Citizenship* (Bristol: Policy Press, 2000).

Elsey, E. 'Disabled Ex-Servicemen's Experiences of Rehabilitation and Employment after the First World War', *Oral History*, 25 (1997).

Englander, D. 'Soldiers and Social Reform in the First and Second World Wars', *Historical Research*, LXVII (1994).

The Experience of Caring for Elderly and Handicapped Dependants: Survey Report (Manchester: Equal Opportunities Commission, March 1980).

Fawcett, B. *Feminist Perspectives on Disability* (London: Longman, 2000).

Fennell, G., Phillipson, C. and Evers, H. *The Sociology of Old Age* (Milton Keynes: Open University Press, 1988).

Fennell, P. *Treatment Without Consent: Law, Psychiatry and the Treatment of Mentally Disordered People Since 1845* (London: Routledge, 1996).

Finkelstein, V. *Attitudes and Disabled People: Issues for Discussion* (New York: World Rehabilitation Fund, 1980).

Finlayson, G. *Citizen, State and Social Welfare in Britain, 1830–1990* (Oxford: Clarendon Press, 1994).

Forsythe, B., Melling, J. and Adair, R. 'The New Poor Law and the County Pauper Lunatic Asylum: The Devon Experience, 1834–1884', *Social History of Medicine*, 9 (1996).

Foucault, M. *Madness and Civilization: A History of Insanity in the Age of Reason* (London: Tavistock, 1965).

Foucault, M. *Discipline and Punish: The Birth of the Prison* (Harmondsworth: Penguin, 1979).

Freeden, M. 'Eugenics and Progressive Thought: A Study in Ideological Affinity', *Historical Journal*, 22 (1979).

Gerber, D. A. *Disabled Veterans in History* (Ann Arbor: University of Michigan Press, 2000).

Giddens, A. *Modernity and Self-Identity: Self and Society in the Late Modern Age* (Cambridge: Polity, 1991).

Girdlestone, G. R. *The Care and Cure of Crippled Children* (Bristol and London: J. Wright and S. Marshall, 1924).

Gittins, D. *Madness in its Place: Narratives of Severalls Hospital, 1913–1997* (London: Routledge, 1998).

Gleeson, B. 'Disability Studies: A Historical Materialist View', *Disability and Society*, 12 (1997).

Gleeson, B. *Geographies of Disability* (London: Routledge, 1999).

Glendinning, C. *'After Working All These Years': A Response to the Report of the National Insurance Advisory Committee on the 'Household Duties' Test for Non-Contributory Invalidity Pension for Married Women* (London: Disability Alliance, November 1980).

Glendinning, C. *Unshared Care: Parents and their Disabled Children* (London: Routledge & Kegan Paul, 1983).

Goldsmith, S. *Mobility Housing* (London: Department of the Environment, 1974).

Goldsmith, S. *Wheelchair Housing* (London: Department of the Environment, 1975).

Goldsmith, S. and Kirby, K. 'Purpose-Built or Adapted: The Neighbourhood Counts', *Municipal and Public Services Journal* (9 December 1977).

Gooding, C. 'Disability Discrimination Act: From Statute to Practice', *Critical Social Policy*, 20 (2000).

Gordon, C. (ed.) *Michel Foucault Power/Knowledge: Selected Interviews and Other Writings, 1972–1977* (Brighton: Harvester Press, 1980).

Gostin, L. O. *The Mental Health Act 1959: Is It Fair?* (London: MIND, 1978).

Gould, T. *A Summer Plague: Polio and Its Survivors* (New Haven, CT, and London: Yale University Press, 1995).

Grant, B. *The Deaf Advance: A History of the British Deaf Association* (Edinburgh: Pentland Press, 1990).

Guttmann, L. 'History of the National Spinal Injuries Centre, Stoke Mandeville Hospital, Aylesbury', *Paraplegia*, 34 (1967).

Guyatt, M. 'Better Legs: Artificial Limbs for British Veterans of the First World War', *Journal of Design History*, 14 (2001).

Harris, A. I. *Income and Entitlement to Supplementary Benefit* (London: HMSO, 1970.

Harris, A. I with Cox, E. and Smith, C. R. W. *Handicapped and Impaired in Great Britain* (London: HMSO, 1971.

Hitchcock, T., King, P. and Sharpe, P. (eds) *Chronicling Poverty: The Voices and Strategies of the English Poor, 1640–1840* (Basingstoke: Macmillan – now Palgrave Macmillan, 1997).

Horsburgh, M. '"No Sufficient Security": The Reaction of the Poor Law Authorities to Boarding-Out', *Journal of Social Policy*, 12 (1983).

Humphries, S. and Gordon, P. *Out of Sight: The Experience of Disability, 1900–1950* (Plymouth: Northcote House, 1992).

Hunt, A. *The Elderly At Home: A Study of People Aged Sixty-Five and Over Living in the Community in England in 1976* (London: HMSO, 1978).

Hunt, E. E. 'Paupers and Pensioners: Past and Present', *Ageing and Society*, 9 (1990).

Hunter, R. and Macalpine, I. *Psychiatry for the Poor: 1851 Colney Hatch Asylum – Friern Hospital 1973: A Medical and Social History* (London: W. Dawson, 1974).

Hurt, J. S. *Outside the Mainstream: A History of Special Education* (London: Batsford, 1988).

Hyman, M. *The Extra Costs of Disabled Living* (Horsham: National Fund for Research into Crippling Diseases, 1977).

Ignatieff, M. 'Citizenship and Moral Narcissism', *Political Quarterly*, 60 (1989).

Ingram, A. *The Madhouse of Language: Writing and Reading Madness in the Eighteenth Century* (London: Routledge, 1991).

Jack, R. (ed.) *Residential Versus Community Care: The Role of Institutions in Welfare Provision* (Basingstoke: Macmillan – now Palgrave Macmillan, 1998).

Jackson, M. 'Images of Deviance: Visual Representations of Mental Defectives in Early Twentieth-Century Medical Texts', *British Journal for the History of Science*, 28 (1995).

Jackson, M. *The Borderland of Imbecility: Medicine, Society and the Fabrication of the Feeble Mind in Late Victorian and Edwardian England* (Manchester: Manchester University Press, 2000).

Johnson, P. 'The Employment and Retirement of Older Men in England and Wales, 1881–1981', *Economic History Review*, XLVII (1994).

Jones, G. 'Eugenics and Social Policy between the Wars', *Historical Journal*, 25 (1982).

Jones, K. *A History of the Mental Health Services* (London: Routledge & Kegan Paul, 1972).

Jones, K. *Asylums and After: A Revised History of the Mental Health Services: From the Early Eighteenth Century to the 1990s* (London: Athlone, 1993).

Jordan, D. *A New Employment Programme Wanted For Disabled People* (London: Disability Alliance, March 1979).

Keeble, U. *Aids and Adaptations* (London: Bedford Square Press, 1979).

King, D. *In the Name of Liberalism: Illiberal Social Policy in the United States and Britain* (Oxford: Oxford University Press, 1999).

Koven, S. 'Remembering and Dismemberment: Crippled Children, Wounded Soldiers, and the Great War in Great Britain', *American Historical Review*, 99 (1994).

Land, H. *Parity Begins At Home: Women's and Men's Work in the Home and its Effect on their Paid Employment* (Manchester: Equal Opportunities Commission and Social Science Research Council, September 1981).

Lane, D. *The Work Needs of Mentally Handicapped Adults* (London: Disability Alliance, December 1980).

Lane, H. *The Mask of Benevolence: Disabling the Deaf Community* (New York: Vintage, 1993).

Langan, M. (ed.) *Welfare: Needs, Rights and Risks* (London: Routledge, 1998).

Laybourn, K. (ed.) *Social Conditions, Status and Community, 1860–c.1920* (Stroud: Alan Sutton, 1997).

Lees, L. Hollen *The Solidarities of Strangers: The English Poor Laws and the People, 1700–1948* (Cambridge: Cambridge University Press, 1998).

Levitas, R. 'The Concept of Social Exclusion and the New Durkheimian Hegemony', *Critical Social Policy*, 16 (1996).

Lister, R. 'From Equality to Social Inclusion: New Labour and the Welfare State', *Critical Social Policy*, 18 (1998).

Loach, I. *The Price of Deafness: A Review of the Financial and Employment Problems of the Deaf and Hard of Hearing* (London: Disability Alliance, 1976).

Loach, I. and Lister, R. *Second Class Disabled: A Report on the Non-Contributory Invalidity Pension for Married Women* (London: Equal Rights for Disabled Women Campaign, July 1978).

Lonsdale, S. *Job Protection for the Disabled* (London: Low Pay Unit. April 1981).

MacKenzie, C. *Psychiatry for the Rich: A History of Ticehurst Private Asylum, 1792–1917* (London: Routledge, 1992).

Malin, N., Race, D. and Jones, G. *Services for the Mentally Handicapped in Britain* (London: Croom Helm, 1980).

Marks, D. *Disability: Controversial Debates and Psychosocial Perspectives* (London: Routledge, 1999).

Marshall, T. H. *Class, Citizenship and Social Development* (Chicago: University of Chicago Press, 1964).

Marshall, T. H. and Bottomore, T. *Citizenship and Social Class* (London: Pluto, 1992).

Martin, M. 'Medical Knowledge and Medical Practice: Geriatric Medicine in the 1950s', *Social History of Medicine*, 8 (1995).

Means, R. and Smith, R. 'From Public Assistance Institutions to "Sunshine Hotels": Changing State Perceptions About Residential Care for Elderly People, 1939–1948', *Ageing and Society*, 3 (1983).

Means, R. and Smith, R. *From Poor Law to Community Care: The Development of Welfare Services for Elderly People, 1939–1971* (Bristol: Policy Press, 1998).

Mellett, D. J. 'Bureaucracy and Mental Illness: The Commissioners in Lunacy, 1845–90', *Medical History*, 25 (1981).

Melling, J. and Forsythe, B. (eds) *Insanity, Institutions and Society: A Social History of Madness in Comparative Petespective* (London: Routledge, 1999).

Miller, E. J. and Gwynne, G. V. *A Life Apart: A Pilot Study of Residential Institutions for the Physically Handicapped and the Young Chronic Sick* (London: Tavistock, 1972).

Morton, J. *Wheelchair Housing: A Survey of Purpose-Designed Dwellings for Disabled People* (London: Department of the Environment, no date).

Nissell, M. and Bonnerjea, L. *Family Care of the Handicapped Elderly: Who Pays?* (London: Policy Studies Institute, January 1982).

Noble, P. 'Mental Health Services: An Historical Review', *Medicine, Science and the Law*, 21 (1981).

Oliver, M. *Social Work with Disabled People* (Basingstoke: Macmillan, 1983).

Oliver, M. *The Politics of Disablement* (Basingstoke: Macmillan – now Palgrave Macmillan, 1990).

Oliver, M. *Understanding Disability: From Theory to Practice* (Basingstoke: Macmillan – now Palgrave Macmillan, 1996).

Oliver, M. and Barnes, C. *Disabled People and Social Policy: From Exclusion to Inclusion* (London: Longman, 1998).

Orme, H. G. and Brock, W. H. *Leicestershire's Lunatics: The Institutional Care of Leicestershire's Lunatics during the Nineteenth Century* (Leicester: Leicestershire's Museums, Art Galleries and Records Service, 1987).

Oswin, M. *The Empty Hours: A Study of the Week-End Life of Handicapped Children in Institutions* (London: Allen Lane, 1971).

Parker, J. *Local Health and Welfare Services* (London: George Allen & Unwin, 1965).

Parker, J. *Citizenship, Work and Welfare: Searching for the Good Society* (Basingstoke: Macmillan – now Palgrave Macmillan, 1998).

Parry-Jones, W. L. *The Trade in Lunacy: A Study of Private Madhouses in England in the Eighteenth and Nineteenth Centuries* (London: Routledge & Kegan Paul, 1972).

Pelling, M. and Smith, R. M. (eds) *Life, Death and the Elderly: Historical Perspectives* (London: Routledge, 1991).

Percy-Smith, J. (ed.) *Policy Responses to Social Exclusion: Towards Inclusion?* (Buckingham: Open University Press, 2000).

Phillips, G. 'Scottish and English Institutions for the Blind, 1792–1860', *Scottish Historical Review*, LXXIV (1995).

Phillips, H. and Glendinning, C. *Who Benefits?: Report of a Welfare Rights Project with People with Disabilities in North Yorkshire* (London: Disability Alliance, March 1981).

Phillipson, C. *Reconstructing Old Age: New Agendas in Social Theory and Practice* (London: Sage, 1998).

Pomeroy, D., Fewtrell, J., Butler, N. and Gill, R. *Handicapped Children: Their Homes and Lifestyles* (London: Department of the Environment, 1978).

Porter, R. *Mind-Forg'd Manacles: A History of Madness in England from the Restoration to the Regency* (Harmondsworth: Penguin, 1987).

Poverty and Low Incomes Amongst Disabled People (London: Disability Alliance, February 1977).

Reé, J. *I See a Voice: Language, Deafness and the Senses – A Philosophical History* (London: HarperCollins, 1999).

Roulstone, A. 'The Legal Road to Rights?: Disabling Premises, *Obiter Dicta* and the Disability Discrimination Act 1995', *Disability and Society*, 18 (2003).

Sainsbury, S. *Registered As Disabled* (London: Bell, 1970).

Sarup, M. *An Introductory Guide to Post-Structuralism and Postmodernism* (London: Harvester Wheatsheaf, 1993).

Sarup, M. *Identity, Culture and the Postmodern World* (Edinburgh: Edinburgh University Press, 1996).

Schneider, J., Simons, K. and Everatt, G. 'Impact of the National Minimum Wage on Disabled People', *Disability and Society*, 16 (2001).

Scull, A. *Museums of Madness: The Social Organization of Insanity in Nineteenth-Century England* (Harmondsworth: Penguin, 1982).

Scull, A. *The Most Solitary of Afflictions: Madness and Society in Britain, 1700–1900* (New Haven, CT: Yale University Press, 1993).

Skultans, V. *English Madness: Ideas on Insanity, 1580–1890* (London: Routledge & Kegan Paul, 1979).

Smith, L. D. *'Cure, Comfort and Safe Custody': Public Lunatic Asylums in Early Nineteenth-Century England* (London: Leicester University Press, 1999).

Soloway, R. A. *Democracy and Degeneration: Eugenics and the Declining Birthrate in Twentieth Century Britain* (Chapel Hill: University of North Carolina Press, 1995).

Stiker, H.-J. *A History of Disability* (Ann Arbor: University of Michigan Press, 1999).

Stone, D. *The Disabled State* (Basingstoke: Macmillan, 1984).

Stowell, R. *Disabled people on Supplementary Benefit* (London: Disablement Income Group, July 1980).

Sutherland, G. *Ability, Merit and Measurement: Mental Testing and English Education, 1880–1940* (Oxford: Clarendon Press, 1984).

Swain, J., Finkelstein, V., French, S. and Oliver, M. *Disabling Barriers – Enabling Environments* (London: Sage, 1993).

Taylor, D. 'Social Identity and Social Policy', *Journal of Social Policy*, 27 (1998).

Thane, P. *Old Age in English History: Past Experiences, Present Issues* (Oxford: Oxford University Press, 2000).

Thomas, M. G. *The Royal National Institute for the Blind, 1868–1956* (London: Royal National Institute for the Blind, 1957).

Thomson, D. 'Workhouse to Nursing Home: Residential Care of Elderly people in England Since 1840', *Ageing and Society*, 3 (1983).

Thomson, D. 'The Decline of Social Welfare: Falling State Support for the Elderly since Early Victorian Times', *Ageing and Society*, 4 (1984).

Thomson, D. '"I am not my father's keeper": Families and the Elderly in Nineteenth-Century England', *Law and History Review*, 2 (1984).

Thomson, M. *The Problem of Mental Deficiency: Eugenics, Democracy, and Social Policy in Britain, c.1870–1959* (Oxford: Clarendon Press, 1998).

Titmuss, R. M. *Problems of Social Policy* (London: HMSO, 1950).

Tomlinson, S. *The Sociology of Special Education* (London: Routledge & Kegan Paul, 1982).

Topliss, E. *Provision for the Disabled* (Oxford and London: B. Blackwell and M. Robertson, 1975).

Topliss, E. *Survey of Physically Disabled People under Retirement Age Living in Private Households in Southampton* (Southampton: Department of Sociology and Social Policy, University of Southampton, 1976).

Topliss, E. and Gould, B. *A Charter for the Disabled* (Oxford: B. Blackwell and M. Robertson, 1981).

Tosh, J. *The Pursuit of History: Aims, Methods and New Directions in the Study of Modern History* (London: Longman, 1991).

Townsend, P. *The Last Refuge: A Survey of Residential Institutions and Homes for the Aged in England and Wales* (London: Routledge & Kegan Paul, 1964).

Townsend, P. 'The Structured Dependency of the Elderly: A Creation of Social Policy in the Twentieth Century', *Ageing and Society*, 1 (1981).

Tregaskis, C. 'Social Model Theory: The Story So Far . . .', *Disability and Society*, 17 (2002).

Walmsley, J. and Rolph, S. 'Development of Community Care for People with Learning Difficulties, 1913–1945', *Critical Social Policy*, 21 (2001).

Walton, J. K. 'Lunacy in the Industrial Revolution', *Journal of Social History*, 14 (1980).

Watson, F. *Civilization and the Cripple* (London: J. Bale, 1930).

Welshman, J. 'Growing Old in the City: Public Health and the Elderly in Leicester, 1948–1974', *Medical History*, 40 (1996).

Whiteside, N. 'Counting the Cost: Sickness and Disability Among Working People in an Era of Industrial Recession, 1920–1939', *Economic History Review*, XL (1987).

Who Cares for the Carers?: Opportunities for those Caring for the Elderly and Handicapped (Manchester: Equal Opportunities Commission, March 1982).

Wing, J. K. and Olsen, R. (eds) *Community Care for the Mentally Disabled* (Oxford: Oxford University Press, 1979).

Woodhams, C. and Corby, S. 'Defining Disability in Theory and Practice: A Critique of the British Disability Discrimination Act 1995', *Journal of Social Policy*, 32 (2003).

Wright, D. 'Getting out of the Asylum: Understanding the Confinement of the Insane in the Nineteenth Century', *Social History of Medicine*, 10 (1997).

Wright, D. 'Learning Disability and the New Poor Law in England, 1834–1867', *Disability and Society*, 15 (2000).

Wright, D. *Mental Disability in Victorian England: The Earlswood Asylum, 1847–1901* (Oxford: Clarendon Press, 2001).

Wright, D. and Digby, A. (eds) *From Idiocy to Mental Deficiency: Historical Perspectives on People with Learning Difficulties* (London: Routledge, 1996).

Index